Michael Paulkovich

# No Meek Messiah

Christianity's Lies, Laws and Legacy

**No Meek Messiah**
Christianity's Lies, Laws and Legacy
Michael Paulkovich

First Edition




ISBN 0988216116
ISBN-13 978-0-9882161-1-2


Library of Congress Control Number: 2013905177

**Terminology**

AUC - *Ab urbe condita* (ancient Roman calendar system).
BCE - Before Common Era, otherwise known as "BC."
CE - Common Era, or "AD."
*CE1907 - Catholic Encyclopedia,* first edition, 1907-1913.
*CE1986 - Catholic Encyclopedia, Revised and Updated,* 1986.
DRC - The "Douay-Rheims Complete" Bible version.
*EH - Ecclesiastical History* of Eusebius, fourth century CE.
ESV - English Standard version Bible.
ISV - International Standard version of the Bible.
JP - Julian Period calendar system.
KJV - King James Version ("authorized") of the Bible.
NIV - New International Version of the Bible.
NLT - New Living Translation of the Bible.
NRS - New Revised Standard version of the Bible.
NT - New Testament.
OT - Old Testament.

**For Books of the Bible -**

**Old Testament:**

| | |
|---|---|
| 1 Chron | 1 Chronicles |
| 1 Sam | 1 Samuel |
| 2 Chron | 2 Chronicles |
| 2 Sam | 2 Samuel |
| Dt | Deuteronomy |
| Ex | Exodus |
| Ez | Ezekiel |
| Gen | Genesis |
| Isa | Isaiah |
| Judg | Judges |
| Lv | Leviticus |
| Num | Numbers |
| Prov | Proverbs |
| Ps | Psalms |
| Zech | Zechariah |

**New Testament:**

| | |
|---|---|
| 1 Cor | 1 Corinthians |
| 1 Pet | 1 Peter |
| 1 Thess | 1 Thessalonians |
| 1 Tim | 1 Timothy |
| 2 Cor | 2 Corinthians |
| 2 Pet | 2 Peter |
| 2 Tim | 2 Timothy |
| Eph | Ephesians |
| Gal | Galatians |
| Jas | James |
| Jn | John |
| Lk | Luke |
| Mk | Mark |
| Mt | Matthew |
| Rev | Revelation |
| Rom | Romans |

# CONTENTS

# PROLOGUE

## *Answer To Stalin*

To the YouTube commenter who posted the message "I would never rely on the words of an atheist, no matter how much of an expert he is," I *had to* reply, writing: "Why? Is it simple religious bigotry, or your own ignorance about what it means to be an atheist? I suspect it is equal parts of both."

Yes, fighting the righteous and rational fight, even in simple YouTube terms. I am not ashamed of hovering around such sites and contributing my opinions from time to time. It is a good and valuable struggle, no matter how meager or modest, as well as painfully *pro bono*. Strangely, in America concepts of humanism and secularism are often regarded as radical, even malevolent.

I feel I issued forth the appropriate amount of indignation or umbrage or insolence; it was deserved even at risking the appearance that nonbelievers are "mean." We question, we rebuke, we criticize, but we do not burn people while alive for their beliefs, or for non-beliefs.

Personally I consider myself a Secular Humanist or more simply a freethinker, but I have complete respect for those who claim to be agnostics or atheists.

That YouTube comment affirms something I have encountered time and again: there is a strange and almost inexplicable stigma attached to the word *atheist*. Most people equate it with evil. Not merely godless (which is, oddly, an anathema to most) but also lost and pitiable, considered allied with forces originating from "hell"—a mythical place after all.

By way of the famous metaphor, atheists simply do not collect stamps.[I] So why all the suspicion and fear and hate?

I am reminded of George H. W. Bush who said he doubted that atheists should even be considered as U.S. citizens. "This is one nation under God," squawked the pious 43rd president, seemingly unaware of the Bill of Rights.

**The A-Word**. Sam Harris never used the word *atheist* in the first edition of his 2005 book, *The End of Faith*. In later printings he brings up the label, but not until his Afterword, and then solely to address antagonists who had read his first printing then maligning Harris as a heretic who bows to no deities.

Dr. Harris generally does not speak that puerile word in debates or presentations, because he considers it meaningless. "We don't need a word like *atheist*, in the same way we don't need a word for somebody who is not an astrologer" he figures.

I will extend the analogy to include Non-Santaists, A*zeus*ists, and A*thor*ists.

The word *atheist* "invites a variety of misunderstandings," Harris has said. "All we need are words like *reason* and *evidence* and *common sense*—and *bullshit* to put astrologers in their place. And so it could be with religion." Harris believes that the label "atheist" suggests that freethinkers are a "maligned and marginal and cranky interest group" and that it is a bad strategy to rally people to a banner of atheism.[2]

About a decade ago, others attempted to tackle this problem by labeling nonbelievers and freethinkers "Brights," and Richard Dawkins and Dan Dennett embraced the idea. Many freethinkers reject the label (Christopher Hitchens detested it).

In a way, the term "Pastafarian" works better because it is cloaked in humor: it conjures the concept of "atheist" or "anti-theist" or at a minimum, nonbeliever. It is perhaps strange that I would rather be called a Pastafarian than atheist, and I pondered this quandary embarking upon this manuscript, in attempt to discover why I think this way.

Rational and freethinking individuals believe that being humanist or agnostic or atheistic are good things, as we can all be "good without god."[3] Most religions represent artless attempts at philosophy and science, embracing superstitions: ancient guesswork and myths bonded together by the crazy glue of faith. Yet you cannot deny there is a nasty barnacle leached to the word *atheist*—an illegitimate negative stigma. Indeed, a stigma any rational advocate of reason and integrity should strive to annul.

It seems the most frequent opposition to the word *atheist,* and to the innocuous notion of rejecting superstitions and myths, takes the form of an argument regarding Stalin, Pol Pot, and Mao Zedong. Those evil men were atheists and therefore atheism is evil—or so the logic goes.

This juvenile pattern-seeking approach is as dismal as noticing that Stalin, Hitler, and Saddam Hussein all had black mustaches and therefore black mustaches are the cause of their wickedness. (This analogy was first put forth by Professor Dawkins.)

A non sequitur is a non sequitur is—guess what—a non sequitur.

Let us examine Stalinism in particular, an analysis then being applicable to both Chairman Mao and (may I call him this?) Mister Pot.

The obvious and rational riposte is that Stalin never committed his atrocities *in the name of* atheism. No doubt the reader can enumerate countless examples of theistic counterparts wherein atrocious acts of violence and murder were committed solely *in the name of* some god. This is in essence the shrewd and unassailable "Hitchens Challenge"—valid reasoning indeed, but there is much more to consider here.

The political system Stalin instituted was totalitarian, just as the mythical and theocratic structure that Christianity defines. Stalin's Secret Police force conjures both the dystopia that Orwell imagined, as well as the omniscient godhead and eternal prison that Christ endorsed and promoted: *thoughtcrime.* Jesus proclaimed "whosoever looketh on a woman to lust after her hath committed adultery with her already in his heart. And if thy right eye offend thee, pluck it out" (Mt 5:28-29). Your local neighborhood Christian apologist will argue vehemently that Jesus spoke in mere metaphor, but he expressed beliefs that the world would end very soon, and if you lust after a woman—Jesus believed—you will not go to his supposed heaven, but relegated to the second-best afterlife joint.

George Carlin pointed out that he still loves you.

Having been brought up Christian, and even attending Russian orthodox seminary for five years in hopes of achieving priesthood, Stalin was inculcated and inundated from youth with ancient myths, liturgies and the infinitely judgmental belief system of the Bible. This brainwashing surely informed Stalin's worldview and seeded his egotistical psyche with nefarious ideas regarding how, exactly, one may gain control over weaker minds. Moreover this is the type of inculcation that so many ex-Catholics cite as the reason they became atheists (those self-proclaimed "recovering Catholics").

Who could blame Stalin for rejecting his Christian upbringing? Yet he seems to have learned mind control via the Bible and the similarly sinister analogues within Christendom itself.

Compare Stalinism to the Roman Catholic socio-political apparatus. This dictator, Joseph Stalin, considered himself faultless and thus the equivalent of the infallible pope. And the mustachioed Man of Steel was essentially omnipotent: Stalin was *god* within his political system, his own type of religion. Stalinism was based on the notion of a theocracy with roots similar to dictates from mythical heaven (and hell) brought to us via ancient scriptures composed by frightened and ignorant men so many centuries ago.

Orwell's Thought Police are analogous to the astral monarchy imposed by the god of Moses, as well as Judaism's immaculately conceived lovechild, Christianity. One hallmark that affirms that Stalin's regime was in fact both totalitarian and theocratic at its base is the imposition of laws that cannot possibly be obeyed, including controlling minds. Stalin may have learned this simple trick by reading his bible. By way of example, Deuteronomy 18:13 claims humans must be "perfect" and "without spot before the Lord."

The New Testament concurs: "Be ye therefore perfect, even as your Father which is in heaven is perfect" Jesus declares (Mt 5:48). Impossible to obey, and thus totalitarian: the prototypical Catch-22. Stalin's regime is born of such deistic and theocratic and dictatorial antecedents found within religion.

Of course we have more *doubleplusgood* (as Orwell might have phrased it) draconian laws in the original sin concept, this "sin" consisting of nothing more than curiosity and knowledge seeking: characteristics our loving creator supposedly instilled in us, subsequently commanding us to restrain those natural urges. And what, dear God, is sinful about seeking knowledge?

Most believers are unaware of the plethora absurdities, atrocities, genocides, and whimsical tales in their sacred texts.

It is demonstrably true that most Christians simply have not read their own holy book. Bart Ehrman teaches bible study at the University of North Carolina at Chapel Hill, and brilliantly illustrates this point as he relates a pop quiz (or perhaps more accurately an informal poll) he once sprung on the first day of class. To his 360 or so new students in the "buckle of the bible belt" as Professor Ehrman calls it—which he confesses "creates certain interesting moments"—he asked his class:[4]

"How many of you in here would agree with the proposition that the bible is the inspired word of God?"

"Voom!" The entire room raises its hand, Ehrman relates.

"How many of you have read the *Da Vinci Code*?" Voom! The entire room raises its hand.

"How many people have read the entire Bible?" *Scattered hands.* Ehrman cackles with delight at the anemic response, well warranted.

Dr. Ehrman then addresses them saying: "I'm not telling you that I thought God wrote the Bible. *You're* telling *me* that *you* think God wrote the Bible. I can see why you might want to read a book by Dan Brown. If God wrote a book," (Ehrman laughs aloud, almost uncontrollably) "wouldn't you want to see what God had to say?"

This is "one of the mysteries of living in the south," Ehrman chortles.

### Christians are Simply Better
### *Or: Atheists may as well be Rapists*

It is not difficult to recognize that religious prejudice and bigotry have always played pivotal roles throughout history, even in the U.S. as the swing votes that brought George W. Bush into power—twice—were largely rooted in strong religious bias. Christians (including key Supreme Court justices) admired Bush as a born again believer.[5] In my experience born-agains become overwhelmingly conservative and judgmental; they try to convert friends and family; and believe with even more unctuous enthusiasm and callow conviction in their holy book, a puerile text overflowing with syllogisms and terror and immorality. A book which they rarely have read in its entirety.

The majority of religious people consider "believers" to be better than nonbelievers. *Much better.* A 2011 poll discovered that atheists are the least trusted group, on par with rapists:[6]

> A new study by the University of B.C. says religious people distrust atheists more than they do persons from other religious groups, gays and feminists. The study found that the only group religious people distrust as much as atheists are rapists.

On the other hand the study found that atheists are not similarly prejudiced: "Atheists don't necessarily favour other atheists over Christians or anyone else. They seem to think that religion is not an important signal for who you can trust."

Years ago I dated a woman who suddenly became born again, right in the middle of our (otherwise wonderful) relationship. It was not a sight for the queasy, but I hung on and tried to make it work. When confronted with a tough decision, she would ask, *What would a good Christian do?*—as if Christians have a monopoly on Goodness. "What would a good *person* do?" I would counter. As you might imagine she regressed toward homophobic and extremely conservative views; she became about as much fun as Jerry Falwell at a Joan Jett concert. It did not last long after that.

Sadly she is gone, now with Jesus.[7]

Like Christendom, Stalin's regime practiced propaganda and censorship. Christians are typically spoon-fed the few "good" parts of the Bible by church leaders, while the absurd, the evil and the contradictory are chiefly kept secret. Most of the Bible is an embarrassment to any wise pastor or priest, and also an embarrassment, one would think, to the supposed son of God, Jesus the Christ.

What Sunday Bible Study would teach of Jesus' racism, and patently immoral beliefs? How many true Christians are aware Jesus refused to heal non-Hebrews (Mt 10 and 15); that the NT praises genocide (Acts 13); that Jesus accused people of thought crimes (Mt 5)?

Most Christians think that only the Old Testament condones killing of disobedient children, strangely unaware that Jesus agrees with this immoral parenting perspective (Mk 7 and Mt 15).

Thus the majority of Christian votaries are simply unaware of the fact that they are unaware. A policy of obscurantism has ever been one of the underlying secrets of the Christian Church.

The masses have been kept ignorant whenever and wherever possible. Christian monks burned books for centuries, and most popes forbade reading books—including the Bible.[8 9] Stalin thus took his cues from the very belief system imposed upon him in his youth, the same superstitious and dictatorial and murderous racket: Bible edicts that have plagued mankind for well over 1600 years.

This gentle Christian Church has always had a wise, wicked, and self-interested fondness for fascism and censorship. The 1229 Council of Toulouse prohibited reading the Bible by laity. In 1270 the king of Aragon, James I, passed a law wherein all people were required to turn their Bibles in to the bishop to be burned; the penalty for not doing so was that they would be declared heretics.[10] Heretics, of course, were killed by Christians whenever discovered. Perhaps such histories inspired Ray Bradbury to compose his *Fahrenheit 451.*

On March 24, 1564 papal bull *Dominici gregis custodiae* forbade all translations of the Greek New Testament because "...much danger, generally arises from reading them." Also in the 16th century the church allowed a Latin "Vatablus's Bible" to be read only by "pious and learned men."

The practices of propaganda and censorship and forgery that originated *ex cathedra* from Christianity over centuries were mirrored exactly by Stalin, enacting censorship and immoral edicts that paralleled the equally immoral bulla of papal origin.

Thus Stalin learned from Christendom precisely how to control his subjects. While he had eventually become a nonbeliever, an atheist, his reign was a religious and theocratic one. His regime is undeniably analogous to the supposed heavenly hierarchy, as well as earthly Christendom we observe in history. Stalin was the pope and more: he suffered from what Ernest Jones termed the "God Complex" and assembled his political machine according to the archetype imposed upon him from youth—a monster of religious doctrine and mind control.

Stalin's regime killed millions, and Stalin purportedly became an atheist. This is perhaps why I prefer the moniker *Pastafarian*: Stalin was raised Christian and turned atheist. Thus, a *Christian*, later an atheist—and not a Pastafarian—was this mass-murderer.

And, if you will notice, Stalin sported a black mustache.

**Fixing the Psalms**. No doubt you are aware of the sanctimonious psalmist who belched the words, "the fool hath said in his heart, there is no God." Many Christians are fond of using this as some sort of childish "proof" that atheists are ignorant fools. It seems to me it is time to correct Psalm 14 (being nearly identical to Psalm 53). The entire first verse, in the KJV, goes: "The fool hath said in his heart, There is no God. Corrupt are they, and have done abominable iniquity: there is none that doeth good."

Here is my proposed correction:

> The fool hath said in his heart, "I *know* there is a God, and just one God. I know his name, I know his mind and his plans for me. I know where we came from and what happens after we die. I know if I merely believe in God I shall live forever in paradise. And all I have to do is pray to God, and all my wishes will come true."

**What is in a Name?** Atheism is evil because Stalin was a Christian who had become an atheist? Stalinism was a fascist church, a religious regime, a theocracy—modeled on Christendom, with Mr. Mustache as God. Stalin learned from religion, and anticipated Orwell and a nightmarish and religious state ministry.

These are points to be brought up by any freethinker whenever confronted with an unctuous antagonist who embodies ignorance regarding the meaning and specific beliefs—or lack thereof, by definition—of an atheist. Similarly one should bring these points when presented with the logical fallacy that connects atheism of Stalin, Pol Pot, and Mao with their reigns of totalitarian terror and subjugation, fashioned from the theocratic, not the secular.

Atheism is a rational concept, the natural and default and *reasonable* position among any young person not yet inculcated with manmade dogma. Every baby is born as an atheist.

As Richard Dawkins pondered at the March 2012 Reason Rally in D.C., "How could anyone rally *against* reason? How is it *necessary* to have a Rally for Reason?"

There is irrational bigotry regarding naturalist perceptions and freethinking notions that do not embrace the idea that real life is meaningless unless we have a supernatural overlord to judge us after our brief sojourn in this existence, so that "He" may relegate us to some mythical afterlife. This belief system posits that our ultimate fate lies either in a faraway land that is overwhelmingly wonderful, or—if this creator and dictator did a poor job in conjuring us—quite the opposite.

Stalin the man was evil and his regime was immoral; he was, for lack of a better term, soulless. But Stalinism was a *religious* system and thus, as with most religions, unambiguously immoral.

I agree with the late Christopher Hitchens: religion poisons everything. But I have to grant exception to Jains, Buddhists, Bahá'í, Mithraists, and Homaranismo.[II]

# INTRODUCTION

Religion has had a free ride and self-proclaimed reign, enjoying unwarranted respect for far too long. Largely, religion is based on nothing more than myths and ancient and ignorant speculation regarding nature and history and morality. Most of the primitive religious hypotheses turned out, eventually, to be completely wrong.[12] We have much better scientific theories and moral tenets today. Yet revered and sacrosanct texts like the Bible espouse hundreds and even thousands of false sciences and invented histories and primitive moralities. Why grant any respect to such a dreadful cobbling of falsehoods and malfeasance?

Similarly, the supposedly meek and mild protagonist of the New Testament has been lauded much undue praise. One may admit that Jesus said a few—*very few*—nice things; yet for the most part this character was no humble or wise prophet. The Bible is proof.

If you disagree and believe Jesus was noble and just, then you simply have not read the Bible, or have not done so with honesty.

Of course this presupposes that the Bible holds an accurate account of the things Jesus said. Perhaps he was a gentle and peaceful man (if he even existed), and not the violent and immoral creature recorded in the Gospels.

One of the most fascinating things I find about Christians is that the vast majority have not read their Bible. Many *think* they have; they are exposed to certain parts on Sundays, even as dedicated attendees of weekly Bible Study. But most are completely unaware, for instance, that the New Testament traces the parenthood of Jesus to mythical "Adam and Eve." *The genealogy in the Bible shows that Jesus comes from the line of David* they will tell you, surprised if shown that the Bible claims an explicit connection from Jesus back to the tall and ignorant tales of Genesis.

Christianity *absolutely depends* on mythical "Adam." Without Adam, Eve, and a talking snake, Jesus' mission is moot and pointless and void. Christians are generally oblivious of this because they have been shown a genealogy in Matthew (which only goes back to "Abraham"), and are rarely if ever exposed to Luke's disparate and childlike version—which if true would negate all of evolution and in fact most known history and science. According to the anonymous author of Luke, a mere seventy-five generations separate "Adam"—and the beginning of the universe—from the birth of Jesus some 2,000 years ago.

And Saint Paul proclaims that the "original sin" of Adam is *the reason* for Jesus' miraculous and essential sojourn from heaven to our blue and sinful planet: his mission—Jesus' *raison d'etre* and the fount and glory of Christianity—is built upon nothing more than ancient and infantile Hebrew myth.

Devout churchgoers are certainly not taught of the racist, violent, immoral, and juvenile beliefs of Jesus.

Yes, *racist, violent,* and in fact *juvenile.* In this book I pull no passion punches: Jesus was no meek messiah, and little if any of the Bible represents factual history. Moreover, Christianity is no peaceful religion, no gentle church. Thus this book is not just about Jesus, it is and must be about the Bible and the appalling history of Christendom based on biblical teachings, thus addressing my subtitle: Lies, Laws and Legacy.

The "virgin mother" claim was simply ancient pre-Christian forgery, or perhaps a plagiarism from earlier cults. Christianity is—demonstrably—mostly a gaggle of borrowings gathered from many prior myths. I am not the first to make some of these claims, but I believe I offer unique and reliable and entertaining perspectives, as well as solid facts and new views regarding these important matters.

I am not taking an approach deliberately provocative or to incite controversy. That would be too easy. I am providing as much evidence as I can against religion in the form of logic, history and humanism.

Now, when I use the word *religion*—word number one of this Introduction—I paint with a wide and arbitrary brush. There are some very respectable religions as mentioned in my Prologue, Homaranismo being among my favorites.

On the other hand Christianity has been the bane of mankind. This book is an examination—and an indictment—of Christendom and the Bible.

Hundreds of millions of people believe today, without any proof whatsoever, in some deity and fantastic stories of even a "son" of this deity and related supernatural spirits. People of various world religions buy into mythical figures like Yahweh, Allah, Jesus, a Holy Ghost, angels, devils, Vishnu, Krishna, Buddha—although I must say I have little beef against the last three.

Followers of the Abrahamic religions have been indoctrinated with a belief system that declares that their current life—*this reality*—is of little importance, and only the next life ("heaven") is truly meaningful because it lasts forever, or so they have been told. Thus many gladly wage Jihad, or kill those who do not believe in their "true" god. Jihadists and even many Christian believers yearning for the "rapture" consider themselves to be God's .007, licensed to kill in the name of His Majesty's Spiritual Service.

But it is not as simple as that. There is another issue, as underscored by the 1937 Fritz Lang film *You Only Live Once*. Similarly, Harold Ramis brilliantly demonstrated in *Groundhog Day* that humanist and selfless endeavors represent the most effective paths toward life fulfillment.

Of course I do not claim Lang or Ramis harbor the greatest of philosophical insight regarding fervor or zeal, or any kind of humanism or routes toward fulfillment. The life Socrates lived presents perhaps a near perfect example: a man who believed that one should always learn and improve oneself to live life to the fullest. Ramis epitomized Socratic philosophy on the silver screen, adding his usual humor.

As another contemporary example, Richard Dawkins answered a similar quandary with his customary eloquence and logic in a CNN television interview when asked how he would characterize atheism (let us forget for a moment that the term *atheism* is rather ill-defined and outdated,[13] making just as much sense as the aforementioned concept of A*thor*ism). Dawkins explained:

> If you're an atheist, you believe this is the only life you're going to get. It's a precious life. It's a beautiful life. It's something that we should live to the full, to the end of our days. Whereas if you're religious and you believe there is another life somehow, that means you don't live this life to the full, because you think you're going to get another one—that's an awfully negative way to live a life. Being an atheist frees you up to live this life properly, happily, and fully.

This is perhaps a more thorough exposition upon a point crudely attempted by T. S. Eliot: "Life you may evade, Death you shall not." Eliot, a Christian and true believer surely was making a much different and deluded point, but once stripped of any superstitious and fearful undertones his words as they stand can be interpreted to the benefit of a rational and secular philosophy.

However, the wise words of Epicurus render Eliot even more impotent by comparison: "Death does not concern us, because as long as we exist, death is not here. And when it does come, we no longer exist."

Most dutiful dogmata are wrapped up in unproven beliefs, often being dangerous, deadly, even genocidal.

A Muslim woman who straps a bomb to her torso to engage in martyrdom—and I use the example of a woman so there can be no confusion that her goal might be sexual (she has no quest for 72 virgins, one may presume)—likely does so because some essential needs are not being met. She might live in a socially and politically bigoted environment, and feels frustrated in her societal role. At some level she believes killing herself, along with other random enemies or infidels will give her more pleasure than pain—*even though in the next microsecond she knows she will die*. She needs, like we all do, to feel significant. In her mind, killing others accomplishes this, even though she ends her own life with the very same act.

I was tempted to describe her suicide as "the ultimate sacrifice." But in the mind of such a martyr there befalls no sacrifice—she believes her actions are just and that this life is expendable, being replaced and in fact improved upon by the next "eternal" one. She is positive that she will, immediately after having committed both mass murder and suicide, be transported metaphysically to a

Utopian existence. This is not the idea Sir Thomas More had in mind.

I believe that people like Ted Kaczynski (the Unabomber), creators of computer viruses, and "taggers" (graffiti artists) largely act out of frustration or a need to feel significant. Similarly, youths who join gangs seek, among other things, a feeling of significance. In the case of Osama bin Laden, his need for importance was fueled by an almost unparalleled, malignant narcissism—in Freudian terms pure ego without any superego whatsoever to keep his psyche in check. He was a special case: a world-class psychopath, one for the history books as well as psychology texts to be studied and revised for decades.

Convicted murderer Mark David Chapman explained: "I killed John Lennon because I couldn't handle being a nobody anymore." Now he is indeed somebody. Chapman's legacy: locked up, a pathetic footnote in history.

I was raised under Christian inculcation, brainwashed as a youngster against my will. I shook it all off around age ten. Then in adulthood I finally read the Bible (few Christians have actually done so, as adroitly demonstrated in the Prologue by Prof. Ehrman, and backed up by many studies), and I examined the history of religions in great depth, including their influence on civilization. One evening not so long ago I had a discussion with a very dear and brilliant friend about authors such as Thomas Paine, Bertrand Russell and Sam Harris. My pal, a freethinking secularist, asked me why people would bother to attack religions in written word. That sparked me to go home that evening and write an article I gave the working title "20 reasons to bash religion." After a short night of contemplation, the project turned into "20,000 reasons to bash religion," and eventually became this book, which could legitimately be titled *Two Hundred Million Reasons to Bash Religion*.[14]

Most people are simply unaware of the depth and breadth and global scope of religious barbarity, as well as the mythical origins of revered belief systems. They have heard of a few atrocities such as the Crusades, Salem Witch Trials, and Inquisition, oblivious to the plethora others, and the millions upon millions of victims. Many people think that persecution of so-called "witches" was a short-lived and relatively insignificant series of events—a couple hundred, maybe a thousand witches killed. Ever hear of the Cathars, or the Stedingers? Thirty Years War? Deutscher Bauernkrieg?

Very possibly you have. How about ongoing, contemporary persecution of "witches" based on nothing more than authoritative Christian scripture?

The vast majority of Christians also believe Jesus was a peaceful and even *perfect* being. Upon undertaking the task of reading the Bible one learns this is not remotely true. If a believing Christian actually reads the New Testament with honesty—even just the four Gospels—while indeed cringing, he or she would realize the truth: Jesus was just an average man at best, a fallible and simple human who believed all the superstitions of the ancient Hebrews. His philosophical offerings were, frankly, mostly foolish and largely immoral, as I shall demonstrate. Jesus actually thought the "devil" causes illness;[15] he believed in a magical pole that cures snakebites; he recommended chopping off your hands and pulling your eyes out, and advised "take no thought for the morrow" because *prayer* is all you need. These are not metaphors or parables or scriptures taken out of context. These are *in context* lessons from Jesus.

And Jesus truly believed the world would come to its ultimate terminus very, very soon, this divine "prophecy" conveyed by the omniscient son of God some 2,000 years ago.[16]

To his credit Jesus proclaimed, "A new commandment I give unto you, That ye love one another; as I have loved you, that ye also love one another" (Jn 13:34). Kudos to Jesus for that. However, this loving outlook (if both redundant and vague) seems obvious and even innate within our nature, our brotherhood and human solidarity. Not to mention that many philosophers realized this peaceful precept long before Jesus supposedly gave this commandment—being, as the reader shall see, contradictory to so many other questionable commandments issued by this prince of grace and glory.

Christianity is based on little more than ancient Egyptian, Babylonian, Persian, Roman and Hebrew myths, along with a mixture of first century writings and many *ad hoc* fictions concocted by superstitious hucksters long after Jesus' time. What followed were some clever, as well as many feeble-minded embellishments upon the original Jesus tales; then transliterations, copyist errors, mistranslations, forgeries and mendacities introduced by monks and editors, resulting in a mutated text and many dozens of differing Bible versions even today.

I prefer to keep this introduction relatively brief. I don a tour-guide hat in Part I to offer an inside look into the grotesque sausage-making factory of Christendom through the many centuries—the *Timeline,* beginning with the origins of religions, followed by ugly and immoral abuse of wacky Christian tenets across two millennia—including forgeries and the invention of wicked and sanctimonious Christian "laws."

I then continue in Parts II through IV to shore up claims regarding the Timeline narrative, providing arguments and considerations on various topics related to the religion—its wild tales, its primitive and backward notions of ethics and morality, as well as a critical examination of the Bible itself. Occasionally some facts are mentioned more than once, largely for those who choose to read only certain chapters, or brought to the reader to further support the particular theme or hypothesis at hand.

Thus I examine Christendom with scrutiny, taking into account the philosophical, social and historical aspects of the religion: its mechanics, its influence on mankind, and its consequences. It also makes sense to critically analyze the Holy Bible for the same reason one might criticize the "science" behind astrology, as Christianity and astrology are born of similar superstitious ilk: no science, and very few true and contemplative moral philosophies. However, astrology has quite benign consequences and no comparable violent history, whereas Christianity's effects have been malignant on the grandest scale. I therefore leave astrology alone and gladly examine dogma. Why not, after all, piss in the punch bowl of the perennial, pious party that is religion? It has wrought so much more agonizing and bloody detriment than benefit or peace or prosperity.

There is, of course, a compelling reason to leave it all alone. As Dave Barry[17] remarked, "The problem with writing about religion is that you run the risk of offending sincerely religious people, and then they come after you with machetes." With some trepidation I nevertheless proceed.

♦ ♦ ♦

The story of Christendom begins many centuries before Jesus with the belief systems of the Egyptians, Babylonians, Persians and other superstitious and sweaty and dusty neighbors, each revering and fearing many gods and goddesses—from which Hebrews and Christians would later borrow most of their spiritual notions, extravagant stories, and magical liturgies.

# PART I. CHRISTIAN TIMELINE

## 30th Century BCE

Let us set sail for the ancient era before **2900 BCE** along the eastern Mediterranean and the Nile delta, as Egyptian priests record their spiritual beliefs on papyrus texts and temple walls. Egyptians would invent—and believe in—almost 1,500 gods over many centuries.[18] As anyone can ascertain from translations of Egyptian texts, their shamans propounded that Horus, the son of God and successor of Ra, is born of virgin mother Isis.[19] Horus is the avenger of God, and we discover "all that liveth" are subject to Him. Horus delivered himself from evil, and promises to guide you to heaven. There was a miracle of seven loaves supplied by the son of God. We find that Egyptians had an anti-pork diet: as with the Hebrews (albeit many centuries thereafter), porcine vittles just ain't kosher in ancient Egypt.[20] Horus is the Prince of Eternity, Lord of mankind. Horus purified his soul with mikvah or baptism. He preaches a communion, and the blood of Horus' mother is magical and holy. Like Jesus supposedly did, Horus cured the blind, and the carpenters of New Testament fiction copied that particular miracle right down to the very method: Jesus used his *saliva* (Mk 8:23) just as Horus had supposedly done. If you doubt any of this, obtain a translation of the Egyptian *Book of the Dead*[21] and other Egyptian texts to see for yourself.

Horus is just one of the many early archetypes for Jesus, covered in detail in Part III of this book.

The planet Saturn appears in the night sky seemingly similar to the millions of stars, but upon close and constant observation one perceives that, unlike the stars, Saturn undergoes strange elliptical, looping movements, as do all planets from the viewpoint of our orbiting and rotating blue and white home planet. Thousands of years before Christianity, Egyptians noticed Saturn's travels and thus proclaimed this wandering white flare to be a god, naming him Rephan or Remphan.[22] This was eventually propagated in Hebrew scriptures and elevated to the Bible in Amos 5:26 as Ραιφαν (Raiphan) in the Septuagint (ancient Greek version of the Old Testament), sometimes translated as *Chiun* (KJV) or *Kaiwan* (NRS),[23] [24] as well as appearing in the New Testament in Acts chapter seven.

Ancient Egyptians, thousands of years before Jesus, also worship Baal-zephon, the Lord of the North, a deity who makes his way to the Bible in Exodus 14 and Numbers 33. The Bible admits to the existence of many dozens of deities, including star-gods, the moon-god, and sun-god, all being sentient supernatural overlords in both OT and NT.

## 17th Century BCE

Some 1700 years before Jesus, Babylonians worship the god who created the universe: Marduk. Our heavenly creator Marduk kills firstborn god Kingu (an obvious antecedent to the Cain-Abel "Murder She Wrote" tale later borrowed by Hebrews) and uses Kingu's blood to create the Babylonian version of the man who Egyptians long before had called "Atum," and who Hebrews would eventually appropriate using a nearly identical appellation, *Adam*.[25]

Marduk then demotes Kingu's army of demons to the underworld, a Babylonian precursor to the hades or "hell fire" where loving Jesus damns you to, if you merely do not believe in him.

Over a thousand years later Hebrews would borrow this story from Babylon and smuggle it westward to Israel to profess virtually identical circumstances in their Genesis tales, with much of the mythology finding its way to the sayings of Jesus as well: Jesus believes all the ancient Hebrew superstitions as if factual. The OT thus cannot be dismissed by Christians—it is essential to their convictions and creeds.

The *Enuma Elish* is an ancient Babylonian text that tells of Lord Marduk working with other gods to create light, the heavens, dry land, the sun and the moon.[26] [27] [28] Beloved Marduk shows up in the Christian Bible in Jeremiah 50:2—

> Announce and proclaim among the nations, lift up a banner and proclaim it; keep nothing back, but say, "Babylon will be captured; Bel will be put to shame, Marduk filled with terror. Her images will be put to shame and her idols filled with terror." [NIV]

Babylonians of this time period also worship Marduk's son Nebo (or Nebu), of whom we read in the Bible in Numbers 32.

A god who is slain as a surrogate for Marduk is called Baal-hamon. Reference to him shows up in the Bible, in Song of Solomon 8:11 as a place name: King Solomon has his vineyard there. Ancient Hebrews performed a communion, eating Baal-hamon's body in *hamantaschen* cakes, a ritual still practiced today among Jews during the Purim holiday.[29]

Over 1200 years later, Babylonian fan fiction would be rewritten, this time having Apostles consume Christ cakes in place of Baal-hamon biscuits.

## 12th Century BCE

From the Canaanite religion before **1200 BCE** we have three important deities: El Elyon, Asherah and Baal.

El Elyon (sometimes El Shaddai), "God most high" or "God Almighty" is father of all other gods.[30] And there are, apparently, so many gods. His wife Asherah is Mistress of the gods and sometimes identified as a Moon goddess, "Lady Who Traverses the Sea."[31] [32]

Baal is god of storms and fertility.[33] All three Canaanite gods eventually make it to Hebrew scriptures, and thus to Christianity.

Second Kings 23:4 in the Bible mentions both Baal and Asherah, with some versions translating Asherah to "the grove":

> The king ordered Hilkiah the high priest, the priests next in rank and the doorkeepers to remove from the temple of the LORD all the articles made for Baal and Asherah and all the starry hosts. He burned them outside Jerusalem in the fields of the Kidron Valley and took the ashes to Bethel. (NIV)

And then we have the King James "Authorized" Bible version:

> And the king commanded Hilkiah the high priest, and the priests of the second order, and the keepers of the door, to bring forth

> out of the temple of the LORD all the vessels that were made for Baal, and for the ***grove***, and for all the host of heaven: and he burned them without Jerusalem in the fields of Kidron, and carried the ashes of them unto Bethel. (KJV)

Asherah is revealed in the Bible in Deuteronomy 16, 1 Kings 15 & 16, 2 Kings 21, and 2 Chronicles 15 among others.

Baal shows up in Judges (2 and 6) and First Kings (16 and 18), to name a few. References to El Shaddai are ubiquitous in the Bible, especially with the stories in Genesis 12, 17, 18 and 28. From Genesis 17:1,

> When Abram was ninety-nine years old, the LORD appeared to him and said, "I am El-Shaddai -- 'God Almighty.' Serve me faithfully and live a blameless life. [NLT]

## 9th Century BCE

Between **900 BCE - 500 BCE** Hebrews borrow many laws, rituals, religious beliefs—and scores of gods—from Egyptians, Persians, Canaanites, Babylonians and others to create their bible, the Tanakh. In its various initial incarnations it professes polytheistic notions. The ancient Hebrew writers show an impressive knowledge of deities worshiped near their own sandy expanse. Beliefs in several dozen gods are still found in modern Bibles, both OT and NT: see the chapter "Polytheism in the Bible" on p. 263.

The Tanakh architects thus borrow from earlier religions the creation myths, forbidden fruit, flood stories, anti-pork diet and baptism, as well as prophesied Messiahs and resurrection of the dead. All this, of course, will be propagated from Judaism to Christianity in the fourth century CE and onwards as Ecumenical Councils prefix their Christian canon with the Tanakh, dubbed (perhaps condescendingly) "Old Testament."

Long before the fabrication of the Christian Bible, Hebrews would attempt, little by little, to remove polytheist references from their scriptures in effort to whittle their numinous beliefs down to one god; yet many polytheist concepts remain.

**Terminology**. At this point it is important to distinguish between terms regarding several types of religious text.

The Torah, also the *Pentateuch,* generally refers to the first five books of the Tanakh: Genesis, Exodus, Leviticus, Numbers, Deuteronomy—sometimes called the "Five Books of Moses."

The Tanakh in essence was the ancient Hebrew term for the book that Christians would borrow to prefix to their Bible—the "Old Testament." The Torah is thus a subset of the Tanakh.

The Septuagint, often abbreviated "LXX" for its erroneous "seventy" etymology, was a translation of the Tanakh from Hebrew to Greek, c. 300-250 BCE.

*Scripture* differs from "canon"—a scripture is any writing not having been universally agreed upon: semifluid, evolving, unofficial, but usually considered in some way divine or undeniably true. When applied to religion, the word *scripture* refers to writing that cultists believe came from or was inspired by God. Scriptures can become *canonized* when some authoritative group agrees upon the acceptance of certain writings, while often excluding others from their canon. Thus the Christian canon was developed when Roman leaders met with Church officials to agree upon which scriptures should belong in their Bible. In a similar way, the Catholic Church uses the term "canonization" when it officially promotes ordinary men or women to sainthood.

The word "Gospel" usually means the books of Matthew, Mark, Luke and John, often "the four Gospels." Other books of the NT are various epistles (letters), plus "Acts of the Apostles" and "Revelation," the final book in the Christian Bible.

## Sixth Century BCE

Mitra/Mithras worship is widespread in the Roman Empire and Asia Minor several centuries before the apparent Jesus era. Its history has a long and complicated path: first from Aryan tribes of the Russian steppes, **500-600 BCE** (and perhaps from centuries earlier) then bleeding into Indians and Persians and Hittites, next westward overland to the Phrygians—concurrently transmitted by sailors via maritime influence, and finally to Romans, many of whom wholeheartedly embraced the religion, long before the time of Jesus.

The traditionally accepted Roman Mithras connection from ancient Persia (Mitra or Mithra) has been examined in recent decades, still under debate.[34] The connection can hardly be denied: in bas-reliefs and statues, Mithras of Roman tradition always wears Persian trousers and a Phrygian cap, and his torch-bearing aides Cautes and Cautopates don the same headgear from Phrygia. If Mithraism landed in the coastal town of Tarsus transmitted by sailors, it seems also that it had migrated westward overland through Persia and Turkey, and even took other paths as far south as Egypt, centuries BCE.

As will be shown, there are many aspects within the cult of Mithras worship that were later borrowed by the carpenters of Christianity. Mitra/Mithras is the son of God, born upon the Winter Solstice (c. December 25) of a virgin mother as supposedly witnessed by shepherds[35] who came to offer gifts. He had twelve disciples, and Lord Mithra promised that faithful followers would live forever. Details and evidence are provided in Part III (p. 169), supported even by the original *Catholic Encyclopedia* and many other venerable and reliable historical and archaeological sources.

Christian mythology was forged and modified and cobbled together by dishonest perpetrators—as well as merely superstitious or ignorant actors—over many centuries.

## 3rd Century BCE

Around **300-250 BCE** after Alexander's conquests, thousands of Jews settle in Alexandria, the intellectual center of the western world. Greek is the universal language, while Hebrew had lapsed into a *lingua mortua*: dead even in synagogues. As the 1907 *Catholic Encyclopedia* ("*CE1907*") avers,[36] Alexandrian Hebrews desperately desire a Greek version of their holy laws and "histories." Various resident Jews fluent in both tongues translate the Tanakh (itself, of course, a book of myths) into the new *lingua franca*. The results: unofficial scrap-versions rendered in Greek. They are rogue and ordinary, merely translations from Hebrew to Greek.

You may well ask: "merely" translations—what could be wrong with that? Well, in those times and among those peoples, only the *mystical* could truly impress: a talking donkey, a burning bush, Yahweh handing Moses a sacred tablet. Even earthquakes, droughts and rainbows were, to them, "signs of God." *Ordinary men* translating a *sacred book* bordered on blasphemy.

Later, around 200 BCE, an anonymous Jew would come to this realization and forge a letter supposedly from an Alexandrian official, Aristeas, addressed to the Greek king of Egypt.[37] It claims religious leaders had commissioned a Tanakh translation by 72 men (thus the *Septuagint*: "sept" from "seventy"). The letter alleges that one exceptional Greek Tanakh translation was in fact proven divine, reviewed by priests, princes, and laity, all agreeing perfect conformity with the Hebrew original. All this is admitted by *CE1907*.[38] This (untrue) story was also related as if factual by dubious "historian" Flavius Josephus late in the first century, in his *Antiquities*, XII:2. The reader shall see that Josephus is not at all to be trusted.

This is a momentous pivot-point. The Septuagint, some 300 years before Christ, sabotages the future Jesus concept: the immaculate maternity, and *magical* paternity, as it is all later discovered to be a fakery. This is Christianity's vatic *fount*, its main spring, broken long before the cult even poked its haloed head out of its mythical manger. The Septuagint version—*not the Hebrew*

*Tanakh*—was incorporated into our Bible as the Old Testament, as conceded by *CE1907*.[39] [40]

How accurate was the translation of the Hebrew Bible into Greek, presenting the world with the sacrosanct Septuagint? Harshly honest with itself up to this point, *CE1907* abruptly aborts its analysis. Within this narrative it dare not continue to the next, obvious step—that the Christian Old Testament, derived from the Septuagint forgery, offers a falsified prophesy: the supposed savior *born of a virgin*. Over the many centuries, linguists and Bible scholars have compared the original Hebrew to the Greek translation, and *CE1907* largely ignores the rather unfortunate conflicts.

The Septuagint altered the Hebrew tales in several prime convictions, forming the bogus basis for Christianity's "Virgin Mary," as well as its monotheistic (later, triune) beliefs. The original Hebrew text, Isaiah, reads (in transliteration): *Hinneh ha-almah harah ve-yeldeth ben ve-karath shem-o immanuel*. It means "a young woman is with child, and bears a son naming him Immanuel." It was altered in three important ways, concocting three lies:

*Lie number one: virgin*. The word *almah* essentially means adolescent girl, a young woman who has reached puberty, with no implication regarding matters of hymenal concern: in other words, *maiden*. Virginity/virgin in Hebrew is *bethulah*.[41] The Septuagint changed *almah* to the Greek παϱθένος (*parthenos*, virgin),[42] and altered definite article *ha* (English: *the*) to the indefinite *a*.[43] They thus transformed "the young woman" to "a virgin." Why would anyone alter their own holy texts in such a way? It seems Septuagint forgers (as well as later New Testament writers) were forlorn in their need for a messiah matching up with so many previously revered sons of God, also born of virgins: Attis, Dionysus, Prometheus, Horus, Hercules, Buddha and Krishna, for example. Thus they might concoct a story of the *newest* messiah that is more believable if the mother of their savior was virginal, having procreative plumbing that was somehow "one-way."[44]

*Lie number two: prophesy*. Isaiah spoke in present participle—not future tense—of "ha-almah" (the young woman) who *is* (not *would become*) with child; she later named him "Emmanuel." In this fiasco of forgeries we cannot ignore the fact that Jesus was not named

"Emmanuel." It seems Jesus was named "Jesus." Christian apologists navigate through the craziest of hoops and labyrinths in attempt to square both the false prophesy and the obvious moniker mistake.[45]

*Lie number three: monotheism.* It seems ancient Hebrews had become suspect of their worship of more than one deity. Perhaps the "real" God was mad at them, they thought. The Septuagint forger(s) attempted to "fix" Hebrew polytheism. When the word *elohim* (plural, *gods*) was used in their Torah, they changed it to Θεος (*Theos,* "God"; plural would be Θεοι). The original Genesis 1:1 in Hebrew reads: *Bereshith bara elohim et hashamayim ve'et ha'arets* (In beginning *gods* created the heavens and the earth).

These pseudo-septuaginters were not one hundred percent successful in washing away polytheism to revamp revered scripture. Traces remain of the Hebrew god referring to himself in the plural (all examples from KJV): Genesis 1:26 - "And God said, Let *us* make man in *our image,* after *our* likeness." Genesis 3:5, "and ye shall be as *gods.*" Genesis 11:7, "let *us* go down, and there confound their language..." Exodus 15:11, "... O Lord, among *the gods...*" Exodus 18:11, "the Lord is greater than all *gods...*" Deuteronomy 10:17, "For the Lord your God is God of *gods,*" et cetera. The Old Testament is thus a poly-monotheist blend. As is the NT, as I shall demonstrate.

Remnants of pagan polytheism and celestial adoration are evident—even rampant—in Genesis, later interpreted by Josephus in *Antiquities* (Bk 2, II:3). In a "vision" supposedly sent by God to Joseph, son of Jacob: "the sun took with him the moon," writes Flavius Josephus, "and the rest of the stars, and came down to the earth, and bowed down [to Joseph]... the moon and sun were like his mother and father... the stars were like his brethren, since they were eleven in number, as were the stars that receive their power from the sun and moon" (see Gen 37:9). Genesis 6 relates stories of many "sons of God" who copulated with mere mortal females (apparently this is where "giants" came from). And, of course, we cannot ignore the supernatural being called "Satan"—the concept of the "devil" is ubiquitous in the Bible. Just how many gods, god-sons, and god-like demiurges are there, for Christ's sake?

You may be surprised: more on this in Part IV.

**Mithra, Savior Born Again.** Around **250 BCE** Persian Mithraism lands in Tarsus. The great historian Plutarch would later write, in 75 CE, that pirates introduced Mitra/Mithras to the Roman world in Cilicia early in the first century BCE (Plutarch, *Parallel Lives,* "Life of Pompey," §24-25), flourishing in Tarsus (coincidentally and suspiciously St. Paul's hometown—much more on this later).[46] Today we know the actual arrival was much earlier—there is evidence of Mithraic worship in the Roman world before 200 BCE.[47] Archaeologists have recently discovered a papyrus from the 3rd century BCE referencing a Roman Mithraeum; historian Roger Beck comments that "the early date is remarkable."[48] For more on this subject see the chapter "Mithra/Mithras" in Part III (page 169).

Plutarch was probably right about the location, Tarsus, but the date of Mithras introduction to the Roman Empire was clearly several centuries before that which Plutarch was aware.

You might be familiar with these words: "He who will not eat of my body and drink of my blood, so that he will be made on with me and I with him, the same shall not know salvation." If you are in fact familiar, it may be because you have read the ancient Mithraic texts. It is more likely you have heard another similar phrase,[49] slightly altered by Christian writers, John 6:54, unapologetically taken from the earlier Mithraic, usurped by much later Christians: "Whoso eateth my flesh, and drinketh my blood, hath eternal life; and I will raise him up at the last day."[50] The ancient Egyptian sacrament of communion was widely copied by various nations and cults, for reasons perhaps only trained psychologists can explain. It is absolutely beyond me why anybody would desire a dead man's spirit be reified as his physical body, then—in what Catholics would eventually call the "Eucharist"—literally eat his flesh and drink his blood.[51] In the Fourth Lateran Council of 1215, Catholic authorities would take it upon themselves to improve upon the supposed words of the supposed Christ by creating their own mystical and magical interpretation of Egyptian and Mithraic communion, inventing the notion of "transubstantiation."[52] In this act of hooey and hocus-pocus, Christians are taught to believe that the wine and bread physically, molecularly, supernaturally transform into the body and blood of Jesus. Then they eat and drink it.

I beg your pardon, but that sounds identical to primitive cannibalism and ancient blood rituals.

Later, in a letter eventually designated as First Corinthians (15:4), Saul/Paul would write that Jesus rose the third day "according to the scriptures."[53] Which *scriptures* does he mean? Saul cannot mean his Hebrew Tanakh, because those scriptures contain no such "third day" prophesy about a Messiah.[54] Nor can he mean the Christian Bible, as that mendacious work would not be concocted until centuries after his own time. Saul can only be referring to something like Mithraic or Egyptian or Sandan scriptures. No others make sense for Saul—geographically, philosophically, or chronologically. Saul's "third day" reference may well have come from the Mithraic scriptures or oral traditions: Mithras (long before "Jesus") was killed then resurrected on "the third day."[55 56 57]

## Second Century BCE

Around **196 BCE** an innocuous Egyptian dedication of temples and priests is decreed and chiseled on slabs, one of which is placed in a ziggurat along the Nile delta. This *Rosetta Stone* would eventually be uncovered in modernity in 1799 and change the world of archeology and history. After linguistic analysis, historians would be able to translate and understand the ancient hieroglyphics to discover that a prime source for Bible tales and modern articles of faith was thus of Egyptian origin.

## First Century BCE

**Mary, c. 20 BCE**. The Bible indicates neither when "Mary" was born nor how old she was when she gave birth to the son of the Almighty. In fact the Gospels mention almost nothing about Jesus' parentage and maternal interactions, the Holy Mother's name appearing fewer than a handful of times, depending perhaps upon the size of your own palm.[58] And of course, nowhere but in the shaky scriptures do we find mention of Mary: no historian of the era ever recorded her. Or her "son."

Apparently the blessed "virgin"—we now know better—was an innocent and very young maiden when impregnated, whether magically or otherwise, and hence my 20 BCE guess for her year of birth. In fact given the times, perhaps 12 BCE may be more realistic. That is, if this ethereal mother of a supposed Christ even existed.

The much boiled-down and distilled single volume 1986 "revised" *Catholic Encyclopedia* ("CE1986")[59] insists Mary "did not lose her virginity, either physical or spiritual."[60] It claims "rationalists and others" attack the virginity story "because of reference in the gospel to the 'brethren' of our Lord"—those damned *rationalists*, and annoying *others*. Thus, this "encyclopedia" not only claims Jesus was in fact born of virgin mother, but that Mary never had sex with her husband even after the birth of Jesus, their "firstborn"—not my word, but of the Bible, Matthew 1:25. As we have seen, the "virgin birth" was an ancient forgery or simplistic mistake: pure fiction. The stork that delivered Jesus was an ordinary one, not a magical gossamer and haloed birdie on a holy mission from heaven.

Yet the *CE1986* insists Mary had only one child, proposing that any reference in the New Testament to Jesus' brothers actually meant *cousins*; yet no evidence is given. Mary "had no other children after the virginal birth," we are told. One must wonder, then, how they would explain "James the Lord's brother" (Gal 1:19); and especially, what a frustrated and confused husband Joseph must have been. Moreover, Matthew 1:25 implies that after Jesus was born, Joseph and Mary did, in fact, get it on.[61]

In **9 BCE** the Provincial Assembly of Asia Minor writes a resolution to honor Emperor Caesar Augustus, *Letter of the Proconsul to the Cities of Asia*. Augustus was considered the son of God who came down to us in human form, only to return to heaven upon his eventual death:[62] [63]

> Whereas the Providence which has guided our whole existence and which has shown such care and liberty, has brought our life to the peak of perfection in giving to us Augustus Caesar, whom It filled with virtue for the welfare of mankind, and who, being sent to us and to our descendants as a savior, has put an end to war and has set all things in order; and whereas having become visible, Caesar has fulfilled the hopes of all earlier times ...not only in surpassing all the benefactors who preceded him but also

> in leaving to his successors no hope of surpassing him; and whereas, finally, that the birthday of the God [Augustus] has been for the whole world the beginning of the gospel concerning him, therefore, let all reckon a new era beginning from the date of his birth, and let his birthday mark the beginning of the new year.[64]

Keywords: *perfection, virtue, welfare, savior, gospel*—not to mention the birthday of the "God" Augustus marking the beginning of the new year.

Roman Emperors were considered deities in ancient times; not much has changed. Even in the 20th century Hirohito, emperor of Japan, was considered by his subjects to be a god, and not demoted to a slightly lower status of demigod until Japan's defeat in 1945.

The rulers—and the dear departed rulers—of North Korea are also, supposedly, all deities: Kim Jong-il (dead), his father Kim Il-sung (long dead), and Kim Jong-un, the third and still living fraction of a Korean component of divine Trinity.

**4 BCE — *or 6 CE.*** The first day of our first century *Anno Domini* is designated January 1 AD, or (the secular term of preference) 1 CE, *Common Era*. It is based on the estimated, supposed birthdate of Jesus: the Gregorian calendar was invented in the sixteenth century, based on Christian mythology. Yet there exists no evidence of the actual year of this messiah's birth. Christians celebrate the Christ nativity every December 25th, a date borrowed from many prior sons of God, being the Winter Solstice, a magical date revered by ancient pagans and then appropriated by Christianity.

In the movie *Back to the Future*, Doc Emmett Brown muses that if he wanted to "witness the birth of Christ" he would set his DeLorean time machine for December 25, 0000. Laughable for many reasons. Momentarily I must disregard the errors: the film ranks among my favorites.

No apostle mentioned the birthdate of Jesus (or, in fact, *any* date whatsoever, either in JP or AUC, the dating systems of the time), despite elaborate and contradictory stories and genealogies.

So nowhere does the Bible give a date for Jesus' birth, and one must admit that if it did propose any such report, the information would nevertheless be spurious, mythical at best, much like claiming a birthdate of Hercules or Robin Hood. Or for that matter the birthdate of Don Quixote.

Neither did any first century extra-biblical writer record *anything* about Jesus. The Jesus tales are found only within the rickety stories of the Bible—never in any reliable historical records of the time.

First century dating systems were quite unlike our present Gregorian calendar, and I am not picking at nits when I point out that December 25, 0000 never occurred—there was no year zero. The annum that followed 1 BCE is termed 1 CE. For perhaps obvious reasons, the primitive and pious populace of the time was frightened by the concept of *zero.*

Largely those are mere technicalities. But for the Christ stories to be true, Jesus had to have been born both *before* 4 BCE (for Herod to be king of Israel, as he died 4 BCE; see Mt 2:1), and *after* 6 CE (when Quirinius was governor of Syria; Lk 2:1-7).

Yet one wobbly hypothesis *could* relinquish a certain benefit of doubt: indeed the Bible cannot be "inerrant" as so many apologists demand, but the Jesus birth claim could be 50% correct—that is to say, one date or the other, but not both.

The supposed date of his crucifixion raises even more inevitable and vexing problems for true believers.

## First Century CE

Almost exactly two thousand years ago an outspoken evangelist roams the Mediterranean somewhere around Egypt and Judea, preaching to the masses. Whether you are a believer or not, this is undisputed history and this rabble-rousing proselytizer flourished around the time we designate as **20-33 CE**. You may have guessed the name of the man of whom I speak: Carabbas.

A flighty prophet among so many thousands of the time, Carabbas is a fanatic early first century ascetic who historian Philo Judaeus terms a "madman." A character of memorable élan, Carabbas often appeals to the masses while stark naked as recorded by exalted Philo, eyewitness to the Carabbasian spectacles.[65] This true story was borrowed by Christians to portray ancient Romans in their supposed mockery of supposed Jesus calling him in the Bible

"King of the Jews."[66] The trick of changing "Carabbas" to biblical "Barabbas" is evident, and the plagiarism is shameless and obvious when one compares Philo's *Flaccus* against Matthew 27:

> *Flaccus* VI.36— There was a certain madman named Carabbas, afflicted... with an intermittent and more gentle kind [of madness]...
>
> Mt 27:26— Then he released to them Barabbas: and having scourged Jesus, delivered him unto them to be crucified.
>
> *Flaccus* VI.37-38— and they, driving the poor wretch as far as the public gymnasium, and setting him up there on high that he might be seen by everybody, flattened out a leaf of papyrus and put it on his head instead of a diadem, and clothed the rest of his body with a common door mat instead of a cloak...
>
> Mt 27:27-28— Then the soldiers of the governor, taking Jesus into the hall, gathered together unto him the whole band. And stripping him, they put a scarlet cloak about him.
>
> *Flaccus* VI.39— Then from the multitude of those who were standing around there arose a wonderful shout of men calling out Maris; and this is the name by which it is said that they call the *Kings among the Syrians...*
>
> Mt 27:29— And platting a crown of thorns, they put it upon his head, and a reed in his right hand. And bowing the knee before him, they mocked him, saying: Hail, *King of the Jews*.

This is how fables often are often manufactured then later revered: borrowings from earlier reliable works, recycled in attempt to instill some sort of inherited validity.

During the first century CE there was another man who was unquestionably just and noble, wearing a white robe and preaching to masses and performing miracles including (apparently) healing the sick and raising the dead. He seems to have been the most gentle, caring, and moral of men of the period—perhaps of *all time.* His acts and travels are well documented. I speak of a magical, saintly prophet among men, referred to as the son of God: Apollonius of Tyana.

A prophet of divine birth, Apollonius led a life of unparalleled saintliness. Traveling and preaching during the first century, he offered wise advice to kings and dignitaries of many lands. He healed the sick (they say), was worshiped as a God, and was (they say) the son of God. Whether or not he actually performed miracles, his life was indeed exemplary, and amongst the kindest and most selfless ever known. See the chapter on Apollonius in Part III (page 176).

There were many other saintly men and miracle-workers of ancient times in the centuries BCE—Pythagoras, Empedocles, Aristeas, Hermotimos, Epimenides, Abaris—all of whom were real characters of history and apparently benevolent god-men. It would seem that southern Europe and the Near East were crawling with miracle-workers and glorious magicians. Fascinating men, to be sure.

Then we have another one, named *Jesus*. Contrary to many claims I have seen, the name *Jesus* was not rare, but quite common in first century Middle East. Flavius Josephus covered more than just a handful of men named *Jesus* (English transliteration of Greek *Iêsous, Iêsoun, Iêsou,* depending upon grammatical inflection). In his *Jewish Wars,* Josephus wrote of Jesus son of Sapphias (II, 20:4), Jesus son of Shaphat (III, 9:7), Jesus son of Gamalas (IV, 3:9), and Jesus son of Ananus (VI, 5:3). In his *Antiquities,* Josephus wrote of:

Jesus brother of John —Bk XI, Ch. 7
Jesus brother of Onias, aka Jason—Bk XII, Ch. 5:1
Jesus son of Phabet—Bk XV, 9:3
Jesus son of Sie—Bk. XVII, 13.1
Jesus son of Damneus—Bk XX, Ch. 9:1
Jesus son of Gamaliel—Bk. XX, 9:4
Jesus son of Josadek—Bk. XX, 10:1

In his autobiography, Josephus wrote of many more men named Jesus. It might seem surprising that nowhere did he write of any "Jesus of Nazareth" or, depending upon which section of the Bible you might select, "Jesus of Bethlehem"—and never of any "Jesus son of Mary" or "Jesus son of Joseph." This, despite the fact that prolific writer Josephus (b. 37 CE) lived shortly after the life of "Jesus Christ"—in the same geographical region, right around the corner from the source of biblical tales and famed "miracles."

In the first and second centuries we have many "christs." Note that the word *christ* simply means anointed with oils, being a servant of God, or (supposed) messiah. The list of christs includes a certain Theudas; a Judas of Galilee; a Bar Kochba; and a christ-like Samaritan. There was a Jesus son of Sirach, who created a collection of sayings. There was a priest, Jesus son of Schiach, who wrote *Ecclesiasticus*, being a favorite of Herod's son Archelaus.[67] [68]

Moreover, prior to the first century minor messiahs and prophets include Amos, Habakkuk, Haggai, Hosea, Joel, Jonah, Malachi, Micah, Nahum, Obadiah, Zechariah, and Zephaniah, and more.

The book of 1 Kings (18:4) mentions Obadiah hiding *a hundred* prophets in a cave. The number of supposed "prophets" in those times seems staggering. Who in the Near East was *not* a prophet? Obadiah's pet dog may have been a prophet, for all that we mere mortals may know.

There were four hundred and fifty prophets of Baal, and four hundred "prophets of the groves" or "prophets of Asherah" (*groves* in some Bible versions, goddess *Asherah* in others: 1 Kings 18:19). In the late first century, Josephus recorded a Simon of Peraea, another "King of the Jews," a messiah, a christ. Before Passover, Romans killed him and crucified his followers outside Jerusalem.[69]

We have Manaheim, son of Judas of Galilee. And a savior, John of Gischala; and Simon bar Giora, and Jonathan the weaver—all prophets.[70]

Shabbetai Zevi of Smyrna was a seventeenth century messiah whose cult had a hundred thousand followers.[71] Is it worth mentioning quite recent "saviors" such as David Koresh, or "Reverend" Jim Jones of Kool-Aid Town, Guyana? How about another twentieth century savior, William M. Branham, whose followers believed he was God in human form?[72]

By my count we have almost 1,000 wanna-be christs even *prior* to the first century:

**Hebrew Prophets:**

Theudas
Judas of Galilee
Bar Kochba
A Christ-like Samaritan
Jesus, son of Sirach

Jesus, son of Schiach
12 named Minor Prophets
100 hidden by Obadiah
450 "prophets of Baal"
400 "prophets of the groves"
Simon of Peraea
= at least 969 "true christs" prior to Jesus

Regarding the chimerical Jesus Christ fellow, firebrand of all firebrands, contemporary to both Carabbas and Apollonius and to so many other true prophets (and pseudo-prophets)—no historical, epigraphic, iconographic, or archaeological evidence suggests that Jesus *ever existed*, as man, or (surely) as a god, or "son of God." See "Mystery of the Silent Historians" in Part IV for a detailed analysis.

It seems we have an overwhelming body of evidence to inveigh *against* an actual Jesus Christ, either as a living man, or as son of the god of the New Testament—perhaps more accurately "New Superstition."

Thus one may term this mythical entity a *phantom messiah*. We must unveil Christianity for what it truly is: essentially equivalent to ancient Persian, Egyptian, Babylonian, Roman, Greek, Norse, and other religious make-believe stories. Christianity is mere mythology, superstition, and some wishful thinking, along with ontological conjecture that is in fact not *wishful* at all, but quite hideous—including notions of a theologically devised astral dictator who has the power to torture his living creations for eternity, at his own tawdry whim.

One can believe with little doubt the historicity of the obscure character Carabbas. He is documented by historian Philo Judaeus whose works are unquestioned. Philo was a revered and honest writer of first century Alexandria, of exactly the same time as Jesus, traveling the same geographical region. He had no reason to invent a Carabbas, a man he mentions only briefly. As shown above, Carabbas was appropriated into the stories of the New Testament under a slightly modified moniker. Yet Philo never wrote of—nor apparently ever heard of—Jesus of Nazareth, Philo's contemporary and noble neighbor to his north who supposedly performed miracles of global expanse (e.g. Mt 27).[73]

Of the historical man Apollonius, Sage of Tyana, one can believe so much more than the Jesus character. Evidences of Apollonius' life are extensive. Yet over the centuries, Christians strove to destroy Apollonius' writings and biographies[74]—his teachings and acts being vastly superior in all respects to those of Jesus.

Carabbas and Apollonius were real men. And, like the Jesus Christ character, they were, of course, not gods. They had no supernatural powers. Historians ascribed miraculous, god-like abilities to Apollonius—like so many prophets and christs of those times and long before.

It is much more difficult to foist the Jesus Christ character as being authentic, as either a man or god, but somehow that is what time (and the powerful Church across almost two millennia) has brought to us. Historical records and archaeological evidence from the first and second centuries prove that the stories of Jesus Christ were fictions and forgeries, and nothing more than local oral traditions much like those of Zeus, Dionysus, Horus, Mithras, and later Robin Hood or Paul Bunyan—Robin Hood being perhaps the most likely historical figure among that lot.

How were church founders and subsequent Christian leaders able to dupe their subjects into believing the "fact" and "history" of Jesus Christ and sustain the beliefs over these two thousand years—especially in view of the thousands of contradictions and bald-faced mendacities of the Bible, in both the Old and New Testaments, and so much historical evidence that readily expose the lies?

This is an easy question to answer. Childhood inculcation is their first method and best friend—in fact, Christianity's *BFF,* a comrade they surely shall always rely upon. Next, fear and threats of supernatural entrapment were precious tools used by the Church throughout the ages, and up to present day. The ontological and soteriological *eternal worship and torture* concepts have been vital companions of Christian authority for propagation of the cult.

You know the drill: 1. Teach Jesus tales to children when they are too young to question, too naïve to think for themselves; 2.

Convince them that to question the teaching means that God will have them tortured *for eternity.*

What you may not be aware of is a *Number three,* when the Roman Empire and the Church colluded to declare all non-Christian cults (as well as non-belief) illegal under penalty of death, beginning as early as the fourth century, then enforced with fire and sword and inhuman torture for some 1500 years that would follow.

Christianity has always been a religion based on intimidation—and, of course, based on one of the many mythical "sons of god." If you believe the Jesus stories and pay weekly monies to the church, they promise you will live forever. If you do not believe in Jesus, his "father" will have you tortured eternally in a hideous afterlife, a made-up place called "Hell"—a powerful tool and image of valuable employ to propagate the ancient cult even to this day.

All this should seem an embarrassment to humanity and to modernity, and especially to all clear-headed Christians.

**Meek Lamb of God**. Jesus, they say, embarked on his ministry around the year **30 CE**, plus or minus. The dates of his life—his birth, his brief ministry, his death—have a historical variance and uncertainty of at least ten years, perhaps even a hundred.[75] [76] [77] If he existed at all, we really have no idea when or where Jesus lived.

This good shepherd, this lamb of God is revered worldwide. Even secular and anti-theist Richard Dawkins admired Jesus, saying he was "ahead of his time." Jesus describes *himself* as meek and gentle (Mt 11:29),[78] and Paul—the artist formerly known as Saul and self-proclaimed "apostle" who never met Jesus—claims the same (2 Cor 10:1).[79]

Yet "meek" Jesus boasted he was "greater than Solomon" (Mt 12:42),[80] saying he "came not to send peace, but a sword" (Mt 10:34), and "to send fire on the earth" (Lk 12:49). Jesus desperately needs your praise (Mt 10:37),[81] and advises savage whipping of your disobedient slaves (Lk 12:47).[82]

*Wait a second:* gentle and perfect Jesus never condemns slavery, and actually recommends whipping of slaves?

Yes. It's in the Bible, and these are not "out of context."

Hungry for nourishment, Jesus son of God loses his temper because an out-of-season fig tree bears no fruit—so he magically destroys it by remote-control or some sort of black magic (Mt 21:19).[83]

Jesus commands you to hate your family, and hate your own life, or you are unworthy:[84]

> If any man come to me, and hate not his father, and mother, and wife, and children, and brethren, and sisters, yea, and his own life also, he cannot be my disciple. - Luke 14:26

These are scriptures never taught in Sunday school or mentioned at the typical sermon—and this is merely the tip of Jesus' "meek" iceberg and the supposed peace and perfection of Christian philosophies. For more, see "The Life and Morals of Jesus of Nazareth" in Part IV (page 245).

Like many Christians, a born-again friend once told me to forget the Old Testament because "Jesus came along and changed everything." Only a very selective reading of the NT can adduce such an assertion. I must point out that Jesus believed in Noah's Ark (Mt 24:37, and Lk 17:27), Adam & Eve and their son Abel (Lk 3:38 and Lk 11:51), Jonah living in a fish or whale (Mt 12:40), and Lot's wife turning into salt (Lk 17:31-32). Jesus even bought into the absurd notion (Jn 3:14) that a magical pole proffered by the OT (Num 21:9) could cure snakebites merely by gazing upon it.

Thus Jeff Foxworthy might well ask, Was Jesus smarter than a fifth grader?

Dim and gullible and superstitious was this figure of Judean folklore, it seems, believing all the absurd tales of the Hebrew Tanakh. Upon reading the Bible, one must be honest: Jesus was not "meek" nor was he in any way a wise Messiah.

Moreover upon any review of history it is painfully obvious that Christendom has been anything but a gentle and peaceful church.

**Death of Jesus**. Modern scholarship places Jesus' crucifixion somewhere between the years **25-36 CE**. The supposed age upon his death, thirty or so, poses inescapable problems for Christian belief. We have John 8:57, "The Jews therefore said to him: Thou art not yet fifty years old." From such statement one logically infers Jesus was in his forties, and early churches claimed *just that*—he was forty-nine upon his death, in stark contradiction to the Gospels.[85] In that case, he died c. 45 or 55 CE.

Reinach observed that "The founder of the library in Jerusalem, about 210, even contended that Jesus had died in 58 under Nero!" Also regarding his death, it seems strange that Acts 10 (KJV, NIV, ESV, ISV, others) states "Jesus of Nazareth [was] slew and hanged on a tree" rather than being crucified on a cross as claimed in the gospels of Matthew, Mark, Luke and John—as well as Paul's letters, in almost all Bible versions.

Was he nailed up and crucified, as we see time and again on the silver screen, or lynched on a tree as the Bible claims elsewhere?

**Saul of Tarsus**. It seems around **40 CE**, Saul, a simple man later beatified and canonized as "Saint Paul" by the powerful and authoritative Church has some wild visions. He sees spectacular lights "from heaven" and experiences hallucinations: "whether in the body, I cannot tell... [only] God knoweth" (2 Cor 12:2).[86] His deluded (perhaps chemically inundated) brain concludes that those visions *must be* of a Palestinian evangelical rabbi he had heard of, named Jesus. All scriptural evidence portrays Saul as a gullible and superstitious man—as well as much less than honest.

Decades later and in his dotage, c. **55-60 CE**, Saul would finally write of his hallucinations—or in English translation, *revelations* (ἀποκαλύψεως, Gal 1:11-17). One wonders why he waited so long to record the most important events in his life. His exploits are also claimed in Acts 9:3-4, 12:7-10, 16:29, 22:1-22, and 26:13-16, written over twenty years after Saul's death, none to be trusted.[87]

Saul seems to know almost nothing about Jesus. He never writes of Jesus' birth, life, geographical location, time period, or any act by Jesus claimed in the Gospels. Saul is completely unaware of all magical miracle claims, unaware of the time and the location of his savior, and ignorant of the supposed virgin mother. Largely he wishes for a Messiah, and claims his savior was called Jesus.

Saul writes, around **55 CE**, "When I was a child, I spake as a child, I understood as a child, I thought as a child: but when I became a man, I put away childish things" (1 Cor 13). One wonders why Saul could not put away the childish notion of a prophesied savior, sent on a mission to redeem mankind from what Saul called "Adam's transgression" (Rom 5).

That's right: in the Bible, Saul actually believes in a sneaky serpent, a fictional forbidden fruit, and everything Genesis says.[88] As does Jesus.

"Jesus empowered the Apostles to drive out devils," asserts *CE1986* (161), and that the Israelites practiced "magical arts" (366).[89] According to *CE1986*, "Christ has the power over the devil and evil spirits and can free souls and bodies from their domination." Yet *CE1986* refers to magic as "superstition," and that it is "contrary to the virtue of religion and the theological virtue of hope." Missing from *CE1986* is any article specifically on witches, wizards, or sorcerers. Yet millions were caught up in the Christian maelstrom over the centuries, tortured and murdered with full papal precedent and sanction. The reason for all this, along the centuries, lies primarily in Exodus 22:18, "Thou shalt not suffer a witch to live."

Exodus is not the only biblical authority promoting hatred of the fictional entity called the "witch" (or *wizard,* or *sorcerer,* depending upon which of the many Bible versions you might choose). You will find the same malignant beliefs promoted in Deuteronomy 18:10-12, Leviticus 20:27, 2 Chronicles 33:6, Micah 5:12, and 1 Samuel 28:3.

Saul/Paul in Galatians 5:19-21 joins the Old Testament anti-witchcraft credo. But let's face it: Paul is (he alleges) a devoted Hebrew,[90] full of credulity and misogyny. Paul will "suffer not a woman to teach."

Neither would St. Cyril, it seems—torture and death being Hypatia's fifth-century punishment for teaching science, math, and philosophy, as we shall see.

Around **60-70 CE** in Egypt, Pamphila writes her immense work of history, *summikton historikon hupomnematon logoi,* but she apparently never heard of Jesus the Christ, whose words went to "the ends of the whole world" (Rom 10) nor is she aware of the "darkness over all the land," and the zombie army conjured by Jesus (Mt 27), this supposedly having occurred a mere thirty or so years before Pamphila's extensive and revered works.

Similarly the famous historian Plutarch (46-125) writes around the year **75** of Mithras worship in the Roman Empire, but strangely is unaware of Jesus and his worldwide miracles. Plutarch, living in the region, first and second century, seems ignorant even of Christians in general.

**Lost Gospel of *Q*.** Bible scholars largely agree that at some unknown date—all we can surmise is that it was before the *Gospel According to Matthew*[91] which was probably written around 80-95—some author designated today as "Q" (from German *Quelle*, or "source") records sayings of a self-proclaimed messiah or of multiple evangelicals, later incorporated into both Matthew and Luke, thus claiming to have originated by the Jesus character.

I must limit this discussion to a brief description of *Q* theory,[92] but the hypothesis is, in essence, that textual analysis of the Jesus speeches that Matthew and Luke both agree upon (sometimes with verbatim phrasing, yet sometimes in total opposition) must come from some common *written* source. The authors of these two gospels, late in the first century (possibly even of the second) certainly were not present during the supposed time of the Jesus sermons. And the two gospels match too closely in certain passages to be simply attributed to oral tradition—thus the theory of an actual *Q* text, of date and origin unknown.

Nevertheless none of the Gospels agree on what would seem to be the most important points of Jesus tales: the crucifixion, tomb stories, resurrection, post-resurrection interactions—the prime questions being: who went to the tomb, what they saw there, what they did next, and so forth.[93] Even the Bible genealogies of Jesus have two distinct lineages in almost complete opposition, both obvious works of fiction.

**Mark after *Q*.** Some of Matthew and Luke probably came from earlier Mark, ostensibly not found in *Q*. Moreover, *Q* seems to fold ancient Egyptian and Hellenistic philosophies into its text.[94] This will seem obvious as you read the "Egyptian Origins" chapter, p. 161. But the writer(s) of *Q* also added doomsday prophesies over and above the peaceful antecedents from which it borrowed—perhaps for dramatic effect? One cannot know.

Thus *Q* is not an actual clutter of scrap writings miraculously discovered in some ancient church library or Palestinian cave. *Q* is a "virtual text," a theory developed in the nineteenth century by scholars, and the essence of its possible original form was constructed[95] by analyzing extant scriptures to determine common themes. If you read the synthesized text of *Q* you will find many of the same inane, illogical, even immoral decrees of Jesus that are spelled out in Part IV of this book, in "The Life and Morals of Jesus of Nazareth."[96]

Bible scholars hold the *Q* theory in high regard. I believe that a physical *Q* text did exist, author unknown. Its veracity and who its central character was are unknown today. It may very well have been a collection of sayings by more than one evangelical Hebrew who preached during some ancient times long before the Gospel writers finally recorded their hearsay, and even from long before the supposed time of Jesus.

**Flavius Josephus.** Christian apologists often claim that Josephus wrote of Jesus Christ in the last decade of the first century (writing between **75** and **95 CE**) but this is simply not true. He is usually referred to as a *historian,* this being all too charitable of a title to bestow upon the man, to say both the least and the most of this fabricator of fables. Yet he seems to have recorded some actual facts in his many offerings, but in the first century Josephus is clearly unaware of Christ. See the chapter "Josephus' Coat of Many Colors" in Part IV (page 191). Josephus was unaware of Jesus and of Christianity, his works later altered by Christians.

**Matthew**. Writing in Greek (not Aramaic, the apparent language of Jesus—nor in Hebrew) c. **85-95 CE**[97] and certainly in possession of the fraudulently fabricated Septuagint, some anonymous author (not "Matthew") composes a text eventually (erroneously, or dishonestly) attributed to the Matthew who might have lived during Jesus. This forger, or perhaps some later copyist (St. Jerome perhaps?), makes his first century Christ match the aforementioned "prediction" by the prophet of the Septuagint in Isaiah 7:14: *Therefore the Lord himself shall give you a sign; Behold, a virgin shall conceive, and bear a son, and shall call his name Immanuel.* Matthew employs the same mistranslated word, παϱθένος (parthenos).[98] So the forger of Matthew propagates that same textual corruption, writing: *Behold, a virgin shall be with child, and shall bring forth a son, and they shall call his name Emmanuel, which being interpreted is, God with us.* (Mt 1:23).

As previously mentioned, Jesus was not, in fact, named Emmanuel. Moreover the name "Jesus" (Joshua, or Yeshua) means "Yahweh saves."[99] Not "God with us."

## Second Century

**Pliny the Younger**. Christian apologists often cite Pliny as a contemporary extra-biblical author who supposedly corroborates the Jesus tales. But Pliny was not a Jesus contemporary, having lived from 61 to 112 CE. Nor does he validate any saga of a "Jesus Christ" in any way. He wrote c. **111 CE** in a letter to Rome that Christianity was a "degenerate sort of cult carried to extravagant lengths," being "wretched."[100] He wrote of *Christians,* but apparently never heard of Jesus of Nazareth (or of Bethlehem or wherever). It beats me why Christian apologists so often claim that Pliny wrote of Jesus, or that he was a contemporary: examples include Strobel in *The Case for Jesus*; Guignebert in *Jesus*; Van Voorst in *Jesus Outside the New Testament*; among so many others.

**Tacitus**. Another non-contemporary of Jesus, Tacitus, lived from **56** to **117**. It appears his *Annals* were never quoted by other authors until many centuries afterward. The one passage Christian apologists use to "prove" Tacitus wrote of Jesus, 15:44, is clearly forged. The word "Christ" is interpolated only one time; in other places his word *chrestians* refers to "good people," not "followers of Christ" (nor followers of "Chrest"). Moreover it is completely out of character for Tacitus to refer to a man who he says "suffered the extreme penalty" (executed) as a christ, a messiah.

It has been conjectured that the *Annals* were forged by Poggio Bracciolini as late as the 15th century.[101] [102] [103]

**Apollonius**. As previously mentioned, Apollonius traveled and wrote extensively in the first century, dying around **97** (as Philostratus claimed) or perhaps as late as **120** (as Dzielska hypothesizes). In none of his writings, and indeed none of the various writers who were aware of Apollonius in the first and second century, do we find any reference to Jesus.

Eusebius, in his fourth century *Preparation for the Gospel,* writes of noble Apollonius, quoting his work *On Sacrifices* (*Prep.,* XIII). The life of Apollonius is covered in detail in Part III, p. 176.

**Suetonius.** Caius Suetonius Tranquillus, close friend of the younger Pliny lived c. **70–130** CE. His *Lives,* XXV, mentions a man named "Chrestus," but not "Christ" or "Christus." Apologists often claim Chrestus is Latin for Christ (not true), and thus proof Suetonius wrote of Jesus. In fact Suetonius wrote that this Chrestus lived when Claudius donned the purple—some twenty years too late. Suetonius wrote c. **125** of: "Christians... a class of men given to a new and mischievous superstition" (*Twelve Caesars,* "Nero," XVI). Like Pliny the Younger, Suetonius is aware of Christians, but never heard of Jesus.

**Phlegon.** Living in the second century, none of Phlegon's works survive today. Prolific Christian Father Origen Adamantius may have written that Phlegon wrote of Jesus in *Against Celsus,* II:14. More likely, this is a later interpolation inflicted upon Origen's work. As we know, Eusebius, well familiar with Origen and writing about him in the fourth century, does not record this in his *Ecclesiastical History.* Or anywhere. Thus we may conclude that the corruption of Origen's writings occurred sometime after Eusebius. The integrity of Eusebius and the veracity of his writings have been questioned by many, including Edward Gibbon, and one can see why. Eusebius attempted to cite various "proofs" of the life of Jesus, including his own obvious inventions. Eusebius claimed, for example, that Pontius Pilate sent Emperor Tiberius "an account of the circumstances concerning the resurrection of our Lord from the dead" (*Ecclesiastical History,* II, 2). Can you imagine Pontius Pilate referring to Jesus as "our Lord," or to his "resurrection"?

**Thallus**. We do not know when Thallus (or "Thallos") lived, only that ninth century monk Georgius Syncellus wrote that Julius Africanus (160-240) briefly mentions him. In his *Extract of Chronography*[104] Syncellus claimed that Africanus claimed that Thallus claimed that there was an eclipse in the first century, which, it seems, we are to connect to Matthew 27, alleging with no other evidence that when Jesus died, there was a "darkness over all the land" (*three hours,* mind you: the longest of solar eclipses may last eight minutes). This third-hand, or fourth, or fifth... or tenth or twelfth-hand legend originated by a man who most probably lived in the *second century*, and then brought to us as far ahead and asunder as the *ninth*.[105]

We have no evidence that Africanus ever mentioned Christ or the crucifixion, so we truly have non-sequitur upon non-sequitur. Apologists can claim no proofs of Jesus from Thallus. He possibly wrote of an eclipse (big deal?), but as far as we know Thallus had never heard of Christianity or Jesus.

**Mara bar-Serapion**. Serapion is another source often used by Christian apologists in attempt to prove extra-biblical writings of a Jesus during his time. All that is known of Serapion's date is that he wrote sometime between the Jewish Wars (after 73 CE) and the third century; thus, not a contemporary by a long shot. Moreover he merely wrote a letter to his son mentioning a "wise king" of the Jews, who the Jews "wrongly" executed. Serapion does not mention this wise king's name.

**Lucian**. Satirist and rhetorician Lucian (c.**125-180**) may or may not have written: "...the man who was crucified in Palestine because he introduced this new cult into the world..." Writing late second century, Lucian is far from contemporary, and the act of "introducing cults" or even *claiming to be a messiah*—did not violate Roman law, and certainly was not an offense in the Empire at that time worthy of crucifixion.[106] Only the most heinous of offenses warranted death on the cross. Thus the supposed crucifixion of Jesus for the offense of claiming to be a messiah is one of the most obvious lies of the New Testament. However, in the Myth Department, it is squarely beaten out by Jesus' virgin birth, "miracles," and supposed—physically impossible—"resurrection."

Others long before Jesus who were supposedly resurrected and whisked off to heaven include Elijah, taken up "into heaven by a whirlwind" (2 Kings 2), and Enoch, transported to paradise to "walk with God" while still alive (Gen 5), Star Trek style. Feeble-minded inventions by ignorant and dishonest men, one must conclude.

**Marcion.** Christian father Marcion of Pontus, **144 CE**, claims all existing (second century) copies of Luke had been corrupted by Jewish interpolations, including Jesus being a Hebrew and circumcised at the Jerusalem temple—both, says Marcion, being lies.

A fervent Christian, Marcion claims *Jesus had no childhood,* being zapped down to earth a full-grown man,[107] and that Jesus was not crucified.[108] The views of Marcion are explained by Tertullian (160 – c. 225) in his *Against Marcion,* 1.15:

> But now, how happens it that the Lord has been revealed since the twelfth year of Tiberius Caesar [Tiberius' reign began 14 CE], while no creation of His at all has been discovered up to the fifteenth of the Emperor Severus...

So, Tertullian cites Marcion claiming that Jesus materialized on Earth, *out of nowhere,* around the year now designated as 26 CE (14 CE + 12), thus the beginning of his life and his ministry. This throws several wrenches into the gears of the Jesus timeline, as modern apologists and historians believe Jesus flourished as an evangelical c. 28-36. Wrote Tertullian:

> ...whatever is the (created) substance, it ought at any rate to have made its appearance in company with its own god. But now, how happens it that the Lord has been revealed since the twelfth year of Tiberius Caesar, while no creation of His at all has been discovered up to the fifteenth of the Emperor Severus; although, as being more excellent than the paltry works of the Creator, it should certainly have ceased to conceal itself, when its lord and author no longer lies hid? I ask, therefore, if it was unable to manifest itself in this world, how did its Lord appear in this world? ...But now there arises a question about place, having reference both to the world above and to the God thereof. For, behold, if he has his own world beneath him, above the Creator, he has certainly fixed it in a position, the space of which was empty between his own feet and the Creator's head. Therefore God both Himself occupied local space, and caused the world to occupy local space; and this local space, too, will be greater than God and the world together. For in no case is that which contains not greater than that which is contained... Now, begin to reckon up your gods. There will be local space for a god, not only as being greater than God, but as being also unbegotten and unmade, and therefore eternal, and equal to God, in which God has ever been. Then, inasmuch as He too has fabricated a world out of some underlying material which is unbegotten, and unmade, and contemporaneous with God, just as Marcion holds of the Creator, you reduce this likewise to the dignity of that local space which has enclosed two gods, both God and matter. For matter

> also is a god according to the rule of Deity, being (to be sure) unbegotten, and unmade, and eternal. If, however, it was out of nothing that he made his world, this also (our heretic) will be obliged to predicate of the Creator, to whom he subordinates matter in the substance of the world. But it will be only right that he too should have made his world out of matter, because the same process occurred to him as God which lay before the Creator as equally God. And thus you may, if you please, reckon up so far, three gods as Marcion's, the Maker, local space, and matter. Furthermore, he in like manner makes the Creator a god in local space, which is itself to be appraised on a precisely identical scale of dignity; and to Him as its lord he subordinates matter, which is notwithstanding unbegotten, and unmade, and by reason hereof eternal. With this matter he further associates evil, an unbegotten principle with an unbegotten object, an unmade with an unmade, and an eternal with an eternal; so here he makes a fourth God. Accordingly you have three substances of Deity in the higher instances, and in the lower ones four. When to these are added their Christs the one which appeared in the time of Tiberius, the other which is promised by the Creator Marcion suffers a manifest wrong from those persons who assume that he holds two gods, whereas he implies no less than nine. though he knows it not.

This may seem odd, but read Luke and subtract only chapters one and two (chronicling Jesus' supposed birth and illusory childhood), which clearly are interpolated, quite fictional and out of place, likely having been added long after the original scripture. Then Marcion's reading seems valid.[109] To many early Christians, the prophesied Messiah was a spirit, an idea, a *logos*—a magical essence or "word" from Heaven.

However, that does not exonerate the rest of the Bible or Marcion's thoughts from critical analysis. Having said that, I must point out that Marcion was a brilliant man of his day who also rejected the nonsense of the Old Testament.[110]

**Justin**. We see around **155** Justin Martyr's writings, admitting to the Roman Emperor that the Christ resurrection story was nothing more than a re-telling of Hellenist myths of the son-gods of Jupiter.[111] He wrote, c. 155:

> And when we say also that the Word, who is the first-birth of God, was produced without sexual union, and that He, Jesus Christ, our Teacher, was crucified and died, and rose again, and ascended into heaven, we propound nothing different from what you believe regarding those whom you esteem sons of Jupiter. And if we assert that the Word of God was born of God in a peculiar manner, different from ordinary generation, let this, as said above, be no extraordinary thing to you, who say that Mercury is the angelic word of God. But if any one objects that He was crucified, in this also He is on a par with those reputed sons of Jupiter of yours, who suffered as we have now enumerated. (Justin, *First Apology*, ch. 21-22.)

Justin also writes of the similarities between the ancient Mithraic practice of Eucharist and the new ritual within Christianity, reversing the chronology by attempting to relegate the Mithraic as a later imitation: in fact the Mithraic liturgies came first, centuries before the Christian practice (but long after that of Egyptians).

> And this food is called among us Eucharistia... Which the wicked devils have imitated in the mysteries of Mithras, commanding the same thing to be done. For, that bread and a cup of water are placed with certain incantations in the mystic rites of one who is being initiated, you either know or can learn. (*First Apology*, ch. 66.)

When the cult apologist has no valid cards to play, he must use words like "wicked" and "devils" to attempt to prove his point. The *ad hominem* is also a clue regarding similar desperation.

**Hermas**. A text called *Shepherd of Hermas* was written in the second century, c. **160**, and many of the first Church Fathers had access to it.[112] It was among the most popular books of the time, yet its authorship is unknown.[113] [114] Origen, Eusebius, Jerome and others believed the author was the Hermas mentioned by Paul in Romans 16:14.[115] [116] This is unlikely, as Paul wrote his letters c. 55-60 (and probably died in 67), while Hermas is not penned until late in the second century—over a hundred years later. The text was eventually discarded and relegated to the blasphemous pile of other apocryphal missals, dismissed from Christian canonization and deemed unworthy of the official Holy Bible.[117]

Like so many ancient texts, this book is in my possession. *Shepherd of Hermas* (or *Pastor of Hermas*) professes five *visions*, twelve *commandments*, and ten *similitudes*. It has been called a Christian book, but I strongly disagree. It refers to the "Son of God"[118] (a much older Egyptian and Babylonian and Persian deist concept) but never uses the word "Christ," "Jesus," nor "Christian." This, at least a hundred and fifty years after the supposed birth of the supposed Christ child.

In *Shepherd of Hermas* the unnamed "son of God" is nothing but a simple slave. Of course the Bible never refers to Jesus as a slave. In fact, Jesus recommends savage whipping of slaves (Lk 12:46-48).

**Gellius**. Aulus Gellius writes his historical compendium *Attic Nights* c. **169** in Greece and Rome. Despite its romantic title, *Attic Nights* is quite a boring read, I must say. And Gellius apparently never heard of Jesus or of Christians or miracles, even at this late date—those miracles being of supposed global consequence, and Jesus' worldwide "fame" claimed in the scriptures of a century before.

**Athenagoras**. Christian father Athenagoras writes his Plea for the Christians c. **176**, but is apparently unaware of his savior's name, never writing the word "Jesus." Athenagoras is covered in more detail in the treatment on Bible origins, p. 210.

**Celsus**. The books of Greek philosopher Cornelius Celsus are often embraced by Christians as some sort of proof of Jesus' historicity, writing around **177** against the Christian dogma. Thus he was a century and a half too late to be considered contemporary. The Christian writings had been in circulation for quite a while. So Celsus may have read the tales and commented on them; how is this "proof" he was some sort of Jesus witness?

Do not confuse this Celsus with Aulus Cornelius Celsus, Roman encyclopedist, physician, and prolific writer who was a contemporary of the Christ.[119] Born some 25 years before Jesus, Celsus overlapped both temporal endpoints by living 20 years beyond the supposed crucifixion. This Celsus certainly should have—but did not—write of Jesus, especially since the words of Jesus supposedly went, according to Paul, "unto the ends of the whole world."[120]

One must assume Paul merely meant *his* known world, and not China or Australia or the Americas. Even upon granting only his local ecumene, his claim is quite an absurd stretch: it seems that no historian of that locale and time recorded anything of the supposed miracles, or even of Jesus. But this should seem obvious to any reasonable person—miracles, magic and supernatural events arise only from imaginative minds, not from reality.

Hallucinogenic substances can be another cause of perceived miracles, as we shall see.

## Third Century

In *Octavius*, a text attributed to Marcus Minucius Felix c. **200**, we see an argument for Christianity, yet neither the names "Jesus" nor "Christ" appear in the manuscript. Moreover the narrator—a Christian—*ridicules* the idea that any Christian would believe that the object of their worship was a mortal, human man who was apparently put to death as a criminal.[121] Thus the Christian author of *Octavius* does not believe the Gospel tales![122]

In **201** the city of Edessa is devastated by a great flood, destroying the Christian church and killing over 2,000 people. Using the logic of Jerry Falwell or Pat Robertson, this proves the real God (Thor? Zeus? Poseidon perhaps?) was angry with Christians for believing in their false god.

In **212** Emperor Caracalla issues the *constitutio antoniniana*, declaring all free men in the Roman Empire to be full and legal Roman citizens. This includes all pagans and Jews—yet it will not exonerate them of the "crime" of not being Christian.

The emperor's motives most likely were concerned not with spiritual matters and toleration, but more about monetary considerations. Dio conjectured, writing c. 220:[123]

> This was the reason why he made all the people in his empire Roman citizens; nominally he was honouring them, but his real purpose was to increase his revenues by this means, inasmuch as aliens did not have to pay most of these taxes. But apart from all these burdens, we were also compelled to build at our own expense all sorts of houses for him whenever he set out from

> Rome, and costly lodgings in the middle of even very shortest journeys; yet he not only never lived in them, but in some cases was not destined even to see them.

In **217** Empress Julia Domna takes her own life. Julia had been responsible for passing the memoirs of Damis to Philostratus of Athens, from which most of our information regarding Apollonius has come down. Philostratus would complete his work sometime around 220-230. Even historian Philostratus, centuries after Christ and as late as 247 in Athens is completely unaware of Jesus: in none of his extensive histories is there any reference to Christianity, or Jesus.

In **232** Heraclas is the first Bishop of Alexandria to use the title "Pope," from Greek *papás*, meaning "father."

Sometime around **235-239** Christian father Origen Adamantius directs the composition of the Hexapla: the Old Testament in six columns of six versions and languages or transliterations, an enormous work of some 6,500 pages.[124] Origen is a brilliant man. But he nevertheless propagates the ancient tales, all bloated with myths and guesswork, all quite economical regarding any truths or actual histories. Origen is all too willing to accept myth as reality.

In **240** Lactantius is born; he would later become instrumental in evoking Christianity as the official religion of the Empire, foreshadowing the cause of the Dark Ages and suppression of free thought and science and social progress, for many centuries that would follow.

Christian apologists of our present time are fond of pointing out how "quickly" Christianity gained popularity, and thus (due perhaps to the logical fallacy *argumentum ad populum*) it must be the "one true" religion.[125] At this time around the middle of the third century the population of Christians is a mere 5% of total inhabitants of the empire. Of the clergy: one bishop, 46 presbyters, seven deacons, seven sub-deacons, 42 acolytes, and 50 readers, exorcists, and porters.[126] Of course things will change late in the fourth century, when Christianity becomes the only legal cult, strictly enforced under pain of death.

Sometime between **270** and **300** philosopher Porphyry writes his *Against the Christians*, citing four prime objections to the newfangled cult of (forged) messianic prophesy. Essentially he writes that:[127] (1) The Bible favors the Jews as the "chosen ones"—why would God show particular favor to peoples of any one nation? (2) Christians inconsistently accept or reject Hebrew law, and create crazy fables about a "savior" who was crucified, whom even the Hebrews renounce with disgust. (3) Christians oppose each other's beliefs; it is thus impossible to tell what Christians truly believe. (4) The Christian writings are riddled with contradictions, including Christ performing miracles and healing others but unable to save himself from torture and execution.

One must admit that it is difficult to argue honestly against Porphyry's logic, being valid exegesis at his time in the third century, and even to this day.

## Fourth Century

Early in the fourth century, c. **305,** the Council of Elvira bans marriage between Pagans and Christians, and between Jews and Christians—Jews are not even allowed to eat in the same room with Christians.[128]

Before the fourth century, Christian clerics had been allowed romantic relationships and (*gasp!*) sexual intercourse, and this same Council of Elvira proposed that church clerics remain unmarried and celibate. The 325 Council of Nicaea, in Canon 3, would enforce this position. Later in Rome, 386 CE, the Church officially enacts the unnatural and immoral Christian "laws." The revised and updated *Catholic Encyclopedia* (p. 100) cites Paul's letter in first Corinthians 7:32 as a reason for the laws, as well as Matthew 19:11-12.

> But I would have you without carefulness. He that is unmarried careth for the things that belong to the Lord, how he may please the Lord (I Cor 7:32).

> But he said unto them, All men cannot receive this saying, save they to whom it is given. For there are some eunuchs, which were so born from their mother's womb: and there are some eunuchs, which were made eunuchs of men: and there be eunuchs, which have made themselves eunuchs for the kingdom of heaven's sake. He that is able to receive it, let him receive it. (Mt 19:11-12)

Of course what followed were centuries of testosterone-laden and sexually frustrated priests who would molest thousands, or perhaps millions of innocent children—"rape in the name of Christ" one might rightly say, the 305 CE ecclesiastical Elviral edict being the root of such cultish evil.

It is in fact the consensus among religious scholars and historians that Paul affected the doctrines of Christendom more than did the canonical gospels. The traditional "head of the household" is the *man*, largely due to Paul's misogyny (e.g. Eph 5:22-23).[129] In the 20th century, Justice Antonin Scalia would actually cite Paul's Romans 13 to justify capital punishment.[130]

Imagine the arrogant audacity of one of the highest-ranking U.S. justices referencing an ancient book of superstition and myths to justify a decision of U.S. law.[131] Let us hope Scalia does not invoke Corinthians if a case is brought before the Nine that involves hair length:

> Doth not even nature itself teach you, that, if a man have long hair, it is a shame unto him? But if a woman have long hair, it is a glory to her: for her hair is given her for a covering. (1 Cor 11)

Some passages in Paul's epistles are kind, and sufficiently vague as to find themselves in wedding ceremonies. Take first Corinthians 13:4-5. Depending upon which Bible version you choose, it may say: *Love is patient, love is kind. It does not envy, it does not boast, it is not proud* (NIV).

In a more original form (KJV, the "authorized" version), the word was *charity* rather than a bettered or corrected newer translation, *love*.[132] The significance of this linguistic trick is worth noting: "*Charity suffereth long, and is kind; charity envieth not; charity vaunteth not itself, is not puffed up...*" The KJV version would be meaningless at any wedding ceremony. Is this why it was modified and "updated"? One must ask, Why was the KJV unsuitable for our consumption, needing to be fixed?

I have heard some very loving and optimistic words of Paul quoted at just about every wedding I have attended. Yet if one reads any Bible version one discovers (buried deep-down, *and never preached*) that Paul's advice is not to marry (1 Cor 7:27-38)—because if you do, you will care more for your spouse than for how you "may please the Lord." I wonder why Justice Scalia ignored that sacred warning, marrying Maureen McCarthy. Perhaps legislation should be introduced prohibiting marriage, with Paul's letters to the Corinthians as the undeniable and sacrosanct legal sanction.

Now back to our Timeline. In **310** Maximian is imprisoned, and takes his own life under orders of his son-in-law, Constantine the Great.

Early in the fourth century the Edict of Toleration (**311**) and next, the **313** Edict of Milan are proposed—not by a Christian, but rather by a Pagan leader. Nevertheless they belong in this Christian chronology: established by Emperor Constantine (a sun-worshiper at this point in his life), those edicts promise religious freedom. It is not long after that things change drastically.

*Like, one year after*: in **314** the Council of Ancyra denounces divination and heathen customs. Temples are demolished, and Pagan priests are tortured and murdered.[133] [134]

In **316** Constantine orders the execution of his brother-in-law Bassianus, just one of many family members and friends Constantine would send his thugs to whack without prejudice or question.

**Proto-Crusades.** Historians consider the Crusades as taking place from the 11th to 13th centuries.[135] Actually the Era of the Christian Soldiers may indeed celebrate its incipience some 800 years earlier, marching onward against the Donatists in **317**. John Holland Smith lends his opinion:[136]

> ...12 March 317 deserves to be remembered, for it marked the beginning of the sad mediaeval story of the use of troops to enforce Christian uniformity. Just four years after that, and a decade after the dying Galerius had issued his ruling that "Christians may exist," imperial Catholicism became a truly persecuting religion with the issue of a general order to the army of Africa decreeing the annihilation of the Donatist sect.

Donatists were Christians with slightly different superstitious beliefs than official Catholic views. In 317, Christian military forces wipe the Donatists from the face of our planet because they could not "be converted to the worship of the Catholic communion."[137]

It is probably around **300-325** when Josephus' "histories" are corrupted by Christian forgers, adding the infamous false paragraph in the middle of his *Antiquities* containing the phrase "...Jesus, a wise man (if indeed it is right to call Him a man)" and other distortions and deceitful manipulations.

Around **325** Eusebius of Caesarea completes his *Ecclesiastical History* describing the traditional thinking regarding the Christian religion and processes wherein church leaders considered some scriptures proper, and many others were rejected.[138] [139]

Also early in the fourth century, Roman leaders decide they need a unified religion: a god, *any* viable god, to hold the flagging Empire together. Emperor Constantine had a choice among many deities believed at the time to be true. The *CE1907* admits:[140]

> But it was especially in the western part of the empire that the veneration of Mithras predominated. Would it not be possible to gather all the different nationalities around his altars? Could not *Sol Deus Invictus* [the "invincible sun-god"], to whom even Constantine dedicated his coins for a long time, or *Sol Mithras Deus Invictus*, venerated by Diocletian and Galerius, become the supreme god of the empire?

Among dozens of candidates, Constantine chose one of the newest, a "Jesus," despite the schizophrenic, violent, racist nature of this latest of "saviors."

Constantine could well have selected Mithras as the official god. In fact the Empire had previously done so: Aurelian in 274 CE declared Mithraism the first official Roman religion; Mithras worship had become widespread in Persia and the Empire long before Constantine, long before Jesus.[141] [142]

It is the beginning of a Brave New World. Rome adopted the Jesus cult in the fourth century in failed effort to keep the Empire together and control the masses: "one state, one religion."[143] [144] The results were undeniably internecine, destructive, unfortunate: a complete backfire. A century and a half ago Father Alessandro Gavazzi orated:

> From the moment that papal authority was established, the Church would fall into schisms... Rome preserved her unity, but what unity? A unity of terror, of despotism, of oppression, of cruelty, of inquisition! That is the unity of Rome, and upon that unity stands the supremacy of the Pope![145]

**Emperor Constantine "The Great" looking very relaxed**

Many superstitious and religious writings had been floating around the Levant and within the Empire. Along the centuries various philosophers and cult leaders weighed in from time to time regarding which texts they thought were valid and which were forgeries, or otherwise in some way spurious or of little value. In those times and in that region there were scriptures from Mithras believers, from Sandan followers, from believers in Ra, Horus, Hercules, Maat, Isis, Krishna, and so many other gods, including certain decidedly *human* (yet quite saintly) characters such as Pythagoras and Apollonius.

Eusebius of Caesarea had a box seat at the First Nicaean council of **325**, which truly was a genesis, a catalyst for unifying disparate Christian theologies in attempt to quell petty doctrinal squabbles between presbyters. In Eusebius' early fourth century work *Ecclesiastical History* we are presented an exhaustive list of the hundred or so texts known by church leaders, most of which are ultimately rejected by various Christian authorities (*EH* 3.25-39). Down the garbage chute went "epistle of James and that of Jude, also the second epistle of Peter... Acts of Paul, and the so-called Shepherd [Hermas]... epistle of Barnabas, and the so-called Teachings of the Apostles" and many more. Saintly Apollonius, peaceful Mithras, benevolent Sandan, Lord Horus and others of their time and region were well-known, but rejected.[146] Why did they consider only scriptures concerning this "Jesus" person as being valid—a man who may have roamed an obscure and tiny parcel within dusty Judea three hundred years prior?[147]

As the Empire was not doing so well at that time, Emperor Constantine reasoned that the gods whom his predecessors worshiped must have been impotent and thus false. He brought superstition and anecdotal evidence to bear against the question of divinity. He also had dreams and hallucinations that he applied to this important question—that is, if you can believe Eusebius.[148] Constantine concluded that it was Jesus who magically helped his army beat Maxentius at the famed battle of the Milvian Bridge.[149] The most recent cult thus seemed valid to him. This is a man who apparently believed in the "messages" of his dreams and hallucinations, just as Saul/Paul had done.[150] The first century character Jesus, a man of sandy and feeble and urban myth, was thus sanctified and anointed by the leader of the Roman Empire, hundreds of years after the nonevents that were claimed in the ancient ignorant scriptures.

Thus the Christian Bible would finally crystallize in the fourth century CE—but not at Nicaea in 325, as most people seem to believe.

If one reads the works of Eusebius, one may easily come away with the notion that it was indeed the Council of Nicaea where various scriptures were voted upon—but actually no canonization process occurred there. Yet I am sure the works of Eusebius *are not* why most people seem to think Nicaea was the source of the first official Bible decree. My guess is that the movie *Da Vinci Code* is a large reason, as that much-viewed film proffered an erroneous account of the events at Nicaea.

Perhaps the most effective outcome of that Council was the formulation of the "Nicene Creed," a mind-numbing submission to myth: "We believe in one God, the Father Almighty, Maker of all things visible and invisible... We believe in one God, the Father Almighty, Maker of heaven and earth, and of all things visible and invisible. And in one Lord Jesus Christ, the Son of God, begotten of the Father..."

This was perhaps paraphrased much later by the cowardly lion in *Wizard of Oz*: "I *do* believe in spooks, I *do* believe in spooks, I *do* believe in spooks..."

Canonization of the Bible would indeed occur, in the 397 CE Council of Carthage, making it more or less official. Prior to that time, the writings were hardly sacred or sacrosanct, but merely collected and conversed among superstitious, ignorant and god-fearing (mostly *gods*-fearing) religious leaders. Carthage made the myths official, with many more edicts to follow—both imperial and papal, and always harmful.

The Christian Bible was not the work of a god as claimed (of course), but a work of humans, demonstrably all *male*. After its canonization, over a dozen centuries were required to bring the holy tome to fruition and to semi-stable form at the Council of Trent (1545 to 1563).[151] Nevertheless scores of different "versions" were subsequently produced, each different from all others. One must ask: Which, of the many, is the "correct" Bible version?

How different the world would have turned out if Constantine and his lackeys had chosen Apollonius as their new god—or Mithras, or Buddha. What if they had adopted the peaceful philosophies of Jainism instead of the scatter-brained and *super*-superstitious Christian precepts?

It has been conjectured that had there been no Christianity, there would have been a fierce struggle between the Hellenist and the Mithraic, and Greek Enlightenment would have emerged victorious over supernatural explanations of the universe. Ernest Renan, in his book on Marcus Aurelius, stated that "One could say, had Christianity been terminated in its infancy by some deadly illness, the world would have become Mithraist."[152] And thus peaceful.

The Revised and Updated *Catholic Encyclopedia*, in its article on the "Dark Ages," prefers the term "Age of Faith" instead of *Dark Ages* for this ghastly epoch of, let's face it, retreat from enlightenment, reversal of advancement.[153] To the rear, we marched. Age of Faith? Indeed, "faith" would indeed explain the darkness.

**Forgeries, Oppression, Genocide**. Early in the fourth century, some shifty Christian counterfeits letters supposedly originating in the first century and claiming to be from King Abgar to Jesus; then letters from Jesus to Abgar; Abgar to Emperor Tiberius, and Tiberius to Abgar, attesting to the "healing powers" of Jesus. The writer forged the first letter claiming to be from "Abgar Ouchama to Jesus, the Good Physician Who has appeared in the country of Jerusalem" and petitioning him as follows:

> I have heard of Thee, and of Thy healings... by Thy word openest [the eyes] of the blind, makest the lame to walk, cleansest the lepers, makest the deaf to hear... if was borne in upon me that... either Thou art God, who hast come down from heaven, or else Thou art the Son of God, who bringest all these things to pass... I also learn that the Jews murmer against Thee, and persecute Thee, that they seek to crucify Thee, and to destroy Thee.

Eusebius would report on this in *EH* 1.12 as if it were true. Honest about this matter, the 1907 *Catholic Encyclopedia* uses the words "legendary" and "imaginary" to describe these letters, known as the "Abgar Forgeries."[154]

In **326** Emperor Constantine follows his mommy's orders and destroys the temple of Asclepius in Aigeai Cilicia, as well as temples of goddess Aphrodite in Aphaca, Jerusalem, Mambre, Phoenicia, and Baalbek. In the same year Constantine orders the execution of his wife Fausta, his first-born son Crispus, and has philosopher Sopater put to death.[155] He has his wife killed by steaming her to death in a hot tub like a lobster.[156] "Fausta Newberg" one might say.

In **330** Constantine has his soldiers steal many statues from pagan temples of Greece to be taken to his beloved Constantinople. In **335** he sacks pagan shrines in Asia Minor and Palestine while ordering the crucifixion of "all magicians and soothsayers," including neoplatonist Sopatrus.[157]

In **346** Christians perpetrate violent and bloody persecutions against all non-Christians in Constantinople. In the same year, orator Libanius (c. 314 – c. 394) is accused of being a magician, and banished.[158]

Constantius II orders all "pagan" (that is, non-Christian) temples closed in **353-354**, some being turned into brothels or gambling establishments. He outlaws all methods of divination in **357**.

In Skythopolis (Syria) in **359** Christians organize death camps for the torture and execution of non-Christians from all around the Empire. Thousands of innocents are murdered.

In **363** Emperor Flavius Jovianus orders the Library of Antioch destroyed. An Imperial edict orders death to all Gentiles who worship the wrong gods or practice divination. Three edicts order the confiscation of all properties of Pagan temples, and death for participation in Pagan rituals of any sort.[159] [160]

Athanasius (c. 296–373), Bishop of Alexandria, assembles in **367** the first canon of twenty-seven New Testament books that would come to represent the compendium that most Christian bibles hold to this day.[161] [162] [163] Modern scholars believe he included a tad too many. Among texts claimed to have been written by Paul but were probably not, we have 1 Timothy, 2 Timothy and Titus.[164] [165] [166] Moreover, the book of Revelation is little more than some sort of Judeo-Christian nightmare, or depraved drug trip.[167] The book First Thessalonians was supposedly the first letter from Paul, c. 51 CE. This has been contested; according to Ferdinand Christian Baur,[168] "The lack of doctrine makes the letter unworthy of Paul." And, "The Epistle is a clumsy forgery. The author has worked up his story from Acts. Paul could not have written ii, 14-16. It is far-fetched to compare the woes inflicted by the Jews upon the Church of Thessalonica with the ills they wrought upon the Church of Judea." Baur writes, "The expression 'the wrath hath come upon them unto the end' (ii, 16), naturally refers to the destruction of Jerusalem (A.D. 70)." This so-called epistle of Paul was thus written by some unknown and fraudulent forger many years after Paul's 67 CE death.

In **370** Emperor Valens (328–378) orders violent and expansive persecution of non-Christians in the Eastern Empire. In Antioch, Christian janissaries execute governor Fidustius and priests Hilarius and Patricius, and burn philosopher Simonides alive. Philosopher Maximus is decapitated, apparently for merely thinking the wrong (non-Christian) way. Emperor Valens orders the governor of Asia Minor to perpetrate genocide against all the Hellenes, and to destroy all their writings in **372**.[169]

Christian leaders force the closure of the temple of Asclepius in Epidaurus, Greece, in **375**.[170] In **376** the Catholic Church seizes the

Mithraeum on Vatican Hill in the name of Christ on December 25, the birthday of Mithras.[171] Emperor Theodosius I writes in **381** "Wills of Apostate Christians to be Set Aside"—meaning that non-Christians have no right to bequeath or inherit property.[172]

Priscillian is Bishop of Abila (modern Ávila) in Spain, beheaded in **385** for being a heretic. Christian authorities claim he practiced sorcery, and execute him along with four others.[173]

**Mendacities, Uninterrupted.** Early Christian fathers accepted the Septuagint forgery when they were too ignorant to know better, and later clerical leaders remained unscrupulous, obfuscating the truth from the masses when they finally did know. Around **382 CE** St. Jerome translates the Tanakh into Latin in the Vulgate, as affirmed by *CE1907*, promulgating the Septuagint "virgin" forgery.[174] So, another *pivot-point*: if Jerome is instead honest, he ignores the Greek forgery, stays true to the Hebrew original, and nullifies the virgin birth (restoring the original "young woman" and present tense phrasing); and thus Jerome would render Christianity null, mythical, and void, exposing it as the Bronze Age fiction that it was.

Jerome knows he *must* propagate the lies, else the cult of Christ falls like a palace built of parchment, leaving all Christian clerics jobless and homeless. The Church continued, supported, and covered up all such unethical and self-promoting behaviors for all centuries that followed. Regarding Jerome, *CE1907* states merely, "it is doubtful whether he revised the entire version of the Old Testament according to the Greek of the Septuagint."[175] We *do know*, by comparing the original Hebrew Tanakh to the Septuagint, and against Jerome's vulgate translation, that Matthew 1:22-23 was retained, parroting the faked prophesy in the NT to shore it up with (the Septuagint version of) the OT.

**The Myth made into Law.** It is **391 CE** now as Roman Emperor Theodosius elevates Jesus (posthumously) to divinity, declaring Christianity the only "legitimate" religion of the world, under penalty of death. The ancient *myth* is rendered *law*. This decision by Theodosius is possibly the worst ever made in human history: what followed were century after century of torture and murder in the name of this false, faked, folkloric "prophesied savior" of fictional virgin mother. Within a year after the decree by Theodosius, crazed

Christian monks of Nitria destroy the majestic Alexandrian Library largely because philosophy and science are taught there—not the Bible. In Alexandria these are times of the highest of intellectual pursuits, all quashed by superstitious and ignorant Christians of the most godly and murderous variety: they had the "Holy Bible" on their side.

Christianity thus begins to flex its muscles, perpetrating summary executions, genocides, censorship, eventually causing the Dark Ages. Reading would be banned, witches murdered by millions, and Roman society rapidly would lose the body of people knowledgeable in engineering and science. Christian law even condemns bathing, being a mark of "vanity."[176]

The original Alexandrian Library held almost a million books. It was a center of scholarship and knowledge, accidentally burned around 48-47 BCE. After relocating to the neighboring Serapeum, Alexandrian scholars quickly begin recovering their database anew, copying every written scroll or book they come across to build up their new repository. Then some 200,000 volumes were gifted to the Library by Mark Anthony as a favor to Cleopatra in 41 BCE.[177]

In 391 mad Christian clerics (terribly angered by the fact that *science,* not *Bible studies* were being pursued) storm the library ziggurats (the Mithraeum and the Serapeum), toppling statues, slashing artwork, then burning every library text they found—hundreds of thousands of scrolls and bound books. Crazed Christians raze the most venerable temple of learning and knowledge of the times, like drunken soccer hooligans after losing (or winning) the World Cup.

The *CE1907* attests: "Much havoc was wrought among its treasures when Bishop Theophilus made his attack upon pagan worship at Alexandria... and whatever remained of the library must have perished after the incursion of the Arabs in 641" (vol. 9, 228); and that Theophilus had a Christian church erected on the destroyed Serapeum (vol. 14, 625).

Even our oft-honest and apologetic *CE1907* seems to ignore the writings of Socrates Scholasticus, writing c. 435 CE, not long after the siege. Remember to translate the word "pagan" into "non-Christian."

Such pagans were typically intellectuals, freethinkers, and leading philosophers:[178]

> At the solicitation of Theophilus bishop of Alexandria the emperor issued an order at this time for the demolition of the heathen temples in that city; commanding also that it should be put in execution under the direction of Theophilus. Seizing this opportunity, Theophilus exerted himself to the utmost to expose the pagan mysteries to contempt. And to begin with, he caused the Mithreum to be cleaned out... Then he destroyed the Serapeum [which held the library]... These were therefore razed to the ground, and the images of their gods molten into pots and other convenient utensils for the use of the Alexandrian church... All the images were accordingly broken to pieces, except one statue of the god before mentioned, which Theophilus preserved and set up in a public place; 'Lest,' said he, 'at a future time the heathens should deny that they had ever worshiped such gods.' ... Helladius however boasted in the presence of some that he had slain in that desperate onset nine men with his own hand.

The fantastic library, moved to the Serapeum only to be destroyed by Christians, housed hundreds of thousands of scrolls and books, including evidence of the actual manufactured origins of Christianity. Of the great Alexandrian Library, Thomas Doane wrote:[179]

> In Alexandria, in Egypt, there was an immense library, founded by the Ptolemies. This library was situated in the Alexandrian Museum; the apartments which were allotted for it were beautifully sculptured, and crowded with the choicest statues and pictures; the building was built of marble.
>
> ...It was not destined, however, to remain there many centuries, as this very valuable library was willfully destroyed by the Christian Theophilus, and on the spot where this beautiful temple of Serapis stood, in fact, on its very foundation, was erected a church in honor of the "noble army of martyrs," who had never existed.
>
> ...*Hypatia,* the daughter of Theon, the mathematician, endeavored to continue the old-time instructions. Each day before her academy stood a long train of chariots; her lecture-room was crowded with the wealth and fashion of Alexandria.

The following account of the Christian destruction of the Alexandrian Library is compelling:[180]

> The frenzied people rushed through the streets along the Canopic way, turning into the short street that led to the temple-area of Serapis, meeting other crowds there, before climbing up the great flight of marble steps, led by Bishop Theophilus. They jumped their way across the stone platform and into the temple, where the events of the final tragedy took place.
>
> In their agitated mood, the angry mob took little heed of the gold and silver ornaments, the precious jewels, the priceless bronze and marble statues, the rare murals and tapestries, the carved and painted pillars, granite, many marbles, ebony and scented woods, ivory and exotic furniture; all were smashed to pieces with cries of pleasure. But that was not all: Those shouting men, filled with demoniac delight, then turned to the library, where hundreds of thousands of papyrus rolls and parchments inscribed with ancient wisdom and knowledge were taken off their shelves, torn to pieces, and thrown to the fire.

The Alexandrian Library contained original writings of Sophocles, Euripides, Aeschylus, Plato, Ptolemy, Aristotle, and many thousands of others. Egyptian scholars were thirsty for all writings of the world. Visiting ships were searched—not for drugs, weapons, shoe-bombs, or offensive materials—but for books, scrolls, letters, manifests, writings of any kind. Official scribes copied all that they found, usually keeping the confiscated *originals* for the permanent Library collection and returning *copies* to the owners.[181]

Early Christians destroyed all that knowledge in a devout and righteous and murderous spree at Alexandria in Egypt, Autumn 391 CE. Centuries later, William Caxton introduced Gutenberg's printing press to England, publishing the first book mass-printed there: The Bible, Latin vulgate. The Bishop of London in 1474 said, so afraid of the truth and real history, "If we do not destroy this dangerous invention, it will one day destroy us."[182] Christian leaders were aware that the Bible is largely violent, immoral, and little more than ignorant fiction.

**History and Science Extinguished**. Four hundred years before Christ, the father of medicine Hippocrates had revolutionized health care, dismissing superstitious and religious medical causality, and applying scientific method. Hebrews were told by their Tanakh that the Lord—not any doctor—heals illness. Read for example 2 Chron 16:12-13:

> And Asa in the thirty and ninth year of his reign was diseased in his feet, until his disease was exceeding great: yet in his disease he sought not to the LORD, but to the physicians. And Asa slept with his fathers, and died in the one and fortieth year of his reign.

Jesus claimed that it is your own fault if you get sick (Jesus thought that "sin" causes illness):

> He answered them: He that made me whole, he said to me: Take up thy bed and walk. They asked him therefore: Who is that man who said to thee: Take up thy bed and walk? But he who was healed knew not who it was: for Jesus went aside from the multitude standing in the place. Afterwards, Jesus findeth him in the temple and saith to him: Behold thou art made whole: sin no more, lest some worse thing happen to thee. (Jn 5:11-14)

Jesus and the Apostles also seem to have believed that illness comes from "the devil"—apparently an evil entity who instills your body with medical maladies:

> How God anointed him with the Holy Ghost and with power, who went about doing good and healing all that were oppressed by the devil, for God was with him (Acts 10:38).

The Church dismissed "pagan" books and teachings like those of wise Hippocrates. To the early Christians, faith and junk science trumped any Hellenistic approach, evidence, knowledge, or reliable scholarship. To them, if it was not in the Bible *it was not fact*. Things are not so different among devout Christians today. Visit one of the many "Creation Museums" for example. Dinosaurs have saddles on, and the "museums" welcome people to ride the dinosaurs the way that ancient people (Neanderthal? Flintstone?) surely rode them.

Hundreds of years before the supposed Christ, Romans had constructed advanced bridges, roads, aqueducts, and indoor and outdoor plumbing. Around the fourth to fifth century CE under oppressive Christian rule, Roman society lost the body of people knowledgeable in those engineering skills[183] as millions of instructive texts had been burned by the new Christian authority. Most religious leaders forbade citizens from reading *anything*—in the rare case where any books had survived ubiquitous Christian bonfires.

**Greece's Labors Lost**. Four hundred years before Jesus, Aristotle had invented and put to use a diving bell. The Dark Ages intervened, caused by the rise of the repressive Christian citadel. The first modern diving bell would not be (re-) invented until 1535, by Guglielmo de Lorena.

The "Antikythera mechanism," dating to about 100 BCE, was an analog computer that modeled the positions of the sun, moon, and some planets as observed from Earth. Obscured by Christians of the times, well over a millennium later it was deemed an accurate representation.

Heron of Alexandria had invented a steam engine, a wind wheel, and many other innovations in the first century. The suppression of science and engineering, or any thinking outside the Bible, caused such innovations to be quashed by Christian superiority. In the sixteenth century, the steam engine would be invented "again."

Many other achievements in science and engineering were wiped out at the Alexandrian Library, mostly not recovered until around the time of the industrial revolution. Texts on science, mathematics, engineering, sociology, and philosophy were lost in that incredible repository, as well as other libraries destroyed by cock-sure and self-righteous Christian mobs along the ages. Greek Enlightenment and extensive scientific knowledge had burned in the flames of Christianity, a cult that had become, by that time, strangely cloistered in the corner opposite from Hellenistic ideas and ideals of humanity, scientific progress, truth, and peace.

The Alexandrian Library was so extensive that it has been said its destruction by mad Christians set civilization back by as many as *one to two thousand* years, causing the Dark Ages that followed.[184] If not for the advent and promotion of Christianity, you very well might be reading this book today in a café on Mars among peaceful freethinkers. The crude visuals that follow in this book illustrate the sad truth—the impact of Christianity upon the world.

By the fourth century CE, Christianity had become the official social currency of the waning Roman world. (Stalin, as well at the

National Socialist German Workers' Party, learned much from the example of Christendom.) Christians would spend the next 1,500 years promoting their religion: assassinating, torturing, destroying, or converting all "pagan" peoples and civilizations, claiming for themselves power, treasures, lands, and entire societies, plundering in the name of their Christ.

In the 16th century, Pope Leo X would say "*Godiamoci del papato poichè Dio ce l'ha dato*" ("Let us enjoy the Papacy, as God has given it to us")[185] also admitting, "How much we and our family have profited by the *legend* of Christ, is sufficiently evident to all ages."[186] [187] [188] All those popes, cardinals, bishops, and Christian authorities enjoy lives of extraordinary comfort and wealth. And, it seems, a good deal of *ad arbitrium* child rape, readily at their disposal and within their private holy chambers.

I do not mean to be contumelious toward modern Christians. I am not indicting today's churchgoers, but rather, it is clear that we can lay blame on early Christian leaders and their lemmings—even throughout history—as well as the holy texts, overflowing with nonsensical excuses to commit atrocities. Followers gladly perpetrated wicked God-sanctioned acts in the name of their Lord, especially where power or wealth may be attained. Even if today the Pope admitted to the one truly *honest* thing he could do—resigning from his unnatural pious post and returning the plundered wealth of the Vatican to the peoples of the world—the Church legacy could never be forgiven. Sarah Silverman had a brilliant idea ("sell the Vatican, feed the world") but surely the Papacy is not honest enough, selfless enough, nor humanitarian enough to ever consider her noble proposal.

Would they even contemplate meeting Sarah half way?

## Fifth Century

The *CE1907* concedes that the "*Apostolic Canons*," forged around **400 CE**, were "a collection of ancient ecclesiastical decrees... concerning the government and discipline of the Church... in a word, they are a handy summary of the statutory legislation of the primitive Church. ... they claim to be the very legislation of the

Apostles themselves, at least as promulgated by their great disciple Clement. Nevertheless... their claim to genuine Apostolic origin is quite false and untenable,"—and that they could not have been composed before the year 341 CE (vol. 3, 279-280). The *CE1907* concludes that the "strikingly characteristic style...makes it evident..." that it is "the work of one individual" (vol. 1, 637). *CE1907* admits some Church authority forged the "Canons" to gain power and wealth for the Christian behemoth.

In **401** a mob of Christians at Carthage lynches Gentiles and demolishes temples and Pagan idols. In Gaza, Porphyrius sends Christians to murder Gentiles and knock down nine Pagan temples. In **405** John Chrysostom has his army of Christian monks destroy idols in Palestine, and in **406** he orders the Temple to Artemis destroyed. Chrysostom (aka "Golden-mouth") dies in **407**.[189] [190]

Honorius, emperor of the Western Empire, and Arcadius, emperor of the Eastern Empire, order all pagan sculptures either destroyed or to be taken away in **408**. Christian bishops embark upon book burning and persecution of all non-Christians. Augustine massacres hundreds of pagans in Algeria. In **409** Christian authorities outlaw divination and astrology.[191]

Hypatia, the beautiful and brilliant head Alexandrian librarian, mathematician, and philosopher continued teaching well after her Library's 391 CE destruction.[192] In **415**, pope of Alexandria Saint Cyril concocts vituperative lies and depicts Hypatia as a "*sorceress*," able to cast "magic spells."[193] Cyril plays the proverbial witch card, the Christian ace in the hole, a putrid and infantile hoax played even today. Fanatical monks eventually catch up with Hypatia when she is about sixty years old. They ambush her chariot on her trek homeward, strip her naked, drag her through dusty streets, and torture her to death by skinning her alive.[194] Those Christian leaders then chop up her body and burn her limbs, torso, and her very-recently-detached cranium, flowing with lush locks, plopping all onto their divine bonfire. All this to make sure, I suppose, that not only was she merely dead, but really most sincerely dead.

In **423** Emperor Theodosius II declares the religions of all non-Christians are "demon worship" and all who practice Pagan rites are to be punished by torture and imprisonment. Christians sack the temple to Goddess Athena in Athens.[195] In November **435** a new edict by Theodosius II orders the death penalty for all non-Christians, excluding Jews: attaching the Tanakh to the front of the Christian Bible (given the moniker "Old Testament") seems to have saved quite a large number of Hebrews from their otherwise demise.

In **438** Theodosius II issues his *Novellae* declaring the penalties for heresy. As the *CE1907* discloses, "In the space of fifty seven years sixty-eight enactments were thus promulgated. All manner of heretics were affected by this legislation, and in various ways, by exile, confiscation of property, or death."[196]

From **440** to **450** Christians demolish all "pagan" (non-Christian) monuments, altars and temples of Athens, Olympia, and other Greek cities. In **448** Theodosius II orders burning of all non-Christian books.[197]

The Council of Chalcedon in **451** enacts twenty-eight "disciplinary canons," including exempting priests from military service, shielding all bishops against criminal charges, and forbidding marriage of monks and nuns.[198]

In the latter half of the fifth century Christian leaders execute philosopher Gessius and physician Jacobus. Christians torture and imprison Severianus, Herestios, Zosimus, Isidorus and others. Fanatic father Christian Conon and his followers murder the last non-Christians of Imbros Island. From **482** to **488** Christians exterminate most of the pagans in Asia Minor.[199]

## Sixth Century

The *Symmachian Forgeries* are concocted by Christian leadership so that bishops could be granted impunity from criminal action. The forgeries are promoted by Pope Symmachus (498-514), appearing "between **501** and **508**... The accounts given in all these writings concerning the persecution of Sylvester, the healing [of leprosy, which Constantine never had] and baptism of Constantine,[200] the emperor's gift to the pope, the rights granted to the latter, and the council of 275 bishops at Rome, are entirely legendary."[201]

In **527** emperors Justin and Justinian declare "Pagans Barred from Office and their Real Property Confiscated." They explain:[202]

> It is our intention to restore the existing laws which affect the rest of the heretics of whatever name they are, (and we label as heretic whoever is not a member of the Catholic Church and of our orthodox and holy faith); likewise the pagans who attempt to introduce the worship of many gods, and the Jews and the Samaritans. ... We forbid any of the above-mentioned persons to aspire to any dignity or to acquire civil or military office or to attain to any rank."

In **528** Emperor Justinian orders the execution—by fire, crucifixion, mauling by wild beasts or cutting to pieces—of all who practice sorcery, divination, magic or idolatry, and prohibiting all teachings by non-Christians.[203] Justinian I decrees, **529 CE**, that it is not only illegal to follow Pagan faith but also that apostasy is to be punished *by death*.[204]

In the 6th century, exact date unknown, Christian emperor Justinian writes the law "Baptized Persons who follow Pagan Practices to Suffer Death."[205] The law calls all non-Christians "impious and wicked" and declares, as one may presume from the law's appellation, those who abandon "the worship of the true and only God" are committing an "insane error." Justinian declares death to be the punishment for anyone baptized who then adopts pagan ways: "this we do in all mercy"—or so goes the compassionate Christian decree.

In **529** Emperor Justinian closes all non-Christian schools of philosophy including the Academy of Athens. The *CE1907* admits "From that date Christianity had no rival in Athens."[206] Justinian rules the Empire from 527 to 565, outlawing and closing libraries, schools of philosophy, and all Gentile institutions. Thousands of Pagans are thus persecuted—arrested, tortured and murdered.

In **580** Christian Inquisitors attack a secret Zeus temple in Antioch, arresting all Pagans found there. They are tortured and taken to Constantinople for "trial." Found guilty of heresy, they are all murdered on the cross, including Vice Governor Anatolius; next, a Christian mob drags their bodies through the streets before tossing their corpses into a mass pile, unburied.[207]

In **583** Byzantine Emperor Theodosius (ruled 582 to 602) continues holy proto-crusades, ordering tens of thousands of Hellenes tortured, burned and even torn to pieces by wild animals and torture devices. Christians destroy their shrines, temples and altars.[208]

**Gregory the Anti-Semite**. Archbishop of Constantinople John Chrysostom had declared in the fourth century that it was the duty of all Christians "to hate Jews," claiming Jews "sacrifice their children to Satan."[209] Pope Gregory I (c. 540 – 604 CE) propagates Chrysostom's hate and racism, proclaiming in **599** that Jews are Christ killers.[210] Over many centuries, Christian leaders fabricate outrageous lies, claiming, for instance, that Jews *stabbed communion wafers* (I kid you not) "to kill Christ," and that *Jews* murder Christian children. Christians react to the made-up stories by killing many thousands of Jews.[211] From the 12th to the 15th century, Jews were regularly converted to Christianity by force and under threat of execution, being murdered if they rejected the Christian dogmata.[212] [213]

You probably have a good idea what happened to millions of innocent Jews in the 1940s.

## Seventh Century

The Byzantine emperor offers the Roman Pantheon as a gift to Pope Boniface IV around **608**, converting it to a Christian church.

The Fourth Council of Toledo convenes in **633**, "one of the most important held in Spain" (*CE1907* vol. 14, 758) proclaiming Christianity a really, *really* great thing, while condemning all Jews because they "killed Christ." In Canon 60 the Council proclaims that:[214]

> the sons and daughters of Jews are to be separated from the parents, lest they be likewise involved in their errors. To be placed either in monasteries, or with Christian men and women who fear God, that from their conversation they may learn the worship of the true faith, and thus instructed for the better, may be improved both in morals and belief.

Jews are also prohibited from holding office, or owning Christian slaves, "for it is shameful that the members of Christ should serve the ministers of Antichrist."

An Ecumenical council meets in **681** in Constantinople, condemning monothelitism as heretical, and the council defines Jesus Christ as having two "energies." Monothelitism taught a slightly different view of Jesus that would be of no consequence to any freethinking person able to dismiss the tales as mere myth and made-up "philosophies."

## Eighth Century

Around **751** Christian leaders forge a letter claiming to have been written by "St. Peter" himself—their insidious intention is that it be a prophesy—addressed from (first century) Peter, long dead one may well think, to *eighth century* Pepin, King of the Franks. This criminal forgery of childlike and superstitious foundation reads as follows:[215] [216]

> Peter, elected Apostle by Jesus Christ, Son of the Living God.
>
> I, Peter, summoned to the apostolate by Christ, Son of the Living God, has received from the Divine Might the mission of enlightening the whole world... Wherefore, all those who, having heard my preaching, put it into practice, must believe absolutely that by God's order their sins are cleansed in this world and they shall enter stainless into everlasting life Come ye to the aid of the Roman people, which has been entrusted to me by God. And I, on the day of Judgment, shall prepare for you a splendid dwelling place in the Kingdom of God.
>
> —Signed, Peter, Prince of the Apostles.

Superstitious authorities of the times actually believed the phony communiqué: "Saint Peter" composed his golden letter *from heaven* to influence and arbitrate political and financial transactions on Earth. "When [Pope] Stephen II performed the ceremony of anointing Pepin and his son at St. Denis," admits the *Catholic Encyclopedia,* "it was St. Peter who was regarded as the mystical giver of the secular power."[217] In such patently dishonest ways this corrupt Church would gain power, wealth, and real estate over many centuries.

In **756** Pepin grants the pope temporal jurisdiction over Rome and surrounding areas and thus creates the Papal States, a huge swath of central and northern Italy subsequently controlled by Church authority. Somewhere between **750** and **850** the *Donatio Constantini* ("Donation of Constantine") was "a forged document [supposedly] of Emperor Constantine the Great, by which large privileges and rich possessions were conferred on the pope and the Roman Church. ...It is addressed by Constantine to Sylvester I (314-35)..." The *CE1907* affirms "this document is without doubt a forgery... As early as the 15th century its falsity was known and demonstrated... its genuineness was yet occasionally defended, and the document still further used as authentic...".[218] The forged document was inserted into the False Decretals (discussed below)[219] and upon "the end of the ninth century and during the tenth, extracts from the false decretals begin to be included in canon law collections."[220]

Christian soldiers under papal command thus seize Rome as early as the eighth century after the "Donation" was forged and incorporated into the false decretals and into law (*CE1907* vol. 5, 119),[221] and most of Italy comes under Church control and possession. The city of Rome itself would not be returned to the Italian people until the nineteenth century (*CE1907* vol. 8, 234).[222] As admitted by *CE1907*, "Not until 20 September, 1870, was Rome taken from the popes and made the actual capital of the Kingdom of Italy" (vol. 13, 169).

Emperor Charlemagne (742-814) "constantly attributed his imperial dignity to an act of God, made known, of course, through the agency of the Vicar of Christ..." Under Charlemagne, Saxons are forced to undergo baptism, executed if they refuse. In *one day* in **783**, revered Charlemagne beheads 4,500 Saxons at Verdun because they resisted Charlemagne's concept of "God."[223]

**Charlemagne, his favorite sword, and some crosses**

## Ninth Century

Around **850** the *False Decretals* are published and widely distributed,[224] having been originally forged around 775 to 785. These are papal letters that the Church uses to claim unlimited authority in all matters, using more jackboot tactics to attain selfish goals via underhanded and violent means. Of around a hundred letters in this collection, supposedly from popes over the centuries, all but a scant few were outright forgeries, with perhaps some being genuine and honest. Of these documents, forged by the Church, Abbé Guettée wrote:[225]

> Here is language quite new on the part of Roman bishops, but henceforth destined to become habitual with them. It dates from 785; that is, from the same year when Adrian delivered to Ingelramn, Bishop of Metz, the collection of the *False Decretals.* There is something highly significant in this coincidence. Was it Adrian himself who authorized this work of forgery? We do not know; but it is an incontestable fact that it was in *Rome itself* under the *pontificate of Adrian,* and in the year in which he wrote so haughtily to the Emperor of the East, that this new code of the Papacy is first mentioned in history. Adrian is the true creator of the modern Papacy. Not finding in the traditions of the Church the documents necessary to support his ambitious views, he

> rested them upon apocryphal documents written to suit the occasion, and to legalize all future usurpations of the Roman see. Adrian knew that the *Decretals* contained in the code of Ingelramn were bogus. For he had already given, ten years before, to Charles, King of the Franks, a code of the ancient canons, identical with the generally received collection of Dionysius Exiguus. It was, therefore, between the years 775 and 785 that the *False Decretals* were composed.
>
> The time was favorable to such inventions. In the foreign invasions which had deluged the entire West with blood and covered it with ruins, the libraries of churches and monasteries were destroyed; the clergy were plunged into the deepest ignorance; the East, invaded by the Musselman, now had scarcely any relations with the West. The Papacy profited from these misfortunes, and built up a power half political and half religious upon these ruins, finding no lack of flatterers who did not blush to invent and secretly propagate their forgeries in order to give a divine character to an institution that has ambition for its only source.

The original *Catholic Encyclopedia* admits to astonishing Church guilt across 800 years: "Nowadays every one agrees that these so-called papal letters are forgeries..." and states that "Nevertheless the official edition of the 'Corpus Juris,' in 1580, upheld the genuineness of the false decretals."[226]

At this point in history the Jesus myths are becoming turbo-charged by many impostures forged by men clearly in search of power and wealth. Christian leadership would indeed gain immeasurable influence, global puissance, and vast treasures almost beyond comprehension. Ever been to Vatican City?

In **897** Pope Stephen VII (or VI)[227] places his rival Formosus on trial. The fact that Pope Formosus had died nine months prior does not bother the current pope. Stephen has Formosus' remains dragged from his tomb, dressed, and propped up on a throne. Stephen shouts accusations at Formosus' skeletal remains, and eventually finds the dead man "guilty of all charges"—that is, guilty of being "evil."[228] According to *CE1907:*[229]

> The decision was that the deceased had been unworthy of the pontificate, which he could not have validly received since he

> was bishop of another see. All his measures and acts were annulled, and all the orders conferred by him were declared invalid. The papal vestments were torn from his body; the three fingers which the dead pope had used in consecrations were severed from his right hand; the corpse was cast into a grave in the cemetery for strangers, to be removed after a few days and consigned to the Tiber.

Throughout the proceedings, the defendant Formosus remains silent, and is never heard from again.

## Eleventh Century

In **1022** we foresee a prelude to the wicked oppression of the peaceful Cathars (or Cathari), as Christian forces burn thirteen alive in Orléans, France.[230] Cathars are nonviolent and reverent: they are vegetarians, fervent pacifists—and they are devout Christians. But the crucifixes slung round their herbivorous throats could not save even a one of them from Christian soldiers who would march upon them in the thirteenth century.

In **1076** Catholic priest Ramihrdus of Cambrai expresses his bold opinion: the Church is corrupt. He is declared a heretic and burned alive. His execution leads to local civil war.[231]

In **1096** a powerful Christian militia embarks upon the First *official* Crusade to retake the so-called "Holy Land" from Muslims.[232] Then in 1099 crusaders storm into Jerusalem to overcome non-Christian rule of "their" sacred town. They slaughter tens of thousands, this sanctimonious coup later being dubbed the "Jerusalem Massacre." Islamic *witches*—not earthly *humans*—are charged with the attempt to control the siege, according to the superstitious Christians. Yet the real-life, human Christians prevailed. They killed men, women, and children as long as the attackers were reasonably sure the alleged heretics were not Christian:

> After a general procession which the crusaders made barefooted around the city walls amid the insults and incantations of the Mohammedan sorcerers, the attack began 14 July, 1099. Next day the Christians entered Jerusalem from all sides and slew its

inhabitants regardless of age or sex... Having accomplished their pilgrimage to the Holy Sepulchre, the knights chose as lord of the new conquest Godfrey of Bouillon, who called himself "Defender of the Holy Sepulchre". They had then to repulse an Egyptian army, which was defeated at Ascalon, 12 August, 1099 (*CE1907* vol. 4, 547).

Note that nearly a century later (September 17, 1187), Islamic Sultan Saladin and his "Infidel Hosts" peacefully recaptured Jerusalem. All Christian residents were permitted to quit the town in peace. Joseph Wheless observed that the Christians "began to learn what civilization was" from Saladin, the Muslim.[233]

## Twelfth Century

Peter of Bruys in southeastern France rejects the superstitious notions of infant baptism, transubstantiation, and other absurd and irrational Christian beliefs. He is declared a heretic and in **1135** "burned to death by a band of angry people."[234]

The Second Crusade begins in **1145**, and it is largely a failure, as were most Christian Crusades.

Christian forces burn several Cathars at the stake in Cologne in **1163**; among the five executed is young girl.[235] In **1166** some 30 Cathars from France arrive in England, and are immediately declared heretics. And we know what followers of Jesus have historically done to "heretics":

> ...Henry II ordered that they be burnt on their foreheads with red-hot iron, be beaten with rods in the public square, and then driven off. Moreover, he forbade anyone to give them shelter or otherwise assist them, so that they died partly from hunger and partly from the cold of winter. Duke Philip of Flanders, aided by William of the White Hand, Archbishop of Reims, was particularly severe towards heretics. They caused [in 1183] many citizens in their domains, nobles and commoners, clerics, knights, peasants, spinsters, widows, and married women, to be burnt alive, confiscated their property, and divided it between them.[236]

The Third Crusade begins in **1189** in effort to retake the Holy Land now under Muslim control by Saladin. More or less a draw, it would thus necessitate a fourth attempt at God-inspired land snatching.

Beginning in **1191** King Richard "Dick" I, a righteous Christian, conquers Navarre in Spain, and the city of Acre in Israel. In Acre, Richard executes 2,700 prisoners of war, many of them women and children.[237] Some are disemboweled by order of Richard in a search for possible swallowed gems.[238]

This King Richard "the Lion-Hearted" is not a peaceful and loving Christian, but a ruthless butcher mostly after riches. Before his 1189 coronation, Richard forbade Jews from attending the ceremonies. As a result, hundreds of Jews were murdered by his merciless soldiers.[239] After all, what would a good Christian do? According to *CE1907*, the reverent Richard "heard Mass daily, and on three occasions did penance in a very remarkable way, simply on the impulse of his own distressed conscience."[240]

Pope Innocent III, given name Lotario dei Conti di Segni (Italian, literally "Larry the Conti Guy"), declares in **1198** that anyone who reads the Bible should be stoned to death.[241] If you have read the Christian Bible, you realize the reason: it is nonsensical throughout, proposing immoral advice time and again, declaring that the Lord imposes infinite punishment for finite "crimes," oozing outrageous violence and intolerance, as well as complete ignorance regarding cosmology, history, and morality. See Part IV of this book for much more.

Thus Christian leaders realize that they have plenty to hide, and that the masses must be kept ignorant whenever and wherever possible. Christian monks burn books for centuries, and most popes forbid reading all books—*including the Bible.*[242] [243] The Church has always embraced censorship, as it must. Some seven hundred years later, Heinrich Heine would write his play "Almansor," and in 1823 his character says, wisely, "Where they burn books, so too will they in the end burn human beings.

Note that he was referring to reverent folks burning the Qur'an, a work equally as fictional and violent and immoral as the Bible.

## Thirteenth Century

The Fourth Crusade is perpetrated **1202-04**. Crusaders gather in Venice in October 1202, beginning their unctuous attack *en masse* November 24. They attack Zara and Constantinople, destroying the Library of Constantinople and looting the city's treasures. Pope Innocent III—one of the most evil popes in history, responsible for the murder of well over a million innocents—wrote that he was thoroughly ashamed of his Crusaders for their heinous behavior, grieving that the Crusaders "spared neither religion, nor age, nor sex."[244] As we shall soon see, the incursion against the peaceful Cathars would be guilty of the same offenses on a much grander scale.

In **1209** John, King of England, refuses to accept Stephen Langton as Archbishop of Canterbury (leader of the Church of England), and is therefore excommunicated by Innocent III. Pope Innocent negotiates with Philip II of France to attack England, and closes down all Anglican churches.

In **1209** town leaders in Béziers, France refuse to hand over 222 of their own followers of Jesus to the Christian forces that invade their humble hamlet. Crusaders thus attack Béziers and massacre every person they find. First, soldiers drag seven thousand refugees out of churches, homes and fortresses and summarily execute them. Others are mutilated, blinded, dragged behind horses, *and used for target practice*. The town is then set ablaze. Proud of his accomplishment, papal legate Arnaud Amaury writes to Pope Innocent III,

"Today your Holiness, twenty thousand heretics were put to the sword, regardless of rank, age, or sex."

Could they really have killed, proudly, 20,000? The population of the town at the time was more like 5,000; but outsiders sought refuge in the city, and the Christian soldiers did not limit their rampage to Béziers proper.[245] Arnaud's dreadful claim seems likely.

It is reported that before their genocidal incursion, one Christian soldier asked Arnaud how one may determine which are heretics and which are good Christians. The Abbot responded "Kill them all, God will recognize his own!"[246]

Thus all peaceful peoples in Languedoc and surrounding regions—Cathars or otherwise—would become victims of the holy Christian juggernaut. The Church was opposed to the Cathar dualism concept: that there are two supernatural opposing forces, *Dieu* ("God") and *Mauvais* (Bad, or Evil).[247] If you've read the Bible, it seems the Cathars got it right.

There were beautiful lands for the Church to acquire—if it used the right tactics and could muster sufficient military force.

The *CE1986* states that the Councils of the Church "condemned" the Cathars. It does not elaborate upon what *condemned* means. Chastised? Poked fun at? Excommunicated? The *CE1986* then casually mentions that Cathars "disappeared" by the fourteenth century. The text skips over the fact that Pope Innocent III ordered a genocidal attack against that entire region. In a vile fit of calumny, the pope depicted the Cathars as witches; of being cannibals; desecrating the cross; and having "sexual orgies."[248]

Yet malefic sounds of sibilance emanated only from the Vatican, and not from its contrived enemies living peaceably in France with their pure and righteous ways. The Church murdered over a million innocent Cathars over the period of 35 years—men, women, children.[249] Christian forces wiped them from the face of the planet. At the height of the siege, Christian forces were burning hundreds at the stake at a time. The Cathars did not merely "disappear" as *CE1986* claims. The Christian colossus exterminated them, then annexed much of the beautiful Languedoc region of France—some for the Church, some from northern French nobles. The extravagant *Palais de la Berbie* (construction began in 1228) and the Catholic fortress-cathedral *Sainte Cécile* (began 1282) are just two examples that remain to this day.

**Palais de la Berbie in Albi, France**

In its article on the Crusades we have a more honest offering from *CE1907*, mentioning the "extermination of the Albigensian heresy."[250] I make perhaps a small point here, but clearly this *extermination* is more closely associated with "Witch Hunts," as well as immoral papal decrees—not Crusades.

In its Inquisition article, our *CE1907* informs us:[251]

> In the second half of the twelfth century, however, heresy in the form of Catharism spread in truly alarming fashion, and not only menaced the Church's existence, but undermined the very foundations of Christian society. In opposition to this propaganda there grew up a kind of prescriptive law — at least throughout Germany, France, and Spain — which visited heresy with death by the flames.

In its treatise on the Albigenses, the *CE1907* refers to them as "a Neo-Manichaean sect"[252] admitting that the other name for these peoples, "Catharists," means *pure*. The *CE1907* recognizes that between the 1148 Council of Reims and the 1163 Council of Tours, the Church excommunicated the "heretics of Gascony and Provence" declaring that all Albigenses "should be imprisoned and their property confiscated."[253] The genocide against the Cathars, as admitted by *CE1907*, "spared neither age nor sex" and degenerated "into a war of conquest." *Mere Christianity*, perhaps, dear Mr. Lewis? And Mr. D'Souza, is this what truly is "so great" about Christianity?

Of this Christ-inspired holocaust, Voltaire wrote:[254]

> The Jesuit Daniel, in speaking of these unfortunate individuals in his *History of France*, calls them vile and detestable. It is quite obvious that these people who desire their martyrdom did not have vile morals. There was nothing detestable about them other than the barbaric way in which they were treated, and nothing infamous other than the words of Daniel. One may criticize only the blindness of these oppressed people, who believed that God would reward them because the monks would burn them alive.

"The death penalty was, indeed, inflicted too freely on the Albigenses, but... excesses were sometimes provoked," admits *CE1907*. Honest at great lengths about the corruption and ruthless massacres, our original *Catholic Encyclopedia*, like *CE1986*, sums it up simply and vaguely and innocently, writing "The heresy disappeared about the end of the fourteenth century."

Facebook status: *Disappeared.*

Again, the consequence of that pope's intolerant and tempestuous decree: more than one million innocent Cathars killed by Christians. The land occupied by the Cathars was annexed to local nobles who had supplied soldiers for the papacy, and, of course, much land was claimed for the undying Catholic Church.[255] [256] [257]

And in the 18th century Voltaire would render his considered opinion on this matter: "There was never anything as unjust as the war against the Albigenses."[258]

During his reign, this infallible pope, Innocent III, declares himself the divinely appointed *ruler of the world*. Mr. Innocent the Third also claims authority to annul the Magna Carta of 1215, calling it "contrary to moral law."[259] [260] This is the selfsame revered creed upon which American founders based the Constitution, the unfailing pope quashing both from across the sea and across time.

At this point the Catholic Church is becoming very skillful at religiocide, and goes on to perpetrate massive murders for hundreds of years—illegally and immorally, of course (yet skillfully, a

Christian *cosa nostra*) gaining astounding collections of real estate and riches for the Church, for the Vatican, and for Christian leaders. If you visit their ill-gotten citadels and pay a nominal fee, you are permitted to gaze upon some of their treasures, such as those on display in Vatican City today.

**Ongoing Persecutions**. A Christian movement called the Waldensians arose late in the prior century, and the Church declares them heretics, burning them at the stake beginning in **1211,** first with a mere eighty victims in that year. The Fourth Lateran Council in 1215 would demand extermination of the entire sect, with thousands hunted down and killed by devout Christian soldiers and janissaries over the centuries.[261] [262]

In **1212** a young and deluded shepherd boy from Vendôme France, and a youth from Cologne gather thousands of lads with a plan retake Palestine. Dubbed the "Children's Crusade," some 30,000 to 50,000 pint-sized righteous and robotic Christian soldier-boys march south through France and Italy on their mission from God, finally reaching Brindisi on the boot-heel of Italy, where "merchants sold a number of the children as slaves to the Moors, while nearly all the rest died of hunger and exhaustion" as *CE1907* admits.[263]

Innocent III, perhaps my favorite evil pope among so many malevolent papal candidates, begins the Fifth Crusade in **1213** to take Jerusalem. While being one of those illustrious men declared by the Church to be "infallible," he nevertheless fails. Hundreds of infallible popes would follow in his footsteps, equal to, or even occasionally bettering Pope Innocent in his failings and evil deeds and immoralities.

In **1214** Roger Bacon is born in England. Bacon writes books on science, typically using secret code, as he realizes the Christian Church would impose great punishment (even the death sentence) if they find out he writes *science* rather than Christian beliefs.

Indeed they find out. And Pope Nicholas IV writes: "on the advice of many brethren condemned and rejected the doctrine of the English brother Roger Bacon, Doctor of Divinity, which contains many suspect innovations, by reason of which Roger was imprisoned"—for more than a decade and until his 1294 death.[264]

In **1215** the Fourth Lateran Council in canons lxxviii and lxxix declares, among other things, "Jews and Mohammedans shall wear a special dress to enable them to be distinguished from Christians.[265] Six years later and perhaps not completely satisfied with the canons of 1215, Pope Honorius III writes *Ad nostrum noveritus audientiam* in **1221** requiring Jews to wear special badges when in public, and banning them from holding any public office.[266]

In **1224** Emperor Frederick II orders heretics in Lombard burned at the stake. Pope Gregory IX gives his approval.[267]

The Sixth Crusade begins in **1228** in attempt to regain Jerusalem after the utter failure of the Fifth. This scrimmage was more or less a draw, both sides compromising. Crusades, it seems to me, are tedious, violent and futile labors of love and hate, of life and death. If only they had actually ended long ago. "Sacred" lands are disputed to this day, something the secular and pragmatic mind can barely comprehend—sacred *land?*

The church reinforces its earlier decrees of censorship in the **1229** Council of Toulouse, prohibiting laity from reading the Bible. Later in 1270 the king of Aragon, James I, would pass a law wherein all people are required to turn their Bibles in to the local bishop to be burned; the penalty for not doing so was that they would be declared heretics. Heretics, of course, are disposed of by dutiful Christians whenever discovered.

In **1231** Pope Gregory IX enacts a law:

> ...for Rome that heretics condemned by an ecclesiastical court should be delivered to the secular power to receive their 'due punishment.' This 'due punishment' was death "by fire for the obstinate, and imprisonment for life for the penitent. In pursuance of this law a number of Patarini were arrested in Rome...[268]

Some of the heretics are burned at the stake, others given mercy and merely tortured and imprisoned. Then, often burned alive anyway.

**Satanic Stedingers**. In **1233** the Vatican accuses German Stedingers of being in cahoots with something or someone called "Satan." And something called *the devil*: "The devil appears to them in different shapes," writes infallible Pope Gregory IX, "sometimes as a goose or a duck... the Devil presides at their Sabbaths," the pope proclaims.[269] [270]

Gregory IX thus commands a crusade against the people of Stedingen; and Christian monks, laymen, and prayerful Christian soldiers murder tens of thousands of innocent people. Much like the fate that Christians imposed upon Cathars, the Stedingers are wiped out:, either defending themselves from attack, or after lost battles burned at the stake including—of course—executing innocent women and children. The prime difference between extermination of Cathars and extermination of Stedingers is that the Church murders only about 30,000 Stedingers (that is to say, every last one they could find, excepting those few who might be allowed to repent).

The *CE1907* admits to the intolerance and draconian doctrine of the Church:[271]

> The Stedingers refused to pay tithes and to perform forced labour as serfs. These duties were demanded of them with considerable severity, and Archbishop Gerhard II of Bremen (1219-58) sent troops against them. His army, however, was defeated in 1229, whereupon the Stedingers destroyed churches and monasteries, and ill-treated and killed priests. A synod... accused them... of contempt for the authority of the Church and for the sacraments, as well as of superstitious practices; it also excommunicated them.
>
> The Emperor Frederick II placed the rebels under the ban of the empire, and on 9 Oct., 1232, Gregory IX issued a Bull commanding the Bishops of Lübeck, Minden, and Ratzeburg to preach a crusade against them. An army was collected and advanced against the Stedingers, but it was defeated in the winter of 1232-33. A new crusading army defeated a part of the tribe, but the other part was once more victorious. The pope now issued another Bull, addressed to several bishops of Northern Germany, commanding a fresh crusade, and on 27 May, 1234, the Stedingers were completely defeated near Bremen. The majority of them now submitted; on 24 August, 1236, Gregory IX commanded that they should be relieved from excommunication after performing penance and satisfaction, and should be received again in the Church. The Stedingers were not heretics, but rebels against lawful ecclesiastical and secular authority.

After considerable carnage, some Stedingers are permitted to live—if they convert to Catholicism and only after performing penance. (Homework assignment: define the word *penance*. Does the word have any logical, secular, *real* meaning at all?) During this entire epoch the Papacy seems radioactive, ionizing and exterminating any European population that displeases Church leaders, as pope after pope commits armed forces against witches, devils, and heretics to eradicate millions, all in the name of Jesus the Christ.

This Vicar of Christ, Gregory IX, was just one of the many superstitious popes. Among other odd practices, Gregory gave his visitors a kind of "good luck charm" in the form of a magical talisman to be worn around the neck—he claimed that this apotropaic relic would neutralize all sins. To one Vatican visitor, exalted Gregory wrote:[272]

> We have sent you a small key from the most sacred body of the blessed apostle Peter to convey his blessing, containing iron from his chains, that what had bound his neck for martyrdom may loose yours from all sins. We have given also to the bearer of these presents, to be offered to you, a cross in which there is some of the wood of the Lord's cross, and hairs of the blessed John the Baptist, from which you may ever have the succour of our Saviour through the intercession of His forerunner.

Muslims regain control of Jerusalem in **1244**. Christians respond with the Seventh Crusade, led by Louis IX of France, beginning in **1248.** Louis is captured by Arabs, and an enormous ransom paid for his return.

In **1249** Count Raymund VII of Toulouse sentences eighty heretics to be burned alive without permitting them to recant. "It is impossible to imagine any such [secular] trials before the [Christian] Inquisition courts," admits the *CE1907*.[273]

In **1252** Pope Innocent IV formally approves of torture against suspected witches in papal bull *Ad Exstirpanda* ("to be exterminated"). This pope sanctions most all means of torture as a way to have victims *confess their errors and accuse other heretics whom they know,* providing that the Church torturers do not kill them or break their arms or legs. Writes Innocent IV:[274]

> The head of state or ruler must force all the heretics whom he has in custody, provided he does so without killing them or breaking

> their arms or legs, as actual robbers and murderers of souls and thieves of the sacraments of God and Christian faith, to confess their errors and accuse other heretics whom they know...[275]

Of course, once the accused "witch" had confessed (having been tortured without breaking essential bones), said witch was savagely executed (or *exterminated,* to use the pope's word) and the Church would retain *all material assets,* gaining more wealth and real estate for Christian authorities.

Continuing, we have this pope's "Law 31" which proclaims that the authorities must:

> ...within ten days after the accusation, complete the following tasks: the destruction of the houses, the imposition of the fines, the consigning and dividing-up of the valuables that have been found or seized, all of which have already been described in this decree. He must obtain all fines in coin within three months, and divide them up in the manner to be set forth hereafter, and convict of crime those who cannot pay, and hold them in prison until they can.[276]

In **1264** Thomas Aquinas writes his "Against the Errors of the Greeks" (*Contra errores Graecorum*). His work ponders the Trinity, Holy Spirit, purgatory and the papacy. It is entirely based on forged quotations of earlier Church fathers, including the fraudulent "Thesaurus of Greek Fathers" concocted by an unknown author and approved by Pope Urban IV. These forgeries were used to promote the doctrine of papal primacy and thus gaining more power for the Church.[277] [278]

In **1270** Louis IX, King of France, invokes the Eighth Crusade. During his military actions, Louis dies in Tunis, possibly of bubonic plague. But you can't keep a good Crusader down: the Ninth Crusade is its sequel, **1271–1272**—a dismal failure.

The Church's mad and continual and genocidal oppression of the Cathars is alluded to here in the *CE1907*: "...at Toulouse, the hot-bed of Catharan infection... we meet in **1275** the earliest example of a witch burned to death after judicial sentence of an inquisitor..." The woman was "probably half crazy" and she confessed to "having brought forth a monster after intercourse with an evil spirit." *CE1907* is honest in admitting that the "possibility of such carnal intercourse between human beings and demons was unfortunately accepted by some of the great schoolmen, even, for example, by St. Thomas Aquinas and St. Bonaventure."[279] It lays much of the blame for later witch hunts on Heinrich Kramer and Jakob Sprenger for their 1486 manual:[280]

> Probably the most disastrous episode was the publication... of the book "Malleus Maleficarum"... There can be no doubt that the book, owing to its reproduction by the printing press, exercised great influence... professed (in part fraudulently) to have been approved by the University of Cologne, and it was sensational in the stigma it attached to witchcraft as a worse crime than heresy and in its notable animus against the female sex.

Beginning around **1280** the Inquisitor of Verona begins pronouncing sentences against heretics who had long been dead, ordering their bodies dug up from their graves and subsequently burned.[281] That'll teach 'em.

## Fourteenth Century

Gerard Segarelli, founder of the Christian sect *Apostolici* in Italy is declared a heretic, and devout and god-fearing Christians burn him at the stake in **1300**.[282]

In **1302** the *Bull of the Two Swords* (*Unam sanctam*) is issued by Pope Boniface VIII. "Two powers," one by clergy, the other by civil authority, are to control the Church. The clergy, it claims, represent the ultimate ("spiritual") authority because of its "greatness and sublimity." Secular powers are thus subordinate to the Church. It is a "Divine" authority, granted to—*if you can believe this*—"Saint Peter." Consequently "whoever opposes this power ordained of God opposes the law of God..."[283] And you know what happens when you oppose the "law" of God: Christians kill you, burn your family, raze your village and annex your lands, granting all leftover physical possessions to the Church. King Phillip IV of France is aware of the dangerous level of puissance that Boniface had thus proclaimed for the papacy, and arranges in **1303** an army of 1,600 mercenaries to attack the pope's palaces at Anagni, plundering all while sparing the life of Boniface, who would nevertheless die soon thereafter.

After she refuses marriage offers by local nobles to save her from punishment, Christian inquisitors first torture and kill Friar Dolcino's beautiful wife in **1307** by slow roasting. Her husband, the heretic, is forced to watch her torture, then is pan-seared by fire and red-hot pincers until dead.[284]

One of the last Cathars burned at the stake is Guillaume Bélibaste, as Christians execute him at Villerouge-Termenès in **1321**.[285] It was perhaps **1329** when the last of Cathar men (four) were executed in Carcassonne, then the last woman on February 22, **1325**. Her name was Guillelme Tournier, burned at the stake after three years of Christian incarceration and torture while witnessing the death of all her companions at Languedoc.[286]

Some Cathars had managed to escape Languedoc, and several descendants are discovered by inquisitors on the island of Corsica around 1340, and near Turin in 1388. They are tortured by Catholic authorities into confessing to their "heresy," then executed.[287]

In **1336** Benedict XII issues papal bull *Benedictus Deus*, essentially redefining "heaven" according to his own whim. After one's death, the pope declares, instead of waiting in some unconscious, limbonical state for the Last Judgment (old-school beliefs, according to this pope), departed souls are immediately transported to be with "our Lord and Saviour Jesus Christ into heaven."[288]

In **1382** John Wycliffe translates the Bible into English. He dies in 1384, then is posthumously declared a heretic in 1415 with orders that his books be burned and his bodily remains exhumed, burned, and discarded.[289] Another example of justice, Christian style: they'll come and get ya, whether you're dead or alive.

## Fifteenth Century

Lorenzo Valla proves in **1440** that the *Donatio Constantini* was a forgery. The Church nevertheless would continue to use the document as if authentic for centuries thereafter.[290] Who could blame those men? Their livelihoods are bettered by fraud and obscurantism, rendering the Church morally and ethically and spiritually bankrupt—not financially so. One must ask: is it likely that modern Bible scholars in the Vatican today are aware of *CE1907*, and the plethora forgeries perpetrated by their monstrous *machina*, born of a plagiarized, fictional, re-forged, and further falsified *deus*?

In **1450** Johannes Gutenberg begins his project to mass-produce the Bible. Gutenberg is wise enough to know printing it in English is heresy and punishable by torture and death. Thus he chooses the Vulgate edition in Latin:

> Gutenberg formed a partnership with the wealthy burgher, Johann Fust of Mainz, for the purpose of completing his contrivance and of printing the so-called "42-line Bible", a task which was finished in the years 1453-1455 at the Hof zum Humbrecht.[291]

In **1452** Pope Nicholas V composes—and imposes—papal bull *dum diversas*, encouraging Portugal to trade in negro slaves as well as enslaving Muslims, pagans, and all nonbelievers.[292] He had the Bible on his side, of course: not only does the Good Book never disapprove of slavery, the OT actually legislates it (e.g. Ex 21), and meek and perfect Jesus instructs us regarding how severely we must lash our human chattel (Lk 12:47).

In **1480** King Ferdinand and Queen Isabella establish the Spanish Inquisition, resulting in centuries of Christian oppression of all non-Christians, and especially of Jews. Torture and executions are rampant. Their chief weapons, as related by the Monty Python troupe, are "such diverse elements as: fear, surprise, ruthless efficiency, an almost fanatical devotion to the Pope—and nice red uniforms."

In **1484** Pope Innocent VIII orders witch hunters to burn all witches' pet cats along with the supposed witches.[293] As a result, superstitious Christians begin ritual burning of cats every Easter, Lent and Shrove Tuesday, sanctioned by most every pope throughout Christendom.[294] It seems if you are a cat-lover you cannot possibly be a good Christian.

In **1486** Heinrich Kramer and Jakob Sprenger write the *Malleus Maleficarum*, handbook for witch-hunters. As Robbins observed,[295]

> Malleus Maleficarum ... [is] without question the most important and most sinister work on demonology ever written. It crystallised into a fiercely stringent code previous folklore about black magic with church dogma on heresy, and, if any one work could, opened the floodgates of the inquisatorial hysteria. It sought to make effective the biblical command of Exodus...

Note that Kramer and Sprenger attach papal bull *Summis desiderantes affectibus* to the front of their *Malleus*, indicating the Church's sanctimonious approval of witch killing. Writes Pope Innocent VIII therein:

> ...many persons of both sexes... have abandoned themselves to devils, incubi and succubi, and by their incantations, spells, conjurations... [witches] have slain infants yet in the mother's womb... they do not shrink from committing and perpetrating the foulest abominations and filthiest excesses to the deadly peril of their own souls, whereby they outrage the Divine Majesty and are a cause of scandal and danger to very many.

For more on the *Malleus* and witch hunts see the treatise on page 123.

In **1492** Columbus, as you may already know, sails the ocean blue. Christopher returns and encourages Isabella to continue exploration of the New World—so that, he says, the natives could be "taught the Gospel." (Much more on this is covered in Part II in "Extermination of the Human Beings," p. 114.) In **1493** Pope Alexander VI believes he has the authority to grant the entire New World to Catholic monarchs as he issues papal bull *Inter Caetera*.[296] Fortunately, however, it would turn out that the New World would be overrun and annexed by Christians independent from papal authority, and not recognized as being owned strictly by a central Catholic church. Native Americans, no doubt, rejoice.

Dominican friars Savonarola, Domenico and Silvestro are first excommunicated, then executed in **1498**. A Church council decrees that "each one of the three friars shall be hanged on the cross, and then burned, in order that their souls may be entirely separated from their bodies."[297] Evidently "souls" are not fireproof.

## Sixteenth Century

Martin Luther develops his theologies early in the 16th century, fairly liberated from accepted Catholic dogma, and thus is met with excommunication by the pope and even condemnation as an outlaw by Emperor Charles V. So far so good. In **1522** Luther begins persecuting witches, calling them "the Devil's whores," and shortly thereafter Emperor Charles enacts a criminal code to distinguish between "black" and "white" witchcraft: witchcraft that causes injury is punishable by death, and harmless witchcraft would be punished according to the magnitude of the "crime." Homosexuality and bestiality are included as crimes worthy of capital punishment.[298]

In **1523** in the Notre Dame cathedral in Paris, Jean Vallière, a monk who supported Luther, is executed for heresy.[299]

In **1525** the *Deutscher Bauernkrieg* ("War of the German Peasants") begins; it is a series of religious revolts in the south of Germany. Mostly a rebellion against the fascist and murderous Catholic Church, it results in at least 150,000 deaths, largely those of peaceful farming families oppressed by violent Christian forces.[300] [301] [302]

Also in 1525 William Tyndale completes his translation of the New Testament into English; Tyndale would be executed in 1536 for the crime of "illegal possession of the Bible in English."[303]

In **1529** Swiss Protestant reformers George Blaurock and Hans Langegger are arrested by Innsbruck authorities and tortured, with unusual cruelty, in attempt to gain information concerning other Protestants of the area. The "crime" of not being Catholic had been prosecuted for centuries as you may have noticed. On September 6 they are both executed. The charges against Blaurock are that he abandoned the office of papist priest, did not agree with infant baptism, rejected mass and confession, and disallowed worship of the mother of Christ. For unbelief of myths and superstitions, this wise skeptic is burned alive by devout Christians.[304]

Pope Paul III establishes more Inquisitions in **1542** to combat "heresy."[305] The Inquisitions were brobdingnagian police efforts by the papacy to rationalize the murder—or possibly convert, when inquisitors were in jolly moods—all nonbelievers. The *CE1907* excuses the inquisitions as mere "ecclesiastical legislation."[306] Could there be a more whitewashed euphemism for *religious war*? *CE1907* goes on to proclaim "The Spanish Inquisition deserves neither the exaggerated praise nor the equally exaggerated vilification often bestowed on it." So, the Inquisitions were not so good, and not so bad? Estimated number of murders perpetrated by Christian inquisitors: at least 50,000 human beings, usually tortured then *burned alive* by the Christian clergy. The number of innocent people who were not killed, but merely tortured for days, even weeks by Christian authorities cannot be known. It surely numbers in the millions.

King Henry VIII passes the first witchcraft act in England in **1542** allowing the state to bring suspected witches to trial, and permitting the state to punish witches. Conjuring spirits and casting spells are punishable by death. Perhaps surprisingly, records exist of only one case regarding a "witch" brought to trial under this particular law, later being pardoned.[307] Circumstances in England would soon change drastically for all supposed sorcerors.

In **1545** the Bible finally becomes somewhat stable with the Council of Trent.[308] Further modifications nevertheless continue. As *CE1907* admits, John Mill (1645-1707) estimated "the variants of the New Testament at 30,000, and since the discovery of so many MSS unknown to Mill, this number has greatly increased."[309] Continuing, "Under Sixtus V (1585-90) and Clement VIII (1592-1605) the Latin Vulgate after years of revision attained its present shape."[310]

In **1555** Pope Paul IV issues papal bull *cum nimis absurdum,* relegating Jews to live in a special ghetto, and "subject to other harassing disabilities" (*CE1907* vol. 14, 762). In the same year, church reformers John Rogers and Thomas Cranmer are burned at the stake by Christian forces, for heresy.[311]

The righteous Church of Christ in **1557** creates an "Index of Prohibited Books" whose purpose is, purportedly, "to shield the community from intellectual and moral poison."[312] I insist upon including the "Holy Bible" in my list of books promoting intellectual and moral poison.

In **1563** a second witchcraft act is passed in England, increasing penalties on witches to include forfeiture of all property. Under James VI in Scotland a similar act is passed the same year, inciting brutal witch hunts and barbaric torture.[313]

The "French Wars of Religion" are fought **1562** to **1598** between Protestants (Huguenots) and French Catholics. In the St. Bartholomew's Day massacre of 1572, ten thousand Protestants lose their lives *in one day,* murdered by Catholic soldiers on papal authority.[314] Meanwhile, Europe is not the only continent where Protestants are persecuted for worshiping Christ the wrong way. In Florida in 1565 hundreds of Huguenots and Lutherans—men, women, infants—are executed, declared "enemies" of the holy faith. One of the surviving Huguenots describes it as a massacre "so horrible that one can imagine nothing more barbarous and cruel."[315 316] Total deaths: *two to four million,*[317] warring over the proper way to worship Jesus, the Prince of Glory.

One is reminded of William E. H. Lecky who wrote: "There is no wild beast so ferocious as Christians who differ concerning their faith."

**Continued Censorship**. Consider if you will papal bull *Dominici gregis custodia*e, imposed upon the common laity on March 24, 1564:

> All books condemned by the supreme pontiffs or General Councils before the year 1515, and not comprised in the present index, are nevertheless to be considered as condemned... The books of heresiarchs... or of those who have been, or are, the heads or leaders of heretics, as Luther, Zwingli, Calvin, Balthazar Pacimontanus, Swenchfeld, and other similar ones, are altogether forbidden, whatever may be their names, titles, or subjects. And the books of other heretics, which treat professedly upon religion, are totally condemned... Translations of the *Old Testament* may also be allowed, but only to learned and pious men, at the discretion of the bishop; provided they use them merely as alucidations of the Vulgate version, in order to understand the Holy Scriptures, and not as the sacred text itself. But translations of the *New Testament,* made by authors of the first class of this index, are allowed to no one, since little advantage, but much danger, generally arises from reading them. ...But regulars shall neither read nor purchase [Latin vulgate] Bibles without a special license from their superiors.

In the 16th century the church allowed a Latin "Vatablus's Bible" to be read only by clerics.[318] Who could blame those snake oil purveyors? Reading the Bible has always been dangerous for the Christian infrastructure and the daffy dogmas of the revered cult, as the Church must hide its falseness, violent legacy, and absurdities, all to remain undiscovered by their sheep.

What Catholic priest ever encourages reading the Bible? It is a common stereotype: Catholics read the weekly bulletin but never the Bible. Their belief is simply in a supernatural and pretty god-man who will "save" them, usually resembling Peter O'Toole. Jesus was a Hebrew; shouldn't he more likely resemble Menachem Begin, Gilbert Gottfried, or Woody Allen?[319]

**Sea Sorcerer.** Vice Admiral Francis Drake is revered today for having circumnavigated the globe. While on his voyage in **1578** our esteemed explorer accuses his second in command, Thomas Doughty, of witchcraft. What does Drake do to Doughty the naughty—lashings, court-martial? Francis Drake, later granted knighthood by British royalty, has Doughty beheaded on the spot.[320] Ding dong, the witch is dead.

## Seventeenth Century

In **1600** scientist Giordano Bruno agrees with Copernicus' theory that the planets orbit the sun, as well as proposing there may be an infinite number of other worlds, some likely inhabited. The peaceful and gentle Christian Church burns Bruno alive for his thought crimes.[321] [322]

The "Thirty Years War" takes place from **1618 to 1648**. Once again, Protestants versus Catholics warring throughout most of Europe—yet another example of "you love Mister Jesus differently than we do, so you must die." Estimated deaths: *seven to eight million.*[323] As Dave Barry explained, it ended in 1648 because "the combatants realized that they would either have to stop fighting or change the name of the war."

In **1632** the Church declares Galileo's ideas "contradictory" to scripture. Let's face it, all reality and all science are contradictory to the Bible. Galileo is accused of heresy and placed under house arrest for life—for agreeing with his predecessors that the Earth orbits the Sun, not the other (ancient, erroneous Judeo-Christian) way around. Dismal, yes; but Kismet handed Galileo a much healthier platter than given the late and extra-crispy Bruno.

The Irish Rebellion takes place in **1641**. Big surprise: Christians striving to take over cultures, lands and governments with Jesus on their side, this time in the UK. Estimated murders in the name of Christ: 300,000.

In **1648** James Ussher, a meticulous and intelligent man, attempts to reverse-engineer the Christian timeline of human history. His *Annals* represent an exhaustive effort to connect his life-reality to the "history" represented in the incongruous and laughable events offered in the Bible. Raised by and surrounded by Christians, Ussher believes the literal word of the Bible: that the universe must be really old—at least a couple thousand years, if you can imagine such a wild concept. Ussher would strive to figure out *exactly* how old was the universe. He starts (of course) with Adam and Eve, then their sons. Next, on to Noah (merely "tenth from Adam"—did you know?) and thus he follows the various explicit genealogies presented in the Bible. That those "genealogies" are absurd, and that they contradict one another does not seem to bother Ussher in the least.

Ussher wraps up his historical account of mythical figures in the Bible with real men of history like Bassus and Flavius Silva of the first century CE. Perhaps strangely, he terminates his history of the world, which he wrote in the 17th century, with the year 73 CE—*first century*. To Ussher, this represents all of reality, all world history, and all things of interest in the cosmos. All history up to his time occurred in only 5,600 years according to Ussher. His intellectual lapse is equivalent to believing that a Terran day lasts 37 milliseconds—that is, that a day lasts literally one tenth as long as the blink of an eye. Ussher is in error by a factor of approximately 2.3 million to one in this regard.

Based on the Bible, Ussher arrogantly calculates our universe's beginning as "the evening before October 23, 4004 BC" (a *Dark and Stormy Night*, no doubt)—this being at least 4,000 years after the invention of baked bread, and 30,000 years after woven textiles. Ussher opens his *Annals of the World* writing:

> In the beginning God created the heaven and the earth. (Ge 1:1) The beginning of time, according to our chronology, happened at the start of the evening preceding the 23rd day of October (on the Julian calendar), 4004 BC or 710 JP.[324]

Ussher goes into great detail concerning his computations: "I ignored the stopping of the sun in the days of Joshua and the going back of it in the days of Hezekiah," he proclaims. Ussher actually believes Joshua stopped the sun from "moving"—OT writers, as well as 17th century Ussher believed that the sun moved around the Earth, and not the other (actual) way around. Moreover we learn from the Bible that the sun and moon are sentient gods, and mere mortal Joshua (not omnipotent Yahweh) commanded them to remain still (see the Polytheism chapter on page 263).

Ussher's *Annals of the World* was a "history book" of the time, attempting to assign dates to all major events of the Bible. Ussher has Noah being born in 2948 BCE; then Sunday, November 30, 2349 BCE (I swear I am not joking) was when God commanded Noah to enter the ark in seven days' time. By Friday October 23 of 2348 BCE, "the surface of the earth was now all dry."

This would mean the builders of Stonehenge (who began their engineering efforts around 3100 BCE) clearly were not hindered by the Lord's global deluge of "2349 BC," and continued constructing their boulder-built structures after the flood waters subsided, the Stoners finishing up c. 1600 BCE. Stonehenge construction crews must have worked diligently right on through the worldwide flood, underwater. Or maybe Noah's children finished the work there, after God had drowned all Stonehengers? Ussher, an English scholar, lived right there in the British Isles but is silent on any way to connect Stonehenge *reality* to Noah *mythos*.

Ussher wrote his magnum opus in the 17th century. Yet he chose to end his *Annals* in the year 73 CE ("the end of the Jewish affairs," he claimed; some may indeed beg to differ) rather than continue history to his contemporary days of another 1600 years. This clearly shows that his is a work interested only in "biblical" history, OT-to-NT, and then a couple decades beyond. That's it. Ussher had no passion for reality, or ongoing history. The world began on October 23, 4004 BC, Ussher asserted, and there was little if any interest, to Ussher, in histories after the fabled biblical times of apparent New Testament writers.

In **1660** eighteen persons in Coimbra Portugal are condemned by Christian authorities and burned at the stake, thirteen being women. Overall more than 30,000 "witches" and "heretics" are condemned in Portugal alone during the Spanish Inquisition, with a recorded 1,808 burned at the stake, the large majority of others eventually being reconciled and allowed to live—after imprisonment, trial, and torture by the devout true believers in Christ the savior.[325]

The Salem Witch Trials occur **1692-3**. Heinous, yes, but I am certain you realize they were quite tame compared to the colossal anti-witch decrees and infantile wickedness perpetrated in Europe, unquestionably and completely sanctioned by the Holy Bible. It seems somewhat surprising, I think, that Christians in Salem killed only nineteen "witches" along with a couple of evil sorcerer dogs.[326] [327]

## Eighteenth Century

Dona Beatriz Kimpa Vita, leader of a Christian movement in the Kingdom of Kongo, is burned alive as a heretic by devout Christians in July **1705**.[328] She was simply the wrong brand of Jesus worshiper, it seems.

With Baron Christoph von Graffenried at the helm, European Protestants in **1710** sail to the Province of Carolina in North America. They annex lands occupied by the native Tuscarora tribe and with biblical authority on their side, and enslave the local Indians. Until then the Tuscarora had lived peaceably among European settlers for decades, but are now forced to battle for their lives against the newest of settlers. Over 1,000 tribe members are enslaved and 1,400 killed by those Jesus-loving invaders.[329]

Maria Barbara Carillo, age 97, is burned alive by Christian inquisitors for heresy in **1721** in Madrid. Her crime: being born of Jewish parents—a 97 year old woman, heretic, non-Christian.[330] I am quite sure she learned her lesson after that: stop being Jewish.

Junípero Serra is a strict Catholic disciplinarian, Father of the Alta California Missions beginning **1770**. The Church beatifies him, with blinders on as always, and with an antiseptic historical image of Serra *the monster*. Serra believes pain and suffering are necessary for "spiritual purification." He strives to convert and to reign over the Native American population by ordering punishment of "Indians" at the hands of their own brothers, including intense floggings.[331]

**Statue of Junípero Serra in Mallorca**

Today one may purchase an activity book for children, *Father Junipero Serra: California Missions Founder* by Carole Marsh. It teaches kids that "When he turned 16, [Serra] knew exactly what he wanted to do with his life. He wanted to serve God."[332] The author does not indicate which of the many gods Serra wished to serve, but I can well speculate.

It is almost a complete sugarcoating of the atrocities, yet *some* honesty lurks within Marsh's book—albeit naïve, and as vanilla as can be: "By the mid 1700s, Spanish explorers had conquered a great deal of land in the Americas... Spanish rulers decided that they could defend the land better if it were settled. They sent Spanish priests to build the missions in the New World. The priests also tried to convert the people who already lived there. These were the Native Americans, or Indians." Christian soldiers protecting Serra's missionaries enslaved the Indians and raped the women and young girls regularly and at will.[333] The victims of Serra's deranged piousness revolted in 1775, setting fire to buildings, and killing missionaries.[334]

The slave ship *Zong* sails from Africa toward Jamaica in **1781** and many meet their doom. You may learn its story and strange fate in "Beaten with Many Stripes" in Part II (page 137).

Catholic leaders in Germany in **1786** become aware of the outrageous forgeries churned out by the Church along the centuries and, in the Congress of Ems, finally declare independence from Roman Catholic authority, rejecting much Christian dogma and its myths and "laws."[335]

## Nineteenth Century

In **1840** William Miller, a simple farmer from New York, determines that the world will come to an end in 1843. (Historians today reject his prediction, claiming Miller may have erred.) He distributes his message of the impending "second coming" of Jesus in print. Christians of that time are easily duped. Consequently many families abandon everyday affairs, sometimes giving their homes away and neglecting their businesses and farms. The son of God was due to return to the Earth in all His glory, they were promised, sure of this—so why not give up all Earthly things to welcome the Savior and head off to eternal ecstasy in Heaven?

When the golden year 1843 came round and passed with all earthly reality surprisingly intact, Miller realized he made "an error" and re-computed the End-Times,[336] now being due October 22, 1844—Miller was a thinker. As you might have guessed the autumn of 1844 came and went, embarrassingly *sans le fin du monde*. Many of those simple and credulous Christians who had given away their real estate and material goods returned to their hometowns to retain lawyers in attempt to recoup their gifts in courts of law.[337] The world did not, in fact, end: reality and the heady flow of space-time have been immune to religious superstitions.

**Taiping Rebellion**. Between **1851** and **1864** at least *twenty million* (perhaps fifty million) are killed in China. The causes are religious—and *Christian*: Hong Xiuquan has "visions" and believes he was the brother of a first century character Jesus Christ, so Hong leads a rebellion to install himself as the "Heavenly King" of the empire.[338] [339]

In **1854** Pope Pius IX issues papal bull *ineffabilis deus* declaring that Mary's own conception (that is, the pregnancy of Mary's mother, Jesus' maternal grandmother) was "preserved free from all stain of original sin." This "immaculate conception," a previously unknown tidbit of supernatural parentage, was apparently "revealed by God" to the pope. Catholic leaders, to the best of my investigations, have never pondered fondly on any act of sexual intercourse—publicly, at any rate.

In September **1870** the forged "Donation of Constantine" is finally quashed by Italians, and many territories that were stolen by the Church are restored to a United Italy.[340] Thus, one thousand years after Catholic authorities illegally and illegitimately and fraudulently annexed half of Italy—including the city of Rome—*some* is finally restored to secular and peaceful sovereignty, returned to the descendants of people to whom it had belonged long before.

**Ku Klux Klan**. The KKK are Christian fundamentalists, first forming around the end of the American Civil War. They use Christianity and the Bible as excuses to rationalize violent racism and homophobia. Their record of atrocities includes terrorism, flogging and killing of blacks and whites, burning churches and schools, and intimidating and oppressing Catholics and Jews. To the KKK, it is essential to be not merely Christian but also Protestant, male, and bigoted. A Congressional Committee in **1872** describes them as "a fearful conspiracy against society, committing atrocities and crimes that richly deserve punishment."[341] The KKK chose the Christian cross as their ethereal emblem to symbolize and sanctify their holy cause. KKK members regularly rape black women. As they torture and hang blacks, merely for being black, they would read the Bible aloud. Perhaps they read from Exodus? "Thou shalt not kill" (Ex 20:13). "Keep thee far from a false matter; and the innocent and righteous slay thou not" (Ex 23:7). "Also thou shalt not oppress a stranger: for ye know the heart of a stranger" (Ex 23:9). Or from Deuteronomy: "Thou shalt not hate thy brother in thine heart" (Dt 19:17).

Perhaps they read from the NT? "A new commandment I give unto you, That ye love one another..." (Jn 13:34). Yes, there are in fact *a few* words of peace and love in the Bible, depending upon the version.

**The First Holocausts**. Russia is in turmoil late in the 19th century as Christian leadership metes out anti-Semitic decrees over the course of several decades. Prior to and during the Russian

Revolution, mad Christians violently attack hundreds of Jewish communities with an estimated 60,000 innocent Jews murdered.[342] [343]

**Congo Free State, 1886-1908**. In the late nineteenth century, Leopold II establishes an independent sovereignty, the "Congo Free State" in the Belgian Congo (not to be confused with Republic of the Congo). British consul Roger Casement is sent to Africa to investigate its progress in 1904. Casement discovers enslavement of natives, cold-blooded killings, mutilations, hangings, and atrocious collateral death by poor conditions and lack of health care, leading to the arrest of European officials who had perpetrated the despicable acts. The atrocities were evidently rationalized by "Manifest Destiny" dogmas and politics (see Part II of this book)—*Divine Providence* justifies annexation of lands held by "inferior" races or "heathens," and the Christian Bible approves of slavery throughout. From Casement's report:[344]

> I visited two large villages in the interior... wherein I found that fully half the population now consisted of refugees... I saw and questioned several groups of these people... They went on to declare, when asked why they had fled, that they had endured such illtreatment at the hands of the government soldiers in their own (district) that life had become intolerable; that nothing had remained for them at home but to be killed for failure to bring in a certain amount of rubber or to die from starvation or exposure in their attempts to satisfy the demands made upon them... on the 25th of July (1903) we reached Lukolela, where I spent two days. This district had, when I visited it in 1887, numbered fully 5,000 people; today the population is given, after a careful enumeration, at less than 600. The reasons given me for their decline in numbers were similar to those furnished elsewhere, namely, sleeping-sickness, general ill-health, insufficiency of food, and the methods employed to obtain labour from them by local officials and the exactions levied on them.
>
> At other villages which I visited, I found the tax to consist of baskets, which the inhabitants had to make and deliver weekly as well as, always, a certain amount of foodstuffs. (The natives) were frequently flogged for delay or inability to complete the tally of these baskets, or the weekly supply of food. Several men, including a Chief of one town, showed broad weals across their buttocks, which were evidently recent. One, a lad of 15 o so,

> removing his cloth, showed several scars across his thighs, which he and others around him said had formed part of a weekly payment for a recent shortage in their supply of food.

Estimated deaths: two thirds of the Congo tribe disappeared during Leopold's reign. Before the carnage, the tribe's size was estimated by Henry Morton Stanley as 43 million, although Ewans believes that to be an overestimate.[345] All told, some *20 to 30 million* innocent people were killed by Christian overlords, and over ten million others enslaved and shipped off to new lands to become slaves, mostly to Christian masters.[346] All this happened little more than hundred years ago with Bible leverage on the side of the pious perpetrators.

## Twentieth Century

In a speech in Munich on **April 12, 1922** Adolf Hitler expresses his heartfelt faith:[347]

> My feelings as a Christian points me to my Lord and Savior as a fighter. It points me to the man who once in loneliness, surrounded by a few followers, recognized these Jews for what they were and summoned men to fight against them and who, God's truth! was greatest not as a sufferer but as a fighter. In boundless love as a Christian and as a man I read through the passage which tells us how the Lord at last rose in His might and seized the scourge to drive out of the Temple the brood of vipers and adders. How terrific was his fight against the Jewish poison. Today, after two thousand years, with deepest emotion I recognize more profoundly than ever before the fact that it was for this that He had to shed his blood upon the Cross. As a Christian I have no duty to allow myself to be cheated, but I have the duty to be a fighter for truth and justice? And if there is anything which could demonstrate that we are acting rightly, it is the distress that daily grows. For as a Christian I have also a duty to my own people. And when I look on my people I see them work and work and toil and labour, and at the end of the week they have only for their wages wretchedness and misery. When I go out in the morning and see these men standing in their queues and look into their pinched faces, then I believe I would be no Christian, but a very devil, if I felt no pity for them, if I did not, as did our Lord two thousand

> years ago, turn against those by whom today this poor people are plundered and exposed.

In **1929** the Lateran Treaty between Mussolini and the Papacy establishes Vatican City as a sovereign nation belonging to the Catholic Church. In 2010, on the possibility of Pope Benedict XVI being arrested under charge of concealing evidence of child rape by priests during his prior reign as Cardinal, Christopher Hitchens would note that Vatican lawyers threatened to claim sovereign immunity for the pope. Wrote Hitchens on this prospect:[348]

> The Reichsconcordat—the very first diplomatic agreement between Hitler and a foreign state—gave the Nazis recognition as the rightful rulers of Germany in exchange for Church control over the education of Catholics and (significantly perhaps) the dropping of allegations about priestly child-abuse. In a time when the Vatican freely banned books it deemed dangerous, all discussion was abandoned of a ban on *Mein Kampf*—a book in which Hitler claimed to be doing "the Lord's work."
>
> Lawyers for the Vatican have recently announced that, if claimants try to summon the pope to court as a defendant, they will in turn claim "sovereign immunity" for the pontiff as a head of state. Again this is something they may regret, since millions of people, including many Catholics, are unaware that the "Holy See" or Vatican City, a pathetic rump of real estate covering 0.17 square miles, is the creation of a treaty between the pope and Mussolini in 1929.

Agree or disagree with his politics or polemics, his point is that Vatican City exists in sovereignty solely due to an agreement between an immoral dictatorship and a Church historically in search of theocratic and political and financial advantage—to say the least.

**Kristallnacht**. Twentieth century Germany is predominantly Christian, largely Lutheran—and in **1938** the terror of *Kristallnacht* is directed along religious, Christian and anti-Semitic lines. During the nights of November 9 and 10 in 1938, racist Christians attack synagogues, Jewish businesses, cemeteries, hospitals, schools and homes. The police detain over 30,000 Jewish males—they arrest *victims* of the crimes, not the Christian perpetrators. The Christian culprits burn or damage over 1,000 synagogues, and ransack, loot and destroy about 7,500 Jewish businesses. At least 91 innocent Jews are murdered.

In the **1940s** during World War II we have the Holocaust, with Hitler's mandates, and Heinrich Himmler as his willing adjunct—Treblinka, Amersfoort, Płaszów, Warsaw, Dachau, Auschwitz, etc. Nazis kill at least six million Jews, merely for being Jews. Iranian President Mahmoud Ahmadinejad, of course, will have no such thing today, claiming the Holocaust a "myth." Perhaps someone should take him to a holocaust museum in Dachau or Auschwitz.[349]

During the winter of **1946-47** Arabian shepherds accidentally come upon a cache of cylindrical jars in a cave in Qumran by the Dead Sea.[350] Over the next decade more of these "Dead Sea Scrolls" would be discovered in many other hollows of the area. The writings hail from a period beginning several centuries BCE and right through the first century. Upon this discovery, modern Christians were sure they would find something about Jesus: Qumran is in the heart of his holy yet earthly stomping grounds, twelve miles from Bethlehem. Yet it would turn out that the writers of the scrolls apparently never heard of Jesus.

In **1976** the Vatican finally responds to the many ongoing suggestions to sell some of its priceless treasures to help the poor. The Vatican refuses. Bishop Giovanni Fallani, president of the Pontifical Commission for Sacred Art explains that to sell the Vatican's riches would be tantamount to "the triumph of materialism over spiritualism."

The Pieta is a marble statue of Mary holding the dying Jesus, once having been on display at the 1964 World's Fair and insured for $10 million ($74 million in 2013 dollars). Fallani wrote in the Holy See's weekly magazine *L'Osservatore della Domenica* in 1976:

> One hears until boredom that the Pieta should be sold and thus we would have enough money for housing the poor, to help the poor..."

The Bishop referred to anyone making similar suggestions as "naive polemicists." In the same year the Italian magazine *l'Europeo* investigates the Vatican's real estate holdings, claiming over a fourth of Rome's real estate are owned either directly or indirectly by the Vatican, and referring to the Holy See as "a real empire."[351]

**Argentina's Dirty Little War**. Between **1976** and **1983** the Argentinian military ran the country as a ruthless dictatorship. In a 1984 report issued by the National Commission on Disappeared People,[352] we learn that 9,000 people had died or had "disappeared," having been considered by the junta as "subversive" and enemies of the state. The actual number killed may be closer to 30,000. A man named Christian von Wernich was the Catholic priest you may have heard about who took the confessions of political prisoners and passed information—supposedly secret and sacred—to the police. The good reverend was well aware he was aiding the military's campaign to torture detainees. Finally brought to trial in 2007, von Wernich compared himself to Jesus Christ in his testimony. He was sentenced to life imprisonment, and as he was led to prison a crowd around the courthouse erupted in cheers.[353]

**Faith Heals**. Leroy Jenkins is an ex-convict and charlatan faith-healer. In **1979** he is arrested and found guilty of arson and assault. He had hired men to torch the home of a policeman who had given Jenkins' daughter a ticket, and attempted to have a reporter beaten up for comments in a newspaper article.

As James Randi observed, "it appears that the easy, foolproof way to get rich in America is to learn about twenty quotations from the Bible, dress in an expensive suit with lots of gaudy jewelry, and rent an auditorium. Tell all the lies you want... Beg for money, incessantly." Better than a Ponzi scheme, and—amazingly—quite legal in America. Even tax-exempt.

**Trouble in Lebanon**. The Sabra and Shatila massacre is perpetrated by Christians in **1982**. During the Lebanese Civil War (1975–1990), Israeli Defense Forces allow members of the Lebanese militia into Palestinian refugee camps; the Lebanese militia then massacres civilians in the camps—all they could kill. Israeli soldiers had been assigned to control the perimeters of the camps.[354] In the span of 48 hours beginning September 16, the *Milices chrétiennes unifiées* (Lebanese Unified Christian Militia Forces) murder thousands of civilians in the camps. The victims are innocent non-combatants, both Palestinian and Lebanese civilians.[355] [356] The Christian Lebanese soldiers said they simply "hated all Palestinians."[357] Estimated deaths: as many as 3,500 civilian men, women and children.[358]

**Creationism Dresses for the Prom**. While the term "Intelligent Design" goes back as far as 1847 in an issue of Scientific American, it was not revived until the **1989** book *Of Pandas and People*. The term, sometimes abbreviated ID, is then promoted *en masse* by credulous writers and pundits. This has been called a re-work of Creationism now cloaked "in a cheap tuxedo." The absurd Intelligent Design concept, a defense of Biblical creation myth, was proven in court exactly as such: "born again creationism" one may well say.[359]

**Ethnic Cleansing in Bosnia**. The Bosnian War lasts from **1992** to **1995**. Here we have more religious fighting, characterized by Christian oppression, mass rape, murdering of innocent men, women and children. At least 100,000 are killed.

**Intolerance of Choice**. In February **1994**, Mother Teresa condemns contraception, comparing it to abortion. The supposedly sweet Albanian proprietor of many "houses of the dying" (her term, not mine) preached, "I know that couples have to plan their family and for that there is natural family planning. The way to plan the family is natural family planning, not contraception..." then claiming once a fetus is "destroyed by contraception, abortion follows very easily." This is a woman who once answered the question of what gives her *absolute ecstasy* as follows: "to see a person die with a smile on their face."[360] Mother Teresa was—well, no "Mother Teresa."[361]

Fanatic Christian Paul Jennings Hill murders Dr. John Britton along with his clinic escort James Barrett in **1994**. Hill is later found guilty of murder, and sentenced to death. Prior to Hill's 2003 execution, he said he expected "a great reward in Heaven... I am looking forward to glory."[362] Britton and his colleague James Barrett had been murdered by Reverend Hill almost 10 years prior to his execution. Similar murders include: Dr. David Gunn of Pensacola Florida, murdered in 1993 by Michael F. Griffin;[363] Shannon Lowney and Lee Ann Nichols, clinic receptionists, killed in Massachusetts in 1994 by John Salvi (Salvi also confessed to an earlier attack in Norfolk, Virginia);[364] security guard Robert Sanderson, killed when the Alabama abortion clinic was bombed in 1998 by Eric Robert Rudolph;[365] James Kopp, convicted of the 1998 murder Dr. Barnett Slepian in Amherst, New York;[366] and Dr. George Tiller, killed by Scott Roeder in 2009 in Wichita, Kansas.[367]

**Queer Days**. The Defense of Marriage Act ("DOMA") is enacted in **1996**, designed by the "Christian right" and signed into law by the U.S. Congress. It seeks to limit the rights of gays. DOMA supporters do not disallow gays from marrying; they merely want to make it illegal for gays to marry other gays. To them, it makes perfect sense for a gay man to marry a heterosexual woman. (See the related chapter on page 143.) Pat Robertson, in a **1998** broadcast of *The 700 Club*, says that Florida (state motto: *live long and perspire*) should beware of hurricanes because Disney World held "Gay Days." Robertson counsels, "I would warn Orlando that you're right in the way of some serious hurricanes, and I don't think I'd be waving those [gay pride] flags in God's face if I were you."[368] From religion, come such intellectual giants.

**Headed to Heaven**. Marilyn Lemak executed her three children on March 4, **1999** by feeding them peanut butter laced with overdoses of antidepressants. Then she laid them down and smothered them with her hands. She wanted to kill the children, and herself, so they could all be reunited in Heaven, "a happier place."[369]

## Twenty-first Century

The religious wars ended long ago, and we can no longer blame neoteric Christian belief and practice for the atrocities of their ancient ancestors—right?

Perhaps not. Edward Gibbon hypothesized that Christianity caused the collapse of the Roman Empire and the stagnation of Occidental society, impeding our progress in science and philosophy. I believe he is correct, and the fourth century imperial edict—proclaiming the Christian cult[370] to be the only legal and legitimate belief, under penalty of death—set western civilization back by at least 1000, more likely 1500 years.

Justin Martyr wrote c. 150 CE of any *believer*, "...by the mere fact of his being a Christian he does no wrong" (*First Apology*, VII.) It was not long after this when Christians began to use military force against those of rival divine doctrines. Tactics long ago abandoned?

In November **2001** Ashley Appoo learned that John Leslie McDonald and his wife were atheists. What would Jesus do? Appoo murdered John with an axe, then hacked John's wife nearly to death. A devout Christian, Appoo had Christ on his side, and could do no wrong. The judge disagreed, sentencing him to eighteen years.[371 372]

On October 18, **2004** Arthur Shelton of Detroit discovered that his close friend and roommate Larry Hooper was an atheist. So Shelton murdered his pal without hesitation.[373 374] He first grabbed his handgun to kill Hooper the evil atheist, then went for his shotgun to complete his heavenly objective, blowing Hooper's head clean off. Shelton then called the police. "I'm a Christian and an Eagle Scout and I wouldn't lie," he proclaimed on the phone, "...don't worry about me, I'm fine, but he's the devil." Squad cars and ambulances arrived to view the bloody scene of the ex-Hooper, whose mangled corpse sat upright on his couch, headless, with his wrong-thinking, wicked atheist brain laying on one of his hands.

Isolated incidents, perhaps? Ancient and supposedly spiritual beliefs cannot be all that harmful—not today. Can they?

Sadly, Debra Gindorf had suicidal tendencies. Before taking her own life, she figured her infant children would have a tough time with their mommy gone, so her loving plan was to take them with her to the "next life." In **1985** she fed her children fatal doses of sleeping pills, taking the same for herself. Her suicide note proclaimed she expected to meet her beloved offspring in "heaven." Her children died; Gindorf survived, and spent eighteen years in prison for her murders.[375]

Christina Marie Riggs killed her two children—Justin, 5, and Shelby Alexis, 2—then tried to kill herself in November **1997**. In her last statement before being executed in 2000 for the murders, she proclaimed "now I can be with my babies, as I always intended."[376 377] Seems to me she had *already* been with them, here on earth. Yet the "afterlife" was the only existence of any importance to her.

On Sept. 3, **1998** Khoua Her of St. Paul, Minnesota strangled her children—all six of them—so they would "not have to suffer" in this life, sending them to the next. She claimed her act was a loving one.[378]

On June 20, **2001** Andrea Pia Yates killed all five of her children in Houston, Texas, drowning them one by one in the bathtub. When she was found guilty of murders she said she wanted to be executed, so that she and "Satan" would be destroyed.[379]

In March **2002** Sherry Marie Delker, 27, of Austintown, Ohio ran over her child with a car. She says she killed her six-year-old daughter to send her to a *better place*. Police charged Delker with aggravated murder.[380]

Deanna Laney in May **2003** stoned two of her sons to death and severely injured a third child—Joshua, 8, Luke, 6, and Aaron, one year old. She believed God had instructed her to kill them.[381] Had she been raised, say, Buddhist, Jain, or agnostic, it seems such a delusion would have been virtually impossible to manifest itself.

In **2004** Dena Schlosser saw a news story about a boy who was mauled by a lion, and Schlosser took that as a sign of the apocalypse.[382] So she amputated her eleven-month-old daughter's arms with a knife, killing the infant, and offered the dead child to God. Could a person who did not have religious indoctrination perform such an act for any similar reason?

On July 19 **2005** Magdalena Lopez murdered her two sons—Antonio, 9, and Erik, 2—in Dyer, Indiana by beating them to death with a ten-pound dumbbell because she thought they would be "better off in heaven."[383]

The incidents cited above include only those that I have thus far discovered. Surely there are many more. Would you be surprised to discover cases of religious parents who passively allowed their children to die?

### Religion in the Modern World

Without depressing you too much with gory details, consider parents who, because of religious beliefs, refused to give their children proper medical care, or who kill children via religious rites. Children lost in this manner include Nancy Brewster (age seven), Justin Barnhart (two), Seth Ian Glaser (17 months), Amy Hermanson (seven), Desiree Camren (three), Lukas Long (newborn), Jessica Crank (fifteen), Eric Cottam (fourteen), Michael Boehmer (four), Sonia Hernandez (four), Harrison Johnson (two), Javon Khadan-Newton (15 months old, starved to death because he didn't say "amen"), and Aqsa Parvez (sixteen, beaten to death for refusing to wear a head scarf).

High on gerin oil for far too long, parents Leilani and Dale Neumann watch reverently and with faith as their daughter of eleven years sinks into a diabetic coma. Her parents do the most they consider reasonable: they pray to God. The couple is unaware of the scientific proof (and simple logic) that prayer does not work, and the "power of prayer" is mere superstition, as proven scientifically in many experiments.[384] Their daughter Kara Madeline dies, and the Neumanns are charged with second-degree reckless homicide. The parents show no emotion and had no sadness in losing their daughter, nor when they are found guilty; they claim they have "peace in God."[385]

Then we have the Brown children (Daniel, Jacob, Jeremiah, Jonathan, and Sarah). Their parents are snake-handlers, a Christian sub-cult that spun off merely due to an obscure and babyish Bible verse claiming that Christian belief gives one "power" over serpents (Lk 10:19). All of the Brown children are orphaned after their parents are killed by religious ritual, bitten by a poisonous snake,[386] said serpent most probably a godless atheist.

**The Savior Made Me Do It**

In **2003** in Nebraska, Ivan Henk murders his 4-year-old son, Brendan Gonzales. Henk claims in court that his son Brendan was "the antichrist" and had "666" tattooed on his forehead. Henk believes his son "had the power to sap his strength and make demons circle his bedroom."[387] [388]

Based on his suicide notes, we learn that Joseph Ganshert killed his wife and their two children in **2005** while they slept. Wrote Ganshert, "God asked me to bring my family to heaven." He then killed himself.[389]

In January **2008** Banita Jacks of Washington D.C. is charged with murder. A devout believer, Mrs. Jacks apparently starved and/or murdered her four daughters because she was sure "demons" possessed them.[390]

In April **2008** Donna Marie Redding of Marietta, South Carolina kills her common-law husband. She tells authorities her husband had used the Lord's name in vain too many times. In her court testimony she claims that Jesus told her to murder him.[391] Blasphemy may be, as the bumper sticker informs us, a victimless crime, but it was an offense worthy of the death penalty according to Mrs. Redding—as well as in the ancient Christian world century after century.

**Modern Witchcraft**. Remember the witch hunts? Long ago and far away, past atrocities forgotten? So perhaps we should forgive and forget. Around the world, the Christian Bible is still used to accuse people, usually children, of "witchcraft" and to punish them. Refer to *The Guardian,* Sunday 9 December 2007, "Child 'witches' in Africa"; *Huffington Post,* October 18, 2009, "African Children Denounced As 'Witches' By Christian Pastors"; and *The Guardian,* Friday 31 December 2010, "Why are 'witches' still being burned alive in Ghana?" The scripture normally cited regarding witches is Exodus 22:18, and there are many more. In Ghana, a study found that "accused witches were physically brutalized, tortured, neglected, and in two cases, murdered."[392] In Kinshasa, Congo, "80% of the 20,000 street children... are said to have been accused of being witches."[393] Even to this day the Bible's proclamations against witches are still considered valid by many Christians. In places like Indonesia, Tanzania, the Congo and Ghana superstitious fundamental Christians actively pursue and execute witches, including murdering child "sorcerers."[394] In Malawi, accused witches are routinely jailed.[395]

Present day witch-killers have irrefragable Yahweh on their side with Exodus 22. The New Testament, in Galatians 5, has Paul preaching his own judgmental concurrence: "Now the works of the flesh are manifest, which are these; Adultery, fornication, uncleanness, lasciviousness, Idolatry, *witchcraft...*"

Fortunately most edicts within the scriptures are largely ignored by Christians. Jesus decreed in Luke 14 that you may follow him only if you hate your entire family and hate your own life. I find only trace evidence of modern Christians true to this decree.

Deuteronomy 13 insists that those who worship the sun or moon be stoned to death. Should Andy Williams have been executed for singing "Moon River"? George Harrison, for penning "Here Comes the Sun"? Indeed, religion poisons everything. The atrocious examples presented here demonstrate the monstrous nature of blind faith, the danger of embracing ancient texts as if they offer incontrovertible moral truths.

**Shots at Blacksburg**. University student Seung-Hui Cho had mental problems. Instead of seeking psychiatric help, his mother took him to various churches in search of exorcism to rid his body of demons.[396] In 2007 Cho killed 32 people at the Virginia Polytechnic Institute in Blacksburg, Virginia, wounding 25 others. He then took his own life, effectively, one would think, exorcising those supposed demons in his head.

**Modern Crusades and Crimes**. In the Yelwa Massacre of 2004, Christians killed more than 600 Muslims (having been instigated by Muslims who killed about 80 Christians—truly, an eye for an eye, at least at a very lenient numerical approximation). A study by Nigerian government officials concludes that between 2001 and 2004, over 50,000 had been killed there in religious fighting.

In **2007** the first "Creation Museum" is built in Kentucky, depicting, for example, dinosaurs living among humans, Flintstone-style. As of this writing, over a dozen such "museums" exist around the world.[397]

In **2009** the FDA approves use of embryonic stem cell-based therapy on humans. Christian leaders immediately condemn this concept, claiming "lives are being lost." By this they mean *cells*. Yet, religious objectors do not condemn insecticides, antivirals, or antibiotics (aren't lives being lost?). Moreover, the stem cells otherwise would be tossed out, left to die. Sam Harris mused that opponents to stem cell research believe that "souls live in Petri dishes."[398]

In **2009** Pope Benedict XVI proclaims that condoms are really, *really bad*—worse than AIDS.[399] This ignorant and mendacious pope states that condoms do nothing to prevent the spread of the disease, and can accelerate the spread of AIDS. A Vatican spokesman supported the pope's comments, saying Benedict was "maintaining the position of his predecessors."

# PART II. A CASE AGAINST RELIGION

## Extermination of the Human Beings

When religious motives are used to justify political actions, typically the devoted laity are readily convinced that the purpose is altruistic (that is, in the name of "God") no matter how atrocious the deed. Surely what comes immediately to mind are the Crusades, Inquisition, witch hunts, as well as the September 11 2001 attacks; but the philosophies and convictions that empowered pioneers to murder natives of the Americas were largely motivated by Christianity, and backed by the Bible.

After discovering the New World, Christopher Columbus sailed a course along such supernatural tack as he coaxed Queen Isabella to support his exploits in the Americas so that the queen "might eminently contribute to diffuse the light and truth of the Gospel" upon the Indians.[400] On Nov 6, 1492, Columbus addressed the king and queen, as recorded in his log. Our intrepid captain opined "I am convinced... that if devout religious persons knew their language, they might be converted to Christ, and so hope in our Lord that your Highnesses will decide upon this course with much diligence." His purpose, Columbus proclaimed, was to "Christianize" the Indians.

A scant few years later Isabella is recorded as having said "...it has always been our principal Intention to cause the Light of the Gospel to shine on the People of the New World."[401]

The Dustin Hoffman movie "Little Big Man" had it right: in their own language, the Cheyenne call themselves *Tsitsistas*: essentially "Human Beings." The genocide against the natives of the Americas, and annexation of their *entire continent*, north, central, and south, was claimed to be justified under the banner of *Manifest Destiny*—a term coined by journalist John L. O'Sullivan in 1845:[402]

> The right of our manifest destiny to overspread and to possess the whole continent which providence has given us for the development of the great experiment of liberty and federated self-government.

O'Sullivan explained (that is, excused and rationalized) the Christian settlers' belief that "providence" (God's will) granted European settlers a mission to spread their myths across North America, and to pilfer all new lands they discovered.[403] [404] The Spanish, conquering the human beings of Central and South America, proffered similar explanations: their mission was "to preach the faith of Jesus Christ."[405] Like Jake and Elwood Blues, the Conquistadors were on a mission from God.

*Manifest Destiny* was merely a twinkle in the fifteenth century eyes of Columbus and Isabella. The credo flowered to fuller bloom by 1630 as Reverend John Cotton gave his farewell speech before leaving England for the Massachusetts Bay colony. Cotton departed his home island nation by announcing that the voyage would be a Puritan Christian "errand into the Wilderness" and basing his language on Bible verses, saying: "Moreover I will appoint a place for my people Israel, and will plant them, that they may dwell in a place of their own, and move no more; neither shall the children of wickedness afflict them any more, as beforetime." Cotton was quoting the KJV Bible, 2 Samuel 7:10 verbatim. Here we have ancient and ignorant Hebrew writ, strangely (it seems to me) regarded as true and sacrosanct.

One can readily see an underlying plan to convert the human beings of the New World to Christianity—but more importantly, to usurp their entire continent. Cotton wrote that God makes room for a people three ways:[406]

> ...he casts out the enemies of a people... as in Psalm 44.2... he gives a forreigne people favour in the eyes of any native people... he makes the Countrey though altogether void of inhabitants, yet voyd in that place where they reside. Where there is a vacant place, there is liberty for the sonne of Adam or Noah to come and inhabite, though they neither buy it, nor aske their leaves...

Basically Cotton is saying that his Christian god permits fellow believers to squat and own any empty lands—and the New World offered millions of hectares of prime real estate otherwise "going to waste" with nobody permanently living there. The Manifest Destiny decree sanctioned invasion of all regions unoccupied by *them there godless Injuns*. The settlers went just a tad beyond God's will and simple squatting in their violent ethnic cleansing and wholesale embezzlement of territory.

Historians and the Olde U.S. Governemente often cited the Bible to defend the notion that white Christian men should have providence over the New World. John Winthrop of Massachusetts (1587-1649) justified the annexation of the newly discovered lands by quoting the Good Book. Wrote Winthrop: *And God blessed them, saying: Increase and multiply, and fill the earth, and subdue it, and rule over the fishes of the sea, and the fowls of the air, and all living creatures that move upon the earth.*[407] This is nothing but Bible nonsense, directly from Genesis 1:28, filched in the seventeenth century by Winthrop to justify aggressive invasions of foreign territories and "God-approved" genocide.

Today we teach history to schoolchildren under the euphemisms "Western Expansion" and "Indian Wars" when addressing property appropriation and mass murder. Rarely if ever are the terms "genocide" or "land snatching" rendered in schoolbooks regarding the old west.[408]

In 1823 the Monroe Doctrine pronounced that the United States would no longer interfere with existing European colonies in the New World, and proclaimed that European powers were to leave American colonies alone. Then the U.S. took Florida from the Spanish and forged westward disputing with Great Britain over Oregon's border, taking Texas in 1837, and New Mexico, Arizona, and California in 1848. When the Spanish-American war broke in 1898, America leveraged Manifest Destiny to annex Guam, Puerto Rico, and the Philippines.[409] [410]

The prescript had manifested tens of millions of American natives to their destiny: immediate and eternal graves.

**Noble Conquistadors**. For centuries following Columbus' "discovery" (of a land occupied centuries before, first by Asians and later by scant Scandinavians), Christian forces from Spain, Italy and Portugal invaded Central and South America. The conquistadors (all

Catholic) killed and looted the "inferior" peoples of the southern Americas, always in the name of their savior.

Estimating the population of that region before the time of the Cortés conquest is a bit of a challenge. Various methods are used, including historical texts, archaeological evidence, determining the acres of farmable land in a given region, water supplies, annual yield with adjustment to account for ancient farming techniques, and so on. Karl Sapper puts the pre-Columbian population of the Americas at 50 to 60 million, and Denevan narrows it down to approximately 57 million.[411] The vast majority were murdered by the European invaders.

In *one day* in 1521, in the Battle for Tenochtitlan, the Spaniards and their allies killed or captured 40,000 indigenous peoples.[412] Justification? The conquistadors claimed that the principal reason for the war against the native Mexicans was to preach of Jesus Christ. After all, WWJD?

Estimates of the carnage vary wildly. David Stannard wrote that today "few serious students of the subject would put the hemispheric figure at less than 75,000,000 to 100,000,000..."[413] The consensus seems to be a slightly more conservative number, "only" about fifty million human beings of the Americas slaughtered. In the end, a mere handful of native Americans were *not* killed by European invaders in the name of Manifest Christianity. Many of them today work menial jobs in casinos and hotels; once upon a time their ancestors owned the entire continent.

I must correct myself: their beliefs were much more humble. In their ideology, *the Earth owns us*: "This we know: the earth does not belong to man; man belongs to the earth." — Chief Si'ahl (Duwamish Native American), January 1854.[414]

Perhaps a letter by Cortés to Emperor Charles V captures the piety and callous and inhuman indifference of the conquistadors. Regarding the battle against Guatemoc, Aztec ruler of Tenochtitlan, Cortés wrote (as recorded by Díaz, witness to the events):[415]

> Guatemoc and his captains were captured on the thirteenth day of August at the time of vespers on the day of Senior San Hipolito in the year one thousand five hundred and twenty-one, thanks to

> our Lord Jesus Christ and our Lady the Virgin Santa Maria, His Blessed Mother. Amen.

Yes: those heathens were captured or killed thanks to our Lord Jesus Christ and our Lady the Virgin. Amen indeed, Señor Cortés. Amen.

## Separation of Armageddon and State

"The only thing more dangerous than ignorance is arrogance." — Albert Einstein

Condoleeza Rice famously had to explain why the Bush administration ignored the *President's Daily Brief* of August 6, 2001 entitled "Bin Laden to Strike in US." Beyond that *Daily Brief* lies a menace far more ominous and globally encompassing than the September 11 attacks of 2001.

Bin Laden stated in interviews that it is the "religious duty" of all Muslims to acquire and use weapons of any type, including those of mass destruction—chemical and nuclear.[416] One cannot overstate the importance and gravity of bin Laden's edict against non-Muslim "infidels." Still out there lurk stalwart Al-Qaeda operatives striving to please their godly and depraved overlords by procuring devices as globally destructive as can be. We know from Bin Laden's adjuncts that they are delighted to use any weapon or means against innocent people, against any nationality or religion, and to die for their illogical, inhuman, "holy" cause.

This brings to my mind the scripture in Qur'an 2:191, commanding all Muslims to slay non-Muslims "wherever ye find them."

Yet radical Islam is not alone in such abject delusion. The vast majority—*billions* of people on this Earth—hold a numinous belief that their current life has little if any meaning, and only the next, "eternal" life has any importance: "heaven."

So most go to church or temple now and then as a type of insurance policy. One friend, explaining why she went to Catholic mass on (*most*) Sundays told me "I want to make sure I get into heaven!" This is the perennial *racketeer church*, attendance (and donations) being the weekly "protection payments" to their god. It seems a rather pitiful way to live one's life.

Several verses of the New Testament predicted (falsely of course) the end of the world, claiming it would come within a generation of Jesus' death—e.g. Matthew 23:35-6, Mark 13:25-31. So far, the Bible has been wrong by several millennia.

The Jehovah's Witnesses have been kind and industrious enough to compute the exact year of the Parousia. They know *exactly* when it will occur. Their Watchtower Society's calculation was slightly off, computing it to be 1874. That year came and went without the glorious Rapture they so sincerely desired. They then proposed a new theory, coming up with 1914, a 365-day time period that remained intact until midnight Dec 31 arrived, proving them again wrong. The Witnesses remained undaunted, their next prediction being 1915. Neither Yahweh nor Jesus showed up that year to end the world, as far as I know.

Then the JWs regrouped and re-computed: 1918 seemed right at first, but that didn't work out. Next they predicted 1920 (failure, obviously). Next 1925, then 1941, then 1975, all clearly miscalculations.[417] Perhaps they'll get it right for us one of these centuries. Kudos on the effort, Witnesses!

Back to serious considerations. The morning of September 11 2001 saw nineteen Muslim men fly airplanes into buildings selected by deluded demagogues, murdering thousands. They killed Muslims, Christians, Jews, atheists, all sorts. The suicidal murderers did not know, nor care: dozens of virgins awaited them on the other side of the life/death curtain. Those arrogant men (yes, men; as you know, all the 9/11 terrorists sported a Y chromosome) were *absolutely positive* that in the next moment they would leave this life and be transported to paradise for all eternity replete with throngs of virgin concubines. You will find in the Qur'an, Hadith, and Sunan absolutely no mention of whether those women are intelligent, interesting, or even attractive: clearly the interest of the would-be martyr is that all 72 would possess vaginas unadulterated.

Yet the evening before their murderous rampage, several bin Laden underlings critically crossed Muhammad's religious laws and sinned in Allah's eyes (see Qur'an 5:90), drinking beer after beer in a Florida strip club, and bragging about their impending Jihadist act of religiocide.[418] Did they really believe in the Qur'an, then? I have to think they must have: they followed up the next day with their satanic Al-Qaeda terrorist plan, and killed themselves for their god.

I hope Allah appreciated the human sacrifice! I have to wonder why they thought that their omniscient deity was looking the other way on September 10th as they swilled, mug after mug, the immoral elixir called "beer" at a sinful American entertainment station called a "booby bar."

I am thoroughly convinced that no such supernatural transportation occurred. They sincerely believed they had their particular middle-east god on their side—but the nineteen frustrated and brainwashed boy-terrorists simply died that morning, as did some 3,000 victims of their religious poison. No virgins for them: just a premature end to their lives. The *only life* they would ever be granted was terminated quite prematurely by their own religious indoctrination.

You will never turn on the news and hear a story claiming "Yesterday, another atheist suicide scientist blew himself up, killing dozens and injuring more."

Any group armed with a nuclear weapon, whether Muslim Jihadist or Occidental Head of State who believes in either martyrdom or the Parousia or a "glorious Rapture," clearly presents a threat a million times more dangerous than bin Laden's 9/11 minions. The Nuclear Genie has been out of his plumbum bottle for over half a century and pervades the globe in the form of tens of thousands of plutonium-armed salvos, many protected by questionable security.

In fact some potential weapons of mass destruction require little or no radioactive substance; just a wacko religious extremist willing to abuse a dirty bomb or biological weapon.

Steven Weinberg said "With or without religion, you would have good people doing good things and evil people doing evil things. But for good people to do evil things, that takes religion."[419] This perfectly describes the new fascist Islam, as well as centuries of genocide perpetrated by Christians, with full "legal" support from the Papacy.

Most religious fundamentalists and deranged armageddonists believe that the sooner we all die, the better. Next stop: heaven—

*hallelujah!* Those who have "chosen rightly" believe their god will embrace his faithful sheep, and will leave all others to go straight to hell. Consider the loving, Christian wish of Pope Gregory I who said: "The bliss of the elect in heaven would not be perfect unless they were able to look across the abyss and enjoy the agonies of their brethren in eternal fire"[420] —that Pope is guilty of schadenfreude of infinite breadth. The same sadistic Gregory "the Great" had the library of Palatine Apollo burned, lest its secular literature distract the faithful men from the contemplation of heaven. Gregory condemned all books but the "Holy Bible"; then he forbade *everyone but the clergy from reading the Bible.*[421] Pope Gregory should consider himself fortunate that the Christian mythologies and superstitions are in fact not true, lest he'd be in a hell of a bad place for all eternity.

These facts underscore the many reasons that Church and State must remain separated like matter from antimatter. The "*L*" component in the Drake equation, essentially the number of years an advanced society can hope to last before it destroys itself, clearly is inversely proportional to the religiosity of that society—the more religious (and less freethinking), the faster a society will devolve and self-destruct.

**The Next Polling Cycle**. Having "faith" has forever been presented as being something good and virtuous; but it is not a positive attribute, and nothing to be proud of. It equates to being merely gullible, superstitious, unquestioning.

No matter where you live on this globe, the next time you go to the polls, remember that the best candidates for high offices are *the least faithful.* We desperately need freethinking leaders, not brainwashed believers. Any world leader who sincerely believes he has "God on his side" is capable of bringing about—and is not afraid—of Armageddon.

## Witch Hunts

The prime reason Christians had hunted down and killed "witches" over the centuries: because the Bible tells them so. Of course. As previously mentioned, it is primarily due to the biblical decree "Thou shalt not suffer a witch to live."

It has been estimated that four out of five witches murdered by Christians were female. However, many thousands of men and children were also killed by Christians for being witches or warlocks. They had the Bible to support them.

Christian scripture also inspired tangential offshoot superstitions. Around the seventh century the *Canon Episcopi* appeared, a terse and lackluster flatus of a work, of unknown authorship. It indicted certain "criminal" women as witches, having been seduced by "the devil," and the delusions of those witches were caused by "the Evil One" (whatever or whoever that is). Such a woman is "an infidel and worse than a pagan" according to the *Episcopi*. The whimsical document was considered by Christians for many centuries to be of the highest authority regarding witchcraft.[422]

Next let us consider Heinrich Kramer (*aka* "Institoris"), who wrote the *Malleus Maleficarum* (or *Hexenhammer*, Witch's Hammer), a handbook for witch-hunters, c. 1486, mentioned in my Timeline. Kramer requested papal sanction to prosecute people who he was sure were witches. The malleable and superstitious pope responded with official papal bull *Summis desiderantes affectibus*, instituting into ecclesiastic law the oppression of anyone who might be a witch.

Pope Innocent [*sic*] VIII offered his observations *ex cathedra* in a papal bull, stating that witches "by their incantations, spells, conjurations... have slain infants yet in the mother's womb." The term "bull" seems perfectly appropriate to describe papal excrement over the centuries that has oozed from the Vatican's immense and profane and lowest of intestines. Adding but four letters would render it perfect. From Latin *bulla*, it derives from the clump of clay used to seal any edict signed by the pope. This particular bull by Innocent VIII reeked evil to such a degree as to urge Christians to perform superstitious and murderous mayhem across mythical God's green Earth, century after century.

Devoted and righteous Christians usually burned witches alive for their crime of "sorcery." Most were tortured using elaborate devices of pain—for days, even weeks, then sent to their ultimate bonfires. A few lucky ones met quick death by Christian sword.

My tiny and humble county library but two miles from my home maintains a modern (1971) printing of Kramer's book; so I was readily able to take a gander at those ancient edicts page by page. Kramer mostly suspects women of being witches (*Malleus*, Part 1, Questions IV-XI, and Part 2, Question IV), but this superstitious Christian inquisitor does not rule out men. Kramer claims that a witch's purpose is to "help the devil."

You may laugh today, but a mere five hundred years ago the "devil" was believed by people to be an actual supernatural being, the ultimate underworld antagonist. I am positive that no intelligent person today believes in such a magical evil entity. (I am aware of Pat Robertson's statement about Haiti's "pact" with the devil, and I stand by my statement.[423])

Over eighty percent of "witches" killed in Europe were women, usually burned alive by Church authorities.[424] [425] [426] Meanwhile on the occidental side of the pond a miniscule collection of Americans were conducting something that came to be termed the Salem Witch Trials. While heinous and incomprehensible to modernity, it was tame compared to the colossal wickedness in Europe, all sanctioned by the Bible, OT and NT. Not long after the trials in Salem, many accusers apologized. Court orders demanded monetary compensation to family members of those "witches" wrongly executed.

I don't mean to discount the atrocities in Salem—nineteen humans were wrongly executed for being "witches"—but compare to the millions of Christian witch burnings perpetrated in Europe, commanded by righteous and *infallible* papal authority and "God's words" in the Bible, approved by absolutely any Pope you might care to name throughout the middle ages and centuries beyond.

It seems to me that Moses and Jesus qualify perfectly as wizards, having sorcerer powers: parting the sea, talking to "God," walking on water, raising the dead, abracadabra culinary feats. Shouldn't both Moses and Jesus have been killed, then, for being witches? Come to think of it, perhaps God's earthly subjects got His word right when they nailed up Jesus the witch, some 2,000 years ago (an event not recorded by history).

This jealous and violent Christian god also imposes the death penalty on Sabbath-breakers. One wonders where his priorities are: "Keep you my sabbath: for it is holy unto you: he that shall profane it, shall be put to death... Every one that shall do any work on this day, shall die" (Exodus 31:14). How important and sacred is an arbitrary *day of the week* on which "God" proclaims you must *kill* anybody laboring in any way?

Now, what is the approximate number? How many witches were killed by Christians? Since the Cathars were murdered by Christian forces under the pretense that they were in fact witches, we start with one million, at least. We may add 30,000 more innocent victims with Pope Gregory IX's crusade against the witches of Stedingen. Next, tally also the countless (and sometimes *counted*, as inquisitors often cataloged witch executions in church records) numbers of other men, women, and children, killed over the course of over five centuries, victims of "Christian business as usual" witch hunts, numbering at least 100,000 in Europe.[427] The final count is thus *at least* 1,130,000 and probably much higher. My best guess is three to four million witches were killed by Christians, simply because "the Bible tells them so." Yet it may easily amount to millions more.

It seems surprising that Christians killed only nineteen people (and, as mentioned before, a few devil dogs) in 17th century Salem in the United States. Surely there were dozens, even hundreds or thousands more witches living in Massachusetts, working with the devil and casting their evil spells, who escaped prosecution...? And, just perhaps, many more possessed dogs from Hell.

It was the Holy Bible, and *only* the Bible that enabled such cruelty and mayhem. Without the Bible there could have been no *Canon Episcopi*, no *Malleus Maleficarum*, no *Summis desiderantes affectibus*—and millions of innocents would have been spared the wrath of Christians who hold the Bible as sacrosanct.

## Bible Bunk and Holy Horrors

Those true believers, whom many freethinkers denigrate by labeling them with the sobriquet *Bible thumpers,* can be a tad frustrating—but only if the freethinker lacks a toolbox chocked with formidable, historical, and logical facts. Typical churchgoers tend to ignore history, and even most scripture, and they have read works by apologists who have figured out ways to justify the Bible as a legitimate, moral text. (Anyone who has actually read it with honestly *knows* that it is neither legitimate nor moral.) Their excuses are usually feeble. They ignore the obvious evil and skip over—or are blind to—the many contradictions. I cannot imagine that Sunday Bible studies ever bring up verses wherein Jesus suggests killing disobedient children, whipping slaves, or plucking your eyes out. Nor do they expose his praise of genocide. The Old Testament, as vile and immoral and murderous as it is, is often regarded as noble God's first, failed attempts, his son coming along several millennia later to render things right. Finally.

How does one argue with Bible believers? Well, begin by showing them that the book is riddled with immoral acts, as well as many, *many* contradictions. This proves them wrong about Bible "inerrancy" as well as its ethics. This is often a difficult task, as they have been trained to pull excuses from a quiver full of nonsense, but you, if you are indeed a freethinker, should be at the ready to point out little-known atrocities and evil within their own Holy Book.

Next, bring up horrors perpetrated by Christians in the real world (as opposed to Bible fantasies), done so solely because they had "God on their side."

The Bible is an enabler for evil. It is the job of rational freethinkers to remind believers of the facts they ignore, or are unaware of. Even Jesus—a supposedly perfect soul—propagated tenets contrived by Bronze Age Hebrew men who sought wealth, power, and conquest of women (virgins in particular for some reason) as they concocted "laws" and "histories" in their Tanakh.

Christian apologists begin with the assumption that the Bible must be true (after all, *it says* it is true); then they attempt to find evidence supporting it. This is the opposite of critical thinking and scientific method.

Consider the opinions in a book by Keith Ward enticingly named *Is Religion Dangerous?* When I came across the title I thought perhaps the author was on to something enlightening: that I might learn even more about the dangers of religion than previously aware.

Enlightening, yes, very much—but in a different way I had hoped. Ward (a Christian theologian, it turned out) wastes no time offering his foregone conclusion: religion could not possibly be evil or dangerous. His Introduction, on *page one,* declares such notions "absurd." This is his credo throughout. One may cringe while trudging through such narrow and apologetic interpretations; nevertheless such jaunts can reap rewards by gaining insight into the whirling workings of brains that have been put through a thorough religious wash cycle without any subsequent tumble-dry.

One must treat harmful mendacities with umbrage; deceivers and obscurantists must be called out, refuted. Unctuous believers have infected and ravaged the world too long, and I for one am quite tired of the violence and lies and murders in the name of various "gods."

Beliefs in some superstitions are innocuous; consider for example, astrology, mentioned in my Introduction. Yet strongly held belief in irrational notions that claim to be approved by some sort of all-powerful supernatural overlord often result in the oppression and murder of millions. So: award several points to astrology merely for innocuousness. I do not believe in astrology, but it does not rub or rile me to raise pen or sword, any more than does my neighbor's barking dog. Mere annoyances, both. Self-righteous cults proffering supernatural dogmas, on the other hand, are much more than merely annoying, to say the least.

The impotent philosophies and tawdry exegesis provided by religious apologists rarely surprise the intelligent reader. Ward, for example, refers to the three Abrahamic monotheisms with blinders on: "The God of Judaism, Christianity, and Islam is a being of justice, mercy, and loving-kindness, who commands [*commands*—any hint of mystical dictatorship here?] humans to be just, merciful..." (49).

Surely, Ward—theologian, historian, author and scholar—must be acutely aware of the injustice, racist intolerance, and pervasive violence proffered by the Old Testament, the Qur'an, and even by the apparent words of Jesus. Upon an honest analysis, the more rational mind really cannot conclude that this three-headed numen embodies justice, mercy, and (Myles Coverdale's ancient portmanteau) *loving-kindness*. Your typical Christian Thumpers and Bible Bambis would be well advised to re-read the scriptures and pay attention next time. After all, these are the words of the Almighty and his son!

For example in Numbers 31, Yahweh commands Moses, in one of the many early faith-based initiatives, to exterminate the Midianites, except virgin girls, whom they can keep for themselves. There are no instructions regarding how to distinguish virgins from non-virgins, but "Virgin Inspector" must have been a pretty groovy profession back then. From a man's point of view.

In Deuteronomy 20, the god of the Hebrews declares after defeating enemies you may indeed take their women, but then must kill all males and livestock: "save alive nothing that breatheth," loving Yahweh commands. In Genesis 19:5-8, Lot, a "righteous man" (2 Peter 2:7), sanctions the rape of his daughters. Later (Gen 19:31-6), Lot's daughters get drunk with dear old dad in an incestuous *ménage à troi*.

As previously mentioned, in Luke 14:26 Jesus decrees you may be his disciple only if you hate your entire family, and hate yourself. Ask your Christian interlocutor if she hates herself and her family.

Qur'an 2:6-7 commands you not to aid disbelievers, because Allah made them this way, and He lusts for divine retribution: "theirs will be an awful doom."

There have been hundreds of millions of victims of religion across time. If they were not killed or tortured by religious fanatics, their potential free thoughts were derailed in youth by a superstitious and morbid upbringing. Drinking the blood and eating the flesh of the son of god is one example, being an ancient liturgy pilfered from pagan practice long before Jesus.

Ward's writing is never acrimonious. Nevertheless like the typical believer he lacks the acumen of a logical and freethinking individual. Ward's recollection of the history of religious atrocities—the very point of his book—is spotty at best. To his credit he admits to the iniquities of one of the Hebrew god's many genocidal decrees of Deuteronomy 20:16-17 (extermination of those annoying Hittites, Amorites, Canaanites, Perizzites, Hivites, and Jebusites), calling it "perhaps the worst of all" primitive moral ideas (109). This is an admission regarding his own all-loving creator! However it is not, by far, the worst. This mythical god, in a long line of other legendary deities, commanded many bizarre dictates much more gruesome and immoral than his Deuteronomic decrees. The entire book of Joshua is much more violent and foul.[428]

Moreover, in the New Testament, Jude 1:5-8, Old Testament genocide is praised, and unbelievers are banished to "Hell." Jesus himself speaks highly of father Yahweh's genocidal tantrums in Matthew 11:20-24.[429]

Ward claims that Jesus' Sermon on the Mount countermanded Yahweh's "horrible" (Ward's word, not mine) decrees. Yet he ignores Matthew 5:28-30 and the unholy dicta propounded by Jesus in that same sermon, such as thought crime (112). In his supposedly wise and peaceful pronunciations on that mount, Jesus, son of the Creator, suggests self-mutilation as your only logical recourse: cut off your hand, pull out your eyes, Jesus advises in Matthew 18.

And I thought chopping off the foreskin was a silly superstitious ritual and a crime against nature.

While he does not specify, Ward must be referring to Matthew 5:21-22 on the "mount" for Jesus supposedly annulling violent Deuteronomic philosophies.[430] Yet Jesus contradicts himself repeatedly, sometimes approving Hebrew "law," sometimes dismissing. Jesus often strikes up an intolerant and infinitely judgmental stance. This is something Ward, a supposed expert on Christianity, seems to have missed.

For example in Mark 7:9-13 and Matthew 15:2-6 Jesus agrees with the Old Testament parenting instructions to kill your rebellious or stubborn son.[431] As a Hebrew you are a hypocrite if you do not, so declares Jesus.[432]

Jesus, a perfect being and the son of God, condemns people to *death and eternal hell* simply because they had not repented (Mt 11:20-

23). Loving Jesus often employs the vile trick of infinite blackmail, damning you for eternity if you merely do not follow him (Mt 25:40-46, Mt 10:33, Mt 12:30-31, Mk 3:29, Mk 8:38, Mk 16:16, Lk 12:10, Jn 3:36, Jn 8:24, Jn 12:48, Jn 15:6, etc.). Comedian Bill Hicks pointed out that "eternal suffering awaits anyone who questions god's infinite love."

Long before Hicks, Robert Ingersoll had commented on the ignorant and immoral nonsense of Matthew 25:41, *Depart ye cursed into everlasting fire, prepared for the devil and his angels.* Ingersoll responds to the scriptures, writing "These are the words of eternal love."[433]

Ward misses—or chooses to ignore—Jesus applauding Old Testament ethnic cleansing and his violent proclamations such as "Think not that I am come to send peace on earth: I came not to send peace, but a sword" (Mt 10:34), and "I am come to send fire on the earth" (Lk 12:49). The typical Christian apologist explains away repugnant or contradictory scriptures using wordplay, pseudo-philosophical legerdemain, or pretexts of context and metaphor. Sending fire on the earth is no metaphor: Jesus repeatedly proclaims that the world will come to its scorching terminus within a generation (e.g. Mt 24, Mk 13, and others). See Matthew 13:40-43 for his dismal eschatology.[434]

So much for Jesus "countermanding" God's primitive morals. (Aren't Jesus and God supposed to be the same entity anyway?) Moreover the idea of *anybody*—even the son of God—countermanding God's words is impossible according to the Bible, as God's laws never change, and are "perfect," as in Isaiah 40:8, Psalms 18:30 and 19:7-8, John 10:35 and 1 Peter 1:25.

Page 124 of this apology contains perhaps Ward's most absurd claim: "there are no serious objections to the moral perfection of Jesus." Is he completely unaware of the writings since the Enlightenment? Even believer C. S. Lewis had questioned Christ as being, just perhaps, immoral. Lewis contemplated that the very words of Jesus should cause one to believe he was the "Devil of Hell" and "a madman or something worse." Lewis wavered and waffled, resigning to proclaim Jesus (against all Lewis' own logical arguments) "Lord and God."[435]

With the canon as my witness, I must raise serious objections to any "moral perfection" of Jesus. The words that come to my mind are:

- *ignorant* (e.g. Mt 6:25-6, Mt 6:34, Acts 10:38).
- *contradictory* (Lk 16:16 *vs.* Mt 5:17 *vs.* Rom 6:14 *vs.* Mt 19:17).
- *violent* (Mk 7:10, Jude 1:5-8, Lk 19:27, Mt 11:20-24).
- *unjust* (Lk 12:46-48).
- *unforgiving and devoid of empathy* (Mt 23:14).
- *intolerant and racist* (Mt 10:5-6, Mt 15:22-24, 2 John 1:10, Acts 13:17-19, Jude 1:5-8).
- *illogical and nonsensical* (Mt 5:29-30, Mt 24:37-39, Mt 12:40, Jn 3:14).

Thus, "perfect" does not describe this savior, sent from Heaven in all its misty and golden glory. Such claims are stretches of titanic proportions. Check your Bibles if you got 'em.

Ward asserts "Christians have given up the Torah" (119) and he holds certain New Testament sections as proof. If so, what might Ward think about the words of Jesus supporting so much of it? Christians who dismiss the Old Testament as Hebrew tales or simple parables should read Matthew 12:40, where Jesus believes Jonah lived in a fish; Jude 1:5-8 treating the "Sodom and Gomorrah" myths as if historical; Romans 1:26-27 where Paul supports the *god hates fags* decree of Leviticus 18:22 and 20:13; and John 3:14 wherein Jesus believes in a magical pole that cures snakebites (*cf.* Numbers 21:8-9).

> *Fun Fact*: "Saint" Paul used his craftiness to dupe gullible minds: "But be it so, I did not burden you: nevertheless, being crafty, I caught you with guile" (2 Cor 12:16, KJV)

The New Testament propagates Old Testament racism against non-Hebrews (e.g. Jude 1:5-8 and Acts 13:17-19).[436] [437] The New Testament also declares Lot—the cowardly and incestuous Old Testament character—to be a "righteous" man, in 2 Peter 2:7 (NAS,

NLT, ESV, ISV, NIV, and many other Bible versions; KJV and DRC use the adjective "just" to describe this repugnant patriarch).

Christians have given up the Torah? This is something that we all should surely wish but is not the case. Very often I see Sunday morning televangelists citing Old Testament scriptures as if they accurately reflect history or morality. The History Channel ran a series called "Mysteries of the Bible" examining the Old Testament tales in detail. One episode was about the Cain and Abel saga, "thought to be the world's first murder." This, from *the History Channel,* for crying out loud! I know what the "mysteries" are: Why would anybody still believe this nonsense, in the 21st century?

In his book *Answers to 200 of Life's Most Probing Questions,* Pat Robertson professes that he actually believes in Adam and Eve, the Garden of Eden, and that it "is as good an explanation for what happened as there could be" (55). Darwin, Sagan, and Hawking come to mind as three (of so many) who might just disagree with this childish conclusion. In *What's So Great About Christianity?* dripping with desperate tautology in attempt to prove the universe was created by "God," Dinesh D'Souza quotes from Psalm 19 (p. 131). D'Souza claims that the Christian god did so completely and solely for the sake of *we humans*. Is this not arrogant solipsism? D'Souza actually declares "the biblical account of how the universe was created is substantially correct" (124). This is pure OT BS; nothing more, nothing less.

Clearly most Christians have *not* given up the Torah, and the New Testament supports much of the Old Testament nonsense, a fact denied by Mr. Ward and so many other contemporary apologists.

The prime D'Souza factoid that really gets my goat (not available as a "burnt offering"; so sorry for Yahweh, our bloodthirsty creator) is his ignorant—or mendacious, I do not know which—claim that the total number of deaths due to the Crusades, Inquisition, and Witch Hunts amounts to a mere 200,000 (p. 215). The actual number is closer to five or six million.[438] Toss in the French Wars of Religion (three million killed) and the Thirty Years War (seven to eight million) and the death toll is perhaps fifteen million; and this is not by any means the end of the Christian madness and genocide.

I do not know where Dinesh gets his statistics, but I have a clue: in a debate against Christopher Hitchens he brings up the witch hunts, limiting his argument to Salem.[439] "I finally researched it," D'Souza declares, learning that only eighteen witches were killed there. I was somewhat surprised his adversary did not bring up the over one million Catharist "witches" violently put down by Christian forces; but on that day Hitch had to shoot many fish, wallowing in Dinesh's lame and watery barrel. I am tempted to coin a term, "D'Souzoid" for Dinesh's ventures into malefic depths. Read his books and watch his debates. Every time you encounter a grossly false "fact," relegate it to that pile.

I am sure one can produce even larger stacks consisting of *Foxoids* and *Bibloids*.

While our esteemed Ward reluctantly admits to *some* Christian atrocities such as the Crusades and Inquisitions, he nevertheless excuses them. In chapter three, "Religion and War," Ward claims Christianity had "humanising effects" on the Roman Empire (66). I believe the millions of victims tortured and murdered by Christian oppressors would disagree—if only they could.

Ward ignores the vast majority of perennial Christian transgressions against mankind. He touches upon one or two of their many inhuman horrors now and then, with but brief mention —and of course tepid, even fetid rationalization.

Over the centuries the telltale and unblinking eye of history has witnessed Christians murdering apostates, people of rival religions, and even fellow Christians with trivial spiritual discrepancies. They eradicated millions; for example the Cathars; then the Stedingers; then masses of German Peasants, all excused by biblical jurisprudence, or immoral decrees from religious leaders. Christian monks burned hundreds of thousands of "witches" while alive; approved, and even urged on by *every pope* across many centuries.

Yet Ward (73) actually asserts "no one who has studied history could deny that most wars in human history have not been religious." I had to read that sentence twice; anyone who has studied history realizes *the opposite is true*.

He backpedals: "And in the case of those that have been religious, the religious component has usually been associated with some non-religious, social, ethnic or political component..." What religion has not been infiltrated by social, ethnic, or political components? I can name some, but the three main monotheisms have always had greedy and malevolent cockroaches and termites in their midst.

Christian leaders have suppressed freethought for nearly two thousand years. The total number of lives taken in the name of mythical Jesus? It amounts to tens, even hundreds of millions, and it took Christianity fewer than twenty centuries to accomplish this feat of "moral perfection." Ward seems only slightly aware of such atrocities: his sub-section "The Crusades" covers—I kid you not—*a page and a half* (68-69)! Again this is the very subject of his work, titled—need I remind the reader—*Is Religion Dangerous.*

Christianity had "humanising effects" on the Roman Empire? Clearly the negative effects (torture, slavery, genocide, forgeries, censorship, large-scale annexation, psychological blackmail) far outweigh the weak and sparse and apologetic positives.

Ward claims that "all" religious views are "underpinned by highly sophisticated philosophical arguments" (91). This statement is not only absurd, but sadly hilarious, while hilariously sad. The archetypical believer in Jesus, Krishna, Mohammed, or Yahweh did not arrive upon his or her faith through any kind of "philosophical" analysis, sophisticated or otherwise. The roots of such beliefs and delusions typically lie in childhood brainwashing, instilling unfalsifiable myths in the budding mind while the grey matter is soft and tender and pliable. The true sources behind most ongoing religious, superstitious, and mythical beliefs stem from youthful indoctrination by parents. It is the reason Ward is a Christian, Bin Laden a Muslim, the Dalai Lama a Buddhist.

It is the reason Hitler remained Catholic.

Being so raised, Hitler claimed to be on a mission from his Christian god: "Hence today I believe that I am acting in accordance with the will of the Almighty Creator: by defending myself against the Jew, I am fighting for the work of the Lord" (*Mein Kampf,* vol. 1 ch. 2, "Wiener Lehr - und Leidensjahre").

Any freethinking individual who has studied history can see that religion is, at face value, not merely dangerous but a malignant behemoth guilty of mass murder and perpetual spiritual blackmail. This excludes, of course, the few truly peaceful religions that I revere, such as Mithraism, Jainism, Buddhism, Bahá'í Faith, Universal Unitarian, and Quakerism, as well as Zamenhof's noble Homaranismo experiment. If only such benevolent belief systems were more universally heralded, what an even more wonderful world we would inhabit. I do truly blame Constantine's and other third and fourth century cronies first, for choosing scripture from violent and immoral cults (Hebrew and Christian; too bad they did not pick, say, Buddhism or Mithraism). Then I blame emperor Theodosius I for declaring Christianity the only legal religion of the empire, 391 CE.

Eusebius was also a dishonest and central contributor to the tall tales and subsequent atrocities, all based on myths and oral tradition and nonsense, some scrawled and copied by ignorant cultists, including mendacious Christian fathers.

The previous pope as of this writing, Herr Ratzinger, is also worthy of many books exposing his immoral and illegal actions committed while wrapped in flowing female eveningwear and—in his position as infallible Vicar of Christ—comical headdress.

Christians, Muslims and Moses-believing Hebrews will find that Ward preaches to their choir, and will appreciate his book, as long as they remain ignorant of history and of actual words of violence and intolerance recorded in the Bible, Torah, and Qur'an. No freethinker aware of history will find anything of value in Ward's twenty-first century Christian apology.

Perhaps simply by subtle contrast, Pat Robertson's aforementioned publication offers a laugh on every page. It is like a book report on the Bible written by a nine-year-old.

D'Souza's rants are merely sad and embarrassing: to him, and to humanity. And if anyone offers you Lee Strobel's works, be sure to counter with the truths in the many publications by Robert M. Price, as well as Bart Ehrman, Frank Zindler, and Joseph Wheless.

One must be honest, and sometimes even vitriolic about this subject because Christians cling to claims made by people like Ward, D'Souza, Robertson, William Lane Craig, Frank Turek, Lee Strobel—their heads buried deep in superstitious sand with a generous cherry-picking of the few "good parts" of the Bible (and apparent ignorance of actual history and Bible anathemas). Such beliefs and disjointed obstinance are ultimately dangerous. Never has any act of genocide or suicide-bombing been perpetrated by, for instance, a Jain or a level-headed secularist.

To help convince believers that they are perhaps misguided, the freethinker may simply point them to the evil parts of the Bible, the plethora of contradictions, and the sad, mad results that these religions have exacted across the millennia.

Such a task might seem almost impossible, but take heart. Many true believers have come to their right minds. Contemporary examples include Christians who had sought to become preachers or priests, including Matt Dillahunty, David Smalley, Dan Barker, and Bart Ehrman. They studied the Bible to such a great extent that they finally pulled their heads from Christendom's contradictory and immoral pies of mud and lies to realize it is, in fact, 99 and 44/100% pure: that is, pure bullshit.

One should point out the atrocities, the millions murdered in the name of Jesus and contrast that with the number of people killed by, say, Quakers or Jains. By very definition, Quakers and Jains cannot use their religion to rationalize murder, or any evil action. Yet Christians are able to cite multiple scriptures to "prove" that gays should be killed, that their god supports slavery, that misogyny is a valid moral position, and the notion that Christians should travel the world and preach their religion while annexing all lands occupied by "heathens."

The core of this particular argument can rightly be: if the Bible never existed, then early Hebrews and later Christians could not have claimed god on their side in performing their many immoral and murderous acts, still in practice today. No Crusades, no witch hunts, no Inquisitions, no oppression of gays, apostates, non-virgin brides, or people of other belief systems. If no Bible: peace, prosperity, continuation of Hellenistic enlightenment, and no Dark Ages.

## Beaten with Many Stripes

For hundreds of years, Europeans collaborated with various African tribes to chase down rival men and women on the Dark Continent to transport them to other lands for brutal enslavement. How could good Christians justify such inhuman acts?

The answer is at once simple and pitiful: they used their Good Book. Thus many centuries of slave trades would ensue. Ponder the following Old Testament verses while noting that the term *servant* did not hold the modern "Jeeves" sense of the word, but rather, human chattel:

> And he entreated Abram well for her sake: and he had sheep, and oxen, and he asses, and menservants, and maidservants... (Gen 12:16).
>
> If thou buy an Hebrew servant, six years he shall serve... (Ex 21:2).
>
> And if a man sell his daughter to be a maidservant, she shall not go out as the menservants do. (Ex 21:7.)

The Old Testament thus permits a father to sell his daughter into slavery. Is it possible that repeated rape may follow? Clearly the Bible has no problem demoting your offspring to the status of auctionable property, even sex slaves.

**Came a Righteous Rebel**. Jesus the Messiah changed Old Testament law, right? This is the Christian claim I have seen many times, but I humbly beg to differ.[440] Here are some words from his Apostles:

> "Servants, be obedient to them that are your masters according to the flesh, with fear and trembling... (Eph 6:5-6.)
>
> Let as many servants as are under the yoke count their own masters worthy of all honour... (1 Tim 6:1.)
>
> Servants, be subject to your masters with all fear... (1 Pet 2:18.)

Our church was not a wacky Evangelical, but still required brain check-in at the door, allowing emptied skulls to be filled with

Christian myths and ancient borrowed liturgies. We sung inspirational tunes about a King of Israel who "loved all the little children."

Do you know the song? They had us sing: *Red and yellow, black and white / They're all precious in His sight / Jesus loves the little children of the world!*

According to that spiritual song of amour, Jesus loves all children regardless of race. Let us thus read the recorded words of the son of God himself: "And that servant, which knew his lord's will, and prepared not himself, neither did according to his will, *shall be beaten with many stripes*." To his credit, Jesus meek and mild declares that obedient slaves should not be beaten quite as severely as bad slaves (Lk 12:46-48).[441]

Also to his credit Jesus does not infer that only dark-skinned individuals should be owned as property; Jesus is an equal-opportunity supporter of slavery and righteous lashings.

**Out of Africa**. Europeans were technologically more advanced than Africans, and—perhaps like a boy who burns ants with a magnifying glass—they considered Africans to be lowly entities, surely less than human. Africans were also godless and needed to be "saved" so they could get into heaven. (There are separate water fountains *on high*, no doubt.) That was the job of missionaries: teaching foreigners about Jesus. Ants are of no practical use, but African "savages" are. The task of Christian merchants, then, was to capture godless Africans, transport them, and sell them into slavery. Then let clerics teach them all about Jesus, if they survive the ordeal.

Slavery brought death to millions of African victims via various factors. It is difficult to determine how many died and how many were murdered by their captors or killed by their eventual masters. Let us nevertheless attempt to crunch some of the obscene and nauseating numbers.

The men, women and children captured by European slave-hunters would find their ultimate destinies in many lands, including Europe and Asia, but let us simplify this examination by concentrating on the element of this holocaust that consigned Africans to their new "home" in the Americas. The bulk of casualties occurred during the voyage from Africa to the New World ("Middle Passage") and the death toll can be approximated. It is largely agreed that the total number of Africans taken from their continent to the Americas from the 15th to 19th centuries for enslavement was about ten million.[442] [443] Given that the mortality rate during the voyage averaged around 12 to 15 percent,[444] we arrive by simple arithmetic upon a first-order approximation of the number of deaths: around one and a half million killed due to attrition of Middle Passage.[445]

A fascinating anecdote in this regard lies in the unusual case of the slave ship *Zong*, a vessel crammed to its gills with more than 400 prisoners from western Africa. The *Zong* raised her sails for the westward trek to Jamaica in 1781. Navigational errors and unfortunate weather conditions resulted in a prolonged voyage of four months. As provisions ran low, the captain ordered about 130 sick or dying prisoners tossed overboard.

*Tossed overboard!* Imagine yourself, an African native stolen from your free life, kidnapped from your home and family in your rainforest or savanna, marched forcibly to a vast ocean coast you had never seen. Next you are imprisoned for weeks—even months—in a shack with others of your familiar color, treated as if a despicable animal.

While incarcerated you are fed and watered. After all, the bleach-faced aliens need you alive to eventually toil for them for the rest of your life. Yet your enslavers treat their horses and dogs and hogs with care and compassion a thousand fold more than for you. Granted, they do slaughter and eat their porcine pups.

Eventually you are shackled below decks in a strange ocean-going vessel the likes of which you could not possibly have imagined. You are incarcerated in a waterlogged bilge, packed side-by-side with fellow prisoners without even headroom to stand.[446] After rocking at sea for months, you are forced out of your dank and musty prison, brought topside into the blinding sun. Bedazzled by your sudden transfer from shadow to overwhelming brightness, you consider that your horror may finally be over.

Suddenly you are tossed into the deep Atlantic by those same intimidating pink-skinned monsters who had shackled you and provided you with semi-edible slop. They inflict the sickening last minutes of your life. You await your end, head above water as best you can, rocking among the mountainous waves of an infinite ocean cold and consuming and blue, destined to drown in the brine with no hope, while the oddly-clad alabaster strangers disappear over the horizon.

Christians considered the basic principle of slavery to be sanctioned by their religion. And why not? The Bible not only advocates, but even legislates many aspects of the slave business—and Jesus condoned the ancient tradition, never admonishing it as immoral.

Captain Luke Collingwood, master and commander of the *Zong*, took solace in his commercial insurance policy. He figured he would be paid for his property losses, receiving compensation for any fewer than the full number of more than 400 "savages" originally registered in the ship's African manifest to be ferried across the Atlantic. Collingwood had the prisoners liquidated (literally) because he considered them not humans, but *insured property*.

Captain Collingwood died before the trial[447] and the courts did not award the requested £30 per "lost" (*tossed*) slave, ruling that the voyage had been mismanaged.[448] [449] The outcome of this trial was quite unusual, and the *Zong* incident formed part of the original impetus for the battle to abolish slavery.[450] [451] [452] Murder was never brought up as an issue in the court case: the slaves thrown overboard were clearly less than human according to the courts and Judeo-Christian moral beliefs of the times, as well as times long prior.

I have seen claims that in fact *Christians* led the fight to end slavery in America. It is true. Christians were largely responsible.

Hooray for them? No, this is the logical fallacy *post hoc ergo propter hoc*: "after this, therefore because of this." Such causality is an artificial connection: *of course they were Christians*. It was a crime, punishable by death, not to be Christian for the many centuries that came before. Almost 100% of Americans were Christians. Who else might have stepped up to end slavery, the Cherokee? The Navajo? Or perhaps all those Jews, Hindus, Jains, and Buddhists in America in the 18th and 19th centuries.

What it required were *Americans* to reject the biblical jurisprudence of flesh trading. That most were also Christians is redundant—a non sequitur.

**Capture to Enslavement**. Fade out now, and fade in to the very first phase of incumbent incarceration and servitude beginning in the jungles—the violent hunts, entrapment, capture, and subsequent forced march to the African coast. These caused many thousands of casualties, as did detainment in dungeons and stockades along the shore. Amid malnutrition and dysentery, captured Africans awaited deportation, often sleeping next to dead comrades (those not fortunate enough to attain the status of "slave" in the Americas).[453] [454]

During Middle Passage slaves often organized revolts, usually ending in disaster. It has been estimated that around 100,000 would-be slaves were killed due to such uprisings.[455] One may find it perhaps not much of a surprise to learn that malaria, smallpox, and scurvy also incurred huge death tolls upon the human chattel.

While arrival at a final destination in the Americas meant that the most hazardous phases of their bondage were at an end, there remained dangers, miseries, and new punishments under the yoke of their white Christian overlords. The number of slaves killed by cruel owners or poor conditions is simply not knowable.

Wouldn't it have been ever so nice if Jesus—anywhere in his sermons—had said that slavery of fellow humans is immoral? Jesus might seem to hint at it in Mt 23:10, but this is merely a metaphor in view of the preceding verse.[456] Clearly, slavery should have been considered much more important than, say, Jesus' edict prohibiting you from defending yourself in court (Mt 5:40). Or when he threatened his adoring audience with the absurd tale of Lot's wife turning into salt (Lk 17:31-32). Or turning water into wine, or killing a fig tree, or murdering pigs. One has to wonder how Jesus established his priorities: instead of walking on water, his time would have been better spent preaching, let's say, "Do not buy or sell men, women or children."

It really is that simple.

On that note, one must mention that the son of God never condemned rape, molestation, or incest. In fact the NT praises genocide (Mt 11:21-24, Acts 13:17-19, Jude 1:5-8).

The Bible was the prime enabler for the western slave trades, lasting centuries and enslaving tens of millions, causing unconscionable death tolls and miseries. Modern society has largely renounced biblical support for slavery. The next step seems simple—relegate the *entire* Holy Bible to its proper status: nothing more than a collection of myths and embarrassingly poor attempts at philosophy and moral advice. File under *Fairy Tales.*

That is to say, uncommonly violent and immoral Fairy Tales. How many murders or acts of slavery had the Brothers Grimm imagined in their fanciful stories, compared to the Bible, and the history of Christendom?

## The Jurisprudence of Gay Marriage

Controversy over marriage rights has been a ubiquitous subject in the news and political discourse. "Don't Ask Don't Tell" in the military was repealed September 2011. As of this writing, almost a dozen American states allow same-sex marriage, with others also teetering on the precipice of modernity. These are huge victories, yet we swim among ongoing iniquities.

You'll recall that some members of the U.S. Congress had crusaded adamantly to legislate at the federal level against same-sex marriage, often called "gay marriage" (a term that, as I shall demonstrate, is muddy and ambiguous at best). They aimed to define marriage as a union between a man and a woman.

And they succeeded. Well, *kind of*. The Defense of Marriage Act (DOMA) was authored by Georgia Representative Bob Barr, passed by congress, and signed into law in 1996.

It is not a moral, ethical, or even a logical law. Moreover it is un-American and very poorly defined. There are many problems in terms of human rights, as well as the disturbing simple-minded nature of this legislation. Of course this is not unusual for a law enacted by the U.S. Congress.

**The Obvious Problems**. I shall not dwell on the clear and evident and obvious problems at all, as they are unmistakable to any intelligent reader: such laws discriminate against gays. The discrimination issue has been brought time and again in court. DOMA is unconstitutional; it goes against the very spirit and core of the concepts "all men created equal" (*men*: merely a semantic problem), and "pursuit of happiness." DOMA stumbles over the same loose cobblestones of discrimination that were solved, one would think, by the 19th Amendment (which finally granted the right to vote, even to stupid girls with their icky cooties). Moreover, the DOMA notion is built upon a narrow-minded stack of straw and hasty generalizations, teetering upon rickety antecedents, mostly of religious origin.

**A Labyrinth of Tribulations**. I am sure you have heard one argument, childishly stated, "it was Adam and *Eve*, not Adam and *Steve*." The concept behind this mantra is simplistic, and—one would think—embarrassingly shallow. The Bible tells the Adam and Eve story as if historical fact. It also says a man should not lie with another man (Lev 18:22, the "God hates fags" argument). But the Bible also commands you to kill a bride discovered not to be a virgin (Dt 22:20-21), and Jesus recommends plucking out your eyes if you lust after a woman (Mt 5:28-29). To be a good Christian and blend into modern society one must be very skillful at choosing one's cherries.

If I could address Congress I would ask them, when legislating or judging the rights of citizens, to consider dismissing edicts of ancient and ignorant religious charter.

The fundamental assumption by DOMA supporters lies in its naïve and binary tenet: that there are but two types of *H. sapiens* in the world, a male and a female, each being attracted to one another. Nothing here but guys and gals: we're all heteros on this bus.

Then, fundamentalists must begrudgingly acknowledge two more "types" of humans: the gay man, and the lesbian woman — who are deviant, it would seem, and thus not worthy of the rights of "normal" people, the healthy heteros.

DOMA supporters do not forbid gays to marry (how nice of them); they merely strive to restrict the rights for gays to marry other gays. To them it makes perfect sense for a gay man to marry a woman. This weltanschauung is shallow and fatuous for so many reasons.

*First,* there is something that seems not to have occurred to them: somebody is going to have to define the legal terms *man,* and *woman.* What is the determining factor?

Is it plumbing? If so, what about a castrato—or, John Wayne Bobbitt shortly after his surprise penisectomy? Who are those men "allowed" to marry?

*Second,* what about someone born male, now post-operative and transgender? This person now has breasts, a vagina, and other very female characteristics that were induced surgically or hormonally. Who is this person "allowed" to marry? (The flip-side of the *Chaz Bono* coin, one might say, subject to the same legal conundrum.)

*Third*—and fourth, and fifth—if it is in fact not about anatomical plumbing but about chromosomes, clearly the transgender man who has been rendered physically female—thus now a woman—is allowed, under a DOMA philosophy, to marry only *another woman*. The issue is much more complex when one takes into account gender ambiguous individuals (those who we used to term hermaphrodites), as well as other complications that Mother Nature has gloriously bestowed upon our species.

If indeed chromosomes are the defining factor, there is much more trouble in Republican River City than one might imagine. Normally females have XX sex chromosomes, while males enjoy the XY variety. On this basis a ban against gay marriage would allow an XX person to marry *only* an XY, and vice-versa.

Life is not as simple as some congresspersons, xenophobes, and homophobes seem to think. The world is not—*surprise!*—inhabited only by Ozzies and Harriets. We must consider XXY people (living with Klinefelter's syndrome), XYY syndrome, and women born with three X sex chromosomes—as well as intersex individuals (the aforementioned "hermaphrodites").

Who is an XXY allowed to marry? What about an XYY who is in love with an XXX? What about an XXX woman who is now a post-op male, replete with (let's say, just one) penis, now *sans* functional breasts? And what jurisprudence within DOMA will help guide humanity when science one day discovers previously unknown human nucleotide sequences?

**A Simple Solution**. These DNA and genitalia issues are sticky wickets that most pandering and pious politicians clearly never considered (and probably were never aware). The solution is simple: drop the Adam and Eve bullshit, face scientific realities, and grant equal rights to the full spectrum of "genders" and sexual preferences. There are, in fact, more than two. Or four, or eight or sixteen.[457]

People of faith are still free to mingle religious tradition with their marriage ceremony. In America that is their right. Others may wish a secular service. *Rights* are the issue; the *rites* are not—marry at a church, synagogue, temple, Justice of the Peace, Vegas casino. Bring gods and saints into it, leave them out; that is not the concern.

This is the concern: individuals of appropriate age should be able to marry any consenting person they wish, regardless of private parts, chromosomes, surgeries, hormones, or sexual orientation.

Government should have no say, no sway in any such personal matters—these are very private notions of love and connection. Government must get out of the matchmaker business, especially when its interference *restricts,* rather than *expands* civil rights.

How complicated is that?

**The Dust May Settle**. As of this writing, events have been positive. Some congresspersons have come to realize the idiocy of DOMA. A "Respect for Marriage Act" (H.R. 1116, "RFMA") has been introduced that would repeal DOMA. We shall soon see where Thor's hammers finally fall: perhaps within the realm of discrimination, superstition, and ancient unctuous tradition—or fair, enlightened, and logical legislation. Your guess is as good as mine. I think the smart money is on RFMA.

If DOMA is torn down there will soon be many angry right-wing religious pundits spouting their smug and prejudiced views on the popular Faux News channels. And that is fine by me. They hang themselves with their own "faithful" and narrow-minded words. Always such fun.

## Pretzel Logic

To any freethinker it must seem painfully obvious that the key beliefs and doctrines within Christian dogma are not merely untenable, but make absolutely no sense. A ten-year-old can see through it all—unless inculcated from a much younger age.

Their logic is both circular as well as twisted: thus a pretzel. Moreover one discovers that the Bible espouses many immoral edicts, praises violence, and contradicts itself repeatedly. How can it be that millions still believe such harmful hogwash?

It could be that they simply do not allow their minds to dwell on anything of substance, being distracted by the "I'm saved!" concept, and typically having their thought process derailed by inculcation from childhood. Cognitive dissonance is fueled by fear of death and of the unknown, as Freud postulated.

One is cautioned to avoid direct observation of the sausage manufacture process, apparently being quite revolting. On the other hand the shaping and baking of pretzels is rather benign and easy on the eye. But the twisting of logic and promotion of tautologies are damaging to the victim of religion—and very much more harmful to society—than any grinding and molding of porcine foodstuff. I am not on about Crusades and Inquisitions here; those are subjects covered elsewhere. I merely propose, without arrogance or conceit, that *Christianity makes absolutely no sense.* And I so present my proofs.

Consider the claimed "mission" of Jesus the Christ: his heavenly mandate was to save humankind from "original sin" committed by "Adam," as we find St. Paul acknowledge in Romans chapter five.[458] Thus to believe in the Prime Directive of Jesus, one must also believe in mythical Adam and Eve.[459]

Let's give Christians slack for the moment and drop the requirement for accepting into their philosophy a talking snake, being perhaps mere metaphor.

Doesn't this mean that a *true Christian* cannot believe in evolution? I know many Christians personally who understand and accept the scientific proof of evolution. If they cogitate over the pillars of their Christian belief system for more than a few seconds—

that of the "messiah" born of a virgin and charged with a "mission" sent from "heaven" to "save us" because "Adam" consumed a "forbidden fruit" from a "tree of knowledge" because "Eve" was convinced by some "devil"...

I fear my word processor is going to run out of quotation marks if I continue reasoning along these lines. Suffice it to say that the Adam and Eve story—being but fairy-tale thinking and irrefutably infantile—is not just a critical share of Judaism, but also essential and foundational to Christianity: "original sin."

Next and equally important to Christian beliefs is the ubiquitous *John 3:16* verse that seems to appear on hastily-scribbled cardboard placards within stadium crowds at every American football game, invoking: "For God so loved the world, that he gave his only begotten Son..."

I am afraid that, like so much other Christian piffle, I just don't get it.

And neither should you: where is Jesus today? Buried in a grave, rotting and eaten by maggots? Suffering in hell? Nay. Christians *pray* to Jesus. Their belief has Jesus securely in heaven on "the right hand" of God (Mk 16:19; *why so important which side*? And how do they know?) —bumping shoulders with his cotton-bearded, and jealous and bloodthirsty dad.

Where was *any* sacrifice on God's part in the alleged crucifixion? If the Jews and some Cecil B. DeMille films hadn't killed Jesus, what was the other choice—that Jesus would remain on Earth forever? Is that better for him than Heaven? Or would Jesus have had a limited lifespan? If so, when Jesus dies, what next but off to Heaven?

"He gave his only begotten son" makes no sense whatever. It is reduced to rubble by stating the simple reality of the situation: *Jesus had a bad weekend for your sins.*[460] Where is God's love? In the flood, drowning millions of God's children? Tormenting Job and Abraham? Exterminating Canaanites and Philistines, and so many others? Allowing his "only begotten son" nailed up and tortured?

Holy crap. Where is the sacrifice, and where is the love? A. E. Housman wrote "And malt does more than Milton can, to justify God's ways to a man." Nurse, three liters of malt, *stat*.

At this point the bedrock and lofty columns of the ancient cult are proven ineffectual, childish, and lacking in any and all logic. One could end the argument here and reasonably relegate Christianity to babyish fairy tale status, being silly sausage in the making—and pretzeline in its reasoning—but several more gratifying moments of exegesis await those interested in a free and full inquiry.

Any nominal and even any "true" Christian must also believe that dead people can live again in some magical way, as Paul demands: "But if there be no resurrection of the dead, then is Christ not risen: And if Christ be not risen, then is our preaching vain, and your faith is also vain" (1 Cor 15).

Well, dear and simple and saintly "Paul"—if that is your real name—no person who truly had his or her life forces completely sapped can be again risen; and thus, as you say, your preaching is in fact vain, and your faith is also vain.

**Jesus the Prophet**. For me, the true enigma of Christian ages centers at Nicaea in 325 CE. Constantine gathered hundreds of religious leaders—men who had spent their lives studying various scriptures and scribbles and tall tales, well familiar with it all. Were there any obvious flaws in the revered writings to be discovered and announced by those men?

Eusebius knew his stuff very well, and was knowledgeable of the problems posed by the two "genealogies" of Jesus, one by the anonymous author of Luke, the other in the Gospel of Matthew, also of unknown origin. Eusebius realized they do not match up at all. He addresses this and attempts to account for the differences in his *Ecclesiastical History*, calling it an "alleged" discrepancy (1.7). He admits that other reverent believers of his time had been "zealous to invent some explanation which shall harmonize the two passages," then he goes on to claim he alone can pull off this hocus-pocus. His unctuous mess of wordplay and clumsy legerdemain—just as zealous to invent explanations as his predecessors—do not convince me at all, but that is not my point.[461] I bring this up to underscore the fact that these scholarly Christian fathers were not ignorant of scripture (as opposed to most Christians today); they were quite immersed and well versed, aware of potential problems and conflicts. At the famed council of Nicaea, early Christian fathers gathered, intimately familiar with many dozens of writings—scriptures held by some in attendance as valid and genuinely Christian (whatever that meant at that early epoch). Upon conclusion of their summit they maintained general agreement regarding some scriptures. Contrary to popular belief, there was no vote at Nicaea regarding "valid" or "invalid" scripture, nor any canonization. Much later, Christian leaders eventually dismissed *Hermas, Barnabas, Gospel of Peter, Acts of Peter, Didache,*[462] and almost a hundred more—to the vexation of many pious presbyters of the fourth century, most of whom would have synthesized quite a different "Good Book" if they had their wishes.

So here is my perplexing Enigma of the Ages. These learned and devout men were intimately familiar with Christian writings (and many other religious scriptures) including the four Gospels—so why did they not notice that Jesus' *most paramount prophesy* had not come true? Jesus claimed all of his predictions (including the end of the world, and his own glorious return) would ensue within a "generation" of his time (Mt 23:36, 24:34, 16:27-28, Mk 9:1, Lk 21:32, 1 Thess 4:17).[463]

How could these gallant clerics and bishops, some 300 years after the predicted *second* coming (which should have been circa 45 or 50 CE), not notice that this coming did not, in fact, come? Why did not even one half-clever vicar stand up at Nicaea to declare, perhaps trembling, "Brethren, I have noticed something fishy about this Jesus character..."?

I understand why superstitious and gullible men of the fourth century did not question the need for Adam and Eve and the talking snake for the Jesus narrative to seem factual. But why did they not notice that Jesus was either deluded, or a liar—or perhaps both?

If the *coming* had not yet happened by the year 325, just when did these noble men expect it?

And why is it necessary, in the twenty-first century, to expose this: the groundless and illogical belief system of Christianity, being riddled with so many obvious pits, pockmarks, cavities and caverns? Why do people still believe this nonsense?

You already know the answer, I am sure: youthful indoctrination. Perhaps the most frequent word used in (anti-) biblical polemics and religion-bashing in general is *brainwashing*. That is because brainwashing from youth (perhaps more politely called *inculcation* or *indoctrination* in cordial social circles) is indeed a powerful tool, and is the reason so many harmful and illogical religions have endured and will continue to endure. Teach them while they are young.

So: Blame the parents. And their parents, and their parents, and theirs.

**Immoral Edicts**. So far we have considered many reasons why the very foundations of Christianity are illogical and obviously nothing but infantile myths. That should be enough: the Christian thesis is so full of holes as to be incapable of retaining watery dampness of any volume or value. The building blocks of Christianity—including the prime directive of Jesus, as well as the backstory—make no sense whatsoever, and have proven to be malignant to society on the grandest scale. Just consider the body count.

Let us forget about the whole "virgin birth prophesy" which we have seen was a Septuagint forgery, centuries before Jesus. That concoction is interesting but not a necessary ally in the deconstruction of this crazy cult of death worship.[464] So far in this analysis one *must* believe in Adam and Eve, as well as somehow squaring the inanity of John 3:16 (was there a sacrifice or not?). Also, in order to be a true and loyal Christian, one must ignore the failed prophesies of the perfect son of God.

It seems that Christianity makes no sense logically, and that fact alone should have been enough to stop it dead in its tracks in the year 325. But the Bible also embraces many immoral decrees.

Thus while I have thrashed this Christian horse to death in this chapter alone, let us not yet send its carcass to the glue factory. It needs to be drawn and quartered and hacked into smaller pieces—ironically, perhaps, in the same way Hypatia was dismembered by mad and god-fearing Christians in the fifth century.

The "Moral Teachings Jesus of Nazareth," as Thomas Jefferson put it, are in fact mostly *immoral,* and Jesus' revered Sermon on the Mount counts among his most dreadful rants. His preachments included, from Matthew chapter 6:

> Take no thought for your life, what ye shall eat, or what ye shall drink; nor yet for your body, what ye shall put on. Is not the life more than meat, and the body than raiment? Behold the fowls of the air: for they sow not, neither do they reap, nor gather into barns; yet your heavenly Father feedeth them... Therefore take no thought, saying, What shall we eat?

Jesus thus advises you not to bother to seek food, or to plant crops. Jesus thinks that *God feeds birds*—believing that birds put no effort into hunting for berries, seeds, insects, fish. So why should humans bother hunting, gathering or farming? The heavenly Lord takes care of birds, and takes care of you, and that is all you need to know. Or so thinks Jesus.

He goes on for dozens of verses on the Mount accusing you of thought crimes, recommending you pluck out your eyes, and saying you should take no thought for the morrow because all you have to do is pray and all your wishes will be granted by God (Mt 7:7-8).

Centuries BCE, Epicurus proposed his own wise thoughts, "It is folly for a man to pray to the gods for that which he has the power to obtain by himself."

**Enough Flogging**. Okay, I declare this pied and pious equine dead, chopped and minced, converted to Elmer's well-known sticky white slime. And it was not necessary here to delve into the rest of the violence and plethora contradictions within Christian scripture and practice. I believe this ubiquitous religion is sufficiently deflated and sent on its way by demonstrating that its very foundations stem from ancient myths, and are ridiculous, as well as immoral.

It seems that, if a believing Christian would just take an extra dozen seconds to ponder the inane "mission" of Jesus, or to dwell for a moment or two on the self-contradictory John 3:16, or ponder for more than just an instant upon the Sermon on the Mount, he or she might just realize the truth.

The underpinnings of Christianity are based on ancient myths, and are nonsensical; the teachings of Jesus are infantile, immoral and—as history proves—ultimately much more than simply harmful.

# PART III. CHRISTIAN ROOTS

## Mythology Abuse: Inherit the Hot Air

If millions of people worldwide woke up every Sabbath and attended temples to worship Zeus, Hera and Ares, we'd think nothing of it, except that they are superstitious weirdoes who believe in ancient myths—the way many of us generally regard Mormons and Scientologists. Yet millions today worship the "Father, Son, and Holy Ghost." Christianity's historicity is groundless myth, and readily disproven. It is a man-made hoax. Hebrew and proto-Christian forgers of the New Testament were surprisingly transparent in plagiarizing other religions and mythologies from their desert-dwelling predecessors.

One problem with teaching from the Torah, Bible, or Qur'an is this: it sticks. It sticks in children's minds as *fact*, instead of being thought of as the preposterous thing that it actually is: ancient made-up stories conceived by primitive and frightened minds. Polls show that the majority of Americans believe that Genesis is literally true, and they believe in the absolutely absurd story of Noah's ark. Wouldn't it be lovely if that flood story served some useful purpose, providing wisdom, some sort of uplifting allegory? Unfortunately it is nothing more than ancient fiction, offering no substance, neither spiritual nor factual. It is but mythos and completely without worth.

**Jesus the Rebus**. Beginning generations after Jesus' supposed lifetime, the New Testament was pieced together as a first- and second-century contrivance,[465] canonized several centuries thereafter, then followed by over 1,500 years of more modifications and re-interpretations. For whatever their reasons the first authors of Christianity gathered stories from Hebrew, Egyptian, Persian, Babylonian, Roman, and other ancient legends, dating from hundreds and even thousands of years prior to the apparent time of Jesus.

It is amazing to me that the vast majority of antique religions plagiarized by Christian forgers came from peaceful and beautiful sources—unlike the spiteful, violent, self-righteous Christian contraption that Rome embraced in the fourth century in failed effort to keep the Empire together and control the masses.

Lactantius (c. 240 - c. 320 CE), among others, championed the idea of Christianity as an official state religion[466] so that the Roman votaries could gain power and wealth. In all his brilliance, Lactantius—as Copernicus recorded centuries later—was also certain that the Earth was flat.[467] As most did in his time.

Almost two thousand years ago Christianity became the faith *du jour,* a hybrid superstitious house of cretinous cards built mostly of oral tradition and later committed to papyrus. The Christian cult was able to persist mostly due to perennial oppression and violence. Early Christian leaders abolished free thought and abrogated all things scientific and provable. Irenaeus, Bishop of Lugdunum proclaimed (c. 180 CE) that "all explanations" can be found in the scriptures, which are—his word—"perfect."[468] If those scriptures are perfect, then so was the Holocaust.

Rather, the words "erroneous," "absurd," and "immoral" come to mind.

In his *Epistle to the Philippians* (135 CE), Polycarp seems to make it clear he believes Jesus came to Earth "in the flesh," and that such thought is the one true way one must believe.[469] However this may be a forgery. The *Encyclopedia Biblica* seriously questions the genuineness of Polycarp's *Epistle,* and the *CE1907* also raises the possibility.[470] [471] Upon reading the *Epistle to the Philippians* one cannot help but notice that Polycarp seems completely ignorant of any gospels (he does use the word "apostles" - ἀπόσολοι - twice, II:19 & IV:1). As Waite wrote,

> No mention is made of either of the Gospels Luke, Mark, John or Matthew, by Clement, Ignatius or Polycarp... No reference is made to either of the four gospels, nor to the Acts of the Apostles, nor are there any quotations except such as evangelical writers concede may have been taken from other sources.[472] [473]

Early Christian church leader and author Tertullian, full of vinegar and pith, proclaimed, c. 200 CE:[474]

> Away with all attempts to produce a mottled Christianity of Stoic, Platonic, and dialectic composition! We want no curious disputation after possessing Christ Jesus, no inquisition after enjoying the gospel! *With our faith, we desire no further belief.* For this is our palmary faith, that there is nothing which we ought to believe besides.

Thus Tertullian admits, essentially, "Our heads are happily buried in the sand; please do not enlighten us with reason or facts, as we prefer not to think for ourselves. We choose to believe what we have been *told* to believe by our fathers."

The Book of Enoch was written by Hebrews two hundred years before Jesus, long before the Christ donned his sandals, beard, robe, and imaginary halo. See if you recognize this:

> Blessed are ye, the just and chosen, for your portion is glorious! And the just will be in the light of the sun, and the chosen in the light of everlasting life... And they will seek the light and will find justice... And after that it will be said to the holy, that they should seek in heaven the secrets of justice... (Enoch IX:58)

Compare to Jesus' supposed Sermon on the Mount in Matthew 5, at least two centuries later:

> Blessed are the clean of heart: they shall see God. Be glad and rejoice for your reward is very great in heaven... You are the light of the world... So let your light shine before men, that they may see your good works, and glorify your Father who is in heaven.

So what does this demonstrate? Perhaps that Jesus had merely a cursory remembrance of his Hebrew scriptures. My prime point is that the Sermon on the Mount, from which this hails, is so oft considered to be an amazing "new" philosophy and epiphany, originating from "God's only begotten son." This sermon was not only unoriginal, but largely illogical and immoral, as previously demonstrated.

**Hatred at its Core**. Jesus claims (Lk 14:26) you may be his BFF only if you hate your entire family, and hate yourself, as I previously pointed out. If they decide to follow him, Jesus tells his disciples that their families will hate *and kill* each other (Mt 10:21-22):

> And the brother shall deliver up the brother to death, and the father the child: and the children shall rise up against their parents, and cause them to be put to death. And ye shall be hated of all men for my name's sake: but he that endureth to the end shall be saved.

It seems that to be a true Christian you must hate just about everybody—except perhaps your enemies (Mt 5:44), whom you are commanded to love. Imagine if the Allied Forces simply loved Hitler: "He's just misunderstood." How about if we simply *loved* the Taliban, and Osama bin Laden: boys will be boys. Let's invite the Taliban over for a cup o' tea.

Jesus seems in agreement with his Heavenly Father's wicked parenting instructions of Deuteronomy 21:20-21, to kill your rebellious or stubborn son. Jesus is recorded as proclaiming, "For Moses said, Honor thy father and thy mother; and, Whoso curseth father or mother, let him die the death" (Mk 7:10 and Mt 15:4).

It is often noted that nowhere in the Bible do Yahweh or Jesus condemn slavery. In fact Jesus does quite the opposite, endorsing savage whipping of disobedient slaves in Luke 12:47.

**The Lord's Prayer**. In Matthew 6 and Luke 11 Jesus "teaches" us his "new" way of praying. Perhaps it comes as no surprise that he did not offer The Lord's Prayer as an original message, but rather he simply repeated a prayer from Hebrew literature—at least as best as Jesus could remember (Mt 6:9-15):

> After this manner therefore pray ye: Our Father which art in heaven, Hallowed be thy name. Thy kingdom come. Thy will be done in earth, as it is in heaven. Give us this day our daily bread. And forgive us our debts, as we forgive our debtors. And lead us not into temptation, but deliver us from evil: For thine is the kingdom, and the power, and the glory, for ever. Amen.

The prayer that Jesus claimed as his own comes from the ancient Hebrew:[475]

> Our Father, which art in heaven, be gracious to us, Lord out God; hallowed be thy name, and let the remembrance of thee be glori-

> fied in heaven above, and upon earth here below. Let thy kingdom reign over us, now and for ever. ...And lead us not into temptation, but deliver us from the evil thing. For thine is the kingdom, and thou shalt reign in glory, for ever and for evermore.

**Born Again**. One concept of being "born again" comes from John chapter three: "...Jesus answered and said unto him, Verily, verily, I say unto thee, Except *a man be born again*, he cannot see the kingdom of God...." This supposedly "Christian" concept is borrowed from the ancient religion of the Brahmins, over 1500 years before the birth of Jesus, and older than the five books of Moses.[476]

Next, I present further evidence of the actual NT origins. All the stuff of Christian "history" and dogma is in opposition to verifiable and historical fact.

## Saviors, Sun-Gods and Messiahs

The very word "sacred" comes into question as a meaningful term: is it possible that any belief, any faith, any set of ideas, any landmass, or any *thing* can be "sacred"? Look that word up in your dictionary and see if you can believe, in consideration of 21st (or even 17th) century enlightenment, that this word could possibly make sense in the natural world. The word *cherished* is rather benign. The word *sacrosanct*, once relieved of any religious connotation and magical contamination can also enjoy natural and useful employ.

The idea of *Faith* has long been strangely untouchable, and even revered. Should we laud extra respect upon those who are willing to accept without evidence the supernatural god-stories that were simply passed down to them? For those of "Faith" their evidence is merely the belief of tales relayed by others, usually being parents and ministers—ministers who are rarely shy about requesting and accepting real-world monetary contributions to propagate the supernatural, other-worldly myths that they sell to their sheep, so they may continue to practice their illicit avocation in the greatest of comfort.

For the freethinker, evidence is required; then the individual makes a judgment. The words *brainwashed, phantasmagoric, deluded,* or merely *tricked* serve well to describe the unique consecration and undeserved reverence ascribed to belief in a supervisory god, and the associated son(s) of God, being among the most prevalent dogmata.

I am certainly not the first to notice that almost all ancient mythologies and religions had their origin in primitive concepts of sun worship, and apparent movements of heavenly bodies—the moon, planets, the stars. The ancients took great lengths to investigate, and then eventually beatify the boundaries between the seasons (attributing them to gods), measuring them by the gradual rise and fall of the sun's apparent zenith and nadir throughout the year. Thus the solstices figure prominently in all sun-god religions, including Christianity.

The curious similarities between ancient polytheisms and Christianity are not coincidental. Following are many of the archetypes—some "gods" were real men, yet most were conjures of ancient myths, phantoms, and some were strange and absurd demiurges. The New Testament forgers clearly plagiarized ideas from many of these well-known myths and men.

## Carabbas/Barabbas

In 38 CE in his *On Flaccus*, prolific and revered historian Philo of Alexandria wrote of many major and even minor figures, including the inconsequential man Carabbas, who was a madman of the "gentle kind."[477] Carabbas (a real man, mind you) lived at the same time and near the same place as Jesus. As revealed in the Timeline of Part I, Philo's reportage of Carabbas was borrowed in the Bible to concoct parts of Matthew's chapter 27 fiction.

But wait, there's more.

Gerald Friedlander points out that Philo was a "valuable mine" for the New Testament writers from which they got their "best treasures." Wrote Friedlander:[478]

> Where, then, did the Gospels find the story of the of the mock coronation and crucifixion, and also the name of Barabbas? I venture to think that Philo is the source used by the Evangelists.
>
> Philo has been a valuable mine whence the writers of the New Testament have drawn some of their best treasures. The "Logos," the "Parable of the Prodigal Son," the "Gift of Tongues" (associated with the Pentecost), as well as "Barabbas" have all been derived from Philo. We saw that Philo spoke of the crucifixion of Karabas. It is a very short step from Karabas to Barabbas, if one bears in mind that in Hebrew or Aramaic *K* is very similar to *B*. Moreover, some of the old texts of Matthew speak of "Jesus Barabbas," as contrasted with Jesus, the Son of the Father in Heaven. The Aramaic for "Son of the Father" is *Barabba*. Does this not suggest that originally Jesus and Barabbas were one and the same person?

Charles Bigg shows that Philonism colored the New Testament, affecting subsequent Christian doctrine; and that the books of Paul and James strongly resemble the writings of Philo of Alexandria.[479]

♦ ♦ ♦

Next I propose to show how the story of Jesus Christ was an agglomeration of real men, plus many ancient god-myths. Dozens of common themes will become evident in New Testament sardoodledom. The roots of Christian origins and plagiarisms are well known, but I believe my research brings new evidence to the table.

As Reinach relates:[480]

> The essential feature of [Christianity] consists in an initiation into the cult of a Saviour-god, who assumed human form, taught, suffered, died and rose from the dead; the reward of the initiated is salvation. Such were the religions of Isiris, Dionysos, Orpheus, Adonis, Attis, and the like; such were no doubt many obscure creeds practised in Greece, Asia Minor, and Syria of which we know very little, because they are hardly mentioned in literature. Christianity is the most recent of its class... the only one that has triumphed and survived.

## Egyptian Origins of Judeo-Christian Beliefs

A point often asserted regarding Mormonism is how obviously manmade the religion is. Blatantly so, and the same with Scientology.

Yet one should be quick to point out that *all religions are manmade*. Humans created the various gods, not the other way around. There is no such thing as a "natural religion" or the "one true religion." Revealed wisdoms do not exist; they are manufactured by humans without any true revelation, then related second-hand, third, fourth, and so on.

Which peoples, then, invented ancient liturgies, still practiced, still believed—the revered dogmas, and tall tales of Genesis? Who first imagined concepts such as a son of god, heaven, miracles, kosher food, virgin birth, magical healing of the sick and blind, mikvah/baptism, divine resurrection and communion?

Those who created such myths did so long before the Christian tales. One might well suppose it was the ancient Hebrews.

One would be wrong.

**Archaeological Evidence**. It is rare to discover ancient religious texts that come down to us unadulterated. Early Christians (many generations after the supposed events), scribbled stories of Jesus. Then the texts were transcribed, translated, interpolated, and modified ad infinitum. In the fourth century, committees examined scriptures of all sorts, and various Christian councils formulated the new approved religion of the Empire: Christianity was given the Good Mythkeeping Seal of Approval, and every other cult or philosophy—even unbelief and apostasy—were rendered illegal under penalty of death.

Modifications and interpolations to the Christian scriptures continued unabated for centuries. Over a thousand years later the 1547 Council of Trent rendered the Bible somewhat stable. Next came over fifty different "versions" in English alone.

By stark contrast, over 1,500 years before Christian times, an "Egyptian Bible" was carved in stone and thousands of copies hidden in scrolls, deep within mausoleums and pyramids.[481] Archeologists recovered them in modern times—unsullied texts expressing ancient Egyptian religious beliefs.

Like the Torah and Bible and Qur'an, Egyptian writings embodied mere superstitions, the stuff of mythos; but their texts recorded the true spiritual proclivities held as incontrovertible during the height of the Great Egyptian Empire. This "Egyptian Bible" had remained an underground secret for thousands of years.

Egyptians held strong numinous beliefs. Theirs is among the oldest of recorded religions, and the Judeo-Christian belief systems and Bible stories clearly were borrowed from Egyptians, whence came also—by no coincidence—the Hebrew alphabet.[482] The exercise-in-proof that follows can be repeated by anybody able to read a valid translation of the Egyptian glyphs into his or her native tongue.

Egyptian hieroglyphics date to earlier than 3300 BCE. Over the centuries, the numbers of evanescent Egyptians able to read their glyphs waned, until the fifth century CE when nobody could interpret them. They became simple curiosities, ancient cave art.

Soldiers under Napoleon Bonaparte discovered a glorious black stone slab late in the 18th century, enabling humankind to interpret ancient Egyptian writings and understand their religion. You are aware of this stone, I am sure. Surprisingly, that nugget helps reveal the true source of much of the Old and New Testament stories and related dogmas. Of this, you may not be aware.

**Egyptian Decoder Ring.** Sweating under the Egyptian summer sun with shovel and pick along the Mediterranean coast in 1799, French Army engineer Pierre-François Bouchard unearthed a tablet that would come to be termed the *Rosetta Stone*. As Bouchard wiped sand and mud from the slab, he immediately recognized its significance. The Stone provided incredible insight into Egyptology.

The lands stretching out from the blue-green Mediterranean waters of Bouchard's newfound treasure largely comprise desert sandscapes: Egypt, Lebanon, Israel, Syria, Libya, Jordan, Persia. This frames both the geographic and demographic context to help understand the spread of ancient Egyptian mythologies throughout the "biblical" region, originating before 3300 BCE and making their way to Genesis and eventually to Jesus stories.

The Stone opened a secret door to the past. Modern man would come to discover that this particular sable slab had been chiseled late in ancient Egyptian history, around 196 BCE. Inscribed on it was one message (mostly a dedication of temples and tax exemption for Egyptian priests) in three languages: hieroglyphs at the top, Demotic next, and Greek at the bottom. Egyptian hieroglyphics had long been a mystery, but the Greek text became the magic decoder ring. *Jackpot*, 1799.

**The Rosetta Stone**

Using the stone, Jean-François Champollion worked with others to decipher the glyphs, forgotten for thirteen centuries. When the teams finally cracked the code they were also able to read Egyptian writings elsewhere, including pyramid texts. The hieroglyphics scrawled in pyramid scrolls and hammered into temple walls were not simply depictions of birdmen and street mimes with arthritis and dislocated limbs; the pictographs have phonetic and syntactical structure and meaning. They disclosed ancient epistemic and religious zeitgeist—Egyptian knowledge, histories, and spiritual beliefs in detail.

Those Egyptian texts expose the primary roots of Judaism and Christianity.

Do not simply believe me. Borrow from your library a translation of the Egyptian *Book of the Dead.* Primarily I cite interpretations by Renouf, Faulkner, and Budge. A direct and pellucid connection is evident: the tales and liturgies of the Tanakh—as well as those of the New Testament—were plagiarisms of mystical and supernatural conjecture, much borrowed from Egyptian belief.

**Judeo-Christian Roots**. The ontological scriptures of the *Book of the Dead* promise peaceful transition to the "next" life, being an aegis for any Egyptian soul knock-knock-knocking on heaven's door. That book and various other Egyptian artifacts provide extensive insight regarding their desperate and fearful beliefs.

Fifteen centuries before Jesus, the Egyptians worshiped a saintly savior named Horus. The Egyptian missals present proofs of the origins of Judeo-Christian mythologies, *res ipsa loquitur.*

The Book of the Dead consists of many "spells." Consider these divine convictions: Born of mother Isis, Horus is the avenger of God, who is his father (Spells 17 and 92). "All that liveth" are subject to Horus (Spell 78). Horus delivered himself from evil (Spell 42), and Spell 92 promises to guide you to heaven. In Spells 52 and 53 we learn a miracle of "seven loaves" supplied by the son of god.

Horus was born of mother Isis (who transformed into *Neith* or *Nephthys,* Spell 17)—a virgin, like so many mothers of sun-gods: Attis, Buddha, Dionysus, Krishna, Perseus, Prometheus, Mithras, Hercules, and of course, Jesus.

In Spell 112 we discover an anti-pork diet. As in the later Hebrew religion, pork was forbidden among ancient Egyptians.

Horus is the Prince of Eternity, Lord of mankind (Spell 42). Spell 97 tells of Horus purifying his soul with mikvah or baptism. Horus preaches a communion (Spell 19), and the blood of his mother is magical and holy (Spell 156).

From the *Book of the Dead,* read the uplifting beliefs of those illustrious peoples:

> I am Horus, avenger of his father...May the eye of Horus deliver for me my soul... imprison not my soul... it is Heaven that shall hold thee. —*Spell 92,* Renouf translation.

> I have followed Horus, the Lord of all. —*Spell 78,* Faulkner translation.

> I am he...*who dieth not a second time* ...I am Horus, *Prince of Eternity*, a fire before your faces... I have set myself free from all things evil. —*Spell 42,* Renouf.
>
> And Ra said to the gods, "*the swine is an abomination...*" And the swine became an abomination to Horus. —*Spell 112,* Renouf. (*cf.* Lev 11:7 and Dt 14:8)
>
> Said over a consecrated crown placed over the face of the person... there shall be given to him drink and food in presence of this god. Thou shall say it at dawn twice; a great protection is it... —*Spell 19,* Renouf.

Sir Ernest Wallis Budge wrote "...many of the attributes of Isis, the God-mother, the mother of Horus, and of Neith, the goddess of Saïs, are identical with those of Mary the Mother of Christ."[483]

The ancient Hebrew cure for snakebites is a Festivus-type pole with a brass serpent at the top (Numbers 21:9). The New Testament surprises us (perhaps) with the Christian Savior's concord: Jesus believes the OT rubbish (Jn 3:14). Yet thousands of years before, antagonist "Seth" turned into a serpent and went underground, recorded by ancient Egyptians. Sun-god[484] (and Son-of-God) Horus assumed the form of a pole with his head at the top, positioning himself above the snake's hole so Seth "may never again come forth therefrom."[485]

Digging deeper into the Egyptian sands and spiritual beliefs, we find other suspicious connections. The Christian Bible claims Jesus cured the blind (Mk 8:23) and the deaf (Mk 7:32-3). How did Jesus cure them? Jesus spat in their eyes (Mk 8:23), and stuck his fingers in their ears, licking and spitting on his medical patients.

Many centuries before Jesus, Egyptian god Thoth cured Horus' torn-out eye *by spitting on it* (Spell 17).

From the *Pyramid Texts* we learn that Horus loves "those who love him."[486] Centuries later Jesus expresses the same sentiment: "and he that loveth me shall be loved of my Father, and I will love him" (Jn 14:21). Jesus, however, is a bit more jealous and in need of idolization; Matthew 10:37 is one example: "He that loveth father or mother more than me is not worthy of me: and he that loveth son or daughter more than me is not worthy of me."

Jesus apparently had run-ins with the "devil," yet returned to earth unscathed (Mt 4); this is suspiciously similar to Spell 173 wherein Horus was "glorious in the Netherworld."

**More Plagiarisms and Parallels**. Ra and Horus were the same entity, Horus being an incarnation of father God—just like the Yahweh-Jesus connection. Horus was a Savior and Redeemer, crucified after being betrayed.[487]

Spell 97 (Renouf translation) discloses Horus' sincere and moving plea for mikvah or baptism: "...let me be purified in the lake of propitiation and of equipoise; let me plunge into the divine pool beneath the two divine sycamores of Heaven and Earth." The much later Hebrew scripture, Psalm 51, reads "Have mercy upon me, O God, according to thy lovingkindness: according unto the multitude of thy tender mercies blot out my transgressions. Wash me thoroughly from mine iniquity, and cleanse me from my sin."

The Ten Commandments bear a striking resemblance to many verses of the Declaration of Innocence, Spell 125:

> I have not done what the gods detest...
> I have not debased the offering cakes of the gods...
> I have not done falsehood against men...
> I have done no wrong in the Place of Truth...
> I have not learnt that which is not...
> I have done no evil...
> I have not caused pain...
> I have not killed...

It seems probable that 2 Kings 18:27, as well as Malachi 2:1-7 are plagiarisms of Egyptian Spell 53, which is "For not eating feces or drinking urine in the realm of the dead." From Malachi,

> "Behold, I will corrupt your seed, and spread dung upon your faces, even the dung of your solemn feasts..."

From 2 Kings:

> "hath he not sent me to the men which sit on the wall, that they may eat their own dung, and drink their own piss with you?"

**Egyptian Influence on Psalms.** There is a king mentioned in the 45th Psalm that seems to refer to Horus, the Egyptian anointed son of God and conqueror of death.[488] Psalm 23 is a plagiarism from Egyptian texts appealing to Osiris.[489] Psalm 47 is a song referring to resurrection of Osiris at the mountains of Amenta, "God is gone up with a shout" (Ps 47:5), to sit "upon the throne [mountain] of his holiness."[490] Psalm 74 is taken from Egyptian stories of battles, and seems to show the Egyptian origin of Moses parting the sea. The "dragons" of this Psalm are the evil crocodiles of ancient Egypt.[491] Consider also Ezekiel 29:3, which reads:

> Speak, and say, Thus saith the Lord GOD; Behold, I am against thee, Pharaoh king of Egypt, the great dragon that lieth in the midst of his rivers, which hath said, My river [the Nile] is mine own, and I have made it for myself.

**Universe Creation, Jesus Creation**. The Hebrew Creation story was obviously borrowed from the much earlier Egyptian: in the Tomb of Ramesses VI (1,100 BCE),[492] Atum[493] is created in a garden paradise, offered a red fruit by a serpent; and the Atum story includes a tree of knowledge. Nearly identical Atum-fruit-serpent scenes of Egyptian art have been on display at both the Louvre (on the coffin of Penpii), and the Museum at Turin.[494] [495] The "tree of life" and "tree of knowledge" are ancient Egyptian concepts.[496]

History also gives us an "Egyptian Calvary" predating Jesus by over 1300 years. On the north wall of Tutankhamun's tomb, one finds: a physical resurrection scene; an ascension scene with the figure welcomed to heaven by the sky goddess; a trinity scene: God (Osiris), son of God (Horus), and spiritual *Ka*, a holy ghost.[497] [498]

As the *Oxford Essential Guide to Egyptian Mythology* teaches (p. 167),

> The iconography of Horus either influenced or was appropriated in early Christian art. Isis and the baby Horus may often be seen as the precursor for Mary and the infant Jesus; Horus dominating the beasts may have a counterpart in Christ Pantokrator [Jesus of Nazareth] doing the same; and Horus spearing a serpent may survive in the iconography of Saint George defeating the dragon.

**More Egyptian Origins**. As mentioned early in this book, Philo Judaeus of Alexandria was plagiarized in Matthew, and several scholars have shown that his writings were also borrowed to concoct much of the Christian Bible.[499] [500] Elizabeth Evans offers her thoughts:[501]

> Christianity, mainly through the influence of Philo, was merely a continuation and a modification of the philosophy taught by Heraclitdus, Plato, and the Stoics...

It is true: *all religions are manmade*, by definition. But Christianity is somewhat unique, being perhaps the most elaborate, composite, and synthesized (Flying Spaghetti Monster notwithstanding), a melting-pot of ancient mythologies, with iron- and bronze-age superstitions stirred in to create the Christian cauldron of cloudy tales. Suetonius wrote, c. 125 CE: "Christians... a class of men given to a new and mischievous superstition."[502] Recall that the younger Pliny wrote c. 111 that Christianity is "an absurd and extravagant superstition," and a "contagion."[503]

**Conglomeration of Myths**. The original sources for Hebrew and Christian tales and rituals clearly derive from Egyptian, Babylonian, Persian, Roman, and other myths. Many other belief systems were copiously sprinkled thereupon, borrowing from the Hebrews, and Tarsus folklore contributed by "Saint Paul" (synthesized, I contend, from local resurrected gods Mithras and Sandan, well known and celebrated in Paul's town of Tarsus).[504] Other contributing factors stem from Hellenism, the Hindus, Persians, and, as mentioned, Philo Judaeus.

**Egyptian Epilogue**. It is unnecessary to dig deeper than the original Egyptian texts and genuine artifacts to discover that those ancient beliefs inspired both the Hebrew religion, and later tales of Christ. Many holy doctrines and "histories" considered Hebrew or Christian owe their existence to earlier belief systems, primarily from Egypt and Babylon.

If you have any doubts, get hold of the Bible, and Egyptian *Book of the Dead*. These suffice to prove most of my assertions with your own eyes. Of course, deeper research is necessary to support other claims—see the footnotes.

The Torah-Egypt and Jesus-Egypt connections are irrefutable. The ancient Egyptian writings provide proof incontrovertible for the origins of most Judeo-Christian mythologies, and the source of many of their rituals and ongoing beliefs.

## Mithra/Mithras: From Persia to Rome

Worship of Mithras was pervasive in the Roman Empire and the Near East several centuries before Christ. Franz Cumont wrote that the deity, worshiped by Roman soldiers, was an extension of much older Persian god Mithra/Mitra. Cumont's conclusion has been questioned in recent years. I present Mithraism in general agreement with the findings of Cumont, updated as appropriate. In this chapter I use the name "Mithra"—being perhaps Latinized "Mithras" after landing in Tarsus in the Roman empire—honoring the probable nascence of the myth.[505] [506]

Originally a god of Persian and Indian mythology, Mithra had believers from the sixth century BCE—perhaps as early as the twelfth.[507] [508] [509] Belief and worship in Mithra lasted some two thousand years,[510] [511] reaching from Iran and India to as far west as Greece, Italy, even north across the channel to Britain,[512] [513] [514] and in the Roman Empire was perhaps most substantially worshiped in Germania.[515] Mithraism was a beautiful religion, tolerant of other religions, and embraced good fellowship,[516] peace, and joy.[517] The Mithraic ministry was democratic; within its church "senators and slaves rubbed elbows," being a system of strong and pure ethics.[518]

Mithraism was the major competitor to the primary religions in the Near East and Mediterranean in the second through fourth centuries CE—and a big problem for Christianity.

Christians of the second through fourth centuries destroyed Mithraian artifacts whenever discovered. Author Payam Nabarz records the deadly envy that Christianity felt regarding the popular cult of Mithra:[519]

> There is perhaps nothing more telling of Christianity's dislike of its main rival than what was found in the Mithraic temple in Sarrebourg... a human skeleton (a Mithraic priest perhaps) who was chained to the Mithraic altar and the door blocked up. One suspects that the true messages of Christ—love, peace, and goodwill to humankind—were also buried in that temple alongside the nameless Mithraic priest.

I have visited several Mithraea in Europe. The display at the Mithraeum in Riegel (Germany) includes an enormous map indicating the spread of the cult during the Roman Empire, with over 300 still-existing Mithraea throughout Europe that the Christians could not find, or did not completely destroy. Many hundreds of ancient Mithras temples have been discovered: in Italy, Morocco, Algeria, Tunisia, Libya, Egypt, Syria, Turkey, Greece, Bulgaria, Croatia, France, Spain, Portugal, Germany, even throughout Britain. If you have the opportunity, visit one of the Mithras museums in France and pick up the DVD (region 2), *Lumières dans la Nuit,* all about the cult of Mithras.

Plutarch wrote that Mithraism was brought to the Romans by pirates early in the first century BCE,[520] but the actual arrival was well before 200 BCE (we have recently discovered a papyrus from the 3rd century BCE referencing a Roman Mithraeum[521]). Christianity had to go head-to-head with strong and widespread Mithraic belief, from which the Christian forgers plagiarized extensively.[522] [523] [524] [525] Sailors brought Mithraism to Rome, Ostia, Capua, Pozzuoli, the Ticino river, ports along the African coast, and parts of Great Britain.[526]

As Vermaseren states, "...anyone who wishes to understand the development of early Christianity must know something of Mithras."[527]

Around 4,000 BCE, Mithra, the son of God,[528] [529] was born in a cave[530] on December 25[531] [532] [533] of virgin mother Anahita,[534] [535] [536] [537] [538] [539] and He was destined to supervise the middle region between Heaven and Hell.[540] [541] His mission was to live on Earth among humans—teaching, healing, and protecting. Mithra's birth was witnessed by shepherds[542] [543] [544] [545] who came to offer gifts.[546] [547] He had twelve disciples,[548] [549] and Lord Mithra promised that faithful followers would live forever.[550] Mithra was the "Judge of Souls" and "Savior,"[551] being called the "Lamb of God" by his worshipers.[552] He was all-seeing, all-knowing.[553] Mithra rewarded good, and stomped out evil.[554] He was infallible, and through his wanderings and preaching, performed miracles.[555]

Sculptures, bas-reliefs and frescos of Mithra show him killing a bull, which symbolizes him "saving" the world (and a later second-coming to destroy it).[556] [557] The *CE1907* compares this to Jesus sacrificing himself.[558] Note, however, in the "revised and updated" version of the *Catholic Encyclopedia*, Thomas Nelson Publishers have removed the entire article on Mithraism—absent from where it should appear on page 393. Nelson Publishers also omitted the original article on the Library of Alexandria and its destruction by Christian mobs (which should appear on pages 29 and 348). In their defense, the Nelson version is but one volume, whereas the original consists of over a dozen. But a short paragraph on those subjects would have been informative, economical, and, at the least forthcoming.

Our savior Mithra protects good souls against Hell, sending us to the next life, a heaven, a paradise.[559] [560] The *CE1907* claims that Mithraism was "tolerant of every other cult," while admitting that Christianity condemns "every other religion in the world."[561]

Mithra is the enemy of darkness and of evil spirits.[562] His followers purified themselves by baptism with water,[563] washing away moral faults.[564] Sweet Lord Mithra is inseparable from Heaven itself; they are one and the same.[565] The holiest day of the week to the Mithrians is Sunday, the day of the sun.[566] [567]

Centuries before Jesus Christ, Lord Mithra had a "Last Supper"[568] [569] [570] and communion,[571] [572] [573] wherein his followers symbolically drank his blood and ate of his flesh by consuming bread and sacred wine,[574] granting them immortality.[575] Mithra was crucified on a tree between two men,[576] [577] buried in a cave, and some claim the myths have him risen and reappearing in the flesh.[578]

A symbol of holiness placed on the ceremonial bread loaves was a *cross*.[579] [580] Note that in Christian iconography, the figure of a lamb appeared on the cross until 680 when the sixth Ecumenical Council (in its Canon LXXXII) prohibited any future representations of Jesus using a lamb.[581]

Mithra was glorified in festivals annually at the winter solstice, December 25,[582] [583] [584] a "feast day,"[585] [586] and believers celebrated His resurrection each Spring/Easter (March/April).[587]

Like the earthly errand of "Jesus Christ," when Mithra's mission was over, He ascended to Heaven to merge with other deities, to become *the One God*[588] [589] [590] where He protects those who believe in Him.[591] [592]

Although it has been a very long time since Mithra walked the Earth and died (then was resurrected), Mithra will return to Earth one day, and have everybody drink a sacred wine which will give all people immortality.[593] [594] [595]

**Great Flood Parallel.** Mithraists and Sumerians believed in a universal flood[596] that wiped out all humans except one, a man named Ziusudra (or Atrakhasis, later "Noah").[597] Forewarned by the gods of an eminent flood, this Persian Noah built an ark[598] which he filled with his animals.[599] Thus we are all descended from this ark-man, this time being Persian.

**The Rise and Fall of Mithraism.** Mithraism gained popularity very quickly,[600] not just in the East where it originated, but also in the Roman Empire, being propagated somewhat secretively, largely by word of mouth.[601] Still, amidst the secret culture, Mithraism achieved widespread acceptance with many thousands of temples and artifacts being constructed and frequented with piety and praise before their almost complete demise by Christian fanatics in the 4th to 5th centuries. Westward dissemination of the Mithraic religion was strongest in the first and second centuries CE while Christianity was still a new and minor cult.[602]

During the first four centuries CE, Christianity gained competitive popularity against Mithraism. Christianity's expansion can be traced at first to oral accounts many generations after the death of a supposed Jesus Christ; then, to publication and distribution of an early version of the New Testament perhaps late in the second century.[603]

The religion of Mithraism was welcomed and adopted by Roman soldiers, merchants, and administrators.[604] After a few centuries of peaceful Mithras worship in the Empire, Early Christians displaced Mithraism. This was a movement that represented a transfiguration, a theistic synthesis. As Cumont puts it, "the foundation of a new religion in harmony with the prevailing philosophy and political constitution of the [Roman] empire."[605] In the fourth century the Roman Empire selected Christianity as its *official religion*. Then, Christians destroyed all Mithras temples they could find, or sometimes simply converted them to Christian churches, with little argument from Mithraists, largely due to the similarities between Mithraism and the newly invented/plagiarized religion of Christianity.[606]

**No Baby Mithra**. The Christian stories triumphed over the far-reaching body of Mithra mythology, perhaps because Mithraism had no cute "baby Savior," and perhaps because the Mithraists largely excluded women from their religious order.[607] [608] Mithra, while born of a virgin mother, had his naissance from a rock—a rather impersonal mother-son relationship, not to mention a bland nativity scene (imagine your Christmas train circumnavigating an evergreen with baby Mithra emerging from a *rock*, instead of the Jesus nativity in a cute manger scene). Christianity was also a slightly less misogynistic tale. That is, notwithstanding I Timothy 2:11-14: *Let the woman learn in silence with all subjection. But I suffer not a woman to teach, nor to use authority over the man: but to be in silence.* As well as other misogynistic phrases in the NT, and *many* in the OT.

Forgers of Christianity created a more anthropomorphic deity, and thus a religion somewhat believable to the Mid-East simpletons of that time, especially when taught to children.

Jesuism was also a "sexier" tale than Mithraism. What does Mithra look like—have you ever seen him? There are many bas-reliefs of his image; they are mostly shadowy, non-descript. In her film *God Said "Ha"* Julia Sweeney admitted that in her youth she and her girlfriends preferred attending mass at certain Catholic cathedrals because the depiction of Jesus on the wall was much more handsome and sexy than at others! Yet Christianity was indeed a cobbling from Mithraism, Hellenistic myth, Ancient Egyptian and other religions, assembled and published many generations after the Jesus story purportedly took place.

The Christian tale offered an oft-regarded milquetoast fellow named Jesus Christ as its mystagogue in place of the loving Persian god Mithra. Clearly, the scriptures prove that Jesus was violent, infinitely judgmental, oddly immoral, superstitious, and surprisingly spiteful. See the treatment in Part IV, "The Life and Morals of Jesus of Nazareth," p. 245.

The forgers of Christianity appended a Mithra-based mythos onto the Hebrew Tanakh, tossed in Carabbas and other Philonisms, some Egyptian and Babylonian modifications, and some OT retro-fitting. It seems that "Mithra" (Petra) became the fabled St. Peter.[609]

Mostly, of course, Christianity's "popularity" was due to the imperial declaration that Christianity be the only legal religion, with draconian and genocidal enforcement of that law. Decrees by Roman emperors would deal the final blows to Mithraism, and belief in the angelic Lord Mithras mostly died out in the Empire by the fifth century CE. The *Catholic Encyclopedia* states "the laws of Theodosius I [391 CE] signed its death warrant."[610] Followers nevertheless continued to practice Mithraism in secret through the early Middle Ages.[611]

**Give Mithraism A Chance**. It has been conjectured by many that had there been no Christianity, there would have been a fierce struggle between the Hellenist and the Mithraic, and Greek Enlightenment would have emerged victorious over supernatural explanations of the universe, and immoral teachings within Christianity. Larson wrote that, had Christianity not existed, "there would have been no Dark Ages."[612] Mithraists had no scriptural warrant to kill "witches,"[613] and a Mithraic society would not likely have given rise to a totalitarian theocracy like the infallible Vatican.

Enter then, in 362, Emperor Julian "the Apostate" (or perhaps more accurately, "the Rational") who detested religious persecution, restoring the legitimacy of non-Christian ("pagan") religions. Despite seeming to be free thinking, Julian was in fact a Mithraist.[614] If Julian had not been killed in battle shortly thereafter (363 CE), Christianity—at that time having a minor following—probably would have been crushed,[615] and the world may well have become loving and Hellenistic, and Mithraic.[616] [617] [618] [619] A Mithraic world would have embraced peace and Greek enlightenment—instead of fear, oppression, ignorance, witch hunts, violence, and Christian self-loathing.

The celebrated 2,000 year history of Christianity has an incalculable volume of blood on its hands, as well as continuous, wicked suppression of the human spirit. After Julian, the Christians resumed their violent destruction of "pagan" artifacts, including extermination of Mithraism.[620] Vermaseren relates the following story:[621]

> In Rome, about A.D. 400, a number of Christians, armed with axes, forced their way into a Mithraic temple on the Aventine, where they smashed the sculptures and cut gaping holes in the paintings. Once the persecuted, they were now the persecutors, and to their ever-growing numbers Mithras and his followers were regarded as deadly rivals.

Mithraism was, before, during, and well after the lifetime of the mysterious phantom Christ, a peaceful religion, and—to borrow from John Lennon—*bigger than Jesus*.

## Apollonius Tyaneus

Having traveled throughout Syria, Israel, Egypt, Turkey, Greece, and India during the same era that Jesus supposedly preached, Apollonius of Tyana (c. 3 BCE - 97 CE)[622] was considered by many to be the greatest religious figure of the time.[623] According to his prime biographer Flavius Philostratus of Athens, Apollonius was a philosopher, philanthropist, and humanist of the highest degree. He discussed philosophy, morals and religion wherever he roamed, and performed miracles including healing the sick and raising the dead (*Vita Apollonii*, IV.45, and VI.43).

Apollonius and his traveling companion and diligent chronicler, Damis of Hierapolis, set out to make the world a better place. Apollonius was vegetarian in both his diet and his wardrobe: when he did wear shoes, never were they made from animal hides, but from cloth or vines. Jesus, by contrast, stagnated in the sands and stones of Galilee, making wine and killing trees, apparently uninterested in the rest of the world.[624]

While visiting certain faraway lands, Apollonius would chastise their king for various moral transgressions, intervene in local affairs, then depart to continue his journeys after refusing the treasures the king wished to lavish upon him in appreciation of his wise counsel.

While in Alexandria, Apollonius once spotted twelve men being led to execution for robbery; it is claimed he sensed that one had been falsely accused. Apollonius approached the captors with his claim and thus saved the innocent man from the executioners (*VA*, V.24). Yet another magic-man? Of course Apollonius had no supernatural powers. That is absurd. *But Jesus did?*

The detailed chronicle of his life recorded by Philostratus (based on the writings of his acolyte Damis and several others, as well as information Philostratus collected "from the many cities that were devoted to him"—*VA*, I.2) consists of both fact and legend. Other ancient authors wrote of Apollonius, such as Maximus of Aegeae (Hadrian's secretary), Moeragenes,[625] and Lucian, as did Soterichus Oasites, epic poet of the third century.[626] Historian Cassius Dio wrote (around 200-222 CE) of an Apollonius event occurring in Ephesus in 96 CE.[627]

Philostratus wrote his biography of Apollonius around 220 or 230 CE, over a hundred years before the concoction of a canonical Bible. Philostratus was one of the most competent and famous historians of the time, yet nowhere in *any* of his writings do we find a mention of Jesus.[628] Funny, that?

According to the account by Philostratus, Apollonius had a divine birth (*VA*, I.5), practiced celibacy (*VA*, I:13), and cured the ill and the blind (*VA*, I.9). He cleansed entire cities of plague (*VA*, IV.10-11), could foretell the future (*VA*, I.37, IV.6, IV.18, IV.43), spoke to and fed the masses (*VA*, IV.13), was worshiped as a god (*VA*, IV.13; IV.44; and I.19), and was in fact *the son of god* (*VA*, I.6).

Second-century Emperor Marcus Aurelius (121-180 CE) wrote that he learned from Apollonius "to be free with a certainty beyond all chance, not to look to anything else but reason even for a moment."[629] Nowhere in the sayings of Jesus of Nazareth do we see an equivalent gem of dialectic, or remotely sage advice elevating *reason* above blind faith: from Jesus we are in fact gifted quite the opposite.

*Reason*, yes—but Apollonius did not discard all the accepted theological tenets of his day. Like most superstitious people of the times, Apollonius believed in Greek gods. Face it, even the New Testament recognizes goddess Diana (Acts 19),[630] as well as gods Molech (Acts 7), Jupiter and Mercurius (Acts 14), and more.

Like Jesus, Apollonius thought demons could control people (*VA*, IV.20). Yet Apollonius was uncommonly humble, believing that any praise of gods was taking on a subject beyond human power (*VA*, IV.30). He gave a sermon on a mount to the Ephesians, urging them to study only truth, philosophy, and wisdom (*VA*, IV.2). Compare this to Jesus' own mount masterpiece. As just one example, Matthew 5:28-29 wherein he says if you find yourself attracted to a woman, pull out your eyes and piss on your brain.[631] What impetus would humans have, then, to indeed "go forth and multiply" (as ostensibly commanded by the god of Moses) *without* feeling some physical attraction? Upon my first thorough reading of the New Testament, I came away with the realization that Jesus considers an erect penis to be an abomination of lowly status on par with pigs, or fig trees bearing no fruit. I see concurrence with Paul: "Now concerning the things whereof ye wrote unto me: It is good for a man not to touch a woman" (1 Cor 7:1).

And you know god not only hates fags (Lev 18:22), but also dykes (Rom 1:21-26).

Now back to our philanthropic Pythagorean protagonist. If you read the *Vita Apollonii* you shall see that Apollonius' compassion and righteous deeds are simply unparalleled. Had the writings of Damis, Maximus of Aegeae, Moeragenes, Lucian, Soterichus Oasites, and others been widely distributed and allowed to come down to us through history without being suppressed by Christian censorship—thus perhaps motivating and inciting a large-scale cult of Apollonius—there would probably not have been the violent Christian histories and superstitions propagated through the centuries up to our current time. Unlike Bible believers, Apollonius followers would have no holy warrant to kill witches or disobedient children or Canaanites. Or *anybody*. Our champion was a benevolent follower of Pythagoras.

In one of his letters to Apollonius, Emperor Titus (39-81 CE) gushed with praise: "... I have indeed taken Jerusalem, but you have captured me."[632] From the steps of the temple in Olympia, Apollonius amazed everyone "not just by his ideas but also by the way he expressed his thoughts" (*VA*, IV.30). When the judges of the Olympic Games requested his presence, Apollonius wrote: "For myself, I would come for the spectacle of the physical struggle, except that I would be abandoning the greater struggle for virtue" as we can see from the Letters of Apollonius still available even today.[633] Emperor Caracalla (188-217 CE) built a temple to Apollonius. Emperor Septimius Severus (145-211 CE), in his court at Rome, had statues erected of both the man Apollonius, and (the chimerical?) Jesus.[634] Emperor Marcus Aurelius reported that he came upon many other statues of Apollonius during his military expeditions.[635]

Apparently even some modern Christians can barely come to terms with the fact that Apollonius, a Jesus contemporary, was a miracle-worker and much more altruistic and saintly than their Christ. The (no doubt Christian) writer of the article on Apollonius in the *Penny Cyclopaedia* claimed, "It is almost needless to remark that the *Life of Apollonius* is a heap of absurdities and impossibilities" yet he admits to the other corroborative texts about our noble sage. Would he have written the same about the Bible?

Apollonius was worshiped for centuries after his death, perhaps most notably by Roman Emperor Alexander Severus who reigned from 222 to 235.[636] Philostratus wrote that Apollonius was the "son of Zeus" (*VA*, I.6); thus he was the son of the Big Guy in the Sky.

Believers in Jesus claimed Apollonius was an imposter, and followers of Apollonius claimed Jesus was the imposter.[637] Will the real Messiah please stand up?

Making the case for a historical Apollonius is slightly problematic because Christian authorities throughout the ages have suppressed as much information and as many artifacts as they could.[638] (After all, how many people do you know who have ever heard of this great man?) Moreover, even modern Christians, apparently offended or frustrated by the idea that such a truly saintly man had rivaled their Christ, strive to debunk Philostratus' account.[639]

Fortunately, the *Vita Apollonii*, works of other historians, and many physical artifacts have escaped Christian censorship and destruction. The hurdles arrayed together in attempts at obfuscation and obscurantism, it turns out, are feeble and easily overcome. We are left with many reliable articles of evidence.

**CSI: Tyana**. Artifacts supporting his historicity include the statues of Apollonius in Rome erected by Emperor Septimius Severus, as well as those recorded by Emperor Marcus Aurelius as previously mentioned. An ancient Sanskrit text was found in India with the names Apollonius (*Apalūnya*), Damis (*Damīśa*), and others mentioned by Philostratus, substantiating the Indian travels of Apollonius and Damis.[640] Among the artifacts in the Adana Archaeology Museum in Turkey is a fragment inscribed with a four-line poem attributed to Apollonius.[641]

A *Book of Wisdom of Apollonius* was written around the fifth century CE, describing a temple of Apollonius in Tyana, a man adored by "all people." The *Historia Augusta* describes the life of Emperor Aurelian, including Aurelian remarking on a statue of Apollonius as his army marched through Tyana. Apollonius' deeds were recorded and preserved in his home city of Tyana, placed in the Apollonius temple, and later referenced in the twelfth century by Tzetzes (yet not extant today).[642]

Some doubters have proposed that Philostratus made up the Damis character as a literary device to aid his chronicle of Apollonius. But one of the richest men in the late second century was a close friend of Vespasian, a man named *Flavius Damianus*—this would precisely be the Roman name given to a descendent of a man named Damis (the family of Damis was very wealthy) if said descendent was so revered to be bestowed praenomen and cognomen.[643]

Julia Domna, wife of Emperor Septimius Severus, possessed the chronicles of Damis (gifted to her by a Damis descendant) and she provided them to Philostratus, asking him to construct a history of Apollonius. Damis had volunteered to accompany Apollonius as companion, chronicler, and guide, as he spoke Persian, Armenian, and Cadusian and was familiar with the geography and land routes to Babylon.[644] In assembling his *Vita Apollonii* Philostratus used the writings of Damis, Maximus of Aegeae, Moeragenes, and others. Before Philostratus, both Lucian and Soterichus Oasites wrote of Apollonius; and Philostratus' work is largely regarded as supplementary to a biography of Apollonius, ἀπομνημονεύματα ("apomnemoneumata") or "memoirs" written by Moeragenes.[645] Moeragenes' work is mentioned by Church Father Origin in *Contra Celsum* (c. 240), but it does not come down to us today.

And it seems that Apollonius did in fact intervene publicly in affairs of the cities he visited, as Philostratus related an incident wherein an angry mob planned to burn alive the governor of Pamphylia, with Apollonius resolving the situation peacefully (*VA*, I.15). This episode is independently corroborated by Maximus.[646]

**Doubting Osmond.** Having said all this, one notes that Osmond de Beauvoir Priaulx expressed his doubts regarding Damis' veracity about the journeys through India.[647] I must however point out that the travels and tales and miracles claimed of Apollonius are much more believable than those told by the authors of the Gospels, much of Apollonius being supported by the attestations and physical proofs provided herein. Christians can only wish they had 1/1,000th the archeological and textual support for their champion as we do in fact have for Apollonius.

**Gentle Jesus**. Greek philosopher Dion of Prusa (39-120 CE) produced his *Orations* in the first to second centuries. Dion once mentioned an unnamed, distinguished first-century philosopher who "enjoyed a reputation greater than any one man has attained for generations," and who admonished the Athenians for gladiator shows at the theater of Dionysus.[648] Might this first century philosopher have been the angelic son of god, Jesus the Christ?

For various reasons, some historians think this distinguished man might be Musonius Rufus, a close friend of Dion. Why not Jesus, then? For the past two millennia, people have been praising Jesus, calling him some remarkable and wonderful things.

Jesus wielded neither quill nor stylus to record his wisdom, whereas Apollonius did so prolifically. Among his works is a *Biography of Pythagoras*, as well as four books *On Sacrifices* (*VA*, III.41). Copies of the letters of Apollonius can be viewed in their original Greek at the US Library of Congress.[649] Emperor Hadrian owned almost all of Apollonius' letters (*VA*, VIII.20).

We must ask again, then: this first-century man of whom Dion of Prusa wrote, this philosopher of greatest reputation—might Dion have been referring to Jesus? This is not at all likely. We see no record of Jesus upbraiding gladiator spectacles in speech—nor did Jesus write *anything* himself. Jesus was not, by any means, a peaceful figure. He said, "Think not that I am come to send peace on earth: I came not to send peace, but a sword" (Mt 10:34). Jesus actually *praised* genocide (Mt 11:21-24, Jude 1:5-8), exposing that the prophesied Hebrew "savior" actually seems to have been a violent racist. As we know from the scriptures, Jesus advised savage whipping of slaves (Lk 12:47).

Jesus demands the utmost of *hatred* from any would-be disciples (Lk 14:26). So why would Jesus decry violence? Certainly Jesus did not have anything to say in this regard. Nor did he ever declare as immoral slavery, pedophilia, rape, genocide, incest—or even those oh-so-violent gladiator games. Jesus had other, less important fish to fry. Or multiply, I suppose.

It seems very likely to me that Dion referred not to Jesus, nor Musonius Rufus, but to Apollonius, especially as we see an exact correlation in a letter from Apollonius, *Epistle Apollonius 70* "To the People of Sais," chastising Athenians for their gladiator shows. Wrote Philostratus (*VA*, 4.22):

> He also corrected the following practice at Athens. The Athenians used to assemble in the theater below the Acropolis and watch human slaughter...This too Apollonius denounced, and when the Athenians summoned him to the assembly, he said he would not enter a place that was impure and full of gore. This he said in a letter, and added: "I am surprised that the goddess has not already left the Acropolis when you pour out blood of this kind for her."

Philostratus adds, "These are the most earnest of his disquisitions at Athens on that occasion that I have discovered."

Perhaps Apollonius was indeed the first-century philosopher about whom Dion raves, and not the man Musonius Rufus, and surely not the seemingly schizophrenic character "Jesus Christ." Or my assertion could be wrong. It has been argued that Dion may have referred to a Roman man; if true, it would probably not be Apollonius.[650]

As an aside I must also point out that both Dion and Musonius lived shortly after "Jesus" and neither man ever wrote of Jesus or of Christians, yet both men certainly should have, if the fantastic tales of Jesus had been true.

**Hail Julia!** If not for Julia Domna, we would probably have very little information about Apollonius. It was at her behest that Philostratus wrote his *Life of Apollonius,* which comes to us in full from almost two thousand years past. Sadly, Julia took her own life before Philostratus could finish his epic work of eight volumes.

The historicity of the genuinely "saintly" (for lack of a better term) figure Apollonius Tyaneus is far stronger than any evidence for one other son-of-god figure supposedly conceived by a miraculous union between a holy ghost and a lowly human virgin. One must assume that this ghost had some magical method of godly sperm delivery: his angelic penis, or a heaven-sent turkey baster, perhaps?

We have only the scantest of clues regarding what shaped young Apollonius, rendering him a man of such wisdom and benevolence. The yokels of Tyana recorded—as Philostratus thus propagated—that on the day of his birth swans danced around his mother in a meadow and a lightning bolt accompanied his divine nativity. We do know his family was wealthy, and he studied philosophy as a youngster, embracing the noble doctrines of Pythagoras. Philostratus wrote that Apollonius did not die, but was resurrected and physically elevated to heaven (*VA*, VIII.30-31).

I surely doubt it; but if Christians claim it for their alleged savior, I feel entitled to hold the same as true for the Sage of Tyanus.

## Mother Maya and Baby Siddhartha

A Hindu God beginning c. 500 BCE, Siddhartha Gautama became the "Buddha"—another Son-O-God, an incarnation of his dad, Vishnu.[651]

Buddha is born December 25[652] of virgin[653] [654] Maya (compare to *Mary*), through a slit on the right side of Maya's torso.[655] A star signaled Buddha's birth,[656] accompanied by angels and auriferous wise men, bearing—what else but gifts of gold.[657] [658] Buddha was instantly baptized,[659] pronounced king of the world[660] and savior of mankind.[661]

**Herod Parallel**. King Bimbasara of Magadha raised an army with the mission to kill Baby Buddha.[662] [663] In most of these stories of gods paralleling the Jesus myths there is a Herod equivalent. Elizabeth Evans puts the historicity of the Bible tale of Herod in perspective:[664]

> The pride and glory of the Romans was their carefully developed and rigorously executed system of law, and no Roman governor would have ventured to destroy a generation of the emperor's subjects at birth without leave and without record. If such a wholesale murder had been accomplished there would have been some mention of the event in profane history, and the silence of three or four evangelists respecting the visit of the Magi and the succeeding massacre by Herod is sufficient proof of the mythical character of the story.

Like Jesus (Lk 2:42), Buddha preached in a temple at age twelve, disappearing until around age thirty becoming wandering sage.[665] [666] Buddha also had about a dozen close acolytes, including a favorite disciple, as well as a "doubter" and a traitor.[667]

*Let the Hero, born of woman, crush the serpent with His heel* is a verse from the Battle Hymn of the Republic. What in the world does it mean? Well, it refers to Bible stories about crushing a snake's head (e.g. Genesis 3:15 and Luke 10:19), actually plagiarized from a Buddha serpent story.[668]

Buddha performed miracles, healed the sick, walked on water and fed masses from a small basket.[669] Some claim that Buddha was crucified and resurrected himself from his tomb.[670] Then his body ascended to Heaven (*Nirvana*). Like Jesus,[671] Buddha did not come to destroy, but to fulfill the old laws.[672] However, to the best of my knowledge Buddha did not contradict himself like Jesus did.[673] Buddha will return to Earth—in judgment, and to restore order and happiness.[674] When Christianity took over the ancient myths, the Catholic Church transfigured many ancients, "Buddha" being assimilated into Christian myth as a "Saint" named Josaphat.[675]

## Mother Semele and Baby Dionysus

Of ancient Greek belief c. 800 BCE, Dionysus is one of my favorite deities, the god of wine, Bacchus being the Roman equivalent. Dionysus, the "twice-born" son of Zeus and Semele,[676] is largely a plagiarism of Egyptian god Osiris.

Brought into this world of a virgin mother in a manger,[677] Dionysus' birth was celebrated annually by Greeks on Rustic Dionysia. Dionysus was the "savior" and "only begotten son of God," the Liberator of Mankind. Your belief in Dionysus will ensure your immortality.[678] See if you can guess when Dionysus was born. If you guessed Santa Clause morning, December 25, you win a candy-cane.[679] [680] [681]

**Herod Parallel.** When Dionysus was brought to Earth, archenemy King Pentheus refused to believe in the coming of a miracle-worker and king arriving from the east. This miracle man would turn out to be Dionysus, and Pentheus banned Dionysus worship.[682]

Dionysus traveled the ancient Middle East (including his home in Palestine) performing miracles, and changed water into wine during his mystical treks.[683] He was a role model for his human worshipers,[684] and promises a joyous afterlife.[685] After being killed (either hanged on a tree or crucified, depending upon who you ask in 800 BCE), Dionysus rose from the dead on March 25th.[686] His followers believed a communion would grant them immortality;[687] they drank wine in rituals, representing his blood.[688] The Dionysia, or Festivals of Dionysus, were held each spring[689] in the month of Elaphebolion (February/March). Hundreds of years before Jesus,

Euripides wrote that Dionysus will return one day with great vengeance.[690]

## Mother Devaki and Baby Krishna

The Hindu deity Krishna first appeared in historical records beginning c. 900 BCE. Being the son of God—an *avatārin*[691] or God in human form—his conception by Mother Devaki was (big surprise) a magical one.[692] [693] Krishna was born (wait for it: another surprise) on December 25.[694] [695] [696] A star in the east[697] [698] informed angels and shepherds of Krishna's birth, presenting the divine baby Krishna with gold, frankincense, fruits, and myrrh.[699]

Yes, the stories are getting old and tiresome. Or perhaps fun and funny as we thoroughly prove the Christian myths were simply plagiarized, like so many others. Modern and clear-minded analysis of ancient texts always prevails. Ancient tales claim that Krishna was the "divine baby and child" and victor over all forms of evil.[700] [701] The Amazing Krishna performed miracles[702] like raising the dead, healing lepers, and curing the deaf and blind.[703] Krishna is the embodiment of Truth and Love,[704] and He promises that his subjects can attain salvation in loving communion with Him.[705]

**Great Flood Parallels.** Krishna worshipers believe in a world-wide flood that covered the highest mountain peaks of the world, coming about because of the sins and corruptions of humanity. There was one man on Earth who was not corrupted, a man many hundreds of years in age: King Satyavrata. He was warned of the impending flood by God (in the form of a fish) and given seven days (seven: same God gave Noah, Gen 7:4) to collect pairs of animals as well as seeds and plants[706] (Yahweh apparently forgot to tell Noah to collect seeds and plants).

**Herod Parallel.** The evil King Kamsa (sometimes *Kansa*) wanted to kill Krishna, because a sage had told Kamsa that Krishna would kill him,[707] so Krishna's father swapped Krishna with another child. King Kamsa went on an infanticidal spree, killing male babies under the age of two,[708] [709] [710] (compare to Mt 2:16-18) so Krishna was taken to Gokula where he spent his childhood.[711]

Krishna, a shepherd, preached sermons and moral lessons, and being the savior of the world, converted his congregation. Like Jesus will supposedly do upon his return (see Rev 20), Krishna crushed a serpent, dancing on its head.[712]

When Krishna was about age 30, a Last Supper was held before his execution, a crucifixion on a tree[713] between two thieves.[714] Krishna arose from the dead, and witnesses saw him ascending to heaven, where he merged with his father, the divine god Vishnu.[715] [716] He will return, he says, "for the protection of the good and the destruction of the evil-doers."[717]

## Mother Gaia and Baby Prometheus

The Greek story of Prometheus comes from a time at least 800 years before the Jesus tales; and the Christian mythologies bear much resemblance. Born December 25 (of course)[718] [719] of mother Gaia, Prometheus descended from heaven. He represented triumph in the face of overwhelming odds.[720] His closest friend, Patraeus[721] [722] (compare to *Peter*) was a fisherman, like Christ's Peter:

> And Jesus, walking by the sea of Galilee, saw two brethren, Simon called Peter, and Andrew his brother, casting a net into the sea: for they were fishers (Mt 4:18).

The fisherman Patraeus forsook Prometheus, and fled.[723] Like Jesus, Prometheus was tortured and crucified, being riveted with "brazen bonds" to a desolate "crag."[724]

## Mother Nana and Baby Attis

Worshiped by Phrygians twelve hundred years before the Jesus apologues, Attis (sometimes *Atys* or *Attys*) was the Greek deity of life, death and resurrection.[725] A shepherd on Earth,[726] Attis is the only begotten son of God.[727] Baby Attis was born in a cave on December 25.[728] [729] His mother Nana (her real name, not Attis's baby-name for his Mum) was a virgin.[730] [731] Nana placed an almond in her bosom to conjure the creation of her god-boy son; the child would be brought into the world miraculously (Pausanias, 7.17). Nana abandoned Attis, and then our "Earth Mother" Cybele adopted him.

The Roman Catholic Church appropriated Our Lady Day (of the Virgin Mary) from Greek celebration day of Phrygian Mother Cybele.[732] Like so many other liturgies and myths plagiarized by Christian fathers.

Ancient Greeks believed that Attis was crucified on a tree.[733] Considered the Savior of mankind, Attis died for our sins.[734] He was resurrected after his crucifixion[735] [736] a few days later.[737] [738] His disciples hailed his resurrection as a promise that they too would have eternal life.[739] Believers annually mourned, and rejoiced the death of Attis, and resurrection at a festival in spring.[740] [741] His followers would use bread as a metaphor for his body, and eat it in worship while symbolizing his blood with wine.[742] [743]

> "People don't come back as *anything*, except Jesus, who came back as bread"—Ned Flanders, *The Simpsons*

**Mother Isis and Baby Horus**. The Egyptian sun-god Horus was described in detail in the chapter "Egyptian Origins of Judeo-Christian Beliefs" (page 161). Like so many other sons of God, there is the proverbial:

**Herod Parallel:** An evil enemy, Seth (or *Set*), was jealous of Horus and strove to kill him.[744] [745] His mother hid the child for protection.[746] [747]

♦ ♦ ♦

**Jesus - Yesus - Yeshua - Horus.** It has been conjectured that the name *Jesus* is a mutation of earlier *Horus*. Phonetically the theory holds viable and reasonable water, considering the transliteration of letters J, Y, and H. Think: Spanish *Jesus* ("Hay-zoos"), Germanic *Jesu* ("Yay-zoo"), as well as Hebrew "H" or "Ch" (as in חנוכה, *Chanukah*) and Arabic ح and خ.[748] Another theory holds that the name of the Phoenician god "Jes" (*the sun personified*) was Latinized by adding suffix "us."

**Mother Mary and Baby Jesus, Epilogue.** One can readily see that the Mary and Jesus stories were plagiarized from ancient tales, cobbled by first- and second-century men to create the newest stories of yet another "Son of God." Second-wave (post-Nicaean) Christians claimed that the similarities of Jesus with other prior gods were the work of *Satan.* (Yes, ancient ignorant people actually believed there was a "devil" and his name was Satan.)

Kuhn sums up the naïve confusion that ancient peoples underwent:[749]

> The Christians of the third and fourth centuries were plagued to distraction by the recurrent appearance of evidence that revealed the disconcerting identity of the Gospel narrative in many places with incidents in the "lives" of Horus, Izdubar, Mithra, Sabazius, Adonis, Witoba, Hercules, Marduk, Krishna, Buddha and other divine messengers to early nations. They answered the challenge of this situation with desperate allegations that the similarity was the work of the devil!

The Christian explanation for the existence of earlier religions that were similar to the Judeo-Christian was that they were "the work of the devil."[750] Of course they could not make the claim that the other cults plagiarized Christianity, since the Christian myths came about long after those "pagan" myths. Charles Morris wrote:[751]

> The worshipers did not know whence came their gods. We, who can approach the subject without prejudice and bigotry, and to whom mythology has ceased to be sacred, can easily trace their origin, and point out nearly every step of their unfoldment.

Many centuries passed, and again became "legal" to practice religions other than Christianity, or to not believe any of them. Historians were quick to write of the "mysterious" similarities between those various ancient Gods and mythical Jesus, generally without receiving the death sentence from the Church. In the 19th century, writers also pointed out that early Christians like Marcion did not believe in the crucifixion.

One of the later 19th c. texts, a book called *Aryan Sun-Myths,* was analyzed in 1890. A doubtful reviewer performed his task by simply opening randomly to page 71, then wrote:[752]

> Seldom is more arrant nonsense and fiction than the above found on less than two [71-72] small pages! ...When the 112th page is

> reached, no reader can be surprised to find "that the crucifixion was not commonly believed in among early Christians."

After reading just a few pages, the reviewer—obviously a believing Christian—dismisses the entire book as bunkum, inferring inerrancy of the Bible: "After this, no confusion of authorities can excite remark." Clearly that reviewer was not capable of withstanding any criticism of his own religious inculcation, his head plunged deep into the biblical mud. To this Christian critic, any author questioning the Bible is barely worthy of consideration.

Perhaps this is no surprise, but the same issue of that journal reviewed *Sermons and Addresses* by Reverend Jacob Merrill Manning, Pastor of Old South Church in Boston, praising the "tone of godly simplicity and sincerity" of these Christian sermons.[753]

Clearly the human-made Christian story, born in the Levant and spreading throughout Europe like a cancer, was a plagiarism of many older (equally human-made) myths from other cultures from all sides, east, west, north, south. Just as obvious, it was not merely *human* but also *male*-made. The major "gods" from the ancient myths are all men, as are all main players in Christianity—except, necessarily, the mother; miraculously in so many religions *always a virgin*. Trained psychiatrists and sociologists are better equipped than I to explain this strange literary device.

The scriptures devalue the stature of women throughout—e.g. Genesis 3:16,[754] first Corinthians 14:34-36,[755] first Peter 3:1[756]—and the Catholic Church disempowers women completely, granting clerical rank to no female. Of course nuns, in a disturbing decree (or metaphor?) are free to "marry" Jesus—from the *CE1907* vol. 11, 164: "*From the earliest times they were called the spouses of Christ.*"

Yet, of course, nuns cannot touch Christ's (or anybody's) penis. Within Judaism and Christianity the right to touch penises of strangers seems to have shifted from women to the domain of mohels and priests.

# PART IV. THE BIBLE

## Josephus' Coat of Many Colors

Jewish historian Josephus was quite the teller of tales between 75 and 95 CE. He also wrote, perhaps, some history. Any writing of Josephus must first be corroborated by reliable historians before being taken seriously. Here are three examples why.

1. Josephus wrote of some sort of magical, laser-like plant called "baarus" (*Jewish War*, VII, IV:3):

> Its colour is like that of flame, and toward evening it sends out a certain ray like lightening: it is not easily taken by such as would do it, but recedes from their hands, nor will yield itself to be taken quietly, until either the urine of a woman, or blood, be poured upon it; nay, even then it is certain death to those that touch it, unless anyone take and hang the root itself down from his hand, and so carry it away. It may also be taken another way, without danger, which is this: they dig a trench quite round about it, till the hidden part of the root be very small, then they tie a dog about it, and, when the dog tries hard to follow him that tied him, this root is easily plucked up, but the dog dies immediately, as if it were instead of the man that would take the plant away; nor after this need anyone be afraid of taking it into their hands. Yet, after all this pains in getting, it is only valuable on account of one virtue it hath, that if it be only brought to sick persons, it quickly drives away those called demons, which are no other than the spirits of the wicked, that enter into any men that are alive and kill them, unless they can obtain some help against them.

2. Josephus actually believes Lot's wife was turned into a pillar of Morton's NaCl, and this first-century con artist claims to have witnessed this amazing salt-henge (*Antiquities*, 1, XI:4).:

> But Lot, upon God's informing him of the future destruction of the Sodomites, went away, taking with him his wife and daugh-

> ters, who were two, and still virgins; for those that were betrothed to them were above the thoughts of going, and deemed that Lot's words were trifling. God then cast a thunderbolt upon the city, and set it on fire, with its inhabitants; and laid waste the country with the like burning, as I formerly said when I wrote the Jewish War. But Lot's wife continually turning back to view the city as she went from it, and being too nicely inquisitive what would become of it, although God had forbidden her so to do, was changed into a pillar of salt; for I have seen it, and it remains at this day.

3. Josephus writes at great length about "Adam and Eve," claiming to know much more about their legendary life and times than even provided by his sacred Torah. He claims (*Antiquities*, I, I:4) that *all* animals in "Eden" were able to speak—not being limited to the well-known talking snake nonsense. Josephus wrote that God punished Adam "because he weakly submitted to the counsel of his wife." All snakes of future generations were rendered mute by the Almighty, says Josephus, "out of indignation at his malicious disposition towards Adam." He claims God (who else?) "inserted poison under [the snake's] tongue," apparently unaware of non-poisonous serpentines.

Moreover I ask the reader to consider, in view of the above "histories" written by Josephus, his preface to *Antiquities*:[757]

> ...I shall accurately describe what is contained in our records... and this without adding any thing to what is therein contained, or taking away any thing therefrom.

Giving the title "historian" to Flavius Josephus is like calling Jon Stewart a newscaster. (Note, please, that I adore Jon Stewart, and believe he would agree with my statement.)

Josephus was indeed an author of his own fictions: a liar. One may excuse *some* of his indulgences and hyperboles by terming his work "apologetic historiography." But he was not an honest nor diligent writer.[758]

Josephus' flimsy and questionable "histories" would later be interpolated by Christian copyists and forgers, inserting false statements including the perhaps famous paragraph that speaks of "Jesus, a wise man, if it be lawful to call him a man." As we shall see,

Josephus would never have made such a remark regarding a self-proclaimed prophet. Moreover, Josephus did not follow up to expound upon this glowing paragraph as one would expect had he been a believer, as the corrupted text infers.

Read Josephus yourself, in context with the rest of his work. You will readily see that the "Jesus/wise man" words could not have been written by Josephus. The corrupted *Antiquities of the Jews* that comes down to us includes the following forged paragraph:[759]

> Now there was about this time Jesus, a wise man, if it be lawful to call him a man; for he was a doer of wonderful works, a teacher of such men as receive the truth with pleasure. He drew over to him both many of the Jews and many of the Gentiles. He was [the] Christ. And when Pilate, at the suggestion of the principal men amongst us, had condemned him to the cross, those that loved him at the first did not forsake him; for he appeared to them alive again the third day; as the divine prophets had foretold these and ten thousand other wonderful things concerning him. And the tribe of Christians, so named from him, are not extinct at this day.

This paragraph sticks out like a 7-foot Scandinavian in a Beijing market compared to the rest of the text. Before this segment, Josephus is writing about Pilate, then—almost as a side-bar—he mentions "Christ," saying he was a man ("*if it be lawful to call him a man*") who arose after "the third day." Next, Josephus casually goes on to write about the temple of Isis at Rome. This is a total non sequitur. That paragraph is clearly an interpolation by later Christians attempting to demonstrate that first century historian Josephus was aware of Jesus. Had Josephus actually known anything of the supposed Jesus stories and believed them, he surely would have dropped all his other research to find out all he could about the Miracle Man, hunting down apostles and their comrades and offspring, to spend the rest of his life writing exhaustively and even exclusively about Jesus the Christ, miracle worker and Messiah and son of God.

Josephus did nothing of the sort.

In this forged segment, Josephus absolutely praises this Jesus. Unless presented with solid evidence, Josephus would never have done so; in his *Jewish Wars*, II 13:4-6, he makes it clear he detests all men claiming to be prophets:

> There was also another body of wicked men gotten together, not so impure in their actions, but more wicked in their intentions, which laid waste the happy state of the city no less than did these murderers. These were such men as deceived and deluded the people under pretense of Divine inspiration... But there was an Egyptian false prophet that did the Jews more mischief than the former; for he was a cheat, and pretended to be a prophet also...

Nowhere does Josephus mention Jesus of Nazareth, Jesus of Bethlehem, Jesus son of Mary, or Jesus son of Joseph, despite the fact that Josephus lived shortly after the supposed time of Jesus, and in the same geographical region—right around the stony corner from the places of biblical tales and supposed miracles.

In his *Antiquities* Josephus mentions "James, brother of Jesus." The words "who was called Christ" were added by a Christian forger at some point in Book XX. How can we be sure this is also a forgery? A century after Josephus, Christian father Origen writes *Contra Celsum,* lamenting in I:XLVII that Josephus does not believe Jesus was "the Christ"—whereas the interpolation in *Antiquities* claims that he so believed.

These supposed references by Josephus deserve thorough discussion because many Christian apologists use that paragraph and others in attempt to prove that Josephus wrote about Jesus Christ, such apologists apparently unaware of Origen. They read in Josephus' *Antiquities*:

> Festus was now dead, and Albinus was but upon the road; so he assembled the sanhedrim of judges, and brought before them the brother of Jesus, who was called Christ, whose name was James... (XX, 9:1)

*Voila*! Jesus of the Bible had a brother named Joseph (forget that so many Christians claim *no* Jesus siblings), and so did another man named "Jesus" in *Antiquities*—and thus there is an extra-biblical reference to Jesus Christ, by Josephus! Unfortunately, Christian apologists often fail to read the entire paragraph, which ends "when he had ruled but three months, and made Jesus, the son of Damneus, high priest."

Josephus was obviously writing of a Jesus *son of Damneus*, who coincidentally had a brother James. Not Jesus of the Bible, not a man "who was called Christ," as proven by Origen's words.[760]

Bible scholar Van Voorst quotes a small part of the Josephus paragraph in his book:[761]

> ...so he assembled the sanhedrim of judges, and brought before them the brother of Jesus, who was called Christ... whose name was James, and some others. When he had accused them as breakers of the law, he delivered them to be stoned.

That's it. He doesn't print the rest of the paragraph; Van Voorst follows this *half of a paragraph* with "The overwhelming majority of scholars holds that the words 'the brother of Jesus called Christ' are authentic, as the entire passage in which it is found...(25)"

One wonders if Van Voorst has ever taken time to read to the end of that paragraph to learn that this particular man whose name is "Jesus" is the son of Damneus. The word "Damneus" does not even appear in Van Voorst's book as far as I can determine. To his credit, his footnote 25 reads "for a recent argument against its authenticity, see Twelftree, "Jesus in Jewish Traditions," 299-301.[762]

Christian Pastor Lee Strobel perpetrates the same obfuscation (or mere ignorance?) in *The Case For Christ*, as do others. Perhaps they are honest but unaware of Origen's lamentations? Or maybe they both believe that Josephus is speaking of two different men, both named Jesus, but not differentiated between them in the writing of Josephus. I cannot speak for those authors.

Note that Van Voorst is professor at Western Theological Seminary, affiliated with the Reformed Church in America. He would likely be barred from teaching at the Seminary unless he professes Bible inerrantism.[763] Some modern-day Crusaders (included are Pastors Lee Strobel and Douglas Wilson) are obliged to propagate apologetics, as if the tired old arguments were rational and supported by science and history. Their arguments usually are not.

To the typical Christian apologist, especially the Seminary student or professor, the Bible *must* represent reliable history—not a collection of primitive myths and plagiarisms from neighboring cults, as would seem obvious to any clear-headed historian or scholar. Thus the apologist would be obligated to use obscurantism on Josephus to help the case for a historical Jesus Christ. Van Voorst's "overwhelming majority" claim shows he is apparently unaware of Origen, as well as Josephus' hatred of men who "deceived and deluded the people under pretense of Divine inspiration," as scrawled in Josephus' *Jewish Wars*.

Early Christian fathers other than Origen had read Josephus, and wrote of his works, yet they do not mention any "proof" within Josephus. Thus for this reason and so many others, it was clearly a later interpolation. We can triangulate the approximate date of the textual modification: sometime after 248 (the date of *Contra Celsum*) and before 324, when we first see the "Christ" reference. Personally, I agree with the theory that the forgery was at the hand of Eusebius,[764] another very deceitful writer, as was "historian" Josephus.

One may attempt to reconstruct the original, unadulterated Josephus. Considering that *Contra Celsum* proves Origen had read an honest version of Josephus devoid of any reference to a Jesus called *Christ*, and thus the "who was called Christ" phrase was a later forgery, Josephus' original text most probably was written as such:

> ...Albinus was but upon the road; so he assembled the sanhedrim of judges, and brought before them the brother of Jesus **the son of Damneus**, whose name was James, and some others... Agrippa took the high priesthood from him, when he had ruled but three months, and made Jesus, the son of Damneus, high priest.

The Christian forger had just enough room to erase the first instance of "the son of Damneus" and change it to:

> ...Albinus was but upon the road; so he assembled the sanhedrim of judges, and brought before them the brother of Jesus **who was called Christ**, whose name was James, and some others... Agrippa took the high priesthood from him, when he had ruled but three months, and made Jesus, the son of Damneus, high priest.

The perpetrator of that forgery somehow missed the reference at the end, it seems, that shows Josephus was in fact writing of the son of Damneus.

Now, when I say he had "enough room," that is because there are proven examples where seemingly reliable extant texts have been shown to have words or letters erased (inks scraped away from the papyrus or vellum surface) and new ones added. Using modern techniques like ultraviolet or x-ray spectroscopy, the underlying original letters can now be seen in various modified works. And note that my example above, in English, is admittedly a crude illustration of "enough room," as *Antiquities* was written in Greek. But the point is valid, and forgers readily find ways to insert words to perpetrate their desires.

On the other hand, for any *copyist* of Josephus, the matter of "enough room" is moot, as the copyist is making a new version of an older text on a different piece of writing material, thus free to pull back the curtains that protect truth, and able to copy *and reinterpret* anything he feels will bolster Christian historicity.

Regarding Eusebius' *EH* 2.23.21-24 on the supposed martyrdom of James within the *Antiquities* of Josephus, esteemed author and theologian John Painter admits that these texts "were transmitted by Christian scribes," and "there was ample opportunity for tampering with the text" and that there are only three texts containing this particular passage in *Antiquities*. Painter continues, saying:[765]

> Origin expresses surprise that Josephus, "disbelieving in Jesus as Christ," should write respectfully about James, his brother.

Painter also wrote "it seems not to have been in the form now found in all extant texts" thus admitting Christian corruptions of the Josephan text along the centuries. Strangely, I often see Christian apologists citing Painter in attempts to *prove* Jesus historicity. This sort of argument involves taking the author out of context, and cherry-picking his text.

In his *Ecclesiastical History* 2.23.4-18, Eusebius apparently writes, in the fourth century, of Josephus' supposed claim: "And these things happened to the Jews to avenge James the Just, who was the brother of Jesus the so-called Christ, for the Jews killed him in spite of his great righteousness." Chilton and Evans observe:

> This passage is found nowhere in the MSS of the works of Josephus. The tone is Christian and exudes a whiff of anti-Judaism. It is probably based on Josephus' comment regarding the fate of Herod Antipas' army after the execution of John the Baptist (cf. *Ant.* 18.5.2 §116-117).[766]

Thus we have the words of Origin and other clear proofs that the writings of Josephus were interpolated, with his original texts having *no mention* of the Jesus of the Bible. Moreover Eusebius is untrustworthy (and his works corrupted), so his remarks on Josephus, and more importantly Josephus' own first century works, cannot be considered as extra-biblical accounts of the Jesus tales.

Perhaps one of the most fascinating aspects of this line of argument and reasoning, from both sides—either for Josephus writing of Jesus, or the interpolations—can be described as follows. Josephus wrote *Antiquities* around the year 93 CE, some 60 years after the supposed crucifixion, 38 or so years after Paul's Epistles, and decades after the hypothetical *Q* text was in circulation. Modern Christians, in desperate effort to prove Jesus actually existed, latch onto Josephus as perhaps their most promising yet frantic attempt to show that some contemporary non-Christian wrote of the Jesus sagas. Yet even if true, all it would mean in the bottom and pathetic line of all these investigations and straw-grasping is that Josephus may have seen the writings of Paul, or of the anonymous authors of early gospel sources. Nothing more.

Christian apologists have had a most difficult time proving *even this* tenuous Josephus case—which if it were even true is meaningless for a Jesus historicity.

The men gathered at early Ecumenical Councils were well aware of Josephus' works and, it seems, should have included at least some of his writings into their agreed-upon scriptures if Josephus had in fact corroborated *any* of the Jesus accounts. Clearly they did not. Eusebius mentions Josephus' viewpoints on "God" in his *Preparation of the Gospels* (VIII:VII) as well as Josephus' "history" of the global flood (IX:XI), but nothing connecting Josephus to Jesus. Yet, even Mithras cult beliefs were under consideration by early Christians: "...Pallas, who made an excellent collection concerning the mysteries of Mithras in the time of Emperor Adrian" as Eusebius wrote (IV:XVI). Eusebius also mentions Zeus and Hera (IV:XV). Eusebius mentions Greek god Apollo dozens of times in his *Preparation.*

Yet, somehow, Roman leadership chose the rickety Jesus character as their heavenly hero.

## Mystery of the Silent Historians

Christian belief holds that a prophet predicted by the Old Testament actually materialized: an angelic boy of virgin birth, brought forth some two millennia prior to our present time. Hundreds of millions believe this prophet preached to multitudes (for almost four years if you believe John; less than one year according to the three others) and was crucified and resurrected, being the *true son of God,* on a mission to save us from "original sin" (e.g. Rom 5:12-15). Are any of the tales of Jesus historical, or are they simply the stuff of mythos like Zeus, Odin, Noah, and Adam and Eve?

Many geographical references in the Bible are erroneous, as are its histories, truth claims, and sciences. Anachronisms are rampant, and internal contradictions number in the thousands. There is absolutely no evidence to support any shred or thread of the spectacular stories woven into the gospels. Even the non-supernatural (that is, possibly believable) stories have no basis in verifiable or corroborative fact. The famed "virgin birth" prophesy was unconscionable fraud as we have seen, along with many acts of forgery and censorship perpetrated by the Church of Rome.

The reader is undoubtedly aware of other works exposing extensive biblical errancy, as well as inexcusable Church violence and corruption. I embarked upon this particular endeavor to expose something deeper: a seemingly inexplicable "silence" even more mysterious and extensive than previously claimed. My prime point is that the more we investigate and the more we dig, the more we discover how feeble and tenuous are any claims that this Jesus person *even existed.*

You may have seen lists of ancient writers who were mysteriously silent on this god-son saga. In his 1909 work *The Christ,* John Remsburg developed one of the lengthiest, citing forty-two ancient authors, many contemporary to Jesus, others writing shortly afterwards. But Dio Chrystostom and Dion of Prusa are one and the same—thus Remsburg erred, actually offering but forty-one. Many writers have parroted Remsburg, usually propagating that error.

I undertook a task to discover how exhaustive Remsburg's list truly is. Might there be more writers of those times and locale who should have written about Jesus, but did not?

**Those Who Wrote of Jesus.** Among the many manuscripts known from the first and second centuries, undoubtedly modern Christians would have discovered *every word* that might help prove the historicity of the Christ tales. Despite the 2,000 year window of opportunity, no such magic stone has been unearthed.

I claim the following as confident proof that, for example, neither Philo nor Thrasyllus (both Jesus contemporaries) ever wrote of Jesus the Christ:

> *It is not necessary to read all known works by Philo or Thrasyllus to discover whether they wrote about Jesus, because if they had done so, Christians would have pounced long ago to tout, with bugles and drumbeats, every such instance. Thus the same applies to the many other writers, contemporary or shortly after the supposed the life and times of Jesus.*

We are often presented with a wearisome list of "contemporary" extra-biblical sources for Jesus (none are even remotely contemporary) proffered by Christian apologists, all easily proven impotent in any support of the ancient tales: Josephus, Thallus, Tacitus, Pliny, the Talmud, et cetera, as I have already addressed. Note that the truthful and rational researcher uses the writings of Josephus, Thallus, Tacitus, and both Plinys as evidence *against* a historical Jesus, as Remsburg did—not *for* the supposed historicity, as Strobel and others have done.

Jesus may indeed have been a real man wandering around desert towns in the first century (as the Talmud indicates, claiming Jesus was the bastard son of Pandira: Shabbat 104b).[767] I simply find it fascinating that, among the horde of reliable writers of the times and of that very region, none who is credible ever recorded his life, interactions with the Jewish or Roman world, or any "Biblical" event.

There are no tales of Jesus—*zero*—written by historians contemporary to the time, nor any evidence supporting the claims of "miracles," or even proof of Jesus simply being a charming chap dunked in a river by one of the many first century Johns, preaching to masses two thousand years ago in a jerkwater and largely illiterate region of Judea. Speeches allegedly given by Jesus, and stories of the "apostles" are demonstrably plagiarisms from Hebrew scripture, Egyptian beliefs, oral tradition, and Asian zeitgeist.[768] [769] [770] Elsewhere in this book we have provided many proofs of this. Myriads of facts (along with simple logic, a faculty available to the freethinking mind) disprove the fantastic Jesus Christ stories.

**Setting the Ancient Records Straight**. Let us engage in investigative journalism and forensics. Which scholars of the first century wrote of the character "Jesus"? We should become very much enlightened by the many writers living, geographically and temporally, alongside Jesus.

The Bible claims Jesus' fame "went throughout all Syria" (Mt 4:24), and "all Galilee" (Mk 1:28). Jesus was followed by "great multitudes of people" (Mt 4:25 & 8:1). The NT declares Jesus was famous across the ecumene, and his words went "*unto the ends of the whole world*" as we learn from Paul in Romans 10:18.

Then again, Romans 10:18 (a faint echo filched from Psalm 19:4)[771] is surely among the most hyperbolic of hyperboles ever hyped. It is the converse of veracity, concocted by Paul of Tarsus, a madman who admits he never met Jesus. Paul had frequent delusional visions as recorded in scripture (e.g. Acts 9, 12, 16, 22, 26; Gal 1; and 2 Cor 12). One could well say that Romans 10:18 is, as it were, a lie of biblical proportions.

Yet for a hundred years after the supposed crucifixion, no extra-biblical writer recorded anything of Jesus.

And so I humbly present this list of 126 silent writers, all having lived in that region and during those times or shortly thereafter.[772] If the New Testament offers even a modicum of truth, every one of these should have written something, anything, about the revered Messiah. Yet none had ever heard of this Jesus Christ, prophesied Messiah and King of the Jews—

> Aelius Theon, Albinus, Alcinous, Ammonius of Athens, Alexander of Aegae, Antipater of Thessalonica, Antonius Polemo, Apollonius Dyscolus, Apollonius of Tyana, Appian, Archigenes, Aretaeus, Arrian, Asclepiades of Prusa, Asconius, Aspasius, Atilicinus, Attalus, Bassus of Corinth, C. Cassius Longinus, Calvisius Taurus of Berytus, Cassius Dio, Chaeremon of Alexan-

dria, Claudius Agathemerus, Claudius Ptolemaeus, Cleopatra the physician, Cluvius Rufus, Cn. Cornelius Lentulus Gaetulicus, Cornelius Celsus, Columella, Cornutus, D. Haterius Agrippa, D. Valerius Asiaticus, Damis, Demetrius, Demonax, Demosthenes Philalethes, Dion of Prusa, Domitius Afer, Epictetus, Erotianus, Euphrates of Tyre, Fabius Rusticus, Favorinus, Flaccus, Florus, Fronto, Gellius, Gordius of Tyana, Gnaeus Domitius, Halicarnassensis Dionysius II, Heron of Alexandria, Josephus, Justus of Tiberias, Juvenal, Lesbonax of Mytilene, Lucanus, Lucian, Lysimachus, M. Antonius Pallas, M. Vinicius, Macro, Mam. Aemilius Scaurus, Marcellus Sidetes, Martial, Maximus Tyrius, Moderatus of Gades, Musonius, Nicarchus, Nicomachus Gerasenus, Onasandros, P. Clodius Thrasea Paetus, Palaemon, Pamphila, Pausanias, Pedacus Dioscorides, Persius/Perseus, Petronius, Phaedrus, Philippus of Thessalonica, Philo of Alexandria, Phlegon of Tralles, Pliny the Elder, Pliny the Younger, Plotinus, Plutarch, Pompeius Saturninus, Pomponius Mela, Pomponius Secundus, Potamon of Mytilene, Ptolemy of Mauretania, Q. Curtius Rufus, Quintilian, Rubellius Plautus, Rufus the Ephesian, Saleius Bassus, Scopelian the Sophist, Scribonius, Seneca the Elder, Seneca the Younger, Sex. Afranius Burrus, Sex. Julius Frontinus, Servilius Damocrates, Silius Italicus, Soranus, Soterides of Epidaurus, Sotion, Statius the Elder, Statius the Younger, Suetonius, Sulpicia, T. Aristo, T. Statilius Crito, Tacitus, Thallus, Theon of Smyrna, Thrasyllus of Mendes, Ti. Claudius Pasion, Ti. Julius Alexander, Tiberius, Valerius Flaccus, Valerius Maximus, Vardanes I, Velleius Paterculus, Verginius Flavus, and Vindex.

Within this compendium, no fewer than forty-six offered their writings not merely shortly after the supposed Jesus events, but were nearby and absolutely contemporary to Jesus.

If we take the words of the gospel as true (Jesus' fame went "unto the ends of the whole world"), we could well add first century writers in India and China and Korea to this list—but I have chosen to adopt the more sober and lenient stance: that the tremendous "fame" was not global as proclaimed, but localized to the Near East, a "Jesus vicinity."

Any writer of that time and region, regardless of his or her discipline or specialty—be it history, politics, engineering, law, medicine, or linguistics—would have dropped all works, *everything*, to record the miraculous events that they should have witnessed (but did not), and to investigate and chronicle Jesus.

**Some of the Silent Ones**. Thousands of writers should have witnessed—or at least heard of—the miraculous crucifixion, replete with magic tricks of astral proportions: Jesus (or God?) conjured zombie armies and mysterious global weather phenomena,[773] recorded *not by any historian*, but only in the dubitable scriptures scribbled many decades later.

Late in the first century and in the second, desultory *ex post facto* stories appeared—always proffered by the most unreliable and superstitious of sources, or simply being spurious. Note that the original Mark ends at 16:8, and later Christian forgers added the fanciful resurrection tale.[774] The entire Chapter 21 of John, describing more post-death actions of Jesus, is also a forgery.[775]

I will not bore you with details of each of the aforementioned 126 silent ones, but several deserve additional comment. In general chronological order:

**Thrasyllus**. Tiberius Claudius Thrasyllus lived when Tiberius donned the Purple, and Jesus the halo. An Alexandrian philosopher, grammarian, writer, editor of Plato and Democritus, Thrasyllus died c. 36 CE. Based on his writings, he never heard of Jesus.

**Attalus**. Greek stoic philosopher, orator and writer during Augustus and Tiberius, Attalus was a Jesus contemporary. Seneca the Elder later praised Attalus as the most acute and eloquent philosopher of his day.

**Apollonius of Tyana**. Apollonius was born in Anatolia (modern Turkey). A revered Greek philosopher and Jesus contemporary, he traveled throughout the Levant and Middle East.[776] Apollonius wrote prolifically, authoring many works. He was an admired first century philosopher, a saintly soul. It is clear that neither Apollonius nor his acolyte Damis heard of Christians or of Jesus.

**Seneca**. Roman philosopher Seneca the Younger was an author and politician, living c. 4 BCE - 65 CE. Contemporary to Jesus and educated in Rome, Seneca traveled extensively in Egypt and Near East. Like Apollonius, Seneca was a saintly soul, vegetarian, faithful follower of Pythagoras.

**Musonius**. Roman philosopher Caius Musonius Rufus was a prolific writer of the first century CE, author of many books. He was a teacher of Euphrates (inveterate enemy of Apollonius). Musonius, a contemporary of Jesus, was born c. 14 CE and lived until at least 79 CE. His writings survive to this day. Musonius mentions nothing of Jesus.

**Flaccus**. Jesus contemporary Publius Aulus Avilius Flaccus, chosen by Tiberius in 32 CE to govern Alexandria, is the heinous politician against whom Philo Judaeus railed in his *Contra Flaccus.* Among Flaccus' vast collection of writings, not a one mentions a supposed messiah, son of God, a Jesus, a Christ, or any "Christians"—just as all reliable writers of the first century fail to do.

**Pamphila**. A brilliant and diligent historian from Egypt, Pamphila was a native of Epidaurus during Nero and beyond. In the first century she wrote a history (*summikton historikon hupomnematon logoi*) in 33 books, as well as *An Epitome of Ctesias* (three books), and others. Her works were referenced and quoted by Diogenes Laertius, Sopater, Photius, and Aulus Gellius, among other venerable historians. Pamphila wrote shortly after the supposed Jesus events. She never heard of Jesus, or Christians.

**Plutarch**. Historian Plutarch (46-125), perhaps the most venerable, and one of the most prolific of ancient Greco-Roman writers studied philosophy under Ammonius during Nero's reign. Plutarch is famous for his *Parallel Lives,* voluminous biographies of Romans and Greeks, an important source of information about antiquity. This brilliant historian was unaware of Christians, and never heard of Jesus.

**Gellius**. While in Greece and Rome, Aulus Gellius wrote *Attic Nights* c. 169 in twenty books. He wrote of everything during his period, and all prior histories he came across. I have read *Attic Nights* cover to cover and nowhere do the words *Christ, Jesus,* or *Christian* appear.

**Cassius Dio**. Dio wrote *Roman History* (c. 220) in 80 impressive volumes. While he mentions the peaceful Mithras religion (vol. 63, 5), it is strange indeed that—at this relatively late date—he had never heard of Jesus or of Christianity.

**Forget the Miracles.** In assembling the above tabulation of silent ones I limited my sights to writers quite close by. Yet in taking the Bible at face value—based on claims of far-reaching miracles and fame—I included writers not strictly line-of-sight to Jesus' travels, just as Remsburg had done.[777]

While Jesus apparently did not consider his heaven-sent message important enough to preach it in well-populated and educated regions—Athens or Rome or Alexandria (or Bagdad or Paris or Peking: he was after all, God)—he is said to have traveled to Tyre (Acts 21), Sarepta (Luke 4), Sidon (Acts 27), Jordon (Luke 4), Decapolis (Mt 4), Capernaum (Mt 5), Gergesa (Mt 8), Caesarea (Mt 16), and a few other dusty desert towns of his narrow and modest region. An equivalent trek in the U.S. is from downtown Alexandria Virginia to Damascus Maryland and back—maybe two hundred miles while pausing for a holy head-slosh in the Potomac.

Now let us assume the "ends of the whole world" writ from Paul was hyperbole or perhaps born of ignorance, and that—*of course*—Jesus conjured no global miracles. Thus he was merely a charismatic Hebrew evangelic, famed in Judea and a few surrounding regions, an annoying self-proclaimed preacher who incurred the wrath of Roman officials. In this case, which sources truly should have provided records or evidence regarding the mere mortal, Jesus son of Mary and Joseph?

**Philo Judaeus**. The great Hebrew historian Philo would have been among the best of candidates to record anything of Jesus. Philo lived and traveled smack-dab in the Holy Land, chronicling and wandering the same time and throughout those selfsame sandy hills and stony villages where Jesus walked and talked. Philo was born 20 years before Jesus and lived 20 years beyond the "crucifixion."

Philo spent his life in the Levant. He journeyed several times to Jesus' sandal-trodden stomping grounds (*On Providence,* 2.64). He chronicled contemporaries of Jesus such as Flaccus, Caligula, Pontius Pilate. He mused on the most inconsequential of individuals such as zany Carabbas. Yet Philo—prolific historian, neighbor to Jesus—knew nothing of the storied prophet and rabble-rouser famously brought to trial before Pilate.

**Josephus**. Famed historian Flavius Josephus joined the Essenes c. 53 CE and published *Jewish Wars* c. 95. Josephus had lived in Japhia, *one mile* from Nazareth—yet Josephus never heard of Nazareth, nor of Jesus. His interpolated works are covered elsewhere in this book.

**Justus**. Similarly we have Justus of Tiberias, Hebrew author and historian shortly after Jesus in the latter half of the first century. While his writings are lost, they were extant in the ninth century and in the hands of Christian scholars such as Photius. Photius laments, understandably perplexed, "Justus makes not the least mention of the appearance of Christ, of what things happened to him, or of the wonderful works that he did." Clearly Justus recorded nothing of Jesus. Recall from the Bible that in Gergesa (a non-riparian real estate zone alongside the Sea of Galilee) the "whole city came out to meet Jesus" (Mt 8). Gergesa was a major part of Tiberias, so Justus—*of Tiberias*—certainly must have heard of Jesus, yet wrote nothing. As Louis Feldman wrote, "...not a single fragment of [Justus'] work was deemed worthy of preservation by Christian copyists, presumably because it lacked any reference to Jesus..."[778]

**Saint Paul**. We covered Paul briefly in our Timeline, Paul having experienced "visions" c. 36-40 CE. It is amazing and quite telling how little Paul knows about Jesus. He wrote of Jesus' mother, "a woman" (Gal 4:4), but never *virgin*. Not only had this supposed apostle not met his savior, but Paul seems to know only two important things about Jesus: that he was crucified (then supposedly resurrected), and that Jesus had a brother and mother. That's it. And there were no "500 witnesses" as apologists insist; this was a later insertion.

Paul knows nothing of Jesus' birth, parents, life events, ministry, miracles, apostles, betrayal, or trial. He knows neither *where* nor *when* Jesus lived and died (or "ascended"). Paul seems to consider the crucifixion metaphorical and spiritual, not physical, as he penned "I am crucified with Christ" (Gal 2:19-20). He even acknowledges people may claim "another Jesus" (2 Cor 11:4), and he wrote that Jesus was perhaps not a man, but simply a "spirit" of

God's son (Gal 4:6-14). Unlike the Gospel writers, Paul does not claim Jesus had come to earth; and never says anything of a "second coming," only of a *future* coming, 1 Corinthians 1:7, using the word Παρουσία (*Parousia*, appearance), never "return." The "five hundred" witnesses of the supposed resurrection in 1 Corinthians 15 is a later forgery, not in our earliest and best copies; not the words of Paul.[779]

Paul speaks of a "spiritual body" of Christ, and that "flesh and blood cannot inherit the kingdom of God" (1 Cor 15:44-50), in contrast to Luke 24:39.[780]

Paul's questionable mental health is another important concern, already covered at length.

Paul's letters avow mostly of an unctuous and nebulous "faith in Christ," a tiresome broken record. Paul uses the word *faith* over 200 times in his epistles; how many times did Darwin, Lagrange, or Einstein use that word in their works? Young Paul would have been inculcated with belief in Sandan, mythical founder of his hometown of Tarsus. Sandan was yet another son of god supposedly resurrected after his death.[781]

Perhaps the most telling evidence regarding Paul's imagination and desire for a Messiah arises from Hebrews 8:4:[782]

> For if he [Christ] were on earth, he should not be a priest, seeing that there are priests that offer gifts according to the law.

The phrase *if he were on earth* should raise the eyebrow of even the most devout believer. And note that I have presented the "authorized" King James Version here. Later Bible versions attempt to fix Paul's words and rephrase the cloudy KJV adding "still" or "again" to *if he were.*

Paul was first to write of Jesus (30 years after Jesus' death, mind),[783] and claimed he spent two weeks with supposed eyewitness Peter. One wonders why Paul does not profess to know more—*much, much* more—about Jesus.

**Marcion.** Also mentioned in the Timeline, this second century Christian presbyter denied any "virgin birth," claiming the son of God "came down from heaven" full-grown, having no earthly body, but a "spirit." Again, by deleting chapters one and two from Luke (which he considered spurious), Marcion's reading thus seems valid.

To many early Christians, the Messiah was a spirit, an idea, a *logos*—never a man on earth.[784] And this is what Paul believed.

**Ancient Records**. Never has anyone found, in the detailed records kept by diligent Roman and Greek scribes around Judea, any reference to Jesus of Nazareth. To give the benefit of the doubt, that tiny region was not overrun with Roman legions; on the other hand the Jesus "miracles" are claimed to have been global in nature. Moreover we know his supposed hometown of Nazareth did not have an active settlement until long after the "crucifixion."[785]

**Qumran.** Dead Sea Scroll writers—contemporaneous to Christ and a mere twelve miles from Bethlehem—recorded absolutely nothing of Jesus. Those scrolls were retrieved unadulterated, and first century Qumran writings quite readily disprove the historical Jesus. Dr. Jodi Magness wrote, "Contrary to claims made by a few scholars, no copies of the New Testament (or precursors to it) are represented among the Dead Sea Scrolls."[786]

It seems Christianity was pure fiction, a hoax, largely invented by Saul of Tarsus, a man claiming to be a Hebrew scholar and member of the Pharisees—yet, most probably, Saul was neither.[787]

**Pagan Sources**. *CE1907* suggests that miracles and legends from earlier pagan religions were plagiarized and incorporated into Christian tradition, producing "an abundance of heroes" that "found their way from Hellenism to Christianity."[788] It speaks of "incredible liberty... under the spell of the Renaissance." That damned annoying Renaissance imposed freethought and critical examination upon the rickety "traditions," contradictory philosophies, and immoral tenets and tales of the Bible, a text still being modified and mutated:[789]

> There was a need of a [Bible] revision which is not yet complete..." and "In all these departments forgery and interpolation as well as ignorance had wrought mischief on a grand scale.

**Pascal Shrugged**. Now, all this does not in any way prove that Jesus did not exist. Nor was that my goal. It is nearly impossible to completely *disprove* a Jesus historicity—or for that matter King Arthur or Socrates. One could conceivably *prove* Jesus' existence, something Christians have been desperate yet unable to achieve for all centuries that followed the era of this Hebrew "messiah"—a figure actually *rejected* as messiah by those very same Hebrews who fervently desired such a glorious coming.

We have seen there is no reliable evidence even suggesting that the Jesus described by the New Testament existed at all. The body of proof against this Phantom Messiah seems to be forever mounting, and gives historical Jesus little if any chance of survival even simply as a human—let alone a deity crucified and resurrected, and of direct filial relation to mythical "Adam" as claimed in the Bible (Luke 3).

Many freethinking scholars believe, as I once did, that Jesus actually did exist, being nothing more than an evangelistic and rebellious and mortal Hebrew. After much research I am leaning more and more toward the supposed "unscholarly" side of the argument: that Jesus never existed, and the tales are fictitious, based on made-up prophesies in the Tanakh (later "fulfilled" by NT deceivers); on many myths of other "sons of God" also born of virgins; on wacky eschatological thinking, and culminating in a story based on conglomerations from a few superstitious first and second century bloviators and unctuous hucksters able to distribute their fictions to gullible masses.

After all this research, I now profess to lean more toward the ranks of John Remsburg, Bruno Bauer, Godfrey Higgins, Robert M. Price, Frank Zindler, Michael Martin, John Mackinnon Robertson, Timothy Freke, Peter Gandy, Barbara Walker and others—outliers, all, but a growing group of rationalists.[790] To me it seems most likely that Jesus was little more than urban (or more accurately, provincial) legend.

If presented all these facts, I believe Occam would favor Team Remsburg, while poor Pascal would assume some other "safer" posture.

## Bible Origins and Wild Variations

The god-worshiping and god-fearing men assembled at various early Ecumenical Councils had set out to authorize, and actually "legalize" countless scriptures that some deemed proper and valid, in hopes of including them in a new book that would eventually come to be known as The Holy Bible—a book that is arguably the most socially destructive and most fictitious book ever compiled. Texts rejected by the Church included many dozens of "gospels," and several epistles (e.g., 3 Corinthians, Epistle to the Laodiceans, Epistle to Mary, Acts of Paul and Thecla, and others).[791] Only some twenty scriptures were considered genuine by many of that time.[792] Eusebius reported that primitive presbyters declared the following books worthy of respect.[793]

- Matthew, Mark, Luke, John
- Acts of the Apostles
- Epistles of Paul (thirteen considered valid—today only seven are generally considered Pauline)
- 1 John
- 1 Peter
- Revelation, "if proper."

Thus was born the Christian Bible, fourth century CE, loosely in agreement, it would seem, with several second and third century men who also gathered ancient scriptures to form some kind of hallowed collection of Christian writings, each concatenated against the next, and against the next work of fiction.

The 397 Council of Carthage would make it official, canonizing scribbles and scrawls that were not quite sacred until that time, but had been merely assembled along a few centuries, then scrutinized—by many devout, superstitious and ignorant cult leaders. After the 397 decree, the ancient stories indeed became sacrosanct within the new official Roman cult. It would be the Empire's downfall and the cause of the Dark Ages—the quintessential internecine blunder and momentous turning point in history.

Immediately after Eusebius' words in his *Ecclesiastical History* regarding which scriptures were to be "maintained" and which "rejected" from the soon-to-be canon, Eusebius wrote, in his next chapter, about a "diabolical power" of a magical "Menander the sorcerer"[794] Then Eusebius opines regarding somebody or something that he called "the evil demon."[795] Eusebius is referring, of course, to "the devil," whom he elicits in many places in his *EH.* This might give the reader an idea of the primitive and credulous mind of Eusebius, and just about all others of that era. From such simple and ignorant minds was born, ladies and gentlemen, The Holy Bible.

The Christian Bible was not—of course—the work of God as is oft claimed, but a work of humans. Over a dozen centuries were required to bring the "holy" tome to fruition and semi-stable form. As the authors of the *Catholic Encyclopedia* wrote (the self-proclaimed "foremost Catholic scholars in every part of the world... with the accuracy that satisfies the scholar"):[796]

> The idea of a complete and clear-cut canon of the New Testament existing from the beginning, that is from Apostolic times, has no foundation in history. The Canon of the New Testament, like that of the Old, is the result of a development, of a process at once stimulated by disputes with doubters, both within and without the Church, and retarded by certain obscurities and natural hesitations, and which did not reach its final term until the dogmatic definition of the [*16th century!*] Tridentine Council [Council of Trent].[797]

### Which Bible, Anyway?

Hundreds of Bible versions were created through the centuries that followed, each being different from the previous. Various odd scriptural sources were used, along with inevitable and *ad infinitum* modifications. The steps toward making the contemporary bible (actually, the many *bibles*) included additions, interpretations, errors by copyists, ecclesiastical doctrines, mutations, translations, and unrelated codices—like the evolution of the Psalms, and many more ecumenical councils, creating *so many* versions: Eusebius Bibles, Jerome's Vulgate, Codex Sinaiticus, Vati-canus, Alexandrinus, Ephraemi Rescriptus, Boernerianus, Angelicus, Athous Dionysiou, Amharic, Wycliffe, Gutenberg Bible, Martin Luther, Ostrog, Tyndale, Cover-dale, Thomas Matthews, Psalter, Bishop's, Douay-Rheims,

New Polish, Vatablus, KJV, Uscan, Georgian, Wakuset, St. Cyril's, DRC, Quaker, United Ruthenians, Thomson's, Joseph Smith, WBT, Galla, Krapf St. Matthew, YLT, Darby, ASV, BBE, AMP, RSV-CE, NASB NIV, New King James, Rotherham's, TNIV, NRSV, CEV, MSG, KJ21, NASU, RcV, ESV, NABRE...

...and so forth. As *CE1907* admits (vol. 8, 439): "The earliest of the extant manuscripts [of the New Testament], it is true, do not date back beyond the middle of the fourth century..." In fact, the vast majority (Trobisch claims over 85%)[798] of original Greek manuscripts of the New Testament were produced in the *eleventh century or later*.

**Bible Anachronisms**. When and where was Jesus born? As previously mentioned, for the Bible stories to be true Jesus had to have been born both before 4 BCE (for Herod to be king of Israel), *and* after 6 CE (when Quirinius was governor of Syria). Reading Luke 2:1-4 we learn that before Jesus was born, Joseph and Mary went to Joseph's supposed birthplace, Bethlehem, for enrollment in a census commanded by Caesar Augustus. However no Roman edict *ever* required people to return to their birthplace for a census. To do so would place an absurd burden on all people, not to mention: how would the notice quickly get out to the peoples, commanding them to return home for the census—via CNN? Al Jazeera Aramaic? Yet the Bible professes such an absurd history.

Luke (3:1) places the birth of Jesus at the time of a census by Tiberius while Herod was "tetrarch of Galilee"; yet first century historian Josephus (who possibly knew much better) chronicled this particular census as having been over a decade after Herod's 4 BCE death—around the year 6 or 7 CE.[799]

**More Trouble**. Depending upon which section of the Bible you select, it was perhaps an angel (Mt 28:2) who, after Jesus was crucified, "descended from heaven, and came and rolled back the stone from the door." As we follow the various accounts in this part of the tale, we find "Mary Magdalene and the other Mary" witnessed this angel's miracle. The angel even spoke to them, "Fear not ye," whereupon they departed and brought the news of the resurrection to the disciples who had gathered in Galilee.

Or, not. Mark (Chapter 16) has no explanation how the stone was rolled away, whereupon a somewhat different group of women

(Mary Magdalene, Mary the mother of James, and Salome) find "a young man" inside. Note that "they trembled and were amazed: neither said they any thing to any man; for they were afraid"—they reported their spooky escapade *to no one.* In which case one must wonder, how does the writer of Mark know of this occurrence?

Note that Mark 16:9 to 16:20, chronicling Jesus' supposed post-resurrection appearances, were later additions and can be addressed only as a forgery.[800]

"The inerrancy of the Bible follows as a consequence of... Divine authorship." — *CE1907* vol. 2, 543

In Luke 24 we are told some women found the stone already rolled away, and "*two* men stood by them in shining garments" (24:4-9) whereupon they "returned from the sepulchre, and [*in fact*] told all these things unto the eleven, and to all the rest."

Or perhaps, as revered Christian father Athenagoras claimed in the second century, the son of God (*Jesus*, a name Athenagoras does not seem to know) never appeared on Earth in human form, being a "first product of the father, not as having been brought into existence" (Athenagoras, *A Plea for the Christians,* Ch. X). In Athenagoras' thirty-seven chapters he never uses the word "Jesus," nor "Christ." Athenagoras uses the word "Christian[s]" twenty-two times. Devout Athenagoras never states that Christians believe that the son of God appeared in human form. In fact he stated *the opposite.* He is an early proto-Christian, believing in a "Son of God" concept yet strangely unaware of Jesus the Christ.

That is not to say that Athenagoras' speech to the emperor was anything less than fair, logical, and actually quite brilliant. People were being charged, convicted, and executed merely for having a belief, being "Christian." That is, Jewish members of a new proto-Christian offshoot religion who believed they were anointed (dedicated to the service of God) were persecuted—guilty by association to the name "Christian." Note that the supposedly atrocious persecution of Christians during Nero's time was a later fabrication; but that is another story.

Athenagoras argued:

> "What, therefore, is conceded as the common right of all, we claim for ourselves, that we shall not be hated and punished because we are called christians (for what has the name to do with our being bad men?), but be tried on any charges which may be brought against us, and either be released on our disproving them, or punished if convicted of crime—not for the name."

Yet over a hundred years after the supposed life of Jesus, Athenagoras would write prolifically about Christians and resurrections, but never mention *one thing* of the god-Man "Jesus," who should have been absolutely his most important figure. Like the embarrassing gaps in St. Paul's epistles, Athenagoras does not write of Jesus' life, words, deeds, or miracles. Nor does he write of any kind of crucifixion. He says only what he was taught: that eternal life is gained through one thing, knowing God and the Logos.[801] Athenagoras, a self-proclaimed Christian, never heard of Jesus.

Athenagoras wrote of the morals of the new Christian religion, including reasons why they do not make sacrifices to God: the "Father of this universe does not need blood, nor the odour of burnt-offerings"[802] He was combating, obviously, scriptures such as Leviticus 1:9:

> "The entrails and feet being washed with water. And the priest shall burn them upon the altar for a holocaust, and a sweet savour to the Lord."

I believe Athenagoras was probably a brilliant man. Delusion may manifest itself in even the most gifted among us. We are slightly more capable and intelligent than chimps, yet likely inferior to dolphins in this regard.

The author of Mark has Jesus traveling from Tyre to Sidon, then "through the midst of the coasts of Decapolis" (Mk 7:31, KJV). It is clear this writer is not familiar with the area, as this trek claims he "came upon the sea of Galilee" just before Decapolis. In fact, the sea lies in the opposite direction.

> *Fun fact*: Some Bible writer seems to believe the value of *pi* is exactly three (2 Chron 4:2 and 1 Kings 7:23).

**The Healing Pool**. John (5:2-3) describes a five-sided "healing" pool in Jerusalem.[803] Modern archeologists dug in the spot described by John, and it was proven to be accurate—*the pool is there!* Christian historicity vindicated? No. The problem is, this Pool of Bethesda was constructed after Hadrian, so John had to be describing a structure built after the year 135, which puts Jesus "disciple" John at a time well over a century after Jesus' death. Moreover the pool was supposedly for healing the sick and lame, and washing sheep; but it seems that both sheep and humans might have problems "wading" through a pool thirteen meters (forty feet) deep.[804] Note that one day, a diseased "angel" apparently waded or swam there, contaminating the waters (Jn 5:4).[805] How can an "angel" be diseased?

**Nazareth**. In the NT we are offered the claim that Jesus grew up in Nazareth (Mt 2:23). Archaeological evidence shows no active civilization there until the *second century* CE—coincidentally, around the time the first raw "New Testament" scriptures were apparently concocted and subsequently collected.[806] [807] During the first century, Nazareth was an austere, tiny, and *nameless* sixty-acre patch of flat land and sand inhabited by fewer than five hundred people,[808] mostly ruins, a junk-yard, left over from hundreds of years earlier, having been destroyed by the Assyrians. It would not receive the name "Nazareth" until centuries after the purported Son of God was born. As John Robertson wrote of the Nazareth story, it is "really a pragmatic myth superimposed on the Bethlehem myth. The textual analysis shows that wherever it occurs in the gospels and Acts the name Nazareth has been foisted on the documents."[809] René Salm's *The Myth of Nazareth* covers this topic exhaustively and convincingly.

## The Gospel Truth

"Properly read, the Bible is the most potent force for atheism ever conceived."
— Isaac Asimov

Now let us examine the good book itself and see what we can glean in support of Jesus tales within scripture.

Many Christians assume that four of Jesus' apostles each wrote an account of their experience with him (Matthew, Mark, Luke, John), their writings becoming famous and *absolutely holy and sacrosanct* in the first century. But none of the twelve apostles wrote *anything* as far as we know. Not a word regarding Jesus came about until many generations after the apostles did not, in fact, write their supposed hagiographies.

Who could blame them: there was no reason to record anything! Jesus convinced his followers that the world would end very soon—within "a generation."[810] Thus, after the thorny-crowned martyr, King of the Jews was supposedly crucified (something history has not recorded), the apostles went straight back their temple (as claimed in Lk 24:52-53), continually "praising and blessing God," waiting, expecting, believing the world would soon end, and their Lord would return—any day. Any day now, they thought. Any day. Soon, soon, for sure...

Like Elvis, Godot, Elijah, and Milli Vanilli, Jesus never came back. Not within a generation, and not before his followers would "taste of death" as promised in Mt 16:28 and Mk 9:1.

Bible scholars agree that the four Gospels were written anonymously, and the earliest copies of the texts do not indicate any authorship. Moreover, they were a cobbling of various texts, with writing styles differing from section to section within the same Gospel. According to the *Encyclopedia Biblica*:[811]

> Almost every one of the apostles had a gospel fathered upon him by one early sect or another, if we may judge from the list of

> books condemned in the so-called Gelasian Decree, and from other patristic allusions.

The *Catholic Encyclopedia* states "the existence of numerous and, at times, considerable differences between the four canonical Gospels is a fact which has long been noticed and which all scholars readily admit... the present titles of the Gospels are not traceable to the Evangelists themselves."[812]

Take a look at "The Gospel According to St. Matthew," not written until c. 80 CE at the earliest, possibly as late as 135.[813] All references to the Matthew character are in the *third person.* (In that case, who wrote the book?) For example, Matthew 9:9: *And when Jesus passed on from thence, he saw a man sitting in the custom house, named Matthew; and he saith to him: Follow me. And he arose up and followed him.* Chapter 10 verse 3 lists all twelve apostles in the third person, including "Matthew the publican." This was not the "style in those days" as I have seen Christians claim.[814] "Saint" Paul (in those days, I must point out) always writes from the first person point of view, as do the anonymous authors of all four Gospels. The same is true of Philo Judaeus and other writers of the era.

Eusebius (c. 310) wrote that mere "tradition" is why people accepted that the first book was written by Matthew and the second by Mark.[815] He also wrote "of all the disciples of the Lord, only Matthew and John have left us written memorials."[816] One notes that the name "Luke" appears but twice in the New Testament.

**Drunk and Disorderly.** Saul of Tarsus claimed he saw magical phantasms and spectacular lights shining from "heaven."[817] I think Saul was simply *on something.* Until recent times, scholars hypothesized that Saul's brain was not firing on all cylinders, suffering the delusionary side-effects of malaria, or perhaps epileptic seizures.[818] It is more likely that Saul (later "Paul") was regularly under the influence of a hallucinogen.

Scientific research supports this hypothesis. Rains and climate conditions in the first century were extraordinarily favorable for certain hallucinogenic fungi such as *Claviceps paspali* to flourish in Asia Minor.[819] This is clearly the most likely explanation for Saul's "visions," and Occam would agree, no doubt, sheathing his well-honed blade for use another day. Many other people of that time and locale would have been exposed to hallucinogens upon drinking from the river's edge, or consuming tainted flora or grains.

This could also explain Matthew's fanciful account in 3:13-17 of "God" appearing in the sky during the baptism of Jesus (in a body of water likely inundated with floating hallucinogenic algae), as well as the many stories of miracles. Funny how magical things like that never happen anymore. The most we get these days is a tortilla with a semi-anthropomorphic smudge on it. The unctuous and simple mind concludes it must be Jesus—if bearded—or the "blessed virgin" if effeminate and apparently clean-shaven. I once saw a cloud that looked sort of like Albert Einstein. Does that count as a miracle?

My hands-down favorite "son of god" (among so many candidates) is Apollonius Tyanus, a Jesus contemporary. These hallucinogenic fungi could explain the simple sentence made in the third century by historian Philostratus: "Apollonius says to [the men of Tarsus] in a letter, Stop getting drunk on water [of the Cydnus]."[820]

So Apollonius, a contemporary of Jesus as well as Saul, claims the men of Tarsus—Saul's hometown—were getting drunk on the water of the river Cydnus! It seems that natural waterborne hallucinogens pervaded the region in the first century. This may also explain the oddity in first Timothy 5:23, wherein Saul preaches complete abandonment of $H_2O$ in favor of wine. (Personally, I like the idea, but my doctor disapproves). Perhaps Saul came to realize his out-of-control "visions" were a result of consuming water from the river's edge. Some later versions of the Bible (e.g. NIV, NLT, ESV) attempt to "fix" Saul's "no longer drink water" by changing it to "no longer drink *only* water." Saul's original ideas (Μηκέτι ὑδροπότει ἀλλὰ οἴνῳ ὀλίγῳ, faithfully translated to English in KJV) were not good enough for us, it seems.

Christendom claims Saul among the first NT writers; yet *Saul never met Jesus*. Apparently he spent a fortnight with Peter, long after the crucifixion: "I went to Jerusalem to see Peter: and I tarried with him fifteen days."[821] Surely Saul, tarrying with Peter, would have pestered him *non-stop* about the *son of God*. Or vice-versa, Peter blathering endlessly about Jesus' incredible miracles, portentous medical knowledge, and incisive philosophical lectures.

Clearly this is not the case. Saul never writes about any act performed by Jesus. In fact he seems to know almost nothing of Jesus. Saul speaks of nebulous notions such as "faith" in Jesus, a man Saul never met,[822] "obedience to the faith,"[823] and the grace of "Lord Jesus Christ," this "Lord" being nothing more than a rumor, and, from Saul's point of view, a mere scintillating apparition. This New Testament twaddle cobbled together in the fourth century reads much like the outlandish Homerian tales (which I am much more inclined to believe). If only the NT could hold itself together as rationally and integrally as the *Iliad* and *Odyssey*. Or Dr. Seuss books for that matter.

Saul writes he is "not ashamed of the gospel."[824] As the Bible was not yet written, his "gospel" can refer only to one of two things: some book of scriptures like the Hebrew Torah, or of Mithras, or Sandan; or the "good news" of the prophesied messiah, apparently recently reified. In any case, why would Saul proclaim that he is not ashamed, unless it would seem obvious to the rational observer that he should, in fact, be thoroughly embarrassed and ashamed of this supposed gospel?

Remember Sandan, the mythical founder of Saul's hometown of Tarsus, and the son of god? Mithras, Horus, Hercules, Krishna, and so many other figures were also "the son" of god. Saul surely was taught of Mithras, whose worship had landed in Tarsus a couple centuries before Saul's birth, becoming pervasive by his lifetime.[825] And, of course, of his home-town hero made good, Sandan, as well as Hercules, and probably Horus, just a couple stadia to his south in Egypt. Might these "sons of god" have affected Saul's theology?

**The Importance of Being Snipped**. In Genesis 34:14-17, family Hemor wishes their children to marry those of family Jacob, but only if their sons' weenies had been whittled:

> We cannot do this thing, to give our sister to one that is uncircumcised... if ye will not hearken unto us, to be circumcised; then will we take our daughter, and we will be gone.

Circumcision is, oddly, an essential and earnest "covenant" between the Hebrew god and his penis-chopping clerics. Our creator *damns* the soul of any male who has the audacity to retain genitalia fully intact.[826] (Seems funny that females have been forever spared this bloody ritual within the Christian religion.) It is unfortunate that some Orthodox Jews still practice the grotesque custom of *metzitzah b'peh,* wherein the mohel sucks the blood from the boy's penis with his mouth after circumcision—to "clean" the wound. In 2004, twin boys in Staten Island contracted Type-1 herpes from their superstitious and contaminated rabbi as a result of the "sterilization." One of the infants died.[827] In a more recent case this procedure resulted in the death of an infant of two weeks in September 2011; the hospital recorded the cause of death as "disseminated herpes simplex virus Type 1, complicating ritual circumcision with oral suction."[828]

Saul supposedly visited Lystra and met Timothy. Before leaving, he gave Timmy's penis a holy trim-job (Acts 16:3). If he practiced Hebrew tradition, Paul as mohel would bite Timothy's penis to rip the foreskin off and then suck it to keep it sterile. Parting is such sweet sorrow.

Such oddities notwithstanding, my primary point here is that Paul wrote nothing of Jesus' life, of his apostles, a trial, or any of his many miracles. Saul/Paul was a reverent and devoted Hebrew—or so he claimed—keeping the "sacred" traditions. And apparently fifteen days were insufficient for Paul to learn *anything* about Jesus, the son of *God,* from "eyewitness" Peter. Paul drones on and on, without making one significant, logical, or salient point. His stories and arguments are full of tautologies, superstition, Hebrew dogma, and circular logic. Paul teaches nothing of the life or philosophies of Jesus—a personage or entity whom Paul admits he never met.

Paul's epistles were written in the second half of the first century, 55-60 CE, some 30 years after his "visions" and the supposed crucifixion. One wonders why he waited until the last decade of his life to do so. Something suspicious we find in those letters: Paul boasts of duping gullible minds by "being crafty."[829] On a similar note we have Pope Leo X in the 16th century declaring, "It is well known to all ages how profitable this fable of Christ has been to us."[830]

One can visit Vatican City to witness how profitable the *fable* truly has been. It is clear that the Church grossly underestimates its own wealth. Bankers have estimated the Vatican's disclosed liquid assets at a mere $15 billion. Vatican City comprises 108.8 acres, with each acre valued today at $35 million. This puts its *land value alone* at

$3.8 billion for that—as Christopher Hitchens put it—"pathetic rump of real estate." The estimated real and liquid value, ignoring its plethora ill-gotten treasures, has been estimated at $2 trillion.[831]

I have even seen the raw and recognized wealth of this eternal Ministry of Love estimated at $500 trillion; I believe even this to be a gross underestimate: surely more than ten thousand of its artifacts are, by themselves, absolutely priceless.[832] This would place the value at *priceless times ten thousand,* at a minimum—whatever that may mean. The smallest country in the world is Vatican City. That minuscule, opulent, artificial and arguably illegal "sovereignty" is also one of the richest in the world.[833] Perhaps this is indeed "What's so great about Christianity."

I hope this makes you feel as nauseated as it makes me.

**A Revelation.** Overwhelming is the lack of any evidence for a "Jesus Christ," son of God (or whatever), the alpha and omega, savior and redeemer, wrongly executed (they say) some 2,000 years ago.

Jesus, meek and mild, said his message would drive families apart, "...and a man's foes shall be they of his own household" (Mt 10:35-36). The OT presents similar preachments, "a man's enemies are the men of his own house" (Micah 7:6). As recorded in John 15:6, Jesus promises you this: "If any one abide not in me, he shall be cast forth as a branch and shall wither: and they shall gather him up and cast him into the fire: and he burneth." As we know he came not to bring peace, but "a sword" (Mt 10:34).

It seems the words recorded from this Jesus person accomplished it all. Christianity divides societies, families, nations. It toppled the Roman Empire as Gibbon observed. It murdered tens of millions, as history records; and religion *poisons everything,* as Christopher Hitchens deftly demonstrated time and again.

Jesus is allegedly due back any day with his violent apocalypse, total destruction of humanity. That is something that God the First promised he would never do again after creating the deluge.[834] Yet Jesus (who is *also* "God"), 2,000 years ago, promised *the End of Times* within a generation. It seems the omniscient son of god was off by a couple thousand years... and counting.

It seems remarkable that there is no reliable evidence whatsoever even suggesting that a son-of-god described by the New Testament actually lived at all. In fact, the body of proof gives the historical Christ very little chance of actuality, of historicity. Even if "Jesus, son of Mary" lived two millennia ago, there was certainly nothing special (or at any rate, supernatural) about him. Any freethinking individual realizes this.

It seems most likely that the Jesus character of the Bible is an amalgam of various self-appointed evangelistic Hebrews and other legendary men, much in the manner depicted in *Monty Python's Life of Brian* (blessed are the cheese-makers!). The Bible is almost 100% fiction. Why do millions of people, in the twenty-first century, still believe in this phantom?

Sigmund Freud answered this in part: as long as humans fear death, many will rationalize and fictionalize a comforting "afterlife" concept.[835]

Personally, I hope—and truly believe—that my corpus shall simply expire one day, my encephalon and neural activity cease, with all chemo-electrical synapse activities and sentience dissolving into the void. That is to say, *dead*. Deceased. Gone. An ex-human being.[836]

I agree with Richard Dawkins who proposed that heaven would surely become extremely tedious after the first thousand years or so. Life is lovely, and continues to be both wonderful, and a challenge; next, peace awaits. No heaven, no hell. Meanwhile, let us enjoy, let us do good, let us create, procreate, explore, and embrace life.

And it seems to me that one should actively deny the outlandish supernatural, the ultimately dangerous religious "laws" and accompanying myths. They are poison.

## The Cheapest of Tuxedos

Many devout Christians proclaim they fully believe the Genesis stories—events that even a freethinking eleven year old can grasp are equivalent to fairy tales. They believe it because, as Pastor Douglas Wilson has said, "I'm a Christian, so I believe the Bible."[837]

This includes, Wilson admits, belief in a talking snake and Noah's ark. It seems to me Wilson would be an embarrassment to the more intelligent Christians of the world who are able to dismiss most Old Testament tales as mere metaphor.

Wilson claims it is "self-evident" that "God exists and created the world." He then clarifies: it is self-evident "to those who believe." Seems like a combination of tautology and sophistry, typical among believers: a steaming heap of logical fallacies and fictions.

And this is where Wilson's logic becomes completely arrogant. One could make a fair case for a first cause, an artificer, Einstein's metaphorical god; but Wilson calls this proposed deity not only by name but also *singly*, thus having no copilot. Somehow he *knows* this creator was "God," *one* deity. Wilson, a Christian, also holds that his supposed god had a son, somehow of equivalent divine puissance. And a "Holy Spirit" it seems.

That is the essence of the point at hand: Wilson *knows* the heavenly Patriarch's "name," using the singular. Why not two? Why isn't there another deity, a maternal one, let's say: Mrs. God—after all Wilson believes in a son of God. And, for crying out loud, maybe Mr. and Mrs. God even have a cat and a dog of mystic and metaphysical nature. Why not? How does Wilson know otherwise? "Because the Bible tells me so" is childish reasoning. "Because the brothers Grimm tell me so" makes as much sense.

Have such believers *really* read the Bible? It unequivocally and repeatedly describes a flat, geocentric concept of Earth. "Oh, but that's ancient Hebrew scripture," your typical Christian apologist will argue, proclaiming that we are under "grace"[838] because of Jesus who changed the world.

There are some things Jesus did not change. Let's start with a few laws from the Torah. Jesus agrees (Mk 7 and Mt 15) with Moses' childrearing instructions, to kill rebellious or stubborn children (Dt

21). Being such a benevolent Messiah, Jesus also preached that obedient slaves should be lightly whipped, but recalcitrant slaves should be severely punished (Lk 12). Never did he declare the buying and selling of humans as immoral: we see quite the opposite in both OT and NT. "Keep the commandments" Jesus declared (Mt 19).

By definition, Pastor Wilson must agree with all this evil, all this nonsense: it's in the Bible. And he must also believe in Creationism, or its modern namesake "Intelligent Design," dubbed by those god-damned annoying rationalists as "Creationism in a cheap tuxedo."

In Petersburg Kentucky the famed Bible-inspired "Creation Museum" has large-scale models of dinosaurs in a mock-up of the mythical "Garden of Eden" along with human figures, dinosaurs bearing saddles, and a scale model of Noah's mythical Ark that only children or the deluded believe in. Absurd enough by itself, but the ark also has a Stegosaurus onboard. Such lunacy only sets intellectual momentum abaft by centuries. Petersburg Kentucky thus marks itself as a black hole of human progress.

You may indeed have heard of this famous "museum." Yet many more bastions of servile ignorance have sprung up throughout America (mostly in the south as one might expect) and surprisingly even in Europe. The "Northwest Creation Network" (a think tank that I am dying to dive right into, head first) lists almost two dozen Creation Museums from Florida to California, Canada to Texas.[839] The sheer number of them is depressing to any rational mind.0

**The Creationist's Nightmare**. If you have had the time and inclination to chase down some of the attempts at philosophy and history by groveling pseudo-scientists, you have no doubt encountered Ray Comfort. Ray has a fruit-based proof of god which he hails as the "Atheist's Nightmare." The banana, Comfort explains, is perfectly made by God to be held in the hand. It has a non-slip surface; it has a tab at the top and "when you pull the tab, the contents don't squirt in your face"; it is "just the right shape for the human mouth"; and is even "curved toward the face to make the whole process so much easier."

This, believe it or not, is his "proof" of God.

In one video his deluded acolyte Kirk Cameron sits at his side, silent and smiling in admiration as the Kiwian sage lectures fellow creationists. Cameron is famous for becoming an insufferable born-again Christian around age seventeen on his own Road to Damascus—this dusty boulevard being located in southwest Burbank California one may surmise.

Ray Comfort, by explaining the perfection of the banana's obvious design for human handling and consumption, considers this to be proof that God made everything, and also proof that Comfort is a thinker and philosopher of the highest order. He does not address comestibles in nature that are not as "perfect," such as the coconut or boar or poisonous berries. Nor does he contemplate God's many human design mistakes, like the knee joint, back, esophagus or testicles—or our susceptibility to cancer and microbes. Comfort would have to admit that the design of the human brain is imperfect, because there are lost souls who are unable to see the "obvious" proofs that God exists, and who do not understand that God designed the perfect banana.

To creationists of the world who reason in any manner such as Mr. Comfort: I declare that you may have my brain only when you pry it from my cold, dead cranium.

Ray Comfort was eventually made aware that bananas do not grow in this special shape in nature: the bananas we get from the grocery store have been, well, intelligently designed by farmers over many decades from wild plantains, being different in many ways from their naturally-occurring ancestors. He was only minimally embarrassed upon hearing this news; Comfort's apology declared that "God" gave mankind knowledge to modify plantains.

I would have to imagine that, as a devoted Christian, Comfort condemns both homosexuality and sodomy. I almost pity him on the day someone takes him aside and points out that there is a male appendage, readily modifiable in size and pliability, also easily held in the hand and fitting perfectly in the mouth, matching up with his banana-based tests that confirm God made such things flawless and with oral intake in mind.

However I cannot guarantee that this appendage will not squirt in Ray's face.

## The Old Testament

### *The Good, the Bad, and the Silly*

The Christian Bible includes the ancient Hebrew Tanakh as its Old Testament, presented as if it represents history and lofty moral authority.

One does in fact discover shards and modicums of *good* therein, such as you should not kill (Ex 20:13 and Dt 5:17). Then there is a lot of *bad*: you *must* kill—just by example, Dt 21:20-1, 1 Sam 23, Psalm 135, Jude 1:5-8, Acts 13:17-19, Mt 11:20-23, Mk 7:10, and the entirety of Joshua.

And then we have not only the *silly*, presented here, but also the very ugly: Yahweh's edict that rape victims must marry their rapists (Dt 22); Jesus' advice to whip disobedient slaves savagely (Lk 12); Jesus convicting you of thought crimes (Mt 5); and so much more foul malice.

Most of the Bible is violent, immoral, useless, and silly. The Old Testament presents itself as an easy target for ridicule, but so many people believe it as historical fact (even Jesus thinks the Tanakh presents valid morals and truthful histories) that I feel compelled to take pot shots at those scriptures. Moreover, it is absolutely evil—as well as hilarious. Critical analysis, ridicule, and exegesis are not simply in order, they are necessary, as well as entertaining.

If my tone switches from semi-scholarly to satirical and playful from time to time it is because the Old Testament is largely unworthy of scholarly examination. Lampoonery would be the more appropriate directive of the day.

**Let's Start the Insanity**. Sound scientific method involves gathering facts via observation, then analyzing all variants, drawing temporary conclusions, and holding the apparent facts until proven otherwise. Rethinking, reworking, and reevaluation comprise this process.

A person indoctrinated into one of the main three monotheisms typically proceeds the opposite way: their Holy Book presents supposed "truths"—though unproven and yet accompanied by the same amount of evidence we have for the Easter Bunny. The job of the believer or apologist is to find facts that might seem to support original conclusions, long ago considered obvious and foregone. This embodies both the Foundational Bias and Straw Man logical fallacies, and is something never satisfactorily accomplished by religionists, except in finding unfalsifiable "evidence"—an approach as solid as believing, without reason or proof, in Russell's celestial teapot, the blessed Pink Unicorn, or Our Lord the Flying Spaghetti Monster (sauce be upon Him).

**The Bible Without Blinders**. Quite a boring task, poring through this supposed "good book." The exhortations in that goofy work of fiction are mind-boggling. Honestly, like most people (including most Christians), I had not read it as a youngster, even after my mother handed me one of the many versions. As an adult I finally tackled it. Holy Mithra of Persia, did I read some crazy crap! The Bible appears to be scribbled by drunken psychopaths charged with concocting an elaborate hoax, and it is so full of illogical and pointless ramblings I admit I skimmed over many parts. *Henoch begot Irad, and Irad begot Maviael, and Maviael begot Mathusael, and Mathusael begot Lamech, who took two wives: the name of the one was Ada, and the name of the other Sella. And Ada brought forth Jabel... Sella also brought forth Tubalcain, who was a hammerer and artificer in every work of brass and iron. And the sister of Tubalcain was Noema....* (Gen 4:18-22).

Why bother listing fictional "ancestors" of humankind? I refrain from conjecture but must point out the Bible's contradiction in a letter from Paul to Titus (3:9), commanding God's subjects to ignore genealogies because they are "unprofitable and vain."

Genesis chapter 10 rejoins mankind's phantasmagorical family tree: *Shem, Ham, Japheth, Magog, Madai, Javan, Tubal, Meshech, Tiras, Ashkenaz, Riphath, Togarmah, Javan, Elishah, Tarshish, Kittim, Dodanim...* and (I swear) *Gomer,* who was a Mayberry frat brother of Kevin Bacon, I think. The Bible preaches a holy buttload of epistemic diarrhea, including faux-genealogy and faux-fact. It is full of faux.

And redundant. And redundant. And redundant. It amazes me that people waste their lives committing the loony tome to memory—let alone teaching it as any kind of truth.

Surely it was human nature for ancient peoples worldwide to attempt to explain mysteries of Nature and Creation, just as we strive today, being much more enlightened with scientific method and evidence.

The ancients needed answers, and having none, they simply made things up, weaving fables, inventing supernatural beings—*gods*, even sons of gods and occasionally daughters—to explain the apparently unexplainable. Unfortunately, Bronze Age guesswork by Hebrews (among others), and second/third/fourth century Greco-Roman and Christian legends and oral traditions were written down, eventually printed *en masse* by Johannes Gutenberg. This engendered an artificial validity, being held as undeniable truths—the "argument from authority," one of the most impotent of fallacies. In the case of the Bible, the argument is from just about the *falsest* of authorities (with *Book of Mormon* and *Dianetics* being strong contenders for the Number One slot).

It is a shame of stellar proportions that Gutenberg did not elect to mass-produce for the first time, let's say, Socrates, Aristotle, Heron, Dio, Philostratus, or Homer, instead of the noxious and ultimately dangerous fiction (as history bears out) that is the "Holy" Bible.

Having *faith* is so much easier than thinking for one's self. Some believers, including Swaggart, Falwell, and Augustine of Hippo (unrelated to Hungry Hungry Hippo, our modern-day and benevolent marblevore),[840] claimed the bible is not merely "holy" but also inerrant—and only an impeccable god could have authored such a "perfectly written book." This absurd assertion is an easy straw ark to sink. An obvious target is the fauxful Adam and Eve tale, including the claim that all humanity descended directly from their children—*all three being boys*. Short-sighted and moronic, it shows that original Torah writers could not think far enough ahead to invent a creation tale with a modicum of non-incestuous procreation—and to me, it is amazing that there is even one person over age ten today who considers the Genesis stories to be factual or logical. Yet there are millions of believers.

The evil and jealous god imagined by ancient Hebrews put Adam here first, in what de Tocqueville might have called "God's Great Experiment: Planet Earth." If you follow Genesis, the only way for humankind to procreate was that those sons of "Adam and Eve" had intercourse with their mother, or with some unnamed sister, as Eve is "the mother of all the living" (Gen 3:20).

Specifically, Cain's "wife" (Gen 4:17) must have been Cain's sister, not some non-relation newly conjured by Yahweh. It is not clear whether his brother Seth had sex with his mother or with some unnamed daughter of Eve to bear Seth's son Enos (Gen 4:26).

The Garden of Eden absurdities and other inane biblical tales have been celebrated in film time and again. Regard and revere, if you will, the venerable directors who elevated the tall tales of the OT and NT to the silver screen:

*The King of Kings* (1927), Cecil B. DeMille
*Noah's Ark* (1928), Michael Curtiz
*Lot in Sodom* (1933), James Sibley Watson
*Samson and Delilah* (1949), Cecil B. DeMille
*David and Bathsheba* (1951), Henry King
*Salome* (1953), William Dieterle
*The Silver Chalice* (1954), Victor Saville
*The Ten Commandments* (1956), Cecil B. DeMille
*Solomon and Sheba* (1959), King Vidor
*The Big Fisherman* (1959), Frank Borzage
*King of Kings* (1961), Nicholas Ray
*Sodom and Gomorrah* (1963), Robert Aldrich
*The Greatest Story Ever Told* (1965), George Stevens
*The Bible: In the Beginning...* (1966), John Huston
*The Last Temptation of Christ* (1988), Martin Scorsese
*The Prince of Egypt* (1998), SimonWells
*Noah's Ark* (1999), John Irvin
*The Gospel of John* (2003), Philip Saville
*The Passion of the Christ* (2004), Mel Gibson
*The Nativity Story* (2006), Catherine Hardwicke

Clearly the Indiana Jones movies are also guilty of claiming and glorifying absurd Judeo-Christian supernatural concepts as their prime plot points. Absurd, yes; I am otherwise quite fond of Spielberg's work.

Mel Gibson's odd experiment in apparent Christian sadomasochistic erotica seems to belong to a class of its own.

You are even able to grab piously infected Q-Tips and cram nonsense into your child's innocent earholes with books like *The Beginner's Bible: Timeless Children's Stories* by Kelly Pulley. This book presents, for example, chapters called "A Basket Boat" (the Moses story); Jesus, "The Most Special Baby"; and a tale regarding the Noah fiction giving rise to the earth's "First Rainbow" ever. Oh, how cute! Does the book also teach "timeless" stories like the ethnic cleansing offered in Joshua and Samuel? Such a chapter might well be called "The Most Wonderful of Rapes and Baby Killings."

**Purgamentum ad nauseum**. In Isaiah 1:18 we see a rare offering of sage advice: "Come now, and let us reason together," yet the Bible is as capable of defending itself from intellectual attack as is a candy-filled piñata. Clearly it is no holy offering from any sort of intelligent Creator, and we have not even touched on the flat Earth concept, the geocentric solar system, the genocide, or ovine and caprine sacrifices.

So let's touch on them now. If it pleaseth the court:

**Flat, Geocentric Concept of Earth.** Consider the following "earth sciences" taught by the Bible:

> Fear before him, all the earth: the world also shall be stable, that it be not moved. (1 Chron 16:30)

> The measure thereof is longer than the earth [how "long" is a sphere?], and broader than the sea. (Job 11:9)

> Who shaketh the earth out of her place, and the pillars thereof tremble (Job 9:6).

> Thou hast set all the borders of the earth: thou hast made summer and winter. (Ps 74:17)

> And he shall set up an ensign for the nations, and shall assemble the outcasts of Israel, and gather together the dispersed of Judah from the four corners of the earth. (Isa 11:12)

> For the poles of the earth are the Lord's, and upon them he hath set the world (1 Sam 2:8).
>
> Where wast thou when I laid the foundations of the earth? Tell me if thou hast understanding (Job 38:4).
>
> And didst thou hold the extremities of the earth shaking them, and hast thou shaken the ungodly out of it? (Job 38:13.)

Correct me if I'm wrong, but the Earth is not set upon any "foundation," or pillars; nor does it have "four corners." It was, they say, either "God" or "Moses" who wrote this tripe (or more likely some anonymous ancient primate), and in any case he (definitely a *he*) was a fatuous fabricator of fiction; a mythmaker.

**Animal Sacrifices.** The Bible commands many barbaric and pointless edicts stemming from ancient Pagan practices:

> And if his oblation be a sacrifice of peace offerings, and he will offer of the herd... before the Lord. And he shall lay his hand upon the head of his victim, which shall be slain in the entry of the tabernacle of the testimony: and the sons of Aaron the priests shall pour the blood round about upon the altar. (Lev 3)

This loving Hebrew god is like a zombie; he not only wants to consume your brain (perhaps an obvious point), but desires as much blood he can get his heavenly hands on. He will, after all, make his arrows "drunk with blood" and his sword "shall devour flesh; and that with the blood of the slain and of the captives, from the beginning of revenges upon the enemy…" (Dt 32:42).

Praise the Lord. From Leviticus chapter 17 we are presented this gem:

> Therefore the children of Israel shall bring to the priest their victims, which they kill in the field, that they may be sanctified to the Lord… and they may sacrifice them for peace offerings to the Lord. And the priest shall pour the blood upon the altar of the Lord, at the door of the tabernacle… and shall burn the fat for a sweet odor to the Lord.

Thus as we learn from our bibles, God loves not only the taste of blood but also the "sweet odor" of burning flesh.

**Monthly Visitors**. God spends well over a dozen of His Bible verses commanding how we must separate menstruating women from *clean* society for a week. Two magical turtles or two young pigeons may make things right again for the lass; such are the words of Almighty God:

> The woman, who at the return of the month, hath her issue of blood, shall be separated seven days. Every one that toucheth her, shall be unclean until the evening. And every thing that she sleepeth on, or that she sitteth on in the days of her separation, shall be defiled. He that toucheth her bed shall wash his clothes: and being himself washed with water, shall be unclean until the evening. Whosoever shall touch any vessel on which she sitteth, shall wash his clothes: and himself being washed with water, shall be defiled until the evening. If a man copulateth with her in the time of her flowers, he shall be unclean seven days: and every bed on which he shall sleep, shall be defiled. The woman that hath still issue of blood many days out of her ordinary time, or that ceaseth not to flow after the monthly courses, as long as she is subject to this disease, shall be unclean, in the same manner as if she were in her flowers. Every bed on which she sleepeth, and every vessel on which she sitteth, shall be defiled. Whosoever toucheth them shall wash his clothes: and himself being washed with water, shall be unclean until the evening. If the blood stop and cease to run, she shall count seven days of her purification: And on the eighth day she shall offer for herself to the priest, *two turtles*, or *two young pigeons*, at the door of the tabernacle of the testimony: And he shall offer one for sin, and the other for a holocaust, and he shall pray for her before the Lord, and for the issue of her uncleanness. You shall teach therefore the children of Israel to take heed of uncleanness, that they may not die in their filth, when they shall have defiled my tabernacle that is among them. This is the law of him that hath the issue of seed, and that is defiled by copulation. And of the woman that is separated in her monthly times, or that hath a continual issue of blood, and of the man that sleepeth with her. (Lev 15:19-33)

God's squeamishness regarding the vagina (which He apparently created) seems akin to His hatred of the penis, and the pig, and of non-Hebrews (all of which He also created, and commands to be mutilated or destroyed).

The Bible bans homosexuality and condemns gays to death. Of course, in the modern Middle East the point is moot, as Iranian President Mahmoud Ahmadinejad pronounced, "We don't have homosexuals like [in America]."[841]

**Verses that Pastors Keep Secret**. The Bible is pure fiction—that much is obvious. Yet the job of the priest or pastor, sadly, is to lie for a living and propagate myths, to bring more sheep to his sermons thus adding to his collection plates.

As of this writing, googling the phrase "lying for Jesus" results in 322,000 hits.

If you question the literal word of the absurdities, your religious leader will tell you these are "allegories" or "metaphors" or "parables." But a lie is a lie. Thomas Paine wrote "No man ought to make a living by religion. It is dishonest so to do."

Let us examine more of the Bible's oddities, contradictions, inhumanity, and absolute evil.

The scriptures specifically approve incest and rape. To protect some "angels" who had holed up in Lot's flat by the gates of Sodom, Lot sanctioned rape of his own virgin daughters—a whole *Lot*-o-love. Lot attempted to ward off the crowd of horny men with the offer: "I have two daughters who, as yet, have not known man; I will bring them out to you, *and abuse you them as it shall please you…*" (Gen 19:8).

Why did Lot offer his virgin daughters to the men of Sodom? Well, those men wanted to screw the angels with whom Lot was breaking bread. Going into great detail, the Bible informs us that this bread was in fact unleavened (Gen 19:3).

You might think, Oh, these must have been two gorgeous female angels replete with silver wings and long slender legs; but the crowd asks "Where are the men which came in to thee this night? bring them out unto us, that we may know them."

Not, in deference to Seinfeld writers, that there is anything wrong with that; but I hope you agree that *rape* crosses the moral line, to say the least, whether rape of "angels" or of humans, gender issues notwithstanding.

Just prior to this would-be erotic episode, Lot and the angel-men had peacefully baked a meal and dined together. Apparently angels from Heaven actually need food. Heaven is a weird place; and I admit I do not understand the supernatural abilities of angels. They fly, they hover, they have gossamer wings, they are magical, and angels apparently are powered by unleavened bread.

Later, Lot's daughters get drunk with their father and engage in *ménage à troi* with him because they think they are the only humans left on earth, and must procreate by means of their pious pop (Gen 19):

> Come, let us make him drunk with wine, and let us lie with him… And they made their father drink wine that night: and the elder went in, and lay with her father… And the next day the elder said to the younger: Behold I lay last night with my father, let us make him drink wine also to night, and thou shalt lie with him....

I must admit that in my life there have been times when I was extremely drunk. Of this I am neither proud nor ashamed. Hey: I went to college, and I've been to Vegas, and Oktoberfest in Munich. But never could I become so drunk that I would allow my daughters to have sex with me. Moreover there is a tipping point in the drunkenness of a man whereupon the requisite biological and hydraulic gear simply refuses to bring itself to an elevated state to perform the necessary carnal task at hand, no matter how beautiful your partner (or seducing daughters) may be.

The Bible is cool with incest, as we have seen with the sons of Eve. We also notice that exalted Amram married his aunt: *And Amram took to wife Jochabed his aunt by the father's side: and she bore him Aaron and Moses. And the years of Amram's life, were a hundred and thirty-seven.* (Ex 6:20).

In Zechariah 14:1-2, God promotes rape:

> Behold, the day of the LORD cometh, and thy spoil shall be divided in the midst of thee… and the city shall be taken, and the houses rifled, *and the women ravished*; and half of the city shall go forth into captivity...

In 2 Samuel 12:11 we see more rape sanction:

> Thus saith the LORD, Behold, I will raise up evil against thee out of thine own house, and I will take thy wives before thine eyes, and give them unto thy neighbour, and he shall lie with thy wives in the sight of this sun.

We see God's approval of polygamy in Genesis: 4:18-19, 31:17, 32:22, 36:2, 37:2, as well as Deuteronomy 21:15 and 1 Samuel 1:1-2.

But wait, read of His apparent disapproval, both OT (Dt 17:17) and NT (Mk 10:11). Dear God: *make up your mind!*

Genesis 38 is particularly fun; in a nut-shell, God told Onan to marry his brother's wife, and Onan did, and whenever he had sex with her he pulled out ("he spilled it on the ground, lest that he should give seed to his brother"). God was not cool with Onan's respectful *interruptus,* so God killed Onan.

*Fun Fact:* In the New Testament, Jude praises the genocide of Joshua. See Jude 1:5-8.

**Bible Babble.** Genesis 11 claims that humans built "the Tower of Babel" with the inane idea of *reaching Heaven.* God catches on, clever geezer that he is, and visits Earth "to see the city and the tower" (Gen 11:5). Imagine the old white-bearded God dude checking out the city of Babel, strolling around like he did in the Garden of Eden wondering—with all his omniscience—what his subjects were up to. God then returned to his home, which apparently is a "holy mountain" (Ez 28:14).

All-knowing God eventually sees the Babel trick for what it is with his own eyes, then confounds the builders—*by inventing different languages.* Yes, this is why, according to the Bible, the many languages exist in the world: God doled out new tongues to humans who, up to that point, spoke but one—this being in contradiction to earlier stories of Genesis, 10:5, as well as 10:31.[842]

How intelligent, powerful, and omniscient can this god be, *sincerely worried* that humans could build a bazillion-parsec high structure reaching "Heaven," *and sneak in,* for crying out loud?

**Isn't Slavery Immoral?** Both the OT and the NT expressly approve of slavery. The Old Testament provides mankind with explicit instructions regarding the trafficking of humans. Yahweh not only *does not prohibit* slavery, but provides instructions for its adoption. As a Hebrew (or Christian), you may sell your daughter into slavery: "And if a man sell his daughter to be a maidservant, she shall not go out as the menservants do..." (Ex 21:7).

Proving that Yahweh is not all that hideous of a creator, we find that a slave does not have to be indentured forever, but only six years—unless said human chattel has a wife and kids whom he loves, in which case he will always be a slave, and his master may nail his ear to the door (Ex 21:2-6).[843] While this is not the most evil and vile of biblical edicts, it is indeed quite sick and misguided, and further proof that Christians simply have not read their Bibles.

Jesus, it seems, had an amazing opportunity to change his father's immoral laws, but his impotence (or indifference) is obvious. And Paul wrote: "Servants, be obedient to them that are your masters according to the flesh, with fear and trembling, in singleness of your heart, as unto Christ" (Eph. 6:5). "Whosoever are servants under the yoke, let them count their masters worthy of all honour; lest the name of the Lord and his doctrine be blasphemed" (1 Tim 6:1).

And Peter agrees: "Servants, be subject to your masters with all fear; not only to the good and gentle, but also to the forward" (1 Pet 2:18).

> *Fun Fact:* Judges 12:5-6 records that the Gileadites ask a man to pronounce the word "Scibboleth." He mispronounces it, so they kill him, and 42,000 others.

**Jesus Was a Fun Guy.** Jesus killed a "great herd of swine" just for giggles (Mk 5:11-13). Or perhaps because of some deranged man, who announced his "name is Legion" (Mk 5:9), was infected with "devils." Either way it's a fun story. This shows Jesus hates pork, quite literally.

Jesus gave cute nicknames to a two of his cronies, James and John, calling them the *Boanerges*, or "sons of thunder" (Mk 3:17). One may think it's because James and John were pro wrestlers, but it's simply just the kind of playful guy Jesus was: "And James the son of Zebedee, and John the brother of James; and he surnamed them Boanerges, which is, The sons of thunder."

Jesus even gave nicknames to his sandals (right foot: "Simon the Weasel"; left foot: "Judas Escargot"), and had a habit of referring to Joseph his father (or step-dad?) as "Joey Bag o' Bagels." This is all in the Bible, somewhere in the back, I think.

But seriously: this Bible, this fuzzy yarn makes the head spin with its illogical and puerile premises. I *would* leave it to sixth-graders to deflate the naïve myths further, but the paragraphs above in summary prove it inane, requiring no exposition. Sixth-graders can have recess instead of a screwball homework assignment.

Let's move on to what I call the "*Second* Genesis"—God's realization that he had created one totally screwed-up universe, and his do-over. Roll up your sleeves for the next phase of human "history" which is:

**The Great Flood**—*and God's promise never to do any evil crap again.* If you have not had the inclination—and perhaps the stomach—to endure a reading of the blowhard work of fiction some call "Gospel," prepare to smell some fetid and nutty cow-plop, starting with Genesis 6:5-7—

> And GOD saw that the wickedness of man was great in the earth, and that every imagination of the thoughts of his heart was only evil continually. And it repented the LORD that he had made man on the earth, and it grieved him at his heart. And the LORD said, I will destroy man whom I have created from the face of the earth; both man, and beast, and the creeping thing, and the fowls of the air; for it repenteth me that I have made them.

**Artist's conception of Noah's fabled Ark**

To whom God said this is unclear. Talking to himself again? No matter. Poor old God was seriously distraught, and ready to kill (for having done such a dreadful job in his creation?). The Old Testament could rightly have been named *Kill Humans: Volume 1*.

Who today would believe such wild myths? Well, perhaps more than you'd care to think. The 1986 *Catholic Encyclopedia* reports this tale as if it is historical fact (pp. 157-8, "Deluge"), dismissing the absurd idea of a *worldwide* flood, claiming "only a limited portion of the earth's surface was inundated, but all mankind perished except those in the ark since humans had not spread beyond the region."[844] This joke of an encyclopedia also states, against the consensus of scholars, that Genesis was "written largely by Moses" (237). This is akin to claiming "Frosty the Snowman" was written by Santa Claus.

The Lord and Creator did apparently wreak some raucous wrath, and *a bunch o' rain* was his WMD of choice. What happened to his Copperfieldesque magic abilities? Seems he'd just wave his wand, or press Ctrl-Alt-Del to conjure *Project Universe 2.0*. But the Almighty went *Sorcerer Super-Soaker* on humankind's collective ass. Being an impatient father of mediocre parenting skills (at best), the god created by ancient Hebrews had long since given up on his first miracles and mistakes, Adam and Eve and their progeny. God realized his entire human family tree consisted of nothing but hooligans. Following this pitiful epiphany, he promised suffering, death, and destruction for his Earthly children. He spared Noah's family because Noah was "a just and perfect man" (Gen 6:9), whereas the rest of God's little piggies deserved an extended waterboarding. What they need's a damn good whacking!

Now, Noah was quite the drunkard. That is fine by me. To the best of my knowledge I have never shared a bottle of booze with a "just and perfect man" like Noah, but that sounds like a gasser. And, nice that God does not preclude someone from being *perfect* if he enjoys getting sauced, stripping naked, and passing out (Gen 9:21-25):

> And he drank of the wine, and was drunken; and he was uncovered within his tent. And Ham, the father of Canaan, saw the nakedness of his father... And Noah awoke from his wine, and knew what his younger son had done unto him.

It's not Noah's fault that some untoward act (whatever it may have been) was inflicted upon his person while passed out drunk!

After all, it seems that Jesus himself was also a drunkard, as we read in Mt 11:19 and Lk 7:34.[845] Blessed are the winebibbers.

**Giovanni Bellini's 1515 painting, *Drunkenness of Noah.***

One OT book later, Moses convinces God—again bent on wicked mass homicide—not to butcher Moses' compatriots. The Bible calls god's intent "evil" (Ex 32:14). So, God's various mass murders are in fact not noble and loving, but considered *evil* by God's own words in the Bible. Such discoveries are, admittedly, weirdly gratifying for any freethinker to come across.

Now, the matter of Moses *convincing* God has not escaped me. How perfect is this god if he can be persuaded by one of his human subjects, against God's own perfect, divine (and self-admittedly evil) plans? William Lane Craig, employing some of the most perfectly circular logic ever devised, tells us that *anything God does* is moral, because he is, after all, God.[846] Dr. Craig, philosopher by trade, seems unable to recognize his own logical fallacies, and they are many. Moreover, this devout Christian seems unaware of Exodus 32, declaring God was forced to "repent" his own plans, being *evil* as declared by Christianity's own Book of Godly Goodness.

Back to the zany ark story: the Hebrew god declares even his *animals* turned evil (Gen 6:12, "And God looked upon the earth, and, behold, it was corrupt; for all flesh had corrupted his way upon the earth."). If so, does that mean, dear god, *good animals* go to heaven? Like Lassie? And Toto too? Still, it made sense to the our loving genocidal creator to have Noah gather pairs of (*evil*) animals for the ark, or as I like to call it, BFB, said Big Boat replete with "little rooms" (Gen 6:14, DRC), presumably to isolate species, and other little rooms for Noah's family to sleep, and some to poop and pee in. And perhaps another room to slaughter sheep and oxen as offerings to god while under sail—God loves (nay, *commands*) animal sacrifices as we learn in Exodus 20:24.[847]

Animal *pairs*, did I say? Elsewhere, God ordered Noah to take *seven* male and *seven* female "clean" species (Gen 7:2). This is but one of the thousands of bible contradictions: Genesis 6:19 commands Noah to bring pairs, while in chapter seven of this "perfect" text, the numbers change.

The schism widens, and "the Gospel" is rapidly turning into a steaming pile of unholy manure.

Even before the Dark Ages, many people questioned the size of Noah's BFB. That it could hold the requisite complement of beasts seemed ridiculous even by some believers in the third century. God instructed Noah to build it 300 by 50 cubits. In Bill Cosby's 1963 comedy album, Noah replies to god: "Right. What's a cubit?"

Right. What's a cubit? A cubit is an ancient unit of length, anywhere from ten to thirty inches, depending upon where you find yourself in antiquity, how long your arms are, and which god's voice you hear in your head. Christian apologist Origen Adamantius (c. 182–251) argued that Noah's cubit would have been *Egyptian*, about 20 inches. This makes the ark 500' x 83' and clearly could have held fewer than one hundredth of a percent of all pairs (or fourteens) of the millions of Terran species. At a thousand times the size, Noah's BFB could not have met this absurd god's absurd edict.

Next there is the question of Noah's ability to collect all animals on Earth, which must include all insects, dinosaurs and even unicorns (Num 23, Dt 33, Job 39, Ps 23, Isa 34, more).[848] God gave Noah seven days (Gen 7:1-5), clearly impossible even for Superman of Krypton, in whom I can believe much more than Noah of Ark.

Finally, consider family Noah's post-flood procreation, and thus our own family tree. They had but one choice—bulk incest: awkward, nasty, musky... sinful within Hebrew theology? It is a story of inbreeding just like that of the sons of "Adam" and "Eve."

My guess is that Noah's offspring formed trailer parks and married cousins and sisters. They had chariots up on blocks in their front yards, failing dental health, and no doubt donned mullets. "If yew cain't sacrifice a goat," Jebediah Foxworthy might ponder, "because yer sacred altar is too full of empty beer cans, yew *might* be a son of Noah."

Questions abound. Did Family Noah sweep up the manure during the long cruise? What vegetation survived on earth after being submerged for almost a year, that mankind and all animals might then eat upon disembarking—seaweed and algae? And was there a casino onboard?[849]

More importantly, why would any rational person buy into this piffle, yet dismiss Zeus, Mithras, Thor, Santa, or, say, phrenology or trepanning? I know why, and I'll bet you do too: religious brainwashing from youth. All ancient peoples took wild stabs at answering the enigmas of nature, history, life, death—and they always got it wrong.[850] Noah's Ark is one such wacky example. This Mosaic mosaic does not fit together in any respect: not logically, scientifically, historically, even (for lack of a better term) spiritually. Like so much of the Bible, it is childish and utterly useless for any purpose. Why has it not been relegated to the same heap along with the fictitious gods of Mount Olympus?

We have just as much proof of the Bible stories as we have proof of the reality of elves, nymphs, goblins, ogres, mermaids, genies, leprechauns, unicorns, vampires, wargs, trolls, ghosts, pucas, werewolves, dragons, Bigfoot, jackalopes, almas, griffons, spriggons, fairies, poltergeist, gnomes, hobgoblins, cabbits, sirens, firedrakes, chupacabras, loogaroos, strix, lindworms, boggarts, tundas, papinijuwari, wyrms, waldgeist, angels, aswangs, panotii, gorgons, harpies, gremlins, manticore, hydras, lamias, minotaur, sileni, navs, centaurs, yetis, gegenees, ladons, hyperboreans, chimera, basilisks, myrmecoleons, hippogriffs, bugbears, muscaliets, perytons, grigoris, Cyclopes, tritons, the Loch Ness Monster, Pegasus, and the T-1000 of *Terminator 2* fame.

Now let us move on to the aftermath of the "hundred and fifty day" flood (Gen 7:24). (I'll bet you thought it was only forty days and nights? It's okay, a common mistake.) As the bible is rambling, boring, and often triply redundant (and triply contradictory), I summarize as follows:

Gen 8:21 - god really screwed up, and promises never to do that evil crap again.

Gen 8:22 - god promises that each new day will come forever—he swears!

Gen 9:9-11 - god promises never to do that evil crap again.

Gen 9:12-14 - god makes a rainbow when there are clouds.

Gen 9:15 - god promises (again) never to do that evil crap again.

Gen 9:16 - the rainbow is god's way of not forgetting that he promises never to do that evil crap again.

Gen 9:17 - the rainbow is god's way (again) of promising never to do that evil crap again.

It's funny, because it's true. I can imagine how eons ago such ideas had come to be oral legend. Certainly attempts to explain rainbows, and legends associated with the Epic of Gilgamesh or the Deucalion flood. Still, the bible thing is just total weird-city.

The words of Robert Green Ingersoll come to mind: "Why should I allow that same god to tell me how to raise my kids, who had to drown His own?"

Speaking of drowning your own, remember the dilemma that Andrea Pia Yates bravely faced (from the Timeline, June 2001)? It was—*dum dum DUMM*—Satan. She killed her children, drowning them in the bathtub. She said she wanted to be executed so that she and "Satan" would be destroyed.

Whew! So glad Satan was finally eradicated! Thank you, Andrea.

**Great Flood Hogwash.** I once came across a cartoon on YouTube glorifying the tale of Noah's Ark. Somebody posted a comment: "great for children." This is the temperament of the religionist who was raised with such myths. What, if anything, is "great" about teaching children utter malarkey? Next, someone else posted: "Thank you for uploading this nice fairytale story." Some poor deluded soul replied: "Noah's Ark wasn't a story. It was a historic event." The adjectives that come to my mind rather than "historic" are *fictional* and *absurd* and *childish.* Many movies have been created to honor the "historic" event:

When Noah's Ark Embarked (1917)

Noah's Ark (1928)
Father Noah's Ark (Disney cartoon, 1933)
L' Arche de Noé (1947)
Noah's Ark (1959)
Mel-o-Toons Noah's Ark cartoon (1960)
Keshtye Noah (1968)
Noah's Ark cartoon (1986)
Enchanted Tales: Noah's Ark (1995)
Noah's Ark (1999)
Evan Almighty (2007)

The Old Testament teaches: (1) God, who is perfect, realizes he screwed up when he created a completely evil world (god damn it!) and decides to cleanse it via lots o' rain. (2) After his flood, God, who might not be perfect, realizes he made another mistake in killing everyone except Swiss Family Noah, and admits his cruel blunder. And (3) God, who clearly is quite fallible, must put a rainbow in the sky, without which he would forget his promise, and perpetrate more immoral and murderous rampages.

Thus the Great Flood story reveals a god that is not "perfect and loving," but incompetent, frustrated, unjust, as moody as a drunk adolescent, manifestly immoral and vengeful, with a teetering memory and incomplete knowledge of the many animal species he himself created. These flaws alone should make any believer—whether Christian, Hebrew, or Muslim—at least a little suspicious of the usefulness of their holy books for any purpose, let alone veracity. Yet such lies, feckless "facts" and inconsistencies pervade those wacky books. (Yes, even the Qur'an includes the Noah tale: see Sura 71.)

God's garbage-like disposal of his progeny is unambiguously immoral and psychopathic: *All God's children left behind* one might say. Even exalted Jesus, recorded in Matthew and Luke, buys into the Noah bullshit:

> But as the days of Noe were, so shall also the coming of the Son of man be. For as in the days that were before the flood they were eating and drinking, marrying and giving in marriage, until the day that Noe entered into the ark, And knew not until the flood came, and took them all away; so shall also the coming of the Son of man be. (Mt 24:37-9)

> They did eat, they drank, they married wives, they were given in marriage, until the day that Noe entered into the ark, and the flood came, and destroyed them all. (Lk 17:27)

Comedian Joe Rogan points out that if you tell the Noah's Ark story to an "eight year old retarded boy, he's going to have some questions."

As a side note, a 2005 poll discovered that more than 10 percent of American adults think that Noah's wife was Joan of Arc.[851]

I realize most Christians are not wacky fundamentalists, but claims that the stories are "allegories" or "parables" equally discredit the Bible's usefulness and validity, and must answer to its contradictions and illogic. Which conflicting passages should I believe? Why even have the book, if it is widely open to interpretation, and not true to its own written words? Where do we find any evidence, any valid "gospel"? And where is Waldo?

**The Rapture.** But wait, there's more, and we need only connect the supposed Beginning of the universe with its predicted End to point out yet another bible contradiction. The Book of Revelation (and many "prophesies" by Jesus) predicts the *End Of The World*—locusts, fire, brimstone, earthquakes, suffering, dragons, $500.00 per gallon gas prices—all the wicked stuff we've come to expect of our loving creator. According to someone named John (supposed author of Revelation; yet nobody is sure *which* John), God will once again become riled and pissed at his Earth invention. This John says God will renege the Rainbow Covenant and try again to wipe out his bad-to-the-bone Earthlings. So God lied again.

Oh well. He is GOD, for fuck's sake! He can do and say whatever he wants. And it's always moral, no matter how sick or evil, by definition—just ask William Lane Craig, philosopher extraordinaire.

## The Life and Morals of Jesus of Nazareth

Let us move on from the ancient Hebrew myths and immoral "laws" of the Old Testament and Tanakh to the words of divinity, brotherhood and peace brought to us by the King of Glory, Jesus the Christ. We shall begin with his teachings and knowledge, supported by known facts, science, history, and morality.

**Jesus v. Truth**. Bertrand Russell said "So far as I can remember, there is not one word in the Gospels in praise of intelligence." Now, I admire Russell, but he missed a few things. I have found in the Bible a modicum of praise for men of learning (never for women, of course). 1 Chronicles 26 seems to praise wisdom, as does 1 Chronicles 27. 1 Esdras 7 and Proverbs 16 praise those who are "learned." But that's about it. Here are those verses:

> And the lot of the east fell to Selemias. But to his son Zacharias, a very wise and learned man, the north gate fell by lot. (1 Chron 26:14.)

> And Jonathan David's uncle, a counsellor, a wise and learned man: he and Jahiel the son of Hachamoni were with the king's sons. (1 Chron 27:32.)

> Artaxerxes king of kings to Esdras the priest, the most learned scribe of the law of the God of heaven, greeting. (1 Esdr 7:12.)

> The learned in word shall find good things: and he that trusteth in the Lord is blessed. (Prov 16:20.)

So there you have it. The Bible provides perhaps four expressions praising intelligence—in a book of a million words. However, the fourth example (Prov 16:20), claiming a "learned" man finds good things, is tainted by the follow-up praise in trust in "the Lord"—that is, not to seek evidence, but blind faith of their Lord of superstition, word-of-mouth legend, myth. So, subtract one. Moreover, in taking from the "Tree of Knowledge" Adam and Eve actually sinned!

What terrible consequences have Christians wrought over the millennia, in blind faith of the "gospels?" Is Faith the problem? In particular, is Jesus the problem? The history of Christendom and the immoral preachments of the Savior prove that yes, Jesus (more accurately, the words of the mythical Savior recorded in the Bible) is the *root* of the problem.

During his supposed ministry, Jesus preached in the region spanning from Jerusalem's Atarot airport and roaming perhaps to the McDonald's in downtown Nazareth (which today might serve a Kosher-Pounder for all I know), proclaiming God's holy word. The pilgrimage of Jesus, a man who began his evangelism as a seasoned adult, is summarized in the Bible: *And he came to Nazareth, where he was brought up: and he went into the synagogue, according to his custom, on the sabbath day: and he rose up to read* (Lk 4:16). *And Jesus himself was beginning about the age of thirty years...* (Lk 3:23).

Some of Jesus' supposed life story can be found in Mt 3:13, and Mk 1:9: "Around then he was baptized by John in the river Jordan." Imagine John the Baptist's avocation, rooted in ancient Egyptian superstition. John performed *no constructive task whatever* as far as we know. John's pitiable occupation is based on falsehoods and mysticism. John should be held in the same low esteem as today's palmists, tarot-card readers, priests, pastors, and astrologers. John immersed people in river water, duping them into thinking that some supernatural transformation ensued. That was his profession: dunking people; duping people. I can't imagine his intelligence being anything beyond dimwit-simpleton if he believed in what he did. What commercial enterprise would employ such an individual? I hope, for his sake, his victims were big tippers.

If Jesus is the man-god or god-man so oft held to be, and the New Testament inerrant, clearly Jesus and his disciples would speak only with absolute epistemic wisdom, and Jesus would offer nothing but love and sound advice in sermons. Yet the NT advises you to disregard science and any new evidence, and retain superstitions. "Faith," it seems, trumps truth and knowledge (1 Tim 6:20-1):

> O Timothy, keep that which is committed to thy trust, avoiding the profane novelties of words and oppositions of knowledge falsely so called. Which some promising, have erred concerning the faith. Grace be with thee. Amen.

The word "amen" in the scriptures seems to mean, time and again, "I have spoken, and what I have just said is God's absolute truth. Die and suffer in Hell if you believe otherwise."

Jesus believes the OT myth of Jonah—that he lived inside a fish (or whale?) for three days. From the anonymous author we have Jonah 2:1-3:

> Then Jonah prayed unto the LORD his God out of the fish's belly, And said, I cried by reason of mine affliction unto the LORD, and he heard me; out of the belly of hell cried I, and thou heardest my voice. For thou hadst cast me into the deep, in the midst of the seas; and the floods compassed me about: all thy billows and thy waves passed over me.

Jesus lends his wise opinion (Mt 12:40):

> For as Jonas was three days and three nights in the whale's belly; so shall the Son of man be three days and three nights in the heart of the earth.

Hercules is a mythical Roman figure actually borrowed from Greek Heracles. Hercules was also swallowed by a giant fish at Joppa where Jonah was swallowed, long before the first century and Jesus' supposed time.[852] Like Jonah, Hercules remained under piscatorial incarceration for three days.[853] Heck, who hasn't lived inside an animal, being fish, whale, or bird, for days? I once spent over twenty-four hours straight in the Flamingo playing blackjack in Vegas.

So many of these invented religions were back and forth plagiarisms of one another, being merely man-made myth. I'd prefer to throw in with Hercules, myself, if I had to choose. He seems cool.

"That Jesus Christ was not God is evidence from his own words." - Ethan Allen

As previously mentioned, JC believes that all sick or handicapped people *are being punished because they are evil.* Jesus thinks disease and handicaps are God's way of penalizing "sin" (Jn 5:11-14).

Wouldn't it have been ever so nice—but uncharacteristically prophetic and useful—if Jesus had taught humans something of nutrition, diet, the reasons for scurvy, beriberi, pellagra? Perhaps a lesson on electricity, chemistry, germs, even the benefits of exercise, for example. Of course, he did not. Two thousand years ago nobody knew of such things—not even the *Son of God*. I would be duly impressed if Jesus had said, 2,000 years ago:

> These are the generations of all matter: A first element, which God hath named *hydrogenum*. A second element, four times the weight of the first, God calls *hoeliumum*. The others, my disciples, are for you to discover and name, but know ye that the first element, when twice combined with an eighth, *oexygenum,* comprises the seas of the Earth: water. I am the Lord. Amen.

Even more impressive would have been: "And here is the Periodic Table of the Elements, as I have carved on this tablet." Simple physics and chemistry, yes. But way too complex for Jesus the simpleton of old to know, and, being some sort of stingy and egotistic Soup Nazi, information too useful for God to provide to humans 2000 years ago. The "Ten Commandments" and various other oddball edicts were all that God was capable of granting back then. Superstitious soup for the soul, one might say.

A Heaven-provided Periodic Table might have made me a believing Christian, perhaps. Of course, nothing even remotely like that, no amazing utterance occurs in the bible, neither OT nor NT. Jesus never offers any thought, any "science," or other such proposition that could not have been uttered by absolutely any Bronze Age layperson. Jesus' philosophies are most often simplistic and even nonsensical, vastly inferior to those proposed by Greeks, Egyptians, and Persians, centuries before the Savior supposedly spoke to the masses in Judea.

Jesus said "But when ye pray, use not vain repetitions, as the heathen do" (Mt 6:7), and the *Encyclopedia Biblica* attributes this to Jesus' belief in magic and superstitions.[854]

I mentioned that omniscient Jesus *actually bought* the absurd story that Lot's wife turned into a pillar of sodium chloride while walking away from the city of Sodom.[855] Says Jesus:

> In that hour, he that shall be on the housetop, and his goods in the house, let him not go down to take them away: and he that shall be in the field, in like manner, let him not return back. Remember Lot's wife. (Lk 17:31-2)

"Remember Lot's wife" the J-man commands. Yes; I remember Lot's wife. If I may be so bold to satirize the scriptures in their simple credulity: I also remember a bridge in Brooklyn that Jesus might be interested in purchasing when the Big Kahuna returns. Waterfront property. A great investment. I think I might make a fortune.

The New Testament seems to hold that all humans can control the weather telekinetically (Jas 5:17-18).[856] Well, some humans apparently could do so, such as Pythagoras and Empedocles—that is, if you also believe some *other* urban legends and myths.[857] [858]

Jesus advised Peter to go fishing to find a way to pay his bills, promising Peter would find money in the mouth of a fish. It's a Festivus miracle:

> Jesus saith unto him, Then are the children free. Notwithstanding, lest we should offend them, go thou to the sea, and cast an hook, and take up the fish that first cometh up; and when thou hast opened his mouth, thou shalt find a piece of money: that take, and give unto them for me and thee.. (Mt 17:26-27)

Jesus says humans have no free will, and that God decides who will perish and who will live forever (Rom 8:29-30, Rom 9:11-22, Acts 13:48, Jude 4, 2 Tim 1:9). The Bible also contradicts this, saying we *do* have free will (Dt 30:19, Joshua 24:15). Let us consider these and other many contradictions a bit later.

Although I can find no biblical support, it would not surprise me to discover that Jesus believes if you lose a tooth and put it under your pillow, in the morning you will always find money. "An eye for an eye and a shekel for a tooth" might be the holy words of the Lord.

How nice it would have been if Jesus in his omniscience had made a holy precept *not to kill in the name of religion*. But as we have seen, Jesus largely preached quite the opposite. In contradiction to its many decrees for execution and murder, the NT gives us Matthew 7:12, a version of the ancient Golden Rule. What a wonderful "new" idea! Yet 500 years prior, Pythagoras said "people should associate with one another in such a way as not to make their friends enemies, but to render their enemies friends."[859]

For these and so many other reasons, I have dysphasia regarding the "Holy" Texts: I cannot swallow the mendacities, atrocities, plagiarisms, contradictions, and words of absolute evil. I like wine and beer, but I think scotch tastes like brake fluid; yet, I can more readily swallow *volumes of* scotch (and perhaps brake fluid) more than I can swallow the fictitious bible verses, which cause me projectile regurgitation. Metaphorically.

I agree with Nietzsche: "In Christianity neither morality nor religion come into contact with reality at any point."

Even early Christian father Origen Adamantius, in the third century, questioned the validity of *most of the Bible*. Origen said that the four gospels (M-M-L-J) were the "only undisputed ones in the whole church."[860] Today the four gospels are *also disputed*, being complete falsehoods, fairy tales.

**Jesus v. Jesus**. Grab a Bible and try to find useful advice, scientific or historical fact. If you can, odds are I can show you somewhere else where it preaches the opposite. Many Christian leaders have contended, amazingly, that the Bible is perfect and inerrant. It does in fact say it is. "As for God, his way is perfect; the word of the LORD is tried: he is a buckler to all them that trust in him" (2 Sam 22:31). "All Scripture is given by inspiration of God" (2 Tim. 3:16). "Every word of God is pure" (Prov 30:5).

So, it must be inerrant, perfect! The genuine son of God would thus give only *consistent* advice. It is unthinkable that the Christ might contradict himself, even just once, in this faultless book.

You know what is coming. Let us start with Luke 16:16, wherein Jesus rejects Old Testament laws:

> The law and the prophets were until John. From that time the kingdom of God is preached: and every one useth violence towards it. (Lk 16:16)

Yet he supports those laws in Matthew 19:17:

> Who said to him: Why askest thou me concerning good? One is good, God. But if thou wilt enter into life, keep the commandments.

Then the NT rejects the OT laws:

> For sin shall not have dominion over you: for you are not under the law, but under grace... But thanks be to God, that you were the servants of sin but have obeyed from the heart unto that form of doctrine into which you have been delivered. (Rom 6:14)

Wait. No, Jesus supports them in Matthew 5:17. Hold on, Jesus himself *ends* the law (Rom 10:4).

Hold on... Jesus declares the law can't change (Lk 16:17).

Giving the benefit of the doubt, Jesus probably was not sniffing Galilean glue when he advised his followers to "keep" the Ten Commandments, then enumerated six, getting one wrong (Mt 19:18-19): *He saith unto him, Which? Jesus said, Thou shalt do no murder, Thou shalt not commit adultery, Thou shalt not steal, Thou shalt not bear false witness, Honour thy father and thy mother: and, Thou shalt love thy neighbour as thyself...*

In the perfect bible, Jesus sends his followers out to preach the gospel (but not to non-Hebrews, mind you: *Go ye not into the way of the Gentiles,* Mt. 10:5), and tells them how to prepare for the long journey. Apostle Matthew claims he commanded them to go barefoot (10:10). Mark, however, says Jesus advised Birkenstocks (6:8).

Jesus requires that all his human subjects be *perfect,* like God (Mt 5:48). In James 3:17, he contradicts himself, saying God is full of mercy, and thus he does not require us to be perfect. In Tobius 3:13, God forgives mankind's imperfections, yet in Deuteronomy 18:13 the Bible claims humans must be "perfect" and "without spot before the Lord." Being "perfect" seems a difficult task. Was even Jesus perfect?

Compare Jonah 1:17 to Matthew 12:40. The OT has Jonah swallowed by a piscine ("great fish" in KJV), while the NT texts have him swallowed by an aquatic mammal ("whale" in KJV, κήτους in Greek). This is not surprising, as God also does not know the difference between the avifauna he created, and his chiropterans (Lev 11:13-19):

> Of birds these are they which you must not eat, and which are to be avoided by you: The eagle, and the griffon, and the osprey. And the kite, and the vulture, according to their kind. And all that is of the raven kind, according to their likeness. The ostrich, and the owl, and the larus, and the hawk according to its kind. The screech owl, and the cormorant, and the ibis. And the swan,

> and the bittern, and the porphyrion. The heron, and the charadroin according to its kind, the houp also, *and the bat.*

So, God doesn't know his bats from his birds. Perhaps he has birds in his belfry.

More nonsense and contradictions follow. Wise men followed a star "in the East" to find the baby King of the Jews—yet, the men came *from* the East to Jerusalem (Mt 2:1-2), which must, in fact, place the star not in the East, *but in the West,* unless the "star" was but a couple miles (as opposed to light-years) above Earth. A star "in the East" would have the men walking *eastward* to follow it. The ancient Bible writers of course knew nothing of cosmology.

Jesus, omnipotent and perfect son of God, needed an angel to appear to him to give him power: *And there appeared an angel unto him from heaven, strengthening him.* (Lk 22:43). Was this another angel who was powered by unleavened bread?

Even down to his final hours (on Earth, that is), we have outrageous contradictions. Nailed to the cross, Matthew claims that omnipotent Jesus whined, "My God, my God, why hast thou forsaken me?" (Mt 27:46). At least Jesus died doing what he loved: playing the part of the victim. (This phrase was in fact lifted word-for-word from Ps 22:1 by the anonymous writer of Matthew.)

Luke, however, has him saying "Father, into thy hands I commend my spirit" before flying off to heaven (Lk 23:46) to be with that same God who had "forsaken" him. And Jesus is somehow the very same entity: God, Jesus, Holy Spirit. Moreover this happens to be a plagiarism of Psalm 31: "Into thine hand I commit my spirit: thou hast redeemed me, O LORD God of truth."

*If we believe absurdities, we shall commit atrocities*—Voltaire

**Jesus v. Morality**. Jesus is regarded by Christians as being full of Love and Peace; but only if you believe in him (and if you are Hebrew, according to the NT); otherwise Jesus will have you tortured in Hell for all eternity. Praise the Lord.

Jesus was not all that good of a fella; his evil ways are skipped over in the typical Sunday sermon. Even anti-religionist Bill Maher got it all wrong saying "Jesus is one of the greatest role models I can think of." Ask a pastor why he does not preach anything from the following verses.

The New Testament praises the OT genocide of Joshua 2-12, in Jude 1:5-8. And Jesus and his Apostles are *all for* ethnic cleansing, as long as Hebrews are on the top rung: "The God of this people of Israel chose our fathers, and exalted the people... And when he had destroyed seven nations in the land of Chanaan, he divided their land to them by lot" (Acts 13:17-19).

As mentioned previously, the NT approves of slavery—1 Timothy 6:1, Titus 2:9-10, Ephesians 6:5-6, and 1 Peter 2:18. However, in Timothy 1:10, if you interpret the word "menstealers" to mean "slave dealers," you merely have yet another of the farrago of bible contradictions.

Jesus agrees (Mk 7:10 and Mt 15:4) with Deuteronomy's jurisprudence *condemning to death* a rebellious or stubborn son (Dt 21:20-1). Obviously, then, Jesus has read Deuteronomy. Does he agree with 22:28-9, wherein the penalty for rape is money paid to the rape victim's father, and the female rape victim must marry her rapist (Dt 22:28-9)?

> If a man find a damsel that is a virgin, which is not betrothed, and lay hold on her, and lie with her, and they be found; Then the man that lay with her shall give unto the damsel's father fifty shekels of silver, and she shall be his wife; because he hath humbled her, he may not put her away all his days.

Here is the bizarre backwards beauty of this Judeo-Christian bylaw: the homeliest boy in the village can simply rape a beautiful girl, she being a virgin; then, under meager monetary obligation he confers upon the father a dowry and is guaranteed marriage to his love interest (more accurately, *rape victim*) after which he may legally rape his wife any time and as often as he wants, for the rest of his life. Mazel tov to the happy couple.

And here is the equally bizarre alternative: perhaps the girl (with permission of her father) decides not to marry this rapist. In this case she must remain unmarried for the rest of her life, because she is no longer a virgin; if she marries, her horrid hymen secret will be discovered, and it will be the duty of all villagers to stone her to death as we learn from Dt 22:21.

Another point about Deuteronomy 22—while the penalty for forced rape is minimal (even *immoral* and beneficial to the rapist), *consensual* pre- or extra-marital sex and *consensual* post-marital adultery are penalized by execution (Dt 22:22-24):

> If a man lie with another man's wife, they shall both die, that is to say, the adulterer and the adulteress: and thou shalt take away the evil out of Israel. If a man have espoused a damsel that is a virgin, and some one find her in the city, and lie with her, Thou shalt bring them both out to the gate of that city, and they shall be stoned [to death]: the damsel, because she cried not out, being in the city: the man, because he hath humbled his neighbour's wife. And thou shalt take away the evil from the midst of thee.

The nasty Old Testament God rewards the violent criminal, while condemning consenting adults to death. The Bible's laws are blatantly immoral, and full of contradictions. The Bible declares *Thou Shalt Not Kill,* then enumerates so many absurd reasons to kill. What's it going to be then, J?

Jesus came to cast fire on the earth (Lk 12:49). He cited a parable of "a certain nobleman" ending in "But those mine enemies, which would not that I should reign over them, bring hither, and slay them before me" (Lk 19:27). This is the "Parable of the Talents" (talents are valuable coins), which also appears in Mt 25:14-30. The text in Luke is rather ambiguous. Here is the KJV version:

> [23] Wherefore then gavest not thou my money into the bank, that at my coming I might have required mine own with usury? [24] And he said unto them that stood by, Take from him the pound, and give it to him that hath ten pounds. [25] (And they said unto him, Lord, he hath ten pounds.) [26] For I say unto you, That unto every one which hath shall be given; and from him that hath not, even that he hath shall be taken away from him. [27] But

> those mine enemies, which would not that I should reign over them, bring hither, and slay them before me. [28] And when he had thus spoken, he went before, ascending up to Jerusalem.

The anti-theist often cites this scripture claiming it was Jesus who said "slay them before me," and it appears that way above. But earlier in the parable, Jesus says the citizens hated the nobleman, declaring they "will not have this man to reign over us." So score one point for Jesus: it was not he who made the murderous proclamation. Nevertheless one must ask what is the purpose of a parable wherein the noble slave-owner sentences people to death for hating him? In Matthew's version, the parable ends with the nobleman saying "And cast ye the unprofitable servant into outer darkness: there shall be weeping and gnashing of teeth." The Bible is full of violence and torture, and Jesus' point here *should have been, but was not* that this nobleman was evil. Jesus appears to hold this man up as a wise lord who knew best what to do with money, and with his slaves. Is that what Jesus was about, dispensing advice regarding investments and human chattel?

Jesus unambiguously condemns to death *and Hell* the Lebanese people who disliked his preaching, and simply because "they had not done penance" (Mt 11:20-23). Funny how often JC forgets about TSNK.

The NT (2 Cor 6:14-5) declares that non-Christians are infidels; thus, following Deuteronomy (13:6-9), *non-Christians must be executed,* as they "serve other gods." So the Bible demands execution of all non-Jews (which would include Christians), then demands execution of all non-Christians (which would include Jews).

And we have Jesus convicting you of thought crimes in Matthew 5:28, your only recourse being to pull your eyes out.

The writer of 2 John says (1:7) that non-Christians are antichrists: "For many seducers are gone out into the world who confess not that Jesus Christ is come in the flesh. This is a seducer and an antichrist," and "Whosoever revolteth and continueth not in the doctrine of Christ hath not God" (1:9). Sorry, Jains, Buddhists, Jews, non-theists—while you may seem very good and peaceful, you are actually godless and evil.

Jesus of Nazareth, perfect son of God, seems to have approved of threats and even torture. Examples follow:

> And his lord was wroth, and delivered him to the tormentors, till he should pay all that was due unto him. So likewise shall my heavenly Father do also unto you, if ye from your hearts forgive not every one his brother their trespasses. (Mt 18:34-35).
>
> Then the king said to the waiters: Bind his hands and feet, and cast him into the exterior darkness. There shall be weeping and gnashing of teeth (Mt 22:13).
>
> The lord of that servant shall come in a day that he hopeth not and at an hour that he knoweth not: And shall separate him and appoint his portion with the hypocrites. There shall be weeping and gnashing of teeth (Mt 24:50-1).
>
> And that servant, who knew the will of his lord and prepared not himself and did not according to his will, shall be beaten with many stripes (Lk 12:47).

I know; Christian apologists will read the above scriptures and declare "*you took them out of context*!" Or, another favorite, the "metaphor" or "parable" excuses. Why could not Jesus, son of God and our savior, have been perfectly clear and unambiguous?

Jesus condemns people to hell if they call others a *fool,* Mt 5:22:

> But I say unto you, That whosoever is angry with his brother without a cause shall be in danger of the judgment: and whosoever shall say to his brother, Raca, shall be in danger of the council: but whosoever shall say, Thou fool [Greek: μωρέ], shall be in danger of hell fire.

Yet, *Jesus himself calls people fools*. Was he therefore sent to hell for eternity (Mt 23:17 and Lk 11:40)?

> Ye fools [μωρέ /μωροὶ] and blind: for whether is greater, the gold, or the temple that sanctifieth the gold? Ye fools, did not he that made that which is without make that which is within also?

While reading the Bible, Stewie Griffin (of "Family Guy") proclaimed "I love God; he's so deliciously evil!" Stewie's observation was preceded 60 years by Winston Churchill's son Randolph. While in the military, friends challenged Randolph on a bet to read the Bible, mostly in hopes of shutting up the obnoxious and loquacious lad for a few weeks.[861] The plan backfired on his colleagues. One of his challengers was Evelyn Waugh who wrote to his friend Nancy Mitford in 1944:[862]

> In the hope of keeping him quiet for a few hours Freddy & I have bet Randolph £20 that he cannot read the whole bible in a fortnight. It would have been worth it at the price. Unhappily it has not had the result we hoped. He has never read any of it before and is hideously excited; keeps reading quotations aloud "I say I bet you didn't know this came from the Bible..." or merely slapping his side and chortling "God, isn't God a shit!"[863]

Quoting Psalms 135:27, "*Give glory to the Lord of lords: for his mercy endureth forever*"—bible evidence overwhelmingly to the contrary—Jesus, wasn't Jesus a *shit!*

Yes, Give glory to the Lord. The Old Testament repeats the phrase "I am the Lord" no fewer than one hundred and forty times. Reminders of God's greatness and rueful need of idolization permeate the scriptures. Bertrand Russell points out that Jesus has a "vindictive fury against those people who would not listen to his preaching."

I've seen so many people who erroneously state "*Love* was Jesus' central message." Clearly it was not. His prime advice can be summed up as follows:

- Drop everything right now, do nothing.[864]
- Leave your family. Also, *hate them*.[865]
- Follow me, I am the greatest man ever.[866]
- The world will end very soon.[867]
- Only fellow Hebrews are worth saving.[868]
- I can get you into Heaven.[869]
- *Or,* I can send you to Hell forever.[870]
- I'll be back.[871]
- SOON![872]

Face it, *God the First* wipes out his humans, and commands genocide and rape. *God the Second* damns you to eternal hell if you do not believe in him—or even if you simply have never heard of him. Thank you, Jesus. Thank you, Lord.

**Revelation**. An angel says in the book of Revelation, "And adore ye him that made heaven and earth" (14:7)—which further shows that "this God Person" (as Douglas Adams called him) is an egotistical non-entity in need of constant reassurance from the beings he supposedly made in His image. Reminders of God being very great and in pathetic need of idolization permeate the Good Book. Just one example:

> Saying with a loud voice: *Fear the Lord and give him honour,* because the hour of his judgment is come. And *adore ye him* that made heaven and earth, the sea and the fountains of waters. (Rev 14:7)

Homework assignment: Read the Bible, and count every time that it indicates that God is great, or that we should praise him.

An even better idea: Don't; and have a martini instead.

Indeed, *adore ye* this God who throws super-sized temper tantrums and kills indiscriminately, sometimes apologizing and promising never to do it again (as he did with the great flood). Next, *sometime soon,* he vows to repeat His acts of monstrous violence and murder—this time, he promises more than just an extreme weather phenomenon. His final act includes fire, brimstone, earthquakes, and a seven-headed dragon. Worship these Gospel verses from "Revelation," aka, the Apocalypse of St. John the Apostle (or some other John, as its authorship is unsure):[873]

> 9:17. And thus I saw the horses in the vision. And they that sat on them had breastplates of fire and of hyacinth and of brimstone. And the heads of the horses were as the heads of lions: and from their mouths proceeded fire and smoke and brimstone.
>
> 9:18. And by these three plagues was slain the third part of men, by the fire and by the smoke and by the brimstone which issued out of their mouths.
>
> 9:19. For the power of the horses is in their mouths and in their tails. For, their tails are like to serpents and have heads: and with them they hurt.
>
> 11:13. And at that hour there was made a great earthquake: and the tenth part of the city fell. And there were slain in the earthquake, names of men, seven thousand: and the rest were cast into a fear and gave glory to the God of heaven.
>
> 11:14. The second woe is past: and behold the third woe will come quickly.

11:18. And the nations were angry: and thy wrath is come. And the time of the dead, that they should be judged and that thou shouldest render reward to thy servants the prophets and the saints, and to them that fear thy name, little and great: and shouldest destroy them who have corrupted the earth.

11:19. And the temple of God was opened in heaven: and the ark of his testament was seen in his temple. And there were lightnings and voices and an earthquake and great hail.

12:3. And there was seen another sign in heaven. And behold a great red dragon, having seven heads and ten horns and on his heads seven diadems.

Please accept my apologies for not delving into the possible "interpretations" of these verses, perhaps being parables, or metaphors. They are obviously not worth wasting any time in analysis. There is nothing sacrosanct, metaphorical, or in any way exceptional about them. They are not parables nor brilliant poetry, but mere gibberish, an ancient *madman's dream* that, had it gone unrecorded, would have rendered the world a much better place. We are continually poisoned by this mote of semi-Christian scripture, handed down along the centuries for no logical nor philosophical reason whatsoever.

The God of the Bible has contradicted himself so many times and shown himself to be such an ignorant and vengeful fool, that the igneous and dark and fiery words of "St. John" simply put the last nails in the coffin: The Bible was, long prior to any of the papal bulls, itself *pure bull.*

Since the "historical facts" of the Bible all were purported to have occurred (but did not happen at all) only within the geographical area well-known to the Bible constructors (the Near East: the Ecumene, the "entire world" to those people), one can only extrapolate that John's apocalyptic events, prophesies, will also happen *only there,* in the general area the Levant. I feel somewhat safe then, living on the other side of the globe. When Jesus returns, He will still be completely ignorant of geography outside his freshman wanderings around Galilee. The mythical "end of the world" will simply affect the Near and Middle East! So, steer clear of Israel, Syria, and Egypt over the next generation.[874] After that, all will be cool; but the area around Judea will, it seems, consist of nothing more than a smoldering crater. Nevertheless, that crater will, I imagine, still be a holy one.

The Church is a *Machina ex Deus* that bases its existence, purpose, and philosophy on the Holy Bible, a Frankenstein-like text that appears to have been cobbled together by dozens of different morons who didn't attend the weekly meetings. As Mark Twain said, "It ain't the parts of the Bible that I can't understand that bother me, it is the parts that I do understand."

John, the supposed author of Revelation, wrote that "a Lamb stood upon mount Sion"—of course! Where else would *anything at all* happen on Earth according to Bible authors, but somewhere between Anatolia, Egypt, and Assyria? The lamb certainly could not stand on Broadway, or Moscow, or Perth! "Saint" John and other writers of the Bible did not know of Japan, Bermuda, the Americas, Hawaii, or Australia, but they were, of course, well familiar with the Near East, the "whole world" in the view of those simpletons, where everything in "recorded history" had taken place, from Adam and Eve, to Noah, to Solomon, to Jesus. Imagine how magical if John had written: "*a Lamb stood upon the grand icy continent at the south pole of the Earth, living peaceably among the penguins thereof*"—but of course, he knew nothing of any geography much farther south than Cairo.

Paul thinks (Rom 10:18) that the *entire world has been exposed to Christ's teachings*: "But I say: Have they not heard? Yes, verily: Their sound hath gone forth into all the earth: and their words unto the ends of the whole world." Paul supposedly wrote those words, some nineteen centuries ago. To Paul, the known "ends of the whole world" would be Gaza, Damascus, and Jerusalem. All walking distance from his hometown of Tarsus.

The Bible is the most absurd, simple, *sad,* and destructive text ever created. If the Bible offered some information that was presage, profound, truly scientific, or original, like concepts of DNA or germs or nutrition, the book may indeed hold some water, being perhaps worthy of apotheosis. But it consistently spews the opposite. 1 Corinthians 15:39 shows its distinct ignorance of DNA: "All flesh is not the same flesh: but one is the flesh of men, another of beasts, other of birds, another of fishes." Another example comes from

Leviticus 11:13-19 (mentioned previously) where God thinks that bats are birds.

**Why Humans Wrote The Bible.** The Bible is clearly man-made (who-else-made, after all?). God did not type up a nonsensical tome, then fax it to Earth. So, why did humans write such a strange and unbelievable book? This Q/A session has an obvious path. Ancient Hebrews longed for an *Earth User's Manual* for the same reasons the Greeks needed to invent Zeus and various gods and demigods; why American Indians had Tull 'Kale, and why Vishnu was invented by... the other kind of Indians, over there in India. All those ancient peoples attempted to answer the most profound of questions: Where did we come from? Why does stuff happen? Where do we go after we die?

You might just as well believe the divinations of Mattel's Magic Eight-Ball, as the "Holy Bible" cannot pull off the hat trick:

> ***Q:* Where do we come from? *A:*** God created the universe 6,000 years ago, *population two,* thinking it an adequately populated world. After Adam and Eve "sinned," they were allowed to copulate and had three sons, Moe, Larry, and Curly (wait, wait, don't tell me: it was Cain, Abel & Dim, Dim being really dim)—and those boys are the forefathers of all humanity.
>
> ***Q:* Why does crap happen? *A:*** Because God gets mad when people of His creation screw up. That's why he throws super-sized temper tantrums and kills indiscriminately. He sometimes apologizes for his mistakes, promising *never* to do it again. *Then he does it again.* That is why unexplainable bad crap happens: lightning, floods, disease, hurricanes, cancer, Hitler, premature balding, Disco, Rap, Sarah Palin.
>
> ***Q:* Where do we go after we die? *A:*** If you are an "A+" student, off to Heaven, wearing silver wings and living for eternity in bliss, playing the harp. However, if you had impure thoughts, labored on the Sabbath, died as an infant, or ate bacon, lobster, *or griffon,* you are destined to an eternity of intense punishment by God.

The Bible's teachings are infantile, self-contradictory, evil, and, in fact, worthless. So many of the verses cancel so many others out, such that it could be pared down to matchbook size:

- God created you, making you wicked and depraved, and you must repent all your life.
- Do not eat pigs, lobsters, shrimp, or sharks.
- Do not kill anybody.
- Kill all non-Jews.
- Kill all non-Christians.
- God loves you.
- God will get you someday, you evil bastard.

*Fun fact*: Jesus says If a woman becomes widowed, then re-marries, she is an adulterer (Mk 10:12).

## Polytheism in the Bible

Immediately upon opening my front door—and prior to any possibility of timely and polite introductions—a round and pink and smiling woman asked, "Did you know God has a first name?"

There stood before me two beaming Jehovah's Witnesses enthusiastically peddling their particular brand of gerin oil. "His full name is Jehovah God!" she continued, delighted about such notion. She seemed to imply that God is not simply a vague and mysterious white-bearded patriarch of the clouds who watches over us in infinite judgment. A good God salesperson *should* personify her deity, so that one can relate: Mister God has a first name, like we do! How cute is that?

Trying to be funny, I asked them what God's middle name was;[875] both Witnesses giggled obsequiously and moved on to their sincere preachments and an invitation to join weekly worship. Uninterested, I quickly dismissed them, sending the duo down the street and to their next victims.

In a way they were right about that one fact, His "first name." You will find God referring to Himself as "Jehovah" in Darby, ASV, YLT; but in other Bible versions as "Yahweh," or simply "the Lord." These are equivalent epithets; no cognomen controversy here. *Jehovah* equals *Yahweh,* equals *El,* equals *God, the Lord.* The One God, differently named here and there. Alas, this is not my current concern.

For no particular reason I prefer to refer to the divine dictator of Judeo-Christian beliefs as Yahweh. As we know from the Bible, He is a green-eyed and violent Deus, commanding "Thou shalt have no other gods before me" (Ex 20), death being His punishment for worshiping any other (Dt 17).

What does He mean, "other gods"? Is there not just the one—regardless what His real first name might be? Christianity is, after all, a monotheistic religion.

Or is it? Psalm 135 commands us to "Give glory to the Lord of lords." The Bible uses the definite article: "*the* Lord." It also says He is the "God *of gods*" (Dt 10), implying Jehovah H. God is, it seems, the *main god,* and there exist others that are rivals, or perhaps merely subordinate cohorts presiding from their own thrones On High (or slightly less elevated Highs). Are there any "other gods" mentioned in the Bible?

You betcha. Bertrand Russell described the Bible as "words written long ago by ignorant men." While I agree, I admit that I am impressed with the knowledge those men had regarding the many deities worshiped by their Hebrew ancestors and even by other nations. The OT presents us with a goddess named **Ashtoreth** (or Astarte) in 1 Kings 11, and 2 Kings 23. She is the Hebrew goddess of love and fertility, a pleasant notion; but also goddess of war.[876] The Bible claims she ruled over the Zidonians (people of Zidon, Lebanon). The main god, Yahweh, became infuriatingly jealous because those bastards, including righteous Solomon, had forsaken *Him* to worship *Her*. As a side note I feel compelled to mention that wise and great Solomon had 700 wives, 300 concubines and many "princesses" (1 Kings 11:3). And he wasn't even Mormon.

Old Testament scriptures are not alone in claims of other gods and goddesses. The New Testament holds a belief in **Diana**, who is "great," a goddess who "all Asia and the world worshippeth" (Acts 19).[877] Yet "her magnificence should be destroyed." What a shame, she sounds nice enough. Again from the New Testament we see that *gods* "come down to us in the likeness of men" and we see the deities **Jupiter** and **Mercurius** mentioned: see Acts 14.[878]

These are not the only supplemental gods admitted by the New Testament. Yahweh and Jesus have many biblical rivals on Olympus (or Mount Sinai, or Nebo, or whatever land enthrones all those deities). Perhaps surprisingly, Saint Paul admits (1 Cor 8:5) "there be gods many, and lords many." He follows up by claiming "But to us there is but one God, the Father." He's saying to ignore all the other gods that he admits do in fact exist. (Newer Bible versions change "there be gods many" to "there may be many so-called gods" as well as other attempts to "fix" Paul's original thoughts.)

**Goddess Diana: She's *great!***

It seems we are *meant* to worship and serve various deities including the sun, moon, and stars. Or perhaps we are *not allowed* to worship those astral gods—depending upon which scriptures you accept as sacrosanct:

> And lest thou lift up thine eyes unto heaven, and when thou seest the sun, and the moon, and the stars, even all the host of heaven, shouldest be driven to worship them, and serve them, which the Lord thy God hath divided unto all nations under the whole heaven. (Dt 4:19)

> If there be found among you, within any of thy gates which the LORD thy God giveth thee, man or woman, that hath wrought wickedness in the sight of the LORD thy God, in transgressing his covenant, And hath gone and served other gods, and worshiped them, either the sun, or moon, or any of the host of heaven, which I have not commanded. ...Then shalt thou ... stone them with stones, till they die. (Dt 17:2-5)

So: while we are *driven*—by God, our creator—"to worship them, and serve them," Yahweh commands us to kill anyone who does so. Was it not He who also commanded *thou shalt not kill*? Upon a solid reading of the Bible, I have concluded that He meant "thou shalt not kill *Hebrews*." Unless they work on the Sabbath, or perform witchcraft, or worship the sun, or... well, so many other reasons.

All the ancients worldwide concocted wild guesses for everything they could not explain. To them the sun was a god, the moon a goddess. They had no idea where their Sun god went at night, nor why the Moon goddess seemed to take His place.

What causes thunder? What is the rainbow for? Ancient Egyptians, Persians, Norse, Greeks, and Mayans had their theories, always supernatural, always guesswork, always wrong.

The Hebrews made up complex stories to support their own stabs in the dark: the rainbow was a "covenant from God" promising that He would never cause another global flood.

Those primitive men did not know what causes storms and wind and thunder. The second book of Kings introduces us to **Nehushtan** who is the god of Lightning:

> He removed the high places, and brake the images, and cut down the groves [*groves*: meaning goddess Asherah], and brake in pieces the brasen serpent that Moses had made: for unto those days the children of Israel did burn incense to it: and he called it Nehushtan (2 Kings 18:4).

Along with Yahweh, apparently the Sun-god and the Star-gods and goddesses rule the universe as co-deities (Psalm 136), and the *Main God* of the Hebrews is chummy with them, addressing those celestial deities personally: "He telleth the number of the stars; he calleth them all by their names" (Psalm 147). One of the Star-Gods mentioned in the New Testament (Acts 7) is **Remphan** (an Egyptian god identified as Saturn). Famed **Wormwood** is another Christian Star-god of the NT (Rev 8) whom C. S. Lewis appropriated in his *Screwtape Letters*, Wormwood joining uncle Screwtape, contriving to embody the uttermost of anti-Christian mischief: men behaving *very* badly.

Of course, another Star-god led wise men to the blessed nativity scene in that dark and drafty manger (Lk 2:7-14). She shone Her light to the magi, moved across the sky, then She paused right above baby Jesus (Mt 2:9). These celestial spirits seem anthropomorphic as they float in heaven, as we read in Revelation, as the Sun's strength is referred to as "his," not "its." I claim I do not assume too much here: Genesis 37 supports this anthropomorphization, as do many other scriptures.

The Moon is a female entity, a Hebrew goddess (Ezekiel 32, Isaiah 13, others). Not only does the Sun-god bring forth vegetation as one would expect from His light and warmth, but our lovely Moon goddess also brings some earthly benefit for mankind (Dt 33). I like to think Her mysterious gift is romance. (Note that the NRS version deleted this original reference to the Moon in its interpretation of Deuteronomy 33.)

The Sun and Moon are sentient gods, of course. For example they both followed the sanctimonious dictates of noble Joshua in his glorious genocidal exploits:

> Then spake Joshua to the Lord... in the sight of Israel, Sun, stand thou still upon Gibeon; and thou, Moon, in the valley of Ajalon. And the sun stood still, and the moon stayed... (Joshua 10:12-13).

As the psalmist croons (Ps 148), the Angels, the Sun-god, Moon goddess, and Star-gods—being deities slightly lower than Yahweh—should "praise Him." Mankind has a long history of loving and serving the Sun god and the Moon goddess, as attested in Jeremiah 8. The *New Oxford Annotated Bible* admits they are among the "astral deities" of the Bible.

In Second Kings 23, we see acknowledgement of several gods bestowed the blessed title **Baal**; and of the Sun god; of the Moon goddess; and Planet gods, unto whom priests burned incense. We find reference and reverence again to Baal in Numbers 25 and First Kings 16. Then we discover gods **Chemosh** and **Milcom**,[879] whom, along with Baal, you better not worship—*or else.*

Chemosh (sometimes *Shamash*) is the Hebrew Sun-god of Sippar and Moab to whom Solomon (apparently forgetting Yahweh is a jealous god) built a temple of worship:

> Then did Solomon build an high place for Chemosh, the abomination of Moab, in the hill that is before Jerusalem, and for Molech, the abomination of the children of Ammon. (1 Kings 11:7)

Surely you noticed: "*...and for Molech*." Solomon's shrine was not dedicated solely to Chemosh, but also held reverence for Hebrew god **Molech** (sometimes *Moloch*), a deity to whom children were sacrificed as burnt offerings, mentioned also in Leviticus 18 and Acts 7. God, it seems, needs cooked kids.

Within a single verse from Second Kings 17 we uncover a triumvirate of deities: Babylonian fertility goddess **Succoth-benoth;** next, Akkadian god of the underworld **Nergal**; finally Moon goddess **Ashima**. In the next verse the KJV reveals "**Adrammelech** and **Anammelech**, the gods of Sepharvaim," as well as **Nibhaz** and **Tartak**, gods of the Avites. Also within Second Kings we discover Assyrian god **Nisroch** (19:37) and Babylonian Storm-god **Rimmon** (5:18).

**Rahab** (Ps 87, Ps 89) is a sea monster; and let us not forget **Bel**, Babylonian god whose idol was "upon the beasts" (Isaiah 46).

**Who is Baal?** Perhaps the better question is *Who are the Baals*? In the simplex form, *Baal* is a deity who is the consort of mother Ashtoreth (e.g. Judges 2 and 6). Then there are the duplex forms, comprising a quinternion of Baal-*hyphen-something* gods.

Lord **Baal-berith** is mentioned in Judges 8:33 and 9:4. He is the Hebrew "God of the Covenant."

> And it came to pass,[880] as soon as Gideon was dead, that the children of Israel turned again, and went a whoring after Baalim,[881] and made Baal-berith their god.

Joshua introduces **Baal-gad** (chapters 11-13), a Semitic name for Pan the goat-lord:[882]

> Even from the mount Halak, that goeth up to Seir, even unto Baal-gad in the valley of Lebanon under mount Hermon: and all their kings he took, and smote them, and slew them. (Joshua 11:17)

The books of Numbers 25 and Deuteronomy 4 herald **Baal-peor** who is "Lord of the Cleft." **Baal-zephon** of Numbers 33 and Exodus 14 is not only a geographic location, but an Egyptian "Lord of the North."[883]

**Baal-hamon** was an ancient god slain as a surrogate for Babylonian god Marduk. Today Hebrews still perform ritualistic eating of

Baal-hamon's body in their *hamantaschen* cakes during Purim holiday.[884] [885]

**Gods Who Shine Brightest**. The Moon is a sentient goddess residing alongside Yahweh according to Psalm 89, a "faithful witness in heaven." Both the Moon and Sun are presented as attentive, living gods (Psalm 104). However, you should beware the Sun and the Moon, as they are both capable of smiting you (Psalm 120), just as our Main God so often has done to His children.

In Isaiah 24 we learn that the Moon and the Sun have human-like feelings. This should be no surprise, as they are in fact gods anthropomorphized:

> Then the moon shall be confounded, and the sun ashamed, when the LORD of hosts shall reign in mount Zion, and in Jerusalem, and before his ancients gloriously.

Note that the writer of Matthew believes stars are so tiny that they could fall "from heaven," landing on earth (24:29). The author of Revelation (6:13, 8:10, and 9:1) is under a similar misapprehension. Look up at the sky one night. Clearly the stars are but specks of light: miniscule things, dots of blue-white twinkle, yet worthy of worship for their might and gifts and mystery, as gods; yet Lilliputian in stature. Peace be upon them.

**The Prince(s) of Darkness**. Let us consider the Judeo-Christian god **Satan** (1 Chron 21, Job 1 and 2, Psalm 109, Zech 3, Mt 4, Mt 12, Mk 1, Lk 4, and so on). To test Job's faith, this apparently omnipotent and evil deity famously tricked omniscient God into inflicting heartache and pestilence upon Job, a god-fearing and gullible buffoon. Sixty years ago Carl Jung sufficiently answered Job's quandary, inferring that the character of Yahweh was a victim of "severe psychosis"—a logical conclusion that C. S. Lewis was not quite able to grasp.

Satan also tempted God's son Jesus (Mt 4), taking Him to a *very* high mountain, where they both could, despite real-world physics, see "all the kingdoms of the world." Because the Earth was flat. Back then.

Jesus seems to hold belief in Thor or some similar meteorological deity, as he gave nicknames to James and John, calling them the

"Sons of thunder" (Mk 3:17). Or perhaps he was simply making levity and metaphor.

In our enumeration of Judeo-Christian gods, we see there are *two* supernatural devils, as Matthew 12:26 mentions Satan, and in the next verse introduces **Beelzebub**. Milton mused on Beelzebub's subordinate status to Satan; poor fellow.

**Lucifer** (Isaiah 14:12) is in fact not one with Satan; He is the bringer of light, a god who announces the daily birth of the Sun-god.[886] Note that the NRS version has tampered with Isaiah, removing the name Lucifer and interpreting Him as the "Day Star" (meaning Venus). Canaanites called him Shaher; and the Jewish morning service of Sharit still commemorates him.[887]

**Hark the Herald Angels**. Angels are all over the place in the Bible, all possessing God-like powers. Very early in human history, Abram's wife Sarai (or Sarah) had been stricken with faulty fallopian facilities. So Yahweh (too busy to attend the task himself) assigned a subordinate angel to impregnate her maid Hagar. Hagar's son thus belonged to, and was given to Abram, naming him Ishmael (Gen 16).

The scriptures approve incest and rape, as we have seen. To mention just one case (apropos because it involves angels), Lot—to protect some haloed homies sent from heaven who had holed up in Lot's domicile by the gates of Sodom—sanctioned rape of his virgin daughters. The New Testament (2 Pet 2) considers Lot a "righteous man." As we explored before, this righteous dude addressed a crowd of horny men who were desirous to "know" those angels. Uninterested in Lot's *selfless* offer, the Sodomite men simply grumbled and disassembled. Virgin daughters of Lot? Screw that: those men lusted after *angel sex.* Don't we all?

It was not Yahweh but an angel who first appeared to Moses in the fabled incendiary shrubbery of Exodus chapter three. Not until Moses showed suspicion of the bewitching bush did God sigh, throw up his hands and finally agree to appear *himself* in the fiery thicket, announcing simply "Here am I" (Ex 3:4). *Also sprach Yahweh.*

It was not Yahweh alone who assisted the Hebrews in their violent genocide against the "Canaanite, the Amorite, and the Hittite, and the Perizzite, the Hivite, and the Jebusite" (surely those heathen bastards deserved to be slaughtered), but this theocratic military action was led by an angel sent by God to aid in His heavenly bidding (Ex 33).

Both the OT and NT mention perhaps the best-known angel, Gabriel, a heavenly spirit "sent from God" (Dan 8, Lk 1:19, and 1:26).

Another famed angel, Michael, makes a final appearance in Revelation 12: "...there was war in heaven: Michael and his angels fought against the dragon..."

Perhaps most famously, Joseph did not get Mary pregnant. The blessed virgin was *touched by an angel*: the Holy Ghost himself got lucky on that magical and romantic evening (Mt 1:20).

**More Gods of Monotheism**. The book of Numbers makes mention (32:3, 32:38) of Babylonian god **Nebo** who built his eponymous city in Jordan near a peak we refer to as Mount Nebo to this day.

Genesis 6 describes many "sons of God" who took human females as wives, and bore for them *Nephelim* (giants). Born of sons of God, are the Nephelim also deities? I am going to let these behemoths slide, excluding them from our ever-growing manifest of gods claimed within this monotheistic opus.

The god of vegetation **Tammuz**, who died and is always resurrected with each returning season, is introduced in Ezekiel 8:14. One of the months of the Hebrew calendar (harvest time) is named for Tammuz.[888] Incidentally, Tammuz was born of a virgin mother.[889]

Second Kings 23 offers **Asherah**, translated in KJV to "grove," but this god's name is maintained in NSRV, NLV, ESV, NASB, GWT, and other versions. Asherah is a fetish, or a "cultus" goddess.[890] She is the "Lady who traverses the sea"—she is the Moon.[891]

Exalted and all-powerful **Dagon** is a Syrian god of piscatorial form, a Serpent-god and chief rival of Hebrew god Yahweh, from Judges 16:23:

> Then the lords of the Philistines gathered them together for to offer a great sacrifice unto their god, and to rejoice: for they said, Our god hath delivered Samson our enemy into our hand.

Consider again the book of Job where we find several Star-Gods revealed by name: **Orion**, **Mazzaroth**, **Arcturus** and **Pleiades** (the Pleiades actually being *seven* goddesses)

> Canst thou bind the sweet influences of Pleiades, or loose the bands of Orion? Canst thou bring forth Mazzaroth in his season? or canst thou guide Arcturus with his sons? (Job 38:31-2)

**Josephus Weighs In**. In *Antiquities of the Jews,* first century "historian" Flavius Josephus gives his own version of the nonevents that the Torah purports to have occurred. He claims that *gods* destroyed the fabled Tower of Babel (Bk 1, 4:3). He writes of the "gods of Laban" (Bk. 1, 21:2), and "gods of the Midianites (Bk. 4, 6:6).

Josephus believes it all, retelling the story of Adam and Eve and talking snake, Noah's Ark, and the burning bush—"Moses was astonished at what he saw" writes our gullible Josephus (Bk. 2, 12:2). Josephus even believes the "Samson and Delilah" story. Perhaps you understand now why I feel compelled to enclose Josephus' supposed profession of "historian" in quotes. You'll recall that Samson's strength was *in his hair* (Judges 16:13-17). When Delilah Bobbitt cuts it off, it transforms the Samsonite fellow into an insecure 98-pound weakling. Same thing happened when Ted Danson began balding. Thank the gods for hair transplants.

**The God List**. To be technically accurate, we must add two more Christian gods to our compilation: *Jesus,* and the *Holy Ghost*. The Trinity explanation—the rationalization concocted in fourth century Nicaea—lumps them all together in a three-in-one Godhead. Even today Christians unreservedly accept this concept as a logical explanation for belief in a supernatural and conglomerated triumvirate of deities glommed together as one, maintaining the monotheism illusion so crucial to Christendom and its pillars of faith.

We can now collect and catalog the many true gods of Christianity:

Yahweh
Ashtoreth
Diana
Jupiter
Mercurius
Nehushtan
Remphan
Wormwood
Chemosh
Milcom
Molech
Succoth-benoth
Nergal
Ashima
Adrammelech
Nibhaz
Tartak
Nisroch
Rimmon
Rahab
Bel
Baal
Baal-berith
Baal-gad
Baal-peor
Baal-zephon
Baal-hamon
Satan
Beelzebub
Lucifer
Tammuz
Asherah
The Moon Goddess
The Sun-God
Pleiades
Orion
Mazzaroth
Arcturus
Jesus
The Holy Ghost
Angels
Planets
Star-Gods
Anammelech
Nebo

Perhaps Creationists are on to something: the universe is far too complex to have come about by accident. Its insipience may have required a holy host of deities, as one might affirm from this list of Judeo-Christian gods.

I think it is important to stress that these are not all simply ancient gods of the Hebrews and rival tribes, to be forgotten by Christians because they were Old Testament concoctions. Gods and demigods recognized by the New Testament include Diana, Jupiter, Mercurius, Remphan, Wormwood, Gabriel, Molech, an unnamed manger Star-god, the Angel who rolled away the stone, along with Satan, Beelzebub, and of course, many more "Angels" without explicit names. And do not forget Jesus and the Holy Ghost.

Thus we are presented at least forty-three *named* gods of the Bible; and since the Pleiades comprise seven goddesses, we may well add each to the list. This does not include the Planets (all being gods), many unnamed Angels, and innumerable Star-Gods not given specific names in the Bible.

I simply find all of this, without judgment, quite fascinating. Is Christianity a monotheist religion? Their holy book seems to indicate otherwise.

# CONCLUSION

Only a very terse wrap-up should be necessary after all this analysis and exegesis and exposition. Thus I append a succinct, if reedy coda.

It should be clear to even the most devout and inculcated reader that it is all up for Christianity, and in fact has been so for centuries. Its roots and foundation and rituals are borrowed from ancient cults: there is nothing magical or "God-inspired" about them. The "virgin birth prophecy" as well as the immaculate conception claims are fakeries, the former due to an erroneous translation of the Tanakh, the latter a nineteenth century Catholic apologetic contrivance, a desperate retrofitting.

Jesus was no perfect man, no meek or wise messiah: in fact his philosophies were and are largely immoral, often violent, as well as shallow and irrational. There have been many proposed sons of god, and this Jesus person is no more valid or profound than his priestly precursors. In fact, his contemporary Apollonius was unquestionably the superior logician and philosopher.

Christianity was a very minor and inconsequential cult founded late in the first century and then—while still quite minor—forced upon all the people of the Empire, and all rival kingdoms in the fourth century and beyond, as enforceable law with papal sanction.

Christianity has caused more terror and torture and murder than any similar phenomenon.

With its tyrannical preachments and directives for sightless and mindless obedience, the Bible is a violent and utterly useless volume, full of lies and immoral edicts and invented histories, no matter which of the many "versions" you may choose to read—including Thomas Jefferson's radical if gallant abridgment.

The time to stop teaching the tall tales and nonsense to children, frightening them with eternal torture administered by God's minions, has long ago passed. Parents who do so are likely deluded, and most surely are guilty of child abuse of the worst sort.

As Robert Ingersoll wrote, "If a person would follow, today, the teachings of the Old Testament, he would be a criminal. If he would strictly follow the teachings of the New, he would be insane." If I were to have heroes, Ingersoll would be among them, as well as Bertrand Russell and Thomas Paine, and, as you may well have guessed, Christopher Hitchens.

The "Jesus" person I hold among the least of possible heroes: in fact an anti-hero, a deluded mountebank, small-time thinker and quite possibly of fictional origin.

Christianity seems to have been little more than a hoax, fiction, oral legend. Mankind will someday grow up and relegate the Jesus tales to the same stewing pile that consists of Zeus and his son, Hercules.

# EPILOGUE

I would wager that the reader already had been familiar with the Crusades, Inquisitions, Witch Hunts, and many other Christian atrocities, but perhaps not to the extent that I have disclosed. I hope that you come away from this book stating several times, "I never knew that," or perhaps, as Randolph Churchill would remark during his first reading of the Bible, "God, isn't God a shit!"

Or perhaps, "Isn't Christendom a shit."

Bill Maher joked that God is not "a single parent who writes books." Isaac Asimov proclaimed "to surrender to ignorance and call it God has always been premature, and it remains premature today."

At age sixteen, Jessica Ahlquist of Rhode Island did *not* surrender to ignorance, taking a stance against accepted dogma. She created a FaceBook page to support an ACLU action regarding an illegal banner in her school promoting school prayer. Eventually Jessica brought a law suit against the obstinate institution after the Cranston School Committee took up the issue, yet voted to keep the illegal banner on display.

While Jessica was ultimately victorious in the law suit, the brave lass received hate mail and death threats in the interim, and even afterward. State Representative Peter Palumbo called Ahlquist "an evil little thing" on the radio.[892] When flowers were ordered to be delivered to Jessica, many local florists refused to fulfill their occupational and ethical obligation. How very Christian of them.

Jessica's plight drew many supporters, some manufacturing and selling "Evil Little Thing" t-shirts.

At the 2012 Reason Rally on the National Mall in Washington, D.C., Jessica was presented with a check for $62,618 to be used for her college education. The money had been raised from both the t-shirt proceeds and outright donations from her supporters. The "memo" line on the check read: *For Bravery*.

The rally's Master of Ceremonies, Paul Provenza, introduced Jessica, saying:

> Folks, that young lady, for standing up for her beliefs, and for standing up for her rights under the Constitution... was maligned, berated, degraded. It was despicable. She has suffered a lot of Hate.

Provenza then called Jessica to the stage, whereupon she addressed the crowd proclaiming "I have a confession to make. I am *Evil Little Thing.*" That sweet little thing, in front of a crowd of over 20,000, apologized for being the least experienced presenter at the rally, also stating she was "undoubtedly the smallest speaker here."

Now, Jessica is from Rhoda Island, not Mississippi or (as Joe Pesci put it in *My Cousin Vinnie*) Ala-fucking-bama. Yet she informed the crowd, "You can't imagine the things that I've heard in school: I walked down the hall and people said *eww, it's the atheist.*"

With much modestly and eloquence (and a beautiful and sincere smile) she announced,

> What I did can be done by anybody. I've made so many friends and this whole [rational/atheist] community has changed my life... and I could just talk all day about how thankful I am and that wouldn't be enough... for a person who felt completely alone, completely rejected by people in her school... even old friends. This community changed everything... and I know that forever and ever I'll always remember the very first Reason Rally, the biggest secular event in world history. And I'm so glad to be here. I love you, and you're all *Evil Little Things* to me.

She threw a kiss to the huge audience and walked off stage like a well-oiled champ. As the crowd cheered and applauded, Paul Provenza took the microphone again to shout "Jessica Ahlquist! I don't know, maybe it's me, but I think she deserves more love than that." The cheers and whistles and hollers thus grew in volume and passion.

And I was there: umbrella in hand in the rain, with eyes that began to fill with joyful tears, and such a feeling of pride and connection and solidarity.

And a sense of commonly held rationality, mixed among that godless and peaceful crowd of *evil things* in front of a stage full of reasonable and rational presenters, all being "evil" in the eyes of sincere believers.

It is clear that the major religions have plagued the world, stagnated society for centuries, and caused the murder of countless millions. The "Holy" Bible has been the chief enabler for the atrocities. The Bible is without doubt the most hateful, evil and harmful book ever written.

Religion has had its reign, having caused so much harm. Yet it marches on, poisoning civilization. Religion is—thank god—past its most influential and harmful apogee. It survives, but takes its last desperate breaths even now.

I call on Edward Gibbon to wrap this up:

> The popes themselves have indulged a smile at the credulity of the vulgar; but a false and obsolete title still sanctifies their reign; and, by the same fortune which has attended the decretals and the Sibylline Oracles, the edifice has subsisted after the foundations have been undermined (Gibbon, vol. V, 275).

# NOTES

1 "Atheism is a religion" some claim, seemingly in attempt to lower freethought to cultish and religious status. The rejoinder to this nonsense has been formulated, *If atheism is a religion, then not collecting stamps is a hobby*. There are many clever variations on this motif: "...then health is a disease," "then bald is a hair color," "then the off button on my TV is a channel," etc.

2 From "Beyond Belief" 2007.

3 As with any general group of people, there are of course exceptions.

4 Heyns Lecture Series, April 25, 2007.

5 Later we'll discuss Justice Scalia's mind in particular, seemingly infected with cognitive dissonance.

6 Digital Journal, Dec 2, 2011, digitaljournal.com/article/315425 retrieved Mar 8 2013.

7 Living in Richmond, Virginia, I believe.

8 Gavazzi, 25-49.

9 Williams, Henry Smith, 511.

10 Cumming, 158-9.

11 By the way, that YouTube commenter never replied to my remark.

12 The earth is not flat, nor is it the center of the universe. There was no global flood. The universe is much, much older than the ancients had speculated. Thousands of gods have been postulated. Disease is not caused by "devils" or "sin." Humans do not have two human ancestors, "Adam and Eve." Thunder, lightning, floods do not have supernatural causes. Human and animal sacrifices do not "please" any god, and killing children for being disobedient is simply and clearly immoral.

13 The *Catholic Encyclopedia* of 1907 (vol. 2, 40) provides a very honest and lucid definition of the term, without vilification: "...atheism, historically considered, has meant no more in the past than a critical or sceptical denial of the theology of those who have employed the term as one of reproach, and has consequently no one strict philosophical meaning; and though there is no one consistent system in the exposition of which it has a definite place; yet, if we consider it in its broad meaning as merely the opposite of

theism, we will be able to frame such divisions as will make possible a grouping of definite systems under this head. And in so doing so we shall at once be adopting both the historical and the philosophical view. For the common basis of all systems of theism as well as the cardinal tenet of all popular religion at the present day is indubitably a belief in the existence of a personal God, and to deny this tenet is to invite the popular reproach of atheism."

[14] Most of the "reasons" are enumerated in the millions of murders and ruined lives caused by religion.

[15] Thus for many centuries mere mortals believed this, setting back the work of Hippocrates and others, and thus Jesus was responsible for millions of deaths.

[16] Judge Elihu Smails perhaps said it best, in another context: "Well? We're waiting?"

[17] Dave Barry: Pulitzer Prize winner, brilliant humorist, prolific author, atheist.

[18] Wilkinson, 6-8.

[19] For example, Budge, *Book of the Kings of Egypt*, vol. 1, XII-XIII, and vol. I, XVIII.

[20] Note that when the Hebrew God was dictating his kosher food menu to Moses and Aaron, he failed to mention that humans should be, literally, off the table. Seems like the arduous text of Leviticus 11 could have been condensed and even improved upon by simply stating, "Two legs bad, four legs good. But don't eat pigs."

[21] Written beginning c. 1600 BCE.

[22] *Encyclopedia Biblica*, vol. IV, 4031-4032.

[23] See for example Good, et al, vol. X, entry "REM".

[24] For more see Barnes, 426.

[25] Phonetics and linguistics explain the slight variance and apparent coincidence.

[26] Walker, 508, 581-2.

[27] Jordan, 184.

[28] Smith, Homer, 230-1.

[29] Walker, 85-86. Another theory posits that the *hamantaschen* (German for "Haman's pockets") comes from the book of Esther: eating hamantaschen commemorates Haman's evil plans against the Hebrews.

[30] Note that *Encyclopedia Biblica* indicates "Shaddai" in Gen 43:14 is "a Redactor's interpolation" - *EB* vol. II, 3326.

[31] Jordan, 30-31.

[32] Walker, 66.

---

[33] Jordan, 41-42.

[34] See Cumont, Beck, Clauss, Nabarz, Gasquet, Ulansey, etc.

[35] Note that the *Encyclopedia Biblica* discards the Christian "shepherd" story of Luke: "So much having already been shown to be untenable it will perhaps be the more readily conceded that the story of the shepherds (Lk. 2:8-20), though one of great poetic beauty, cannot be regarded as historical." *EB* vol. III, 2964.

[36] *CE1907* vol. 13, 723.

[37] *Encyclopedia Biblica*, vol. IV, 5016.

[38] *CE1907* vol. 13, 722-723.

[39] Trobisch, *The First Edition of the New Testament*, 62.

[40] *CE1907* vol. 13, 722-723.

[41] *Bethulah*: the social condition of virginity; under guardianship of her *ba'al*.

[42] Isaiah 7:14 in the Septuagint - διὰ τοῦτο δώσει κύριος αὐτὸς ὑμῖν σημεῖον. ἰδοὺ ἡ παρθένος ἐν γαστρὶ ἕξει καὶ τέξεται υἱόν, καὶ καλέσεις τὸ ὄνομα αὐτοῦ Ἐμμανουηλ.

[43] The *Encyclopedia Biblica* debunks the virgin birth nonsense as follows: "Nor would Is. 7:14 have been sufficient to account for the origin of such a [virgin birth] doctrine unless the doctrine had commended itself on its own merits. The passage was adduced only as an afterthought, in confirmation. Moreover, it is fitted to serve the purpose at all only in the LXX [Septuagint], and the rendering virgin (παρθένος) must be rejected all the more because pregnancy before marriage is punishable with death according to Dt. 22:20-21, 22:23-24, a law which certainly is not later than Isaiah's time." - *EB*, vol. III, 2964.

[44] In its "Virgin Birth" article (vol. 15, 448-451), *CE1907* professes Catholic dogma holds Christ "incarnate by the Holy Ghost of the Virgin Mary," but later admits Isaiah does not contain a "real prophesy" of the virgin birth, and admits that "Jesus was really the son of Joseph and Mary"; and that there are theories that the Christ/virgin claims came from pagan fables and "extraordinary births of the heroes of other nations."

[45] See *CE1986*, 187 (mendacious about "almah"); and *CE1907*, vol. 15, 464C; and vol. 5, 404.

[46] See also Cumont, *Mysteries of Mithra*, 31-32; and Pörtner, 115.

[47] Cumont, *Mysteries of Mithra*, 34.

[48] Beck, 2050. This is likely Zoroastrian, from Persia, and perhaps not the Roman version, but nevertheless it is Mithraist, and surprisingly quite far west of original Mitra worship of the time.

[49] Gasquet, 84-85.

[50] See Godwin, 28; and Vermaseren, 104.

---

[51] Communion is the "fount and apex of the whole Christian life" according to *CE1986*, p. 198, and "a singular and wondrous conversion of the total substance of bread into the body and the total substance of wine into the blood of Christ, the external appearances only remaining unchanged" (583).

[52] Canon I, "Exposition of the Catholic Faith and of the dogma of Transubstantiation." *CE1907* vol. 9, 18.

[53] Note that in *A Short History* (p. 2), John Robertson wrote that allusions to Jesus being "risen" in 1 Corinthians 15 have "every mark of interpolation" and thus may be the words of a later forger.

[54] Exodus 19 speaks of God Almighty to "come down in the sight of all the people upon mount Sinai" in the third day after speaking to Moses, but nothing about a Messiah.

[55] Bernard, 104.

[56] Condon, 1.

[57] Knight, 60.

[58] Only in Matthew 1, 2, and 13; Mark 6; and Luke 1 & 2 (Luke likely being forgeries); yet never in John, nor in any of Paul's Epistles. Mary, saintly mother of Jesus, is a very minor character of the Bible. Yet I cannot drive from my home to the local grocery store without seeing several concrete or marble statues apparently depicting this holy mother of God positioned, it seems, within a cut-in-half bathtub.

[59] Compare the *CE1986*, a book of one volume, to the impressive two-foot long shelf of *CE1907* in fifteen volumes, composed by venerable historians and scholars.

[60] *CE1986*, 601. One wonders the difference between losing one's "physical" virginity compared to "spiritual" virginity.

[61] Joseph "knew her not till she had brought forth her firstborn son: and he called his name JESUS."

[62] Cartlidge, 5.

[63] Perriman, 106.

[64] For the full text of the inscription we have at Priene, Greece, see Fredrich.

[65] Philo, *On Flaccus*, VI:36 - "There was a certain madman named Carabbas, afflicted not with a wild, savage, and dangerous madness (for that comes on in fits without being expected either by the patient or by bystanders), but with an intermittent and more gentle kind; this man spent all this days and nights naked in the roads, minding neither cold nor heat, the sport of idle children and wanton youths..."

[66] See Price, *Deconstructing*, 242-6.

[67] Tosches, 19.

[68] Kalthoff, 21.

[69] Flavius Josephus, *Jewish War*, 2, 4:1.

[70] Tosches, 19.

[71] Tosches, 19.

[72] Mather, 44.

[73] Mt 27:51-54— "And, behold, the veil of the temple was rent in twain from the top to the bottom; and the earth did quake, and the rocks rent; And the graves were opened; and many bodies of the saints which slept arose, And came out of the graves after his resurrection, and went into the holy city, and appeared unto many. Now when the centurion, and they that were with him, watching Jesus, saw the earthquake, and those things that were done, they feared greatly, saying, Truly this was the Son of God." Note that Luke 23 has the centurion saying merely "Certainly this was a righteous man."

[74] For example, Hotema, 11. More on this in the subchapter on Apollonius.

[75] *CE1907* puts the start of Jesus' ministry between 777-779 AUC, or 24-26 CE, with his death the "fifteenth (or sixteenth) year of Tiberius" admitting a four-year uncertainty, the crucifixion being sometime between 25 and 29 CE. (*CE1907* vol. 8, 377-378.) Some of the more modern sources lean toward slightly later dates.

[76] Ellegård and others place Jesus about 100 years prior to the generally accepted first century time.

[77] Paul, in his Epistles, never hints at any dates for Jesus, nor any geographical locations for his supposed earthly visit. He does not seem to know when or where Jesus may have lived or died.

[78] "Take my yoke upon you, and learn of me; for I am meek and lowly in heart: and ye shall find rest unto your souls." - Mt 11:29.

[79] "Now I Paul myself beseech you by the meekness and gentleness of Christ, who in presence am base among you, but being absent am bold toward you." - Mt 12:42.

[80] "The queen of the south shall rise up in the judgment with this generation, and shall condemn it: for she came from the uttermost parts of the earth to hear the wisdom of Solomon; and, behold, a greater than Solomon is here."

[81] "He that loveth father or mother more than me is not worthy of me: and he that loveth son or daughter more than me is not worthy of me." - Mt 10:37.

[82] "And that servant, which knew his lord's will, and prepared not himself, neither did according to his will, shall be beaten with many stripes." - Lk 12:47.

[83] For some reason Jesus, the son of God, a magical and omnipotent *deity*, needs food, and is angered by a fig tree bearing no fruit.

[84] Christians sometimes claim the word "hate" is an inaccurate translation from the Greek. But the original Greek word in the NT is *miseo*: it means *hate*. For example, our English words *misogynist* and *misanthrope* derive from *miseo:* hate—of *gynia* (women) in the first example, of *anthropos* (mankind) in the second.

[85] Reinach, 242.

[86] The *Encyclopedia Biblica* rips Acts of the Apostles a new one: "According to [Acts] 22:9 his companions see the light from heaven but do not hear the voice of Jesus ; according to 9:7 they hear the voice but see no one and do not fall down ; according to 26:12-18 they fall down indeed with Paul, but it is he alone who sees the heavenly light, and hears the voice. This last account, moreover, represents him as having received at the time an explanation of what had occurred ; according to 22:14, he did not receive the explanation until afterwards, through Ananias.

"Further inconsistencies of statement are to be found when we compare the explanation of the departure from Jerusalem in 9:26-30 with that in 22:17-21 ; the account in I0:44 (etc) with that in 11:15 ... the explanation of the offering in 21:20-26 with that in 24:17 ; the accounts in 21:31-34 22:23-29 23:27 with 28:17, according to which Paul was, in Jerusalem, a prisoner of the Jews and not as yet of the Romans ; the occasion of the appeal to Caesar in 25:9-11 with that in 28:18. The liberation of Paul and .Silas from prison at Philippi (16:23-40) is not only a very startling miracle (with resemblances to what we read in Euripides, Bacchae, 436-441, 502 f., 606-628 [cp Nonnus, Dionysiaca, 45 262-285], regards Acts 16:35-39, in Lucian, Toxaris, 27-33), but is scarcely reconcilable with 1 Thess. 2:2, where the language of the apostle hardly suggests that his 'boldness in God ' was in any measure due to an occurrence of this kind.

"So much for inaccuracies that cannot be attributed to any tendency on the part of the writer. There are others and these of much greater importance which can only be so explained. Before discussing these, let us ascertain clearly what the tendency of the writer is..." - *EB* vol. I, 39.

[87] For example, Maccoby; and Peerbolte, 105.

[88] Regarding Christian fundamentalists believing everything Genesis says, comedian Jimmy Carr opines "I don't even think Phil Collins is a good drummer."

[89] Citing Jeremiah 27:9, Micah 5:11, and Malachi 3:5.

[90] Or so he claims, e.g. 2 Corintians 11:22, and Philippians 3:5. Maccoby makes a strong case that Paul lied about being a Hebrew.

[91] *Not* written by Matthew, mind you.

[92] For more, see for example Mack, *The Lost Gospel.*

[93] *Who looked in Jesus' tomb?* Four different stories. 1. Mary Magdalene and the other Mary (Mathew 28). 2. Mary Magdalene, and Mary the mother of James, and Salome (Mark 16). 3. "the women" (Luke 23-24). 4. "Mary Magdalene" (John 20). *What did they find there?* 1. They found an angel (Mathew 28). 2. They found a young man dressed in a white robe sitting on the right side (Mark 16). 3. They found two men "in shining garments" (Luke 23-24). 4. Mary found nothing (John 20).

[94] Mack, 15-27, and 34-36.

[95] Rather than *constructed,* a more correct term is *synthesized.*

[96] For more details, see Mack, chapter 5 for the sad truth of this misguided and self-proclaimed Messiah.

[97] Possibly much later. Homer Smith puts the Matthew author in the year 140 CE; Ellegård and others also place all the gospels in the second century. When one considers supposed "facts" like, *most historians believe the gospels were written in the first century,* one must realize that in the Western world the vast majority of historians are in fact Christians. They may, therefore, show some bias.

[98] Matthew 1:23 - ἰδοὺ ἡ παρθένος ἐν γαστρὶ ἕξει καὶ τέξεται υἱόν, καὶ καλέσουσιν τὸ ὄνομα αὐτοῦ Ἐμμανουήλ, ὅ ἐστιν μεθερμηνευόμενον μεθ' ἡμῶν ὁ θεός.

[99] E.g. Smith, Homer, 193.

[100] Pliny's *Letters*, bk. 10, Letter XCVII.

[101] Fomenko, 386-94.

[102] Ross.

[103] Brewer, 382.

[104] *CE1907* vol. 6, 463.

[105] It is possible Thallus lived during Augustus and Tiberius as some hypothesize (e.g. Collins, 51; Holladay, 343; *Oxford Classical Dictionary*, 434), and in such case he certainly should have written about Jesus and Christians, but did not do so.

[106] Mason, *Flavius Josephus*, 167.

[107] E.g. Luke 4:31, "And came down to Capernaum, a city of Galilee, and taught them on the sabbath days." Capernaum is northeast of Nazareth (thus it should have said *up*, or *over*; not *down*); Marcion claims Jesus came *down* from Heaven to Capernaum.

[108] See also Dungan, 43.

[109] Luke ch. 3 begins "Now in the fifteenth year of the reign of Tiberius Caesar..." which would make Jesus approximately thirty as we pick up on Jesus' life in his baptism tale, dunked by John the Baptist.

[110] See also Dungan, 44.

---

[111] Admitted by *CE1907* vol. 8, 580-582.

[112] Roberts, Alexander, 3.

[113] Dungan, 186.

[114] Roberts, Alexander, 6.

[115] Eusebius, Bk III, 3.6.

[116] Roberts, Alexander, 6-7.

[117] Note that a Bible version composed in the 4th century, dubbed the *Codex Sinaiticus*, included Shepherd of Hermas.

[118] *Shepherd of Hermas*, Similitude Fifth, e.g. Ch. V & VI.

[119] Targa, V.

[120] Romans 10:18.

[121] M. Minucius Felix, *Octavius*, Ch. 29.

[122] See also *CE1907* vol. 10, 336-7, "Minucius Felix."

[123] Dio, *Roman History*, LXXVIII, 9.

[124] Dungan, 50.

[125] Any clear-headed individual can grasp that there is no true revealed religion: all religions are man-made, some noble, but most being ill-conceived and primitive.

[126] Gibbon, vol. 1, 579.

[127] Dungan, 56-57, comes to basically the same interpretation of Porphyry.

[128] *CE1907* vol. 5, 395-396. Regarding the date, *CE1907* states "The exact year in which it was held is a matter of controversy upon which much has been written. Some copies of its Acts contain a date which corresponds with the year 324 of our reckoning; by some writers the council has accordingly been assigned to that year. Hardouin suggests 313, Mansi 309, and Hefele 305 or 306. Recent opinion... would put the date considerably earlier, from 300 to 303..."

[129] "Wives, submit yourselves unto your own husbands, as unto the Lord. For the husband is the head of the wife, even as Christ is the head of the church: and he is the saviour of the body." This may or may not have been written by Paul.

[130] Whitman, 29-30.

[131] Justice Scalia once stated that "government derives all of its authority from God." (*The Humanist*, March-April 2010, 20.) Scalia, it seems, did not go on to explain, among all the thousands proposed, exactly *which* god he means. As he is Catholic, one must assume he means the jealous and violent monster Yahweh, or perhaps one of the other three Christian deities.

[132] The original word in Greek was ἀγάπη, which could mean affection, affinity, fondness, liking, or love.

[133] Hernandez, 122.

[134] See also *CE1907* vol. 15, 675.
[135] The first *official* Crusade was 1096; second Crusade, 1145, etc.
[136] Smith, J. H., 58.
[137] *Cod. Theod.* xvi, 5, 46; 409.
[138] McDonald, Lee Martin, et al, 12.
[139] Dungan, 126.
[140] *CE1907*, vol. 4, 298.
[141] Panati, 68.
[142] Karageorghis, 189.
[143] Cumont, *Mysteries of Mithra*, 188.
[144] Vermaseren, 188-9.
[145] Gavazzi, 51.
[146] It is perhaps not surprising to discover that many people believe today that the 325 Council of Nicaea canonized the Bible. In *The DaVinci Code* (film version) it is stated that the men there assembled voted on which scriptures should be contained in the new Bible, and one "nay" vote would cause any scripture to be rejected. Indeed, upon reading Eusebius' writings on the Council and on scripture selection, it is easy to come away with the impression that the Bible was canonized at Nicaea. Eusebius was a deceptive author, probably forging and interpolating several texts, and perhaps wrote his works in order to convince readers that the Council was in fact responsible for creating the Bible. The Council was not.
[147] The writings of Josephus, so often employed as a champion of "proof" of Jesus by modern Christian apologists, were scrutinized by early Christian committees, but rejected. It seems likely that just after the Nicaean Council, Eusebius forged the "Jesus" references within Josephus' works.
[148] Eusebius, *Life of Constantine*, Bk. I, Ch. XXXVII: "Constantine, however, filled with compassion on account of all these miseries, began to arm himself with all warlike preparation against the tyranny. Assuming therefore the Supreme God as his patron, and invoking His Christ to be his preserver and aid, and setting the victorious trophy, the salutary symbol, in front of his soldiers and body- guard, he marched with his whole forces, trying to obtain again for the Romans the freedom they had inherited from their ancestors.

And whereas, Maxentius, trusting more in his magic arts than in the affection of his subjects, dared not even advance outside the city gates, (1) but had guarded every place and district and city subject to his tyranny, with large bodies of soldiers, (2) the emperor, confiding in the help of God, advanced against the first and second and third divisions of the tyrant's forces, defeated them all with ease at the first assault, (3) and made his way into the very interior of Italy."

[149] It has also been proposed, and is likely, that Eusebius invented this particular tale for his *Life of Constantine*: in *Ecclesiastical History*, his earlier work, there was no magical vision mentioned.

[150] Eusebius, *Life of Constantine*, Bk. I, Ch. XXIX: "He said, moreover, that he doubted within himself what the import of this apparition could be. And while he continued to ponder and reason on its meaning, night suddenly came on; then in his sleep the Christ of God appeared to him with the same sign which he had seen in the heavens, and commanded him to make a likeness of that sign which he had seen in the heavens, and to use it as a safeguard in all engagements with his enemies."

[151] *CE1907* vol. 3, 274.

[152] Renan, Bk 7, *Marc-Aurèle*, 579. Renan wrote: *on peut dire que, si le christianisme eût été arrête dans sa croissance par quelque maladie mortelle, le monde eût été mithraiaste.*

[153] *CE1986*, 151.

[154] *CE1907*, vol. 1, 42-43.

[155] Sopater's murder: some unknown date, but before 337.

[156] Lietzman vol. III, 138.

[157] Hernandez, 123.

[158] Hernandez, 123.

[159] *CE1907* vol. 16, 27.

[160] Hernandez, 123.

[161] Ehrman, *The New Testament*, 11.

[162] McDonald, et al, 291.

[163] *CE1907* (vol. 2, 35-40) provides a detailed chronology of Athanasius' life.

[164] Ehrman, *Misquoting Jesus*, 181-182.

[165] Dungan, 43.

[166] See also Ehrman, *Jesus Interrupted*, 112.

[167] For example, "And there appeared another wonder in heaven; and behold a great red dragon, having seven heads and ten horns, and seven crowns upon his heads. And his tail drew the third part of the stars of heaven, and did cast them to the earth: and the dragon stood before the woman which was ready to be delivered, for to devour her child as soon as it was born. And she brought forth a man child, who was to rule all nations with a rod of iron: and her child was caught up unto God, and to his throne. And the woman fled into the wilderness, where she hath a place prepared of God, that they should feed her there a thousand two hundred and threescore

days. And there was war in heaven: Michael and his angels fought against the dragon; and the dragon fought and his angels..." - Rev 12.

[168] *CE1907* vol. 14, 630.

[169] Hernandez, 124.

[170] Hernandez, 124.

[171] Walker, Barbara, 665.

[172] *Cod. Theod.* XVI, 7, 1.

[173] Schaff-Herzog, vol. 9, 259.

[174] *CE1907* vol. 8, 341.

[175] *CE1907* vol. 8, 341.

[176] Smith, Homer, 228.

[177] *CE1907* vol. 1, 303.

[178] Socrates Scholasticus, 5:16.

[179] Doane, 438-44, PDF version.

[180] Osman, xi.

[181] *CE1907*, vol. I, "Alexandrian Library".

[182] Taylor, Robert, 33.

[183] e.g. Panati, 131, 328.

[184] e.g. Hatonn, 18-9.

[185] Vallentin, 462.

[186] *CE1907* vol. 9, 163.

[187] Roscoe (388) has Leo saying "It is well known to all ages how profitable this fable of Christ has been to us."

[188] De Camp interprets Leo X as: "what profit has not that fable of christ brought us!"

[189] Hernandez, 128.

[190] Alexander, Edward, 11.

[191] Hernandez, 128.

[192] Dzielska, *Hypatia*, 103.

[193] Watts.

[194] Socrates Scholasticus, *Historia Ecclesiastica*, 7.15.

[195] Hernandez, 128.

[196] *CE1907* vol. 8, 26.

[197] Hernandez, 129.

[198] *CE1907* vol. 3, 555-558.

[199] Hernandez, 129.

[200] A life-long sun-worshiper, Constantine was baptized "Christian" on his deathbed, apparently "just in case"—Pascal's Wager in action.

[201] *CE1907* vol. 14, 370-371.

[202] *Codex Justinianus*, 1.5.12.

[203] Hernandez, 129-130.
[204] *CE1907* vol. 13, 579.
[205] *Codex Justinianus,* 1.11.10.
[206] *CE1907* vol. 2, 43.
[207] Hernandez, 130.
[208] Hernandez, 130.
[209] Alexander, Edward, 11.
[210] Haught, 43.
[211] Haught, 43-52.
[212] Marcus, Jacob Rader, 169.
[213] Smith, David Whitten, 63.
[214] Finn, 83-84.
[215] Coulange, 295.
[216] See also Manhattan.
[217] *CE1907* vol. 11, 663, "Pepin the Short."
[218] *CE1907* vol. 5, 118-119.
[219] *Encyclopedia Britannica,* "Donation of Constantine."
[220] *CE1907* vol. 5, 777-778.
[221] "...the emperor makes a present to the pope and his successors of the Lateran palace, of Rome and the provinces, districts, and towns of Italy and all the Western regions..." - *CE1907* vol. 5, 119, on the "Donation."
[222] "...finally, on 20 September, 1870, Rome, having been taken by force of arms, declared its union with the Kingdom of Italy..." - *CE1907* vol. 8, 234.
[223] *CE1907* vol. 3, 615.
[224] *CE1907* vol. 5, 773-780.
[225] Guettée, 258-262.
[226] *CE1907* vol. 5, 773-780.
[227] Due to historical ambiguities, Stephen VII is sometimes referred to as Steven VI.
[228] Guettée, 343.
[229] *CE1907* vol. 14, 289.
[230] *Time,* "Massacre of the Pure," Friday, Apr. 28, 1961.
[231] Witt, Ronald, 212.
[232] A note on the Crusades: I do not intend to give a detailed history about them. Many other books cover this topic completely; I reservedly present some of the more interesting acts and facts regarding the Christians and their noble Crusades.
[233] Wheless, 545.
[234] McGoldrick, 48.
[235] Brenon, 85.

[236] *CE1907* vol. 8, 29.
[237] Rafiabadi, 157-8.
[238] Haught, 26.
[239] Johns, E. Neville, 84.
[240] *CE1907* vol. 13, 42.
[241] Robertson, Alexander, 214.
[242] Gavazzi, 25-49.
[243] Williams, Henry Smith, vol. VIII, 511.
[244] Innocent III, Letter 126 (July 12, 1205, to the papal legate).
[245] Maseko, 485.
[246] *Time* magazine, "Massacre of the Pure," Friday, Apr. 28, 1961.
[247] Catharist texts in our possession include: 1. The "Cathar Bible" (*la Bible Cathare*) in Occitan (French dialect of Languedoc); a copy is preserved at Lyon, consisting of an Occitan translation of the complete New Testament from the Latin Vulgate. 2. The Book of the Two Principles (*Livre des Deux Principes*), theorizing absolute dualism; we have a copy in Florence. 3. An apocryphal "Last Supper Secret" (*Cène Secrète*) from the eleventh or twelfth century, including "heretic" Catharist dualistic beliefs. 4. The Lyon Ritual (*Rituel de Lyon*) of Catharist liturgies. 5. The "Cathar Treaty" (*Traité cathare*), an anonymous collection of quotations for pastoral use. 6. A "Ritual of Florence" (*Rituel de Florence*), being Latin liturgies. 7. A Ritual of Dublin (*Rituel de Dublin*) in Occitan.
[248] Victor, Jeffrey S., and Russell, Jeffrey Burton.
[249] The "official" period of genocide against the Cathars ended after twenty years with the 1229 Treaty of Paris. The Inquisition was established in that same year primarily to promote the continuation of the genocide, to seek out and execute Cathars wherever Christian authorities could pursue them. As *CE1907* indicates, the Church had wiped out almost every last one by the fourteenth century.
[250] *CE1907* vol. 4, 543 and 550.
[251] *CE1907* vol. 8, 28-29.
[252] In fact they were not Manichaean: "With the new sources, one can be assured that the accusations of Manichaeanism were nothing but Inquisition propaganda." ("*Avec ces sources nouvelles, on se rend compte que les accusations de manichéisme n'étaient que propagande de l'Inquisition.*") - *Le Pointe*, "Cathares: de l'hérésie au mythe," August 10, 2006.
[253] *CE1907* vol. 1, 268.
[254] Voltaire, "Essai sur les mours et l'esprit des nations" (1756) - "Le jésuite Daniel, en parlant de ces infortunés dans son Histoire de France, les appelle infâmes et détestables. Il est bien évident que des hommes qui volaient ainsi

au martyre n'avaient point des mœurs infâmes. Il n'y a sans doute de détestable que la barbarie avec laquelle on les traita, et il n'y a d'infâme que les paroles de Daniel. On peut seulement déplorer l'aveuglement de ces malheureux, qui croyaient que Dieu les récompenserait parce que des moines les faisaient brûler."

[255] Reinach, 76 and 319-320.

[256] *Time*, op. cit.

[257] Levack, 41-42.

[258] "...qu'il n'y avait rien de plus injuste que la guerre contre les Albigeois." Voltaire, op. cit.

[259] Smith, John Holland, 66.

[260] Cheney, Christopher Robert, 378.

[261] Pierson, 113.

[262] Tice, xii.

[263] *CE1907* vol. 4, 550.

[264] *CE1907* vol. 13, 112.

[265] *CE1907* vol. 9, 18.

[266] Thomsett, 118.

[267] *CE1907* vol. 6, 797.

[268] *CE1907* vol. 6, 797.

[269] Mackay, 474.

[270] Gardner, 248.

[271] *CE1907* vol. 14, 283-284.

[272] *Epistles of St. Gregory the Great*, Book IX, Letter 122.

[273] *CE1907* vol. 8, 34.

[274] Innocent IV, Law 25.

[275] From antiquecannabisbook.com/chap2B/Church/Ad_Extirpanda.htm retrieved Mar. 21, 2013.

[276] Innocent IV, Law 31.

[277] *CE1907* vol. 14, 665.

[278] Hillhouse, 90-1.

[279] *CE1907* vol. 15, 675.

[280] *CE1907* vol. 15, 676.

[281] Dean, Trevor, 70.

[282] Megivern, 123.

[283] *CE1907* vol. 15, 126.

[284] Lea, Henry Charles, vol. 3, 115-120.

[285] Weis, Rene.

[286] Brenon, 160-1.

[287] Lea, Henry Charles, vol. 2, 254-256.

[288] Pitstick, 314.
[289] Choi, 45.
[290] *CE1907* vol. 5, 119; and vol. 12, 768.
[291] *CE1907* vol. 7, 90-92.
[292] Thomas, Hugh, 59-65.
[293] Regenstein, 74.
[294] Frazer, 656 (1922 edition).
[295] Robbins, 337.
[296] Johns, Fleur, 22.
[297] Crawford, 235-253.
[298] Guiley, 379.
[299] Kenz, 10.
[300] Blickle, *passim.*
[301] *CE1907* vol. 11, 597-8.
[302] Herzog, vol. III, 432-5 ("Peasant's War").
[303] Hensarling, 35-37.
[304] Estep, 50-54.
[305] "*The*" Inquisition is a false notion. There were several Inquisitions established by the Church of Rome: not merely the famed and much feared Spanish Inquisition.
[306] *CE1907* vol. 8, 26.
[307] Guiley, 380.
[308] *CE1907* vol. 3, 274.
[309] *CE1907* vol. 4, 498.
[310] *CE1907* vol. 12, 769.
[311] Downey *et al*, 68.
[312] *CE1907* vol. 13, 607.
[313] Guiley, 380.
[314] Myers, 379-80.
[315] Bloomfield, 12-14.
[316] Hawthorne, vol. 1, 20.
[317] Knecht, 91.
[318] Council of Trent's "Index of Prohibited Books," Rule 3.
[319] That is, without glasses, and possibly with a beard and longer hair. As far as we know.
[320] Corbett, Julian Stafford, vol. 1, 249-260.
[321] Haught, 66.
[322] Sagan, 86.
[323] Wedgwood, 496.

---

[324] JP = *Julian Period*. 4714 JP = 1 CE, and 1 JP = 4713 BC. For more, see Bond, John James, 258.
[325] Roth, Cecil, 124-126.
[326] Smith, Homer W., 294.
[327] Hill, Frances, 83.
[328] Thornton, John Kelly.
[329] Mobley, 47-58.
[330] Roth, Cecil, 126.
[331] Palou.
[332] Marsh, 1.
[333] Ryba, 117-118.
[334] Palou, 83.
[335] *CE1907* vol. 5, 409-10.
[336] De Patmos, John, *The Great Disappointment of 1844*.
[337] De Patmos; see also Knight, George R., *Millennial Fever and the End of the World*.
[338] Chin, et al.
[339] Reilly.
[340] *CE1907*, vol. 13, 169.
[341] O'Donnell, 7.
[342] Fitzpatrick, 25.
[343] Borrero, 66.
[344] Casement.
[345] Ewans, 238.
[346] Ewans, 24.
[347] *Freethought Today*, April 1990.
[348] *Free Inquiry*, vol. 30 (Aug/Sept 2010), 12.
[349] While they are at it, how about introducing Ahmadinejad to a clothing store other than Good Will, where he appears to buy his Western attire.
[350] Magness, 25-26.
[351] *Associated Press*, January 1 1977, "Vatican Rejects Art Objects Sale To Help The Poor."
[352] The "National Commission on Disappeared People" -- I realize they are desperately in need of a name change.
[353] *The Independent*, David Usborne, "Argentina's disappeared: Father Christian, the priest who did the devil's work." 11 October 2007.
[354] Shahid.
[355] Kapeliouk, 94.
[356] Shahid.
[357] Kapeliouk, 98.

---

[358] Kapeliouk, 94.

[359] Kitzmiller v. Dover Area School District, decided December 2005 by Judge John E. Jones III, a conservative Republican.

[360] *CNN*, "Tony Robbins: Practicing What He Preaches," aired January 7, 2001.

[361] Read *The Missionary Position* or watch "Hell's Angel," both by Hitchens, and you'll understand my own, non-missionary position on Teresa.

[362] *ThirdWay*, "A certain martyr?" by Paul Vallely. Oct 2003. vol. 26, No. 8, p. 5.

[363] LeVay, 370.

[364] *Washington Post*, "Salvi Convicted of Murder in Shootings," March 19, 1996, A01.

[365] *CNN*, "Eric Robert Rudolph: Loner and survivalist," December 11, 2003.

[366] *New York Times*, "Doctor's Killer Tries to Make Abortion the Issue," January 13, 2007.

[367] *Huffington Post*, "George Tiller Killed: Abortion Doctor Shot At Church," 05-31-09.

[368] Bakker, ch. 5.

[369] *ABC-7 Chicago*, "Lemak found guilty of killing three children," December 20, 2001.

[370] Pliny, c. 111 CE, referred to Christianity as a "degenerate sort of cult carried to extravagant lengths," being "wretched" (*Bk. 10, Letter XCVI*, Radice translation). What, exactly, separates a "cult" from a "religion"? Many clever answers have been proposed, with which I shall not bore you.

[371] *The Age*, "Religious axe killer jailed." December 23, 2004.

[372] *Taipei Times*, "Devout atheist-slayer sentenced to jail." Dec 24, 2004.

[373] *World Press*, Science Notes: "Followup to the murder of Larry Hooper." August 28, 2010.

[374] Steven Wells, *Philadelphia Weekly*, "Taking the Christ out of Christmas." Dec. 19, 2007.

[375] *Chicago Tribune*, "Update: Debra Gindorf, 1,710 days later...," December 21, 2007.

[376] *Albany Herald*, "Looking Back Oct. 31," October 31, 2010.

[377] *New York Times*, "Arkansas Executes a Woman Who Killed Both Her Children," May 3, 2000.

[378] *Houston Chronicle News Services*, "Not without precedent," July 1, 2001.

[379] *O, The Oprah Magazine*, "A Cry In the Dark," February 2002.

[380] *Cincinnati Enquirer*, "Woman accused of killing daughter, 6," April 03, 2002.

[381] *Associated Press*, "Doctor says mom who killed sons mentally ill," March 31, 2004.

[382] *USA Today*, "Doctor: Woman says God wanted her to cut baby's arms," February 20, 2006.

[383] In The Court Of Appeals Of Indiana, No.45A03-0609-CR-00411. Appeal From The Lake Superior Court Criminal Division, Room 3 The Honorable Diane Ross Boswell, Judge Cause No. 45G03-0507-MR-00008.

[384] See for example, *Associated Press*, "Power of prayer flunks an unusual test," 2006.

[385] *Free Inquiry*, Oct/Nov 2009, vol. 29 No. 6, 22-23.

[386] *CNN U.S.*, "Custody of snakebite orphans split between grandparents," February 12, 1999.

[387] *KETV*, "Ivan Henk Admits to Killing Brendan Gonzalez," April 29, 2003.

[388] Washburn County Court, case number 2011CM000125.

[389] "Husband apparently kills family, himself no one saw any warning signs in the *nondescript family*." Associated Press, Feb 4, 2005.

[390] *CBS News*, "D.C. Woman: 'Demons' Possessed Slain Girls," Jan. 11, 2008.

[391] *The Greenville News*, "Woman Says Jesus Told Her to Kill Her Husband," May 29, 2008.

[392] *PubMed*, US National Library of Medicine National Institutes of Health, "Child witch hunts in contemporary Ghana," September 2011.

[393] *Wordpress*, February 23, 2011, "Witchcraft, Displacement and Human Rights Network."

[394] IRIN, "Rights: Child witchcraft allegations on the rise," p. 71. Dakar, 16 July 2010.

[395] IRIN, "Malawi: Suspected witches jailed," 6 April 2011.

[396] Associated Press, "Shooter's Mom Asked Church for Help Healing Her Son." May 7, 2007.

[397] *Northwest Creation Network* - nwcreation.net/museums.html - retrieved Mar 2013.

[398] *The Four Horsemen* discussion (2007), Episode 1.

[399] Pullella, Philip, "Vatican Defends Pope Condoms Stand, Criticism Mounts." Reuters, March 18, 2009.

[400] Dennis, vol. III, 361-362.

[401] Sanford, 13.

[402] Stephanson, 42.

[403] Stephanson, 49-50, 58.

[404] See also Sanford, 44; and Weinberg, 74, 77, 85, 111, 149.

[405] Thomas, Hugh, 455.

[406] Sanford, 15-17.

[407] Weinberg, 74.

[408] For example, the textbook *A Patriot's History of the United States from Columbus's Great Discovery to the War on Terror* (Schweikart and Allen) uses the word "genocide" one time—referring to the Nazi holocaust. In *A History of the American People* (Johnson) the word appears once, in the discussion on

the Viet Nam War. In *The Complete Book of U.S. History* (American Education Publishing) the word never appears.

[409] Powers, 173-191.

[410] Drew, 355-68.

[411] Denevan, 1-12.

[412] Thomas, 523.

[413] Stannard, 11.

[414] This quote by Si'ahl is pervasive in our texts, has no evidence of authorship; it nevertheless expresses the philosophy of most Native American tribes.

[415] Díaz, 454.

[416] Kimberly McCloud, et al, *CNS Reports*, "WMD Terrorism and Usama Bin Laden," 7 March 2001.

[417] Boyett, 54.

[418] *Associated Press*, "Manager: Men spewed anti-American sentiments," 14 September 2001.

[419] *New York Times*, April 20, 1999.

[420] Paterson, James, 378.

[421] Smith, Homer W., 228-9, 253.

[422] Johns Hopkins University, *Modern Language Notes*, vol. 23, 82-85.

[423] See The Young Turks episode for Robertson's unreal thoughts, retrieved May 22, 2013: http://www.youtube.com/watch?v=59NCduEhkBM

[424] Schormann, 71.

[425] Levack, 1.

[426] Hansen, 12.

[427] Levack, 22.

[428] Just by example: "And they utterly destroyed all that was in the city, both man and woman, young and old, and ox, and sheep, and ass, with the edge of the sword" (Joshua 6:21) — commanded by god.

[429] "Then began he to upbraid the cities wherein most of his mighty works were done, because they repented not: Woe unto thee, Chorazin! woe unto thee, Bethsaida! for if the mighty works, which were done in you, had been done in Tyre and Sidon, they would have repented long ago in sackcloth and ashes. But I say unto you, It shall be more tolerable for Tyre and Sidon at the day of judgment, than for you. And thou, Capernaum, which art exalted unto heaven, shalt be brought down to hell: for if the mighty works, which have been done in thee, had been done in Sodom, it would have remained until this day. But I say unto you, That it shall be more tolerable for the land of Sodom in the day of judgment, than for thee." - Mt 11:20-24.

430 "Ye have heard that it was said by them of old time, Thou shalt not kill; and whosoever shall kill shall be in danger of the judgment: But I say unto you, That whosoever is angry with his brother without a cause shall be in danger of the judgment: and whosoever shall say to his brother, Raca, shall be in danger of the council: but whosoever shall say, Thou fool, shall be in danger of hell fire." - Mt 5:21-22.

431 "And he said unto them, Full well ye reject the commandment of God, that ye may keep your own tradition. For Moses said, Honour thy father and thy mother; and, Whoso curseth father or mother, let him die the death: But ye say, If a man shall say to his father or mother, It is Corban, that is to say, a gift, by whatsoever thou mightest be profited by me; he shall be free. And ye suffer him no more to do ought for his father or his mother; Making the word of God of none effect through your tradition, which ye have delivered: and many such like things do ye." - Mark 7:9-13.

432 Jesus is big on accusing people of hypocrisy. The word *hypocrite(s)* (ὑποκριταί) appears over a dozen times in the Gospels. He even calls you a hypocrite if you "pray standing in the synagogues" or "in the corners of the streets." - Mt 6:5.

433 Ingersoll, *The works of Robert G. Ingersoll,* Volume 4, 20.

434 "As therefore the tares are gathered and burned in the fire; so shall it be in the end of this world. The Son of man shall send forth his angels, and they shall gather out of his kingdom all things that offend, and them which do iniquity; And shall cast them into a furnace of fire: there shall be wailing and gnashing of teeth. Then shall the righteous shine forth as the sun in the kingdom of their Father. Who hath ears to hear, let him hear." - Mt 13:40-43.

435 C. S. Lewis, *Mere Christianity.*

436 "I will therefore put you in remembrance, though ye once knew this, how that the Lord, having saved the people out of the land of Egypt, afterward destroyed them that believed not. And the angels which kept not their first estate, but left their own habitation, he hath reserved in everlasting chains under darkness unto the judgment of the great day. Even as Sodom and Gomorrha, and the cities about them in like manner, giving themselves over to fornication, and going after strange flesh, are set forth for an example, suffering the vengeance of eternal fire. Likewise also these filthy dreamers defile the flesh, despise dominion, and speak evil of dignities." - Jude 1:5-8

437 "The God of this people of Israel chose our fathers, and exalted the people when they dwelt as strangers in the land of Egypt, and with an high arm brought he them out of it. And about the time of forty years suffered he their manners in the wilderness. And when he had destroyed seven nations

in the land of Chanaan, he divided their land to them by lot." - Acts 13:17-19.

[438] Witch hunts: 4,000,000; Crusades: 1,500,000 at a minimum; Inquisition: at least 50,000 and more likely much higher. Total: around six million, simply for this small segment of religious barbarity.

[439] *CSPAN-2 Book TV*, "Is Christianity the Problem?" November 2007.

[440] Okay, I admit it: not *humbly*, but usually assertively, sometimes arrogantly. This is my prerogative as a freethinking humanist, I contend.

[441] "The lord of that servant will come in a day when he looketh not for him, and at an hour when he is not aware, and will cut him in sunder, and will appoint him his portion with the unbelievers. And that servant, which knew his lord's will, and prepared not himself, neither did according to his will, shall be beaten with many stripes. But he that knew not, and did commit things worthy of stripes, shall be beaten with few stripes. For unto whomsoever much is given, of him shall be much required: and to whom men have committed much, of him they will ask the more."

[442] Franklin, 49.

[443] Postma, 41.

[444] Postma, 35.

[445] See also Taylor, 37, arriving upon approximately the same number.

[446] Phillips, 34-35.

[447] Philip, 189.

[448] Postma, 45.

[449] Taylor, 32.

[450] Walvin, 16-17.

[451] Blake, 166.

[452] Rawley, 257.

[453] Postma, 22-25.

[454] Taylor, 17-19.

[455] Postma, 28.

[456] "And call no man your father upon the earth: for one is your Father, which is in heaven" (Mt 23:9). "Neither be ye called masters: for one is your Master, even Christ" (Mt 23:10).

[457] Taking into account chromosomes, physical characteristics, and sexual orientation there are many "types" of people. Consider just two: (1) XY chromosomes, with penis, male breasts, bisexual; and (2) XXX chromosomes, vagina, female breasts, lesbian. You can see the number of permutations or combinations is large - in fact at least 4*3*2*4 = 96.

---

[458] "Nevertheless death reigned from Adam to Moses, even over them that had not sinned after the similitude of Adam's transgression, who is the figure of him that was to come." - Romans 5:14.

[459] Not to mention "Abel," admitted in the NT to be one of Adam's sons (Mt 23:35), and do not forget the entirety of the fictional "genealogy" of Jesus in Luke ch. 3.

[460] Senator John McCain spent over five years in a Vietnam prison, tortured severely, resulting in permanent damage to his arms. Jesus had it *really easy* by comparison. Moreover we are told Jesus is in "heaven" now. McCain is much more of a savior than "Jesus" it seems to me -- and I am not even a Republican.

[461] Again, one cannot ignore the fact that Luke traces Jesus' bloodline all the way back to the Genesis fairy-tale character "Adam."

[462] Note that the *Didache* foreshadowed the centuries of child rape and cover-ups by church clerics that would follow: "thou shalt not corrupt boys, thou shalt not commit fornication" (Ch. 2), and "be not a liar" (Ch. 3).

[463] Christian apologists typically attempt to redefine that word, *generation*, but this wheel-spinning is both perfidious and pointless, as elsewhere Jesus made the same claims without uttering the word—all will come true, Christ declared, before his followers would "taste of death" (Mt 16:28, Mk 9:1, Lk 9:27). I do believe all people of the first century have in fact tasted of death. This seems to be the reason the legendary "wandering Jew" was concocted.

[464] I consider Christianity to be a cult of death worship because they worship the death of their Savior, as well as their own pending deaths, which will result in transportation to "heaven."

[465] The phrase "unto this day" in Mt 27:8 and 28:15 is also a strong indication that considerable time had passed since the events supposedly being discussed and the time they were written.

[466] Smith, J. H., 17.

[467] Copernicus, Nicolaus, *De revolutionibus orbium coelestium*, 1543 CE.

[468] Irenaeus, *Against Heresies*, 2.XXVII.1

[469] Polycarp, 7:1.

[470] 'Epistle of Polycarp to the Philippians' is the work of an unknown hand, in the spirit of the epistles of Ignatius, though not, in view of the differences in style and language, by the same author, as a sequel to that group, and not, as has been conjectured, with the object of recommending them, or of controverting Docetism. ...The epistle is a well-meant, though by no means important, composition of the edifying order, made up in great part of borrowed words, and in no respect showing much independence, written

after Polycarp's death about the middle of the second century, and before Irenaeus... therefore, about 160 A.D." - *Encyclopedia Biblica*, vol. III, 3713.

[471] *CE1907* vol. 12, 219, "Polycarp" -- "*rejecting the epistle as spurious on account of the anachronism...*"

[472] Waite, 57 and 61.

[473] However this viewpoint is not undisputed; Bible scholar David Trobisch makes a case that Polycarp, an experienced publisher and authoritative figure in the early Christian community, may have published the first edition of the New Testament. Thus, while his *Epistle* is the only work that comes down to us, Polycarp may have been in possession of some Christian writings.

[474] Tertullian, "The Prescription against Heretics" Ch. 7.

[475] Meredith, Evan P., 426.

[476] Meredith, Evan P., 427.

[477] Philo, *On Flaccus*, VI (36-43).

[478] Friedlander, xii.

[479] Bigg, *The Christian Platonists of Alexandria*, 49-50.

[480] Reinach, 228.

[481] Cheyna, vol. II, 1219.

[482] Tylor, 101-102.

[483] Budge, *Gods of the Egyptians*, vol. 2, 220.

[484] Wilkinson, 201.

[485] Budge, *Gods of the Egyptians* vol. 1, 481.

[486] Budge, *The Book of Opening of the Mouth*, vol. 2, 14.

[487] Churchward, 135.

[488] Massey, *Ancient Egypt, the Light of the World*, vol. 1, 472.

[489] Walker, Barbara, 750.

[490] Massey, *Ancient Egypt, the Light of the World*, vol. 1, 472-473.

[491] Massey, *Ancient Egypt, the Light of the World*, vol. 1, 486.

[492] Note that Genesis was written some 500 years later.

[493] As mentioned earlier, compare to Adam; as the glyphs are transliterated phonetically, this comparison is valid.

[494] Lefébure, vol. 9, 176.

[495] Massey, *Gnostic and Historic Christianity*, 113.

[496] Lefébure, Volume 9, 178-9.

[497] Osman, 304-5.

[498] Cotterell, 98, 282.

[499] Bigg, *The Christian Platonists*, 49-50.

[500] Friedlander, xii.

[501] Evans, 54.

[502] Suetonius, *The Twelve Caesars*, "Nero," XVI.

[503] Pliny, *Letter XCVII.*

[504] For more on Mithras and Sandan in Tarsus, see: Plutarch, *The Parallel Lives*, "The Life of Pompey," §24-25; Pörtner, 115; Holzner, 10; and Frazer, vol. IV, 124-127 (1922 printing).

[505] Ware, and Kent, vol. 55, 52-61.

[506] Nabarz, 8-9.

[507] Nabarz, 2.

[508] Vermaseren, 13.

[509] Reinach, 65.

[510] Vermaseren, 13.

[511] In fact the *CE1907* states (vol. 2, 156) that Mithrian virtues ("truth and open-handed generosity") still flourish "exceedingly in the small, but highly intelligent, community" in India.

[512] *CE1907* vol. 10, 402.

[513] Mead, 15.

[514] Godwin, J., 98.

[515] Cumont, *Mysteries of Mithra*, 9, 190.

[516] *CE1907* vol. 10, 402.

[517] *CE1907* vol. 10, 404.

[518] Cumont, *The Oriental Religions in Roman Paganism*, 161 and 199.

[519] Nabarz, 52.

[520] Plutarch, The Parallel Lives, "The Life of Pompey", 24-25.

[521] Beck, 2050.

[522] Reinach, 72-3.

[523] Cumont, *Mysteries of Mithra*, 188.

[524] Smith, J. H., 19.

[525] Morford, 344.

[526] Pörtner, 115.

[527] Vermaseren, 11.

[528] Smith, H. W., 128-9.

[529] Ahura-Mazda (God) and Mithra are called "the two great ones." Rawlinson, 33.

[530] Smith, H. W., 130.

[531] Hall, 38.

[532] *CE1907* vol. 10, 404.

[533] Vermaseren, 75.

[534] Cumont, *Mysteries of Mithra*, 179.

[535] Campbell, vol. 3, 259–61.

[536] McCabe, 49.

[537] Robertson, *Pagan Christs*, 338-9.
[538] Maitland, 63.
[539] Nabarz, 2, 4-6, 19, 48, 100-102.
[540] Cumont, *Mysteries of Mithra*, 127.
[541] *Catholic Encyclopedia*, vol. X, 404 ("Mithraism").
[542] Cumont, *Mysteries of Mithra*, 131.
[543] *Catholic Encyclopedia*, vol. X, 403 ("Mithraism").
[544] Vermaseren, 77.
[545] Campbell, vol. 3, 261.
[546] Nabarz, 19.
[547] Cumont, *Mysteries of Mithra*, 132.
[548] Nabarz, 19.
[549] Beck, R., from Temporini, II 17.4, 2002-2115.
[550] Cumont, *Mysteries of Mithra*, 145-6, 160.
[551] Campbell, vol. 3, 261.
[552] Morris, Charles, 60.
[553] Forty, 94.
[554] Cumont, *Mysteries of Mithra*, 2-5.
[555] Cumont, *Mysteries of Mithra*, 2-6.
[556] *Oxford Classical Dictionary*, 992.
[557] Cumont, *Mysteries of Mithra*, 137, 191-3.
[558] *CE1907*, vol. 10, 404 - "Mithra saved the world by sacrificing a bull; Christ by sacrificing Himself." This particular *CE1907* article then goes on to say "Christ was born of a Virgin" supposedly in contrast to Mithra: "there is nothing to prove that the same was believed of Mithra..." (We see disagreement in Cumont, Campbell, McCabe, Robertson, Maitland and Nabarz, all showing Mithra's mom was a virgin.) Yet *CE1907* admits elsewhere that Jesus was in fact *not* born of a virgin: "Jesus was really the son of Joseph and Mary" and "virgin claims came from pagan fables" (vol. 15, 448-451).
[559] Forty, 94.
[560] Cumont, *Mysteries of Mithra*, 5.
[561] *CE1907*, vol. 10, 404.
[562] Cumont, *Mysteries of Mithra*, 3-6.
[563] Cumont, *Mysteries of Mithra*, 6, 172-3.
[564] Cumont, *The Oriental Religions in Roman Paganism*, 157.
[565] Cumont, *Mysteries of Mithra*, 6-7.
[566] *Catholic Encyclopedia (1907)*, Vol X, 404. ("Mithraism")
[567] Cumont, *Mysteries of Mithra*, 167, 191.
[568] Cumont, *Mysteries of Mithra*, 137-8.

[569] *Catholic Encyclopedia (1907)*, Vol X, 403. ("Mithraism")
[570] Vermaseren, 98-9.
[571] *Oxford Classical Dictionary*, 991.
[572] Cumont, *Mysteries of Mithra*, 158.
[573] Vermaseren, 99-100.
[574] Cumont, *Mysteries of Mithra*, 158.
[575] Cumont, *Mysteries of Mithra*, 160.
[576] Campbell, vol. 3, 260.
[577] Godwin, 106.
[578] Carpenter, 21.
[579] Cumont, *Mysteries of Mithra*, 160.
[580] Godwin, 103.
[581] Smith, William, *et al*, vol. IV, 619.
[582] Smith, J. H., 77.
[583] Cumont, *Mysteries of Mithra*, 167, 191.
[584] Matthews, 52.
[585] Smith, J. H., 24.
[586] Nabarz, 58.
[587] Cumont, *Mysteries of Mithra*, 167.
[588] Forty, 86.
[589] Cumont, *Mysteries of Mithra*, 138-40.
[590] Vermaseren, 105-6.
[591] Cumont, *Mysteries of Mithra*, 140.
[592] *CE1907*, vol. 10, 403.
[593] Wallis, 259.
[594] *CE1907*, vol. 10, 403.
[595] Smith, J. H., 20.
[596] Cumont, *Mysteries of Mithra*, 138, 191.
[597] Walker, 315.
[598] Walker, 315.
[599] Cumont, *Mysteries of Mithra*, 138, 191.
[600] *CE1907*, vol. 10, 402.
[601] Smith, H. W., 130.
[602] Mead, 15.
[603] e.g. Trobisch, David, "Who Published the New Testament?" *Free Inquiry*, Jan 2008, Vol 28, no 1, p 33.
[604] Churchill, Winston, vol. 1, 29.
[605] Cumont, *Mysteries of Mithra*, 187.
[606] Funk & Wagnalls, vol. 17, 412-3.
[607] Cumont, *Mysteries of Mithra*, 173.

[608] Morford, 344.
[609] Smith, Homer W., 227.
[610] *CE1907* vol. 10, 402.
[611] Mead, 16.
[612] Larson, 416.
[613] Unlike Christianity: Ex 22:18, Lv 20:27, Dt 18:10, Lv 19:31, Lv 20:6, Lv 20:27, 1 Sam 28:3, 2 Chron 33:6, Micah 5:12, Gal 5:20.
[614] Vermaseren, 189.
[615] Smith, Homer W., 224-5.
[616] Beck, from Temporini, 614.
[617] Cumont, *The Oriental Religions in Roman Paganism*, 160.
[618] Vermaseren, 188.
[619] Renan, 579.
[620] Clauss, 170.
[621] Vermaseren, 11.
[622] The 3 BCE - 97 CE dates are according to Philostratus. Note that Dzielska with reasonable evidence pushes Apollonius' dates forward by several decades, perhaps born 40 CE and dying in 120 (Dzielska, *Apollonius*, 32-38).
[623] Sator, 82.
[624] John 2 – Jesus turns water into wine. Matthew 21:18-19 seems to indicate Jesus hates figs: "Now in the morning as [Jesus] returned into the city, he hungered. And when he saw a fig tree in the way, he came to it, and found nothing thereon, but leaves only, and said unto it, Let no fruit grow on thee henceforward for ever. And presently the fig tree withered away."
[625] "Moeragenes" or Μοιραγένει in Philostratus, I.3—or "Meragenes," in Waite 103; or "Moiragenes," Dzielska, *Apoll.*, 45.
[626] *Suda*, Sigma 877.
[627] Dio, *History*, 67:18:1.
[628] Herzog concurs, writing, vol. I, 232 - "...there is no evidence that Philostratus had any knowledge of the Gospels and the Acts, and the life of Apostle Paul is a much closer parallel to Apollonius than that of Christ, who was no peripatetic philosopher."
[629] Aurelius, *Meditations*, 1:8.
[630] *Diana* in some versions, *Artemis* (the Greek version of Roman Diana) in others.
[631] Sorry, that second part came from Clarence Beeks in "Trading Places." Jesus commands only that you pull out your eyes. The dogma and superstitions within Christianity are what cause followers to piss on their brains.
[632] Waite, 115.
[633] Jones, Christopher, *Letters*, 25.

[634] Riedweg, 125; and Waite, 112.

[635] Dzielska, *Apollonius,* 58-59.

[636] Sator, 83.

[637] Trickler, 216-217.

[638] See for example Elsner, 660-1.

[639] For example, I came upon a modification to the Wikipedia article on Apollonius in March 2009. Some frustrated vandal modified the article, warning that the information was not to be trusted and "IT CAN HAVE ALL KINDS OF WRONG INFORMATION!!!!!!" (all caps). This edit was corrected with dispatch.

[640] V. Bhattacharya, *The Āgamaśāstra of Gaudapāda,* LXXII-LXXIV. A few years ago I added this fact to Apollonius' Wikipedia entry. And you are welcome.

[641] Bowie, from Temporini, II 16.2, 1687-8.

[642] Dzielska, *Apoll.,* 58.

[643] Bowie, from Temporini, II.16.2, 1670.

[644] Priaulx, 2.

[645] Reitzenstein, 40.

[646] Bowie, from Temporini, II 16.2, 1690.

[647] Priaulx, 62.

[648] Dion, *Oration* 31:122.

[649] Eilhard Lumin, *Ex Officina Commeliniana,* a text from the year 1601 CE: *Epistolae Apollonii Tyanei, Anacharsidis, Euripidis, Theanus, aliorúmque ad eosdem.* Heidelberg: Ex officina Commeliniana, 1601. See LC Control No. 2008570706, call number PA3487 .E4 1601, Jefferson Collection (Rare Book/Special Collections Reading Room [Jefferson LJ239]).

[650] E.g. Bowie, from Temporini, II 16.2, 1688.

[651] "Siddhartha" is a shortened form of "Sarvarthassiddha," meaning *Perfect Prosperity.* See Beal, 54.

[652] Morris, Charles, 153.

[653] Forty, 146.

[654] Morris, Charles, 154.

[655] Proving she is a vaginal-tract virgin, of course.

[656] Jackson, 79.

[657] Whitney, 18, footnote 11.

[658] Hardy, 146. "Golden caskets, ... tiaras...

[659] Whitney, 18.

[660] Hardy, 146.

[661] Doane, 207.

[662] Beal, 103-4.

[663] Evans, Elizabeth, 29.

[664] Evans, Elizabeth, 29.
[665] Campbell, vol. 3, 354.
[666] Whitney, 42, 76.
[667] Evans, 49.
[668] Doane, 11.
[669] Forty, 146.
[670] Doane, 293.
[671] Matthew 5:17: "Do not think that I am come to destroy the law, or the prophets. I am not come to destroy, but to fulfil."
[672] Hardy, 306.
[673] Luke 16:16: "The law and the prophets were until John. From that time the kingdom of God is preached: and every one useth violence towards it." *And so many other similar contradictions.*
[674] Doane, 293.
[675] Smith, Homer W., 227.
[676] Oxford Classical Dictionary, 479.
[677] Otto, 65-7.
[678] Guthrie, W.K.C., 115, 174-5
[679] Morris, Charles, 71.
[680] Burdick, vol. XXVIII, 701.
[681] Forlong, 415.
[682] Buxton, 81.
[683] Lietzmann vol. III, 321.
[684] Oxford Classical Dictionary, 479.
[685] Oxford Classical Dictionary, 479.
[686] Doane, 221.
[687] Guthrie, W.K.C., 180-1.
[688] *Oxford Classical Dictionary*, 480.
[689] *Oxford Classical Dictionary*, 480.
[690] Euripides, *The Bacchae*, lines 548-50.
[691] Williams, George M., 70.
[692] Bharati, Part I, 136, and Part II, 24.
[693] Evans, 28.
[694] Morris, Charles, 37.
[695] Williamson, 21-22.
[696] Tuttle, 225.
[697] Jackson, 79.
[698] Carpenter, 24.
[699] *The Madras Journal of Literature and Science*, Volume 16, 267. Madras: Christian Knowledge Society's Press, 1850.

[700] Williams, George M., 185.
[701] Lipner, 134.
[702] Williams, George M., 187.
[703] Carpenter, 24.
[704] Bharati, Part I, 32.
[705] Lipner, 258.
[706] Bharati, Part I, 170-9.
[707] Lipner, 135-6.
[708] Higgins, vol. 1., 129-30.
[709] Williamson, 22.
[710] Cox, 135.
[711] Williams, George M., 187.
[712] Williams, George M., 187.
[713] Carpenter, 17.
[714] Doane, 186.
[715] Williams, George M., 188
[716] Higgins, vol. 1., 130
[717] Lipner, 134
[718] Morris, Charles, 73; see also 29-30.
[719] Hardwicke, Herbert Junius, "The God Idea," *The Agnostic,* Vol 1. No. 1 (January 1885), p. 445.
[720] Forty, 316.
[721] Taylor, Robert, *The Diegesis*, 193.
[722] Hannay, James Ballantyne, *Symbolism in Relation to Religion*, 302.
[723] Doane, 193.
[724] Buxton, 55.
[725] Forty, 258.
[726] Frazer, 346.
[727] Frazer, 346-349.
[728] Matthews, 55-6.
[729] Hardwicke, Herbert Junius, "The God Idea," *The Agnostic,* Vol 1. No. 1, p. 445 (January 1885).
[730] Jackson, 65.
[731] Frazer, 347.
[732] Morris, Charles, 72-3.
[733] McCabe, *The Myth of the Resurrection,* 14-17.
[734] Jackson 67.
[735] Forty, 72.
[736] Frazer, 351.
[737] McCabe, *The Myth of the Resurrection,* 14.

[738] Godwin, 122.
[739] Frazer, 351-2.
[740] Forty, 258.
[741] Frazer, 346-8.
[742] Pausanias, *Guide to Greece.*
[743] Frazer, 350.
[744] Forty, 46.
[745] Allen, *Horus in the Pyramid Texts*, 12.
[746] Budge, *Gods of the Egyptians*, vol. 2, 206.
[747] Smith, Homer W., 36.
[748] See also Higgins, vol 1., Bk VI, Ch IV.
[749] Kuhn, 35.
[750] Reinach, 73.
[751] Morris, Charles, 14.
[752] *New Englander and Yale Review*, No. CCXXVIII, January 1890 (p. 275-6).
[753] ibid., 280.
[754] "... and thy desire shall be to thy husband, and he shall rule over thee..."
[755] "Let your women keep silence in the churches... And if they will learn any thing, let them ask their husbands at home: for it is a shame for women to speak in the church..."
[756] "... ye wives, be in subjection to your own husbands..."
[757] Josephus, *Antiquities of the Jews*, Preface, 3.
[758] Mason agrees, writing that he was "sloppy at times, sometimes went off on tangents" and "contradicted himself." Mason, *Josephus and the New Testament*, 29-30.
[759] Josephus, *Antiquities of the Jews* (interpolated version), xviii 3.3.
[760] Regarding Damneus, see also Doherty, *Neither God not Man*, 572-5.
[761] Van Voorst, 83.
[762] He's referring to Graham H. Twelftree's article in *Gospel Perspectives: The Jesus Tradition Outside the Gospels*, David Wenham, editor. Sheffield: Sheffield University Press, 1982. As I am literally going to press in a few days I have no time in this edition to follow that up.
[763] See Price, *Case Against*, 60.
[764] For example, Robert M. Price in *The Christ Myth Theory and its Problems*, 31, as well as others.
[765] Painter, 133-134.
[766] Chilton and Evans, 235.
[767] The Talmud writers were quite befuddled regarding Jesus, confusing him with two men: Jesus ben Pandira, and Jesus ben Stada, who were

undoubtedly real. One of them may have been the character that the Jesus stories used as their central character; perhaps, even both.

[768] Walker, Barbara, 750.

[769] Evans, 54.

[770] Friedlander, xii.

[771] "Their line is gone out through all the earth, and their words to the end of the world. In them hath he set a tabernacle for the sun." - Ps 19:4.

[772] See Appendix for references.

[773] "And, behold, the veil of the temple was rent in twain from the top to the bottom; and the earth did quake, and the rocks rent; And the graves were opened; and many bodies of the saints which slept arose, And came out of the graves after his resurrection, and went into the holy city, and appeared unto many. Now when the centurion, and they that were with him, watching Jesus, saw the earthquake, and those things that were done, they feared greatly, saying, Truly this was the Son of God." - Matthew 27:51-4.

[774] Ehrman, *Jesus Interrupted,* 48.

[775] *Encyclopedia Biblica,* vol. 2, 2543.

[776] Note that contrary to Philostratus and traditional belief, Apollonius may indeed have lived slightly after Jesus' supposed time, *almost* a contemporary; see Dzielska, *Apollonius,* 32-38.

[777] The *Encyclopedia Biblica* points out that "real" Jesus would never have performed miracles: "The miracle of the wine at Cana is shown at once to be unhistorical by the express statement that Jesus definitely refused to work 'signs' such as this is expressly called in Jn. 2:11" - *EB,* vol. III, 2966.

[778] Temporini/Feldman, II.21.2, 787.

[779] The "500 witnesses" and "apostles" claims of 1 Corinthians 15 were later interpolations by Christian forgers - e.g. Price, *The Case Against,* 235-239, and Robertson, *A Short History,* 2.

[780] "Behold my hands and my feet, that it is I myself: handle me, and see; for a spirit hath not flesh and bones, as ye see me have" (Lk 24:39).

[781] e.g. Gasquet, 32-33, and Holzner, 10.

[782] That is, if Paul was in fact the disputed author of this revered mote of scripture. Epistle to the Hebrews may well be the work of some other first or second century author.

[783] The *Encyclopedia Biblica* holds the view that Paul wrote *none of the epistles* attributed him (Vol. III, 3625-6), stating: "With respect to the canonical Pauline epistles, the later criticism here under consideration has learned to recognize that they are none of them by Paul; neither fourteen, nor thirteen, nor nine or ten, nor seven or eight, nor yet even the four so long 'universally' regarded as unassailable. They are all, without distinction,

pseudepigrapha, (this, of course, not implying the least depreciation of their contents).

[784] See Dungan, 43-44.

[785] Maccoby is comprehensive on this subject.

[786] Magness, 34.

[787] Maccoby, *passim*.

[788] *CE1907* vol. 9, 130.

[789] *CE1907 vol.* 12, 768.

[790] Noting that George A. Wells, a very respectable historian and Bible expert, has recently retreated from this position; see *Free Inquiry* June/July 2012, vol. 32, No. 4, in his review of Ehrman's *Did Jesus Exist?* Professor Wells now believes "there really was a man Jesus but that we can know very little about him" (p. 59).

[791] Dungan, 69.

[792] Dungan, 83.

[793] Eusebius, *EH,* 3.25.1-7: "The Divine Scriptures that are accepted and those that are not."

[794] *EH*, 3.26.1-4.

[795] *EH*, 3.27.1.

[796] *Catholic Encyclopedia*, Preface.

[797] *CE1907* vol. 3, 274, "Canon of the New Testament".

[798] Trobisch, *Paul's Letter Collection,* 4.

[799] Flavius Josephus, *The Antiquities of the Jews*, XVIII.

[800] Ehrman, *Jesus Interrupted*, 48.

[801] The 1907 *Catholic Encyclopedia* explains that Logos "is the term by which Christian theology in the Greek language designates the Word of God, or Second Person of the Blessed Trinity". (Vol 9, 328-9.)

[802] Athenagoras, *A Plea For The Christians,* Ch. XIII.

[803] "Now there is at Jerusalem by the sheep market a pool, which is called in the Hebrew tongue Bethesda, having five porches. In these lay a great multitude of impotent folk, of blind, halt, withered, waiting for the moving of the water." (Jn 5:2)

[804] Horne, 28-9.

[805] "For an angel went down at a certain season into the pool, and troubled the water: whosoever then first after the troubling of the water stepped in was made whole of whatsoever disease he had." (Jn 5:4)

[806] Taylor, Joan E., 221-65.

[807] Bagatti vol. 1, 272-310.

[808] Chancey, 83.

[809] Robertson, John M., *A Short History of Christianity*, 11.

---

[810] Mt 23:36, 24:34, 16:27-28, Mk 9:1, Lk 21:32, 1 Thess 4:17.
[811] *EB,* Volume I, 259.
[812] *EB,* Volume 6, 658 and 656.
[813] See Ehrman, *Jesus Interrupted,* 287; Smith, Homer, 180; and Ellegård, *passim.*
[814] For example, Watson, 24-25.
[815] Eusebius, *Commentary on the Gospel of Matthew,* VI, 25.4-5.
[816] *EH,* 3.24.5.
[817] Acts 9:3-4, 12:7-10, 16:29, 22:1-22, 26:13-16, Gal 1:11-17, 2 Cor 12:1-3.
[818] E.g. Drolsum, 110; and Borg, 64-67.
[819] Wasson, 33.
[820] *Vita Apollonii,* 1:7.
[821] Galatians 1:18 (DRC).
[822] In 2 Cor 12:2 Paul writes "I knew a man in Christ above fourteen years ago, (whether in the body, I cannot tell; or whether out of the body, I cannot tell: God knoweth;) such an one caught up to the third heaven." He is speaking of his drugged-out experience of an apparition of the "Messiah."
[823] Romans 1:5.
[824] Romans 1:16.
[825] See Hillhouse, 7-8.
[826] Genesis 17:10-14.
[827] *New York Times,* August 26, 2005; and January 6, 2006.
[828] Thomas Zambito, "Infant's Death at Maimonides Hospital Linked to Circumcision," *New York Daily News,* Saturday, March 3, 2012.
[829] 2 Corinthians 12:16—"But be it so, I did not burden you: nevertheless, being crafty, I caught you with guile."
[830] Roscoe, 388; De Camp, 399.
[831] "Pope Benedict XVI is richer than Bill Gates at least 20 times," retrieved Mar 5, 2013 - christianreforms.wordpress.com/2011/01/10/total-wealth-of-vatican
[832] The *Catholic Encyclopedia* of 1907 (vol. 15, 281-286) claimed "The Vatican works of art represent in their entirety an irreplaceable treasure, which is not actively at the disposal of the Curia, but passively in their possession, since the repair and maintenance of these objects make great claims on the resources of the Holy See. Those who proclaim the riches of the Curia should know that, though the works of art are worth many hundred millions, they have no market value. The Holy See, notwithstanding its difficult financial position, values too highly its civilizing mission to divest itself of these treasures, which are being constantly increased." *Many hundreds of millions* in 1907 - let's say just 500 "hundred million" - represents some $1.3 trillion in 2013 dollars, accounting solely for inflation effects on its artwork.

[833] Darryl Eberhart, Editor of ETI & TTT, agrees, writing "Its wealth (e.g., gold, stock shares, banking assets, real estate holdings, precious art treasures and manuscripts, etc.) is incalculable."

[834] Genesis 9:12-14.

[835] Freud, *Die Zukunft einer Illusion.*

[836] One of my editors commented on this point, surprisingly (as he is much younger) recognizing the Pythonic reference, commenting, "Beautiful plumage, though, the Norwegian Blue."

[837] "Collision" interview with Hitchens and Wilson, by Joy Behar.

[838] "grace" - whatever that means.

[839] Northwest Creation Network, *op. cit.*

[840] I have to credit Mike Birbiglia for observing that Hungry Hungry Hippo is a "marblevore."

[841] Ahmadinejad, Addressing New York's Columbia University, September 2007.

[842] "By these were the isles of the Gentiles divided in their lands; every one after his tongue, after their families, in their nations" - Gen 10:5.

[843] "If thou buy an Hebrew servant, six years he shall serve: and in the seventh he shall go out free for nothing. If he came in by himself, he shall go out by himself: if he were married, then his wife shall go out with him. If his master have given him a wife, and she have born him sons or daughters; the wife and her children shall be her master's, and he shall go out by himself. And if the servant shall plainly say, I love my master, my wife, and my children; I will not go out free: Then his master shall bring him unto the judges; he shall also bring him to the door, or unto the door post; and his master shall bore his ear through with an aul; and he shall serve him for ever." - Ex 21:2-6.

[844] The 1986 *Catholic Encyclopedia* seems to claim that, around the fifth century BCE, humankind had not spread beyond Mesopotamia. This, in clear contradiction to known facts.

[845] Mt 11:19: *The Son of man* [Jesus] *came eating and drinking, and they say, Behold a man gluttonous, and a winebibber, a friend of publicans and sinners...*

[846] Just as one example: Notre Dame University debate, 7 April 2011 on the topic *Does Good come from God?* This same speech also proves Dr. Craig does not understand what the word "Atheism" means; he says "Maybe Dr. Harris is right: that Atheism is true." This makes as much sense as saying "if *not watching TV* is true." Perhaps he should look up the word in a dictionary. www.youtube.com/watch?v=wAcdg2RlUJY - 11:10 "If atheism is true" and www.youtube.com/watch?v=uQTZBBkkcxU @14:00 Harris addresses Craig.

[847] "An altar of earth thou shalt make unto me, and shalt sacrifice thereon thy burnt offerings, and thy peace offerings, thy sheep, and thine oxen: in all places where I record my name I will come unto thee, and I will bless thee." - Ex 20:24.

[848] For example, "God brought them out of Egypt; he hath as it were the strength of an unicorn." - Num 23:22.

[849] If so, did they allow doubling down after splitting pairs?

[850] Correct answer: *42*. But I am sure you already know this.

[851] McKibben.

[852] Morris, Robert, 95-100.

[853] Morris, Charles, 69.

[854] *Encyclopedia Biblica*, vol. 3, 2901.

[855] That's the city of *Sodom,* mind you. So close, coincidentally, to *Sodium.*

[856] "Elias was a man subject to like passions as we are, and he prayed earnestly that it might not rain: and it rained not on the earth by the space of three years and six months. And he prayed again, and the heaven gave rain, and the earth brought forth her fruit." - James 5:17-18.

[857] Kingsley, 223.

[858] Riedweg, 2-4.

[859] Diogenes, Bk 8, Life of Pythagoras, XIX.

[860] Dungan, 51.

[861] Richard Dawkins mentioned this in *The God Delusion*, but I had to include it here, as it dovetails so perfectly with Stewie Griffin's similar proclamations.

[862] Evelyn Waugh, author of *Brideshead Revisited,* and Nancy Mitford who wrote *The Pursuit of Love.*

[863] Mosley, 7.

[864] Mt 6.

[865] Lk 14:26.

[866] Mt 12:42, "...and, behold, a greater than Solomon is here."

[867] Mt 23:36, Mt 24:34, Mk 9:1, Lk 21:32, 1 Thess 4:17.

[868] Mt 10:5-6.

[869] Mt 19:21.

[870] Mt 10:33-34, Jn 3:36, Jn 8:24, Jn 12:48, Jn 15:6-7, Mk 16:16 (Note that Mk 16:16 is a later interpolation; it was not part of the original scripture).

[871] Mt 16:27.

[872] Mt 23:35-6, Mk 13:25-31.

[873] It's interesting to note that Martin Luther despised the book of Revelation (Dungan, 136).

[874] See Matthew 23:36.

[875] To the best of my knowledge his middle initial is apparently "H."

[876] Wilkinson, 138-9.

[877] *Diana* in some Bible versions, *Artemis* in others.

[878] That's the KJV. In newer Bible versions, it's usually Zeus and Hermes.

[879] See *Encyclopedia Biblica,* vol. I, 736 for Chemosh. For Milcom: "the national god of the Ammonites" - see *Encyclopedia Biblica,* vol. III, 3085.

[880] Various things are said to "come to pass" over four hundred times in the KJV Bible.

[881] The word *Baalim* means "gods," plural of *Baal,* "god."

[882] Walker, 85.

[883] *Encyclopedia Biblica,* vol. I, 408 widens the scope of Baal-Z to Phoenicia.

[884] In the Bible in Song of Solomon 8:11, Baal-hamon is the name of the place Solomon has his vineyard.

[885] Walker, 85-86.

[886] *Encyclopedia Biblica,* vol. III, 2828.

[887] Walker, 551-552.

[888] *Encyclopedia Biblica,* vol. IV, 4893.

[889] And Tammuz was the "*Christos* or sacred king annually sacrificed in the temple at Jerusalem, attended by women who dedicated him to their Goddess Ishtar-Mari, Queen of Heaven, his mother and bride (Ezekiel 8:14)... Tammuz occupied the central position in the sacred drama at Jerusalem, the New Testament transformed him into a mere apostle of the new dying god, under the Greek form of his name, Thomas." - Walker, 970-971.

[890] *Encyclopedia Biblica,* vol. I, 330.

[891] Walker, 66.

[892] Feel free to send Palumbo mail, calling him anything you like, as long as you use the word "EVIL" to describe him: Representative Peter Palumbo, 67 Kearney Street, Cranston, RI 02920, or email at peter@peterpalumbo.com

# BIBLIOGRAPHY

Alexander, Edward, *The Holocaust and the War of Ideas*. Edison: Transaction Publishers, 1994.

Allegro, John M., *The Dead Sea Scrolls and the Christian Myth*. Amherst: Prometheus Books, 1992.

Allen, Thomas. *Horus in the Pyramid Texts*. University of Chicago Press, 1916.

Bakker, Jay, *Fall to Grace*. New York: Hachette Digital, 2011.

Bagatti, B., *Excavations in Nazareth: from the 12th Century until Today*. Jerusalem: Franciscan Printing Press, 1969.

Barnes, Albert, *Barnes' Notes on the New Testament*. Grand Rapids: Kregel, 1962.

Barry, Dave, *Dave Barry's History of the Millennium (So Far)*. New York: Berkley Publishing, 2008.

Beal, Samuel, *The Romantic Legend of Sâkya Buddha*. London: Trūbner & Co., 1875.

Beck, R., "Mithraism since France Cumont," from Temporini, *Aufstieg und Niedergang der Römischen Welt*, vol. II 17.4; 1986.

Bernard, Raymond W., *From Chrishna To Christ*. Pomeroy: Health Research Books, 1966.

Bharati, Baba Premanand, *Sree Krishna: The Lord of Love*. New York: The Krishna Samaj, 1904.

Bhattacharya, V., *The Āgamaśāstra of Gaudapāda*. Motilal Banarsidass Publ, 1989, Calcutta.

Bigg, Charles, *The Christian Platonists of Alexandria, the 1886 Bampton Lectures*. London: Oxford at the Clarendon Press, 1968.

Bigg, Charles, *The Origins of Christianity*. Oxford University Press, 1909.

Blake, William O., *The History of Slavery and the Slave Trade, Ancient and Modern*. Charleston: Nabu Press, 2010.

Blickle, Peter, *Der Bauernkrieg: Die Revolution des Gemeinen Mannes*. Munich: C. H. Beck, 1998.

Bloomfield, Max, *Bloomfield's Illustrated Historical Guide*. St. Augustine: Max Bloomfield, 1886.

Bond, John James, *Handy-book of Rules and Tables for Verifying Dates with the Christian Era*. Cambridge: Harvard College Library, 1869.

Borg, Marcus J., and Crossan, John Dominic, *The First Paul: Reclaiming the Radical Visionary Behind the Church's Conservative Icon*. New York: HarperOne, 2010.

Borrero, Mauricio, Russia: *A Reference Guide from the Renaissance to the Present*. New York: Facts on File, 2004.

Boyett, Jason, *Pocket Guide to the Apocalypse*. Orlando: Relevant Books, 2005.

Bowie, "Apollonius of Tyana: Tradition and Reality," from Temporini, *Aufstieg und Niedergang der Römischen Welt*, II, 16.2; 1986.

Brenon, Anne. *Les Femmes Cathares*. Paris: Perrin, 1992 & 2004.

Brewer, Ebenezer Cobham, *The Reader's Handbook of Famous Names in Fiction, Allusions, References, Proverbs, Plots, Stories, and Poems*. Philadelphia: J. B. Lippencott, 1899.

Budge, Ernest, *Book of the Kings of Egypt*. London: Kegan Paul, Trench, Truebner & Co., 1908.

Budge, Ernest, *Gods of the Egyptians*. London: Methuen, 1904.

Burdick, Lewis D., "Primary Economical and Political Significance of our Christmas Anniversary," *Dietetic and Hygienic Gazette*, Vol. XXVIII, 1912.

Buxton, Richard, *The Complete World of Greek Mythology*. London: Thames and Hudson, 2004.

Campbell, Joseph. *The Masks of God: Occidental Mythology*. New York: Viking Press, 1970

Carpenter, Edward, *Pagan & Christian Creeds: Their Origin and Meaning*. Sioux Falls: NuVision, 2007.

Cartlidge, David R., and Dungan, David L., *Documents for the Study of the Gospels*. Cartlidge and Dungan, 1994.

Casement, Roger, *Report of the British Consul on the Administration of the Congo Free State*, 1904.

*Catholic Encyclopedia*, first edition. The Encyclopedia Press, 1907-1913.

*Catholic Encyclopedia, Revised and Updated*. Nashville: Thomas Nelson Publishers, 1986.

Chancey, Mark A., *The Myth of a Gentile Galilee*. New York: Cambridge University Press, 2002.

Cheney, Christopher Robert, *Pope Innocent III and England*. Hiersemann, 1976.

Chilton, Bruce, and Evans, Craig A., *James The Just and Christian Origins*. Leiden: Brill, 1999.

Chin, Shunshin, and Fogel, Joshua A., *The Taiping Rebellion*. 1982.

Choi, Andrew, *New Life*. Bloomington: AuthorHouse, 2005.

Churchill, Winston, *A History of the English Speaking Peoples*. New York: Dodd, Mead & Co., 1956.

Churchward, Albert, *The Origin & Evolution of Religion*. Escondido: Book Tree, 2000.

Clauss, Manfred, *The Roman Cult of Mithras*. New York: Routledge, 2001.

Collins, John Joseph, *Between Athens and Jerusalem*. Eerdmans Publishing, 2000.

Condon, R.J., *Our Pagan Christmas*. Austin: American Atheist Press, 1989.

Corbett, Julian Stafford, *Drake and the Tudor Navy*. London: Longmans, Green, and Co., 1898.

Cotterell, Maurice, *The Terracotta Warriors: The Secret Codes of the Emperor's Army*. Bear & Company, 2004.

Coulange, Louis, *Religious Inventions and Frauds*. Kessinger Publishing, 2003.

Crawford, William Henry, *Girolamo Savonarola: a Prophet of Righteousness*. Cincinnati: Jennings and Graham, 1907.

Cumming, Rev. John, *Apocalyptic Sketches*. London: Arthur Hall, Virtue & Co., 1850.

Cumont, Franz, *Astrology and Religion Among the Greeks and Romans*. New York: BiblioBazaar, 2007.

Cumont, Franz, *The Mysteries of Mithra*. New York: Dover Publications, 1956.

Cumont, Franz, *The Oriental Religions in Roman Paganism*. New York: Dover, 1956.

Cumont, Franz, and Latte, Kurt, *Die Mysterien des Mithra - Ein Beitrag zur Religionsgeschichte der römischen Kaiserzeit*. Teubner B.G. GmbH, 1981.

Cutner, Herbert, *Jesus: God, Man or Myth?* Mokelumne Hill Press, 1986.

Dean, Trevor, *The Towns of Italy in the Later Middle Ages*. Manchester University Press, 2000.

Denevan, William M., *The Native Population of the Americans in 1492*. University of Wisconsin Press, 1992.

Dennis, James Shepard, *Christian Missions and Social Progress*. New York: Fleming H. Revell Co., 1906.

De Camp, L. Sprague, *The Ancient Engineers*. New York: Ballentine Books, 1960.

De Patmos, John, *The Great Disappointment of 1844*. Misketonic University Press, 2001.

Díaz, Bernal, del Castillo, *The Discovery and Conquest of Mexico, 1517-1521*. New York: H. Wolff, 1956.

Doane, Thomas William, *Bible Myths and Their Parallels in other Religions*. Cosimo Classics, 2007.

Doherty, Earl, *Neither God not Man*. Ottawa: Age of Reason, 2009.

Downey, Peter, and Shaw, Ben, *Everything You Want to Know about the Bible*. Grand Rapids: Ozdad, 2005.

Drew, Dennis M., and Snow, Donald M., *The Eagle's Talons: the American experience at war*. Montgomery: Maxwell Air Force Base, Air University Press, 1988.

Drolsum, T. Joyner, *Unholy Writ: An Infidel's Critique of the Bible*. Bloomington: AuthorHouse, 2008.

Dungan, David L., *Constantine's Bible*. Minneapolis: Fortress Press, 2007.

Dzielska, Maria, *Apollonius of Tyana in Legend and History*. L'Erma di Bretschneider, 1986.

Dzielska, Maria, *Hypatia of Alexandria*. Cambridge: Harvard University Press, 1996.

Ehrman, Bart, *Jesus, Interrupted*. New York: HarperCollins, 2009.

Ehrman, Bart, *Misquoting Jesus*. New York: HarperOne, 2005.

Ehrman, Bart, *The New Testament*. New York: Oxford University Press, 2012.

Ellegård, Alvar, *Jesus One Hundred Years Before Christ*. New York: Overlook Press, 2002.

Elsner, Jas, "Beyond Compare: Pagan Saint and Christian God in Late Antiquity." *Critical Inquiry*, Spring 2009.

*Encyclopedia Biblica: A Critical Dictionary of the Literary, Political and Religion History, the Archeology, Geography and Natural History of the Bible*. Edited by Thomas Kelly Cheyne and J. Sutherland Black. 1899.

Estep, William Roscoe, *The Anabaptist Story: An Introduction to Sixteenth-Century Anabaptism*. Grand Rapids: Eerdmans Publishing Co., 1975.

Eusebius, *Ecclesiastical History*. Fourth century CE.

Evans, Elizabeth Edson Gibson, *The Christ Myth*. New York: The Truth Seeker Company, 1900.

Ewans, Sir Marti, *European Atrocity, African Catastrophe: Leopold II, the Congo Free State and its Aftermath*. London: RoutledgeCurzon, 2002.

Finn, James, *Sephardim: or, The History of the Jews in Spain and Portugal*. London: Rivington, 1841.

Fitzpatrick, Sheila, *The Russian Revolution*. Oxford University Press, 2001.

Forlong, J. G. R., *Rivers of Life*, Vol. 1. Yorkshire; Celephaïs Press, 2005.

Forty, Jo, *Mythology A Visual Encyclopedia*. London: PRC, 1999

Fomenko, Anatoly, *History: Fiction or Science? Chronology 1*. Bend: Delamere Publishing, 2003.

Franklin, John Hope, *From Slavery to Freedom: A History of African Americans*. New York: McGraw-Hill, 2000.

Frazer, Sir James George, *The Golden Bough*, Oxford: Oxford University Press, 1998.

Fredrich, Carl Johann, and Hiller, Friedrich, *Inschriften von Priene*. Berlin: Gruyter, 1906.

Friedlander, Gerald, *The Jewish Sources of the Sermon on the Mount* (1911). New York: KTAV Publishing, 1969.

Funk & Wagnalls *New Encyclopedia*. Rand McNally, 1983.

Gardner, Gerald Brosseau, *The Meaning of Witchcraft*. Boston: Red Wheel/Weiser, LLC, 2004.

Gasquet, Amédée, *Essai sur le culte et les Mystères de Mithra*. Elibron Classics, 2006.

Gavazzi, Alessandro, *The Lectures Complete of Father Gavazzi, as Delivered in New York* (Reported by Giovanni Battista Nicolini). New York: Dodd, 1854.

Gibbon, Edward, *Decline and Fall of the Roman Empire*. London: Aberdeen University Press, 1901.

Godwin, J., *Mystery Religions in the Ancient World*. San Francisco: Harper & Row, 1981.

Good, John Mason; Gregory, Olinthus; and Bosworth, Newton, *Pantologia: A New Cyclopaedia, Comprehending a Complete Series of Essays*. London: Davidson, 1813.

Guettée, Abbé, *The Papacy: Its Historic Origin and Primitive Relations*. New York: Minos Publishing Co., 1866.

Guiley, Rosemary Ellen, *The Encyclopedia of Witches, Witchcraft and Wicca*. New York: Facts on File, 2008.

Guthrie, W.K.C., *The Greeks and Their Gods*. Boston: Beacon Press, 1954.

Hall, Manly P., *The Secret Teachings of All Ages*. New York: Tarcher/Penguin, 2003.

Hansen, Chadwick, *Witchcraft at Salem*. New York: George Braziller, 1969.

Hardy, R. Spence, *Manual of Buddhism*. Whitefish: Kessinger Publishing, LLC, 2003.

Harris, Sam, *The End of Faith*. New York: Norton, 2004.

Haught, James A., *Holy Horrors*. Amherst: Promethius, 2002.

Hawthorne, Julian, *The History of the United States from 1492 to 1910*. P. F. Collier & Son, 1910.

Hensarling, Reid, *The Biblical Gospel: Its Significance and Impact in Spiritual Renewal*. Bloomington: WestBow Press, 2001.

Hernandez, David, *The Greatest Story Ever Forged (Curse of the Christ Myth)*. Dorrance Publishing, 2009.

Herzog, Johann Jakob, et al., *The New Schaff-Herzog Encyclopedia of Religious Knowledge*. New York: Funk and Wagnalls, 1910.

Hall, Manly P., *The Secret Teachings of All Ages*. New York: Tarcher/Penguin, 2003.

Higgins, Godfrey, *Anacalypsis*. A&B Books, 1992.

Hill, Frances, *The Salem Witch Trials Reader*. New York: DaCapo Press, 2000.

Hillhouse, Alexander, *The Man Who Sold Jesus to the World*. Xlibris, 2010.

Hitchens, Christopher, *god Is Not Great*. New York: Twelve, 2007.

Holladay, Carl R., *Fragments from Hellenistic Jewish Authors*. Scholars Press, 1983.

Holzner, Joseph, *Paul of Tarsus*. Hounslow: Scepter Publishers, 2002.

Horne, Thomas Hartwell, et al, *An Introduction to the Critical Study and Knowledge of the Holy Scriptures*, Vol. 3, 1877.

Hotema, Hilton, *The Mystery Man of the Bible*. Pomeroy: Heath Research, 1967.

Hatonn, Gyeorgos C., *Through Darkness Into Light*. Carson City: America West, 1992.

Ingersoll, Robert G., *The Works of Robert Ingersoll*. C. P. Farrell, 1900.

Jackson, John, *Christianity before Christ*. American Atheist Press, 1985.

Johns, E. Neville, *History of England for Schools*. London: Wm. Isbister, 1882.

Johns, Fleur, *Events: The Force of International Law*. New York: Routledge, 2011.

Johns Hopkins University, *Modern Language Notes*. Vol 23, 1908.

Jones, A. H. M., *The Later Roman Empire. 284-602: A Social, Economic, and Administrative Survey*. Baltimore: The Johns Hopkins University Press, 1986.

Jones, Christopher P., Philostratus, Flavius, *The Life of Apollonius of Tyana, Books 1-IV*. Loeb Classical Library, 2005.

Jordan, Michael, *The Encyclopedia of Gods*. London: Kyle Cathie Ltd., 1992.

June, Lee N., and M. Parker, *Evangelism & Discipleship in African-American Churches*. Grand Rapids: Zondervan, 1999.

Kalthoff, Albert, *The Rise of Christianity*. London: Watts & Co., 1907.

Kapeliouk, Amnon, *Sabra et Chatila: Enquête sur un Massacre*. Paris: Seuil, 1982.

Karageorghis, Vassos, The *Greeks Beyond the Aegean: From Marseilles to Bactria*. Alexander S. Onassis Foundation, 2002.

Kenz, David, *Les Bûchers du Roi: la Culture Protestante des Martyrs (1523-1572)*. Paris: Champ Vallon, 1997.

Kingsley, Peter, *Ancient Philosophy, Mystery, and Magic: Empedocles and Pythagorean Tradition*. New York: Oxford University Press, 1996.

Knecht, Robert, *The French Religious Wars 1562-1598*. Osprey Publishing, Oxford, UK, 2002.

Knight, Christopher, and Butler, Alan, *Solomon's Power Brokers*. New York: Sterling, 2007.

Kuhn, A. B., *Who Is This King of Glory?* Kessinger Publishing, LLC; Facsimile Ed edition, 1992.

Larson, Martin A., *The Story of Christian Origins*, Village, 1977.

Lea, Henry Charles, *A History of the Inquisition of the Middle Ages*. London: MacMillan, 1906.

Lefébure, Par E., "Le Cham et L'Adam Égyptiens," *Transactions of the Society of Biblical Archæology*. London: Office of the Society, 1893.

Levack, Brian, *The Witch-Hunt in Early Modern Europe.* New York: Longman, 1995.

LeVay, Simon, and Valente, Sharon McBride. *Human Sexuality*. Sunderland: Sinauer Associates, Inc., 2008.

Lietzmann, Hans, *A History of the Early Church.* New York: Meridian Books, 1961.

Lipner, Julius, *Hindus: Their Religious Beliefs and Practices*. New York: Routledge, 1998.

Maccoby, Hyam, *The Mythmaker.* New York: Barnes & Noble Books, 1998.

Mack, Burton L., *The Lost Gospel - the Book of Q and Christian Origins.* New York: HarperCollins, 1993.

Mackay, Charles, LL.D., *Extraordinary Popular Delusions and the Madness of Crowds*. New York: Harmony, 1980.

Magness, Jodi, *The Archaelogoy of Qumran and the Dead Sea Scrolls.* Grand Rapids: Eerdmans, 2002.

Maitland, Edward, and Kingsford, Anna, *The Keys of the Creeds*. London: Trürner & Col, 1875.

Manhattan, Avro, *The Vatican billions: Two Thousand Years of Wealth Accumulation from St. Peter to the Space Age*. London: Paravision, 1972.

Marcus, Jacob Rader, and Saperstein, Marc, *The Jew in the Medieval World: a Source Book, 315-1791*. Hebrew Union College Press, 1999.

Marsh, Carole, *Father Junipero Serra: California Missions Founder*. Peachtree City: Gallopade International, 2003.

Maseko, Achim Nkosi, *Church Schism & Corruption*. Durban: Maseko, 2008.

Mason, Steve, *Flavius Josephus: Translation and Commentary*. Boston: Brill, 2001.

Mason, Steve, *Josephus and the New Testament*. Peabody: Hendrickson, 2003.

Massey, Gerald, *Ancient Egypt, the Light of the World.* Sioux Falls: NuVision, 2009.

Massey, Gerald, *Gnostic and Historic Christianity.* Whitefish: Kessinger Publishing, 2005.

Mather, George A., and Nichols, Larry A., *Dictionary of Cults, Sects, Religions, and the Occult*. Grand Rapids: Zondervan, 1993.

Matthews, John, *The Winter Solstice: The Sacred Traditions of Christmas.* Quest, 2003.

McCabe, Joseph, *The Myth of the Resurrection and other essays.* Amherst: Prometheus Books, 1993.

McDonald, Lee Martin, and Sanders, James A, *The Canon Debate.* Grand Rapids: Baker Academic, 2001.

McGoldrick, James Edward, *Baptist Successionism: A Crucial Question in Baptist History.* Lanham: Scarecrow Press, 1994.

McKibben, Bill, *Harper's Magazine,* "The Christian paradox: How a faithful nation gets Jesus wrong," August 2005.

Mead, G.R.S., and Clary, Edward, *The Mysteries of Mithras.* Sequim: Holmes, 2004.

Megivern, James J., *The Death Penalty: An Historical and Theological Survey.* Mahwah: Paulist Press, 1997.

Meredith, Evan P., *The Prophet of Nazareth.* London: F. Farrah, 1864.

Mobley, Joe A., editor, *The Way We Lived in North Carolina.* University of North Carolina Press, 2003.

Morford, Mark P.O., *Classical Mythology.* Longman: New York, 1991

Morris, Charles, *Aryan Sun-Myths: The Origin Of Religions.* Troy: Nims and Knight, 1889.

Morris, Robert, *Bible Witnesses from Bible Lands.* Cambridge: Andover-Harvard Theological Library, 1910.

Mosley, Charlotte, *The Letters of Nancy Mitford and Evelyn Waugh.* New York: Houghton Mifflin Company, 1996.

Myers, Philip Van Ness, *Mediaeval and Modern History.* Cambridge: Athenium Press, 1905.

Nabarz, Payam, *The Mysteries of Mithras.* Rochester: Inner Traditions / Bear & Company, 2005.

Nelli, René, *Écritures cathares.* Paris: Planète, 1968.

O'Donnell, Patrick, *Ku Klux Klan: America's First Terrorists Exposed.* West Orange: Idea Men Productions, 2006.

Osman, Ahmed, *Out of Egypt.* London: Arrow, 1998.

Otto, Walter G, *Dionysus -- Myth and Cult.* Bloomington: Indiana University Press, 1965.

*Oxford Classical Dictionary.* New York: Oxford University Press, 1996.

*Oxford Essential Guide to Egyptian Mythology.* New York: Berkley, 2004.

Painter, John, *Just James: The Brother of Jesus in History and Tradition.* Edinburgh: First Fortress Press, 2005.

Palou, Francis, *Life of Padre Junipero Serra.* Kessinger, 2006.

Panati, Charles, *Extraordinary Origins of Everyday Things*. New York: Harper & Row, 1987.

Paterson, James (pseud. for Croake James), *Curiosities of Christian History*. London: Methuen & Co, 1892.

Pausanias, *Guide to Greece*, second c. CE.

Peerbolte, L.J. Lietaert, *Paul the Missionary*. Leuven: Peeters Publishers, 2003.

*Penny Cyclopaedia of the Society or the Diffusion of Useful Knowledge*, No. 88, Vol. II, London: Charles Knight, 1833.

Perriman, Andrew, *Otherways*. Open Source Theology, 2007.

Philip, Marlene Nourbese, *Zong!* Toronto: Mercury Press, 2008.

Phillips, Ulrich Bonnell, *American Negro Slavery: A Survey of the Supply, Employment and Control of Negro Labor as Determined by the Plantation Regime.* University of Toronto Libraries, 2011.

Pierson, Paul Everett, *The Dynamics of Christian Mission: History Through a Missiological Perspective.* Pasadena: William Carey International Univerity Press, 2009.

Pitstick, Alyssa Lyra, *Light in Darkness: Hans Urs Von Balthasar and the Catholic Doctrine of Christ's Descent into Hell*. Grand Rapids: Eerdmans Publishing, 2007.

Pörtner, Rudolf, *Mit dem Fahrstuhl in die Römerzeit.* Munich: Knaur, 1967.

Postma, Johannes, *The Atlantic Slave Trade*. London: Greenwood Press, 2003.

Powers, H. H., "The War as a Suggestion of Manifest Destiny," *Publ. American Academy of Political and Social Science,* No. 235 (October 4, 1898).

Priaulx, Osmond de Beauvoir, *The Indian Travels of Apollonius of Tyana and the Indian Embassies to Rome*. London: Quaritch, 1873.

Price, Robert M., *Deconstructing Jesus.* Amherst: Prometheus, 2000.

Price, Robert M., *The Case Against the Case for Christ.* Cranford: American Atheist Press, 2010.

Rafiabadi, Dr. Hamid Naseem, *World Religions and Islam*. New Delhi: Sarup & Sons, 2003.

Rawley, James A., and Behren, Stephen D., *The Transatlantic Slave Trade: a History*. University of Nebraska Press, 2009.

Rawlinson, George, *The Religions of the Ancient World.* New York: Humboldt, No. 82, November 1884.

Regenstein, Lewis G., *Replenish the Earth*. New York: Crossroad, 1991.

Reilly, Thomas H., *The Taiping Heavenly Kingdom: Rebellion and the Blasphemy of Empire*. Seattle: University of Washington Press, 2010.

Reinach, Salomon, *Orpheus, a History of Religions*. New York: Liveright, 1933.

Reitzenstein, Richard, *Hellenistische Wundererzählungen*. Leipzig: Tübner, 1906.

Renan, Ernest, *Histoire des Origines du Christianisme*. Paris: Ancienne Mason Michele Levy Frères, 1895.

Riedweg, Christoph, and Rendall, Steven, *Pythagoras: His Life, Teaching, and Influence*. Ithaca: Cornell University Press, 2002.

Robbins, Rossell Hope, *The Encyclopedia of Witchcraft and Demonology*. New York: Crown, 1959.

Robertson, John M., *A Short History of Christianity*. London: Watts & Co., 1902.

Robertson, John M., *Pagan Christs: Studies in Comparative Hierology*. London: Watts & Co., 1903.

Roberts, Alexander, et al, *The Ante-Nicene Fathers*. Grand Rapids: Wm. B. Eerdmans Publishing Co., 1977.

Robertson, Alexander, *The Roman Catholic Church in Italy*. London: Morgan and Scott, 1905.

Rodriguez, Junius P., *Slavery in the United States: A Social, Political, and Historical Encyclopedia*. Santa Barbara: ABC-CLIO, 2007.

Roscoe, William, *The Life and Pontificate of Leo the Tenth*. University Press of the Pacific, 2000.

Ross, J.W., *Tacitus and Bracciolini, the Annals forged in the XVth century*. London: Diprose & Bateman, 1878.

Roth, Cecil, *The Spanish Inquisition*. New York: Norton, 1964.

Russell, Jeffrey Burton, *Witchcraft in the Middle Ages*. Ithaca: Cornell University Press, 1984.

Ryba, Thomas, et al, *The Comity and Grace of Method: Essays in Honor of Edmund F. Perry*. Northwestern University Press, 2004.

Sagan, Carl, *Cosmos*. New York: Random House, 1980.

Salm, René, *The Myth of Nazareth*. Cranford: American Atheist Press, 2008.

Sanford, Charles L., *Manifest Destiny and the Imperialism Question*. New York: John Wiley and Sons, 1974.

Sator, Darwin, *The Crisscross Double-cross*. Victoria: Trafford Publishing, 2002.

Scholasticus, Socrates, *Historia Ecclesiastica*, c. 439.

Schormann, Gerhard, *Hexenprozesse in Deutschland*. Göttingen: Vandenhoeck & Ruprecht, 1981.

Shahid, Leila, "The Sabra and Shatila Massacres: Eye-Witness Reports," *Journal of Palestine Studies*, Vol. 32, No. 1., Autumn, 2002.

Smith, David Whitten, and Burr, Elizabeth Geraldine, *Understanding World Religions: a Road Map for Justice and Peace*. Lanham: Rowman and Littlefield, 2007.

Smith, Homer W., *Man and His Gods*, New York: Grosset & Dunlap, 1957.

Smith, John Holland, *The Great Schism*. London: 1970.

Smith, William, and Wace, Henry, *A Dictionary of Christian Biography, Literature, Sects and Doctrines; During the First Eight Centuries*. London: John Murray, 1887.

Stannard, David. *American Holocaust: The Conquest of the New World*. New York: Oxford University Press, 1993.

Stephanson, Anders, *Manifest Destiny: American Expansion and the Empire of Right*. New York: Hill and Wang, 1995.

Targa, Leonardo, *A Translation of the Eight Books of Aulus Cornelius Celsus on Medicine*. 1840.

Taylor, Eric R., *If We Must Die: Shipboard Insurrections in the Era of the Atlantic Slave Trade.* Louisiana State University Press, 2006.

Taylor, Joan E., *Christians and the Holy Places*. Oxford: Clarendon Press, 1993.

Taylor, Robert, *The Diegesis; being a discovery of the Origin, Evidences, and Early History of Christianity*. London: W. Dugdale, 1845.

Temporini, Hildegard, *Aufstieg und Niedergang der Römischen Welt.* Berlin: Walter de Gruyter, 1986.

Thomas, Hugh, *Conquest: Cortes, Montezuma, and the Fall of Old Mexico*. New York: Simon & Schuster, 1995.

Thomsett, Michael C., *The Inquisition: A History*. Jefferson: McFarland & Co, 2010.

Thornton, John Kelly, *The Kongolese Saint Anthony: Dona Beatriz Kimpa Vita and the Antonian Movement, 1684-1706*. Cambridge University Press, 1998.

Tice, Paul, *History of the Waldenses: From the Earliest Period to the Present Time.* San Diego: The Book Tree, 1999.

Tosches, Nick, *King of the Jews: The Greatest Mob Story Never Told*. New York: Harper, 2006.

Trickler, C. Jack, *A Layman's Guide To: Who Wrote the Books of the Bible?* Bloomington: AuthorHouse, 2006.

Trobisch, David, *The First Edition of the New Testament*. New York: Oxford University Press, 2000.

Trobisch, David, *Paul's Letter Collection*. Bolivar: Quiet Waters Publications, 2001.

Tuttle, Hudson, *Evolution of the God, and Christ Ideas.* Berlin Heights: The Tuttle Publishing Company, 1906.

Tylor, Edward Burnett, *Researches Into the Early History of Mankind and the Development of Civilization*. London: John Murray, 1878.

Ulansey, David, *The Origins of the Mithraic Mysteries: Cosmology and Salvation in the Ancient World*. Oxford University Press, 1989.

Vallentin, Antonina, *Leonardo da Vinci, the Tragic Pursuit of Perfection.* Viking Press, 1938.

Van Voorst, Robert E., *Jesus Outside the New Testament: An Introduction to the Ancient Evidence.* Grand Rapids: Eerdmans, 2000.

Vermaseren, M. J., *Mithras, the Secret God.* New York: Barnes & Noble,1963.

Victor, Jeffrey S., Satanic Panic: the Creation of a Contemporary Legend. Chicago: Open Court, 1993.

Waite, Charles B., *History of the Christian Religion to the Year Two Hundred.* Kessinger, 2003.

Wallis, Wilson D., *Religion in Primitive Society.* New York: Crofts and Co., 1939.

Walker, Barbara, *The Women's Encyclopedia of Myths and Secrets.* New York: HarperOne, 1983.

Walvin, James, *Black Ivory: Slavery in the British Empire.* Hoboken: Wiley-Blackwell, 2001.

Ware, James R., and Kent, Roland G. "The Old Persian Cuneiform Inscriptions of Artaxerxes II and Artaxerxes III". *Transactions and Proceedings of the American Philological Association,* Vol. 55, 1924.

Wasson, R., *Persephone's Quest: Entheogens and the Origins of Religion.* Yale University Press, 1992.

Watson, Richard, *An Apology for the Bible.* Cambridge: Hillard and Brown, 1828.

Watts, Edward Jay, *City and School in Late Antique Athens and Alexandria.* University of California Press, 2008.

Wedgwood, C.V., *The Thirty Years War.* New York: NYRB Classics, 2005.

Weinberg, Albert K., *Manifest Destiny.* Chicago: Quadrangle, 1963.

Weis, Rene, *The Yellow Cross: The Story of the Last Cathars' Rebellion Against the Inquisition (1290-1329).* New York: Random House, 2001.

Wells, G. A., *The Historical Evidence for Jesus.* Amherst: Prometheus, 1988.

Wheless, Joseph, *Forgery in Christianity.* Moscow, Minneapolis: Filiquarian Publishing, LLC, 2007.

Whitman, James, *The Origins of Reasonable Doubt: Theological Roots of the Criminal Trial.* Yale University Press, 2008.

Whitney, Loren Harper, *A Question of Miracles - Parallels in the Lives of Buddha and Jesus.* Chicago: The Library Shelf, 1908.

Wilkinson, Richard H., *The Complete Gods and Goddesses of Ancient Egypt.* New York: Thames and Hudson, 2003.

Williams, George M., *Handbook of Hindu Mythology,* Santa Barbara: ABC-CLIO, 2003.

Williams, Henry Smith, *Historians' History of the World*. London: Hooper and Jackson, 1909.

Williamson, W., *The Great Law*. New York: Longmans, Green and Co, 1899.

Witt, Ronald, *The Two Latin Cultures and the Foundation of Renaissance Humanism in Medieval Italy*. Cambridge University Press, 2012.

# APPENDIX

## References for the "Silent Historians"

**1. Aelius Theon**

Alexandrian sophist and rhetorician of the first century; **Theon** wrote a Treatise on Rhetoric, and many other works. His *Προγυμνάσματα* (Progymnasmata, or tutelage) is extant. Author of commentaries on Apollonius Rhodius and Xenophon.

References: Anderson, R. Dean, 72-73; Smith, William, *A Dict. Gk. Rom. Biogr. Myth,* vol III, 1081.

**2. A. Gellius**

Author and grammarian, 125-180 CE, pupil of Fronto, disciple of Sulpicius Apollinaris. Flourished in Rome; some writers refer to him as *Agellius.* Aulus Gellius wrote *Attic Nights* (169 CE) in twenty books, on philosophers, history, grammar, manners, and current events.

References: Atchity, 305; Clark, 93-4; Dihle, 265; Lietzmann, Vol. 2, 216, 220, 278, 289; Platts, Vol. II, 86, 153-4; Tennemann, 161-3.

**3. A. Cornelius Celsus**

Roman encyclopedist & physician, contemporary of Christ, c. 25-35 BCE to c. 50-60 CE. He "possessed a diversity of talent" and wrote many works on military art, rhetoric, philosophy, agriculture, and medicine.

References: Fowler, 175-6; Middleton, 235-7; Targa, V.

**4. Albinus**

Teacher of Galen, active in Smyrna c. 100-165 CE. Albinus wrote *Διδασκαλικος* (*Didaskalikos,* or Preceptorial), a Platonic work of philosophy. Wrote nothing of Jesus or Christianity.

References: Tennemann, 161-3; Turner, 380.

**5. Alcinous**

Philosopher and author of the second century. Among other works, he authored a book of Platonic doctrine which we have today.

References: Platts, Vol. II, 149; Tennemann, 161-3; Trapp, 158; *Encyclopedia Britannica,* 1910, Vol. 1, 523.

**6. Ammonius of Athens**

Flourished c. 60 CE, Athens, Greece. Writer and philosopher who taught Plutarch, Plutarch living 46-120.

References: Edwards, 940; Long, Vol. I, XXIV; Platts, Vol. II, 83-4; Tennemann, 161-3; Williams, Henry Smith, 401.

**7. Alexander of Aegae**

Alexander was from Aegae, Macedonia -- first century writer, philosopher, and tutor of Emperor Nero.

References: Alberti, 2; Parkinson, Vol. II, 153; *Encyclopedia Britannica*, 1911, 163.

**8. Antipater of Thessalonica**

Poet, contemporary of Christ, author of epigrams in the Greek Anthology, c. 10 BCE - c. 40-50 CE.

References: Bowra, 2, 17; Dodd, 42; Gunnyon, 79.

**9. Antonius Polemo**

Famous sophist author under Trajan and Hadrian, some of his works are available today.

References: Anthon, 444; Mossman, 6-11; Reader, 1, 5; Wells, 235-7.

**10. Apollonius Dyscolus**

Prolific writer of Alexandria. One of the greatest of the Greek grammarians, mid to late second century.

References: Dickey, 73; Luhtala, 78; Swiggers, 233-9.

**11. Apollonius of Tyana**

From Tyana in Anatolia (modern Turkey), Apollonius was a Greek philosopher and contemporary of Christ. He traveled throughout the Levant and Middle East. Besides many letters, Apollonius wrote *On Sacrifices, Life of Pythagoras,* and a will. His primary biographer Philostratus (based primarily on writings by disciple Damis, as well as Maximus of Aegeae, and Moeragenes; places his life 3 BCE to 97 CE, but upon examining his life events, it seems likely Philostratus had skewed the dates slightly retrograde, and Apollonius was born perhaps as late as 20 to 40 CE, living until c. 120. Lucian and Soterichus Oasites also wrote of Apollonius. Philostratus' *Life of Apollonius* is largely regarded as supplementary to a biography of Apollonius, "απομνημονεύματα" by Moiragenes.

References: Dzielska, *Apollonius*, 31-37; Jones, *Phlstr, Apollonius*; Penella; Platts, Vol. II, 87; Reitzenstein, 40.

**12. Appian**

Appian, from Alexandria, lived c. 95 - c. 165 CE. Prolific historian, he traveled the Levant, Egypt, Italy. Wrote *Roman History* in twenty-four books, available today. A distinguished nobleman in both Rome and Egypt, Appian seems completely unaware of Jesus, and of the Christians.

References: Niebuhr; Platts, Vol. II, 104; White.

**13. Archigenes**

Physician born at Apamea in Syria, lived during Domitian, Nerva, and Trajan. Wrote 10 books on fevers, a book on drugs, one on "affected parts," and a treatise on adorning hair; died age 37. Some fragments are still extant, and more information about his writing comes down to us from other ancient historians.

References: Platts, Vol. II, 113; Prioreschi, 170-3; Temporini, II.37.2, 954-8.

**14. Aretaeus**

Aretaeus (Aretæus, Aretaeos) of Cappadocia, Greek physician and author of at least eight books in the first century under Nero or Vespasian; his works are extant.

References: Park, 488; Platts, Vol. II, 114; Prioreschi, 263-76.

**15. Arrian**

Arrian of Nicomedia (Izmit), Greek/Roman historian, lived c. 86 - past 161 CE. Arrian wrote an account of Alexander's expedition, as well as works on philosophy and other subjects. He died during the reign of Marcus Aureleus.

References: Lietzmann, Vol. 2, 27 & 299; Mills, 484; Platts, Vol. II, 148-9; Rooke.

**16. Asclepiades of Prusa**

Famed physician under Hadrian, born 88 CE in Prusa, Asclepiades wrote several books on internal and external medicines.

References: Luck, 189-90; Platts, Vol. II, 114; Thomas, Joseph, 199.

**17. Aspasius**

Peripatetic philosopher, Aspasius was born c. 80 and died c. 150 CE. Wrote commentaries on most of Aristotle's works, some of which are still extant. Also wrote commentaries on Plato.

References: Alberti; Parkinson, 4, 153-4, 166; Trapp, 12, 76-7.

**18. Atilicinus**

Middle of the 1st c. Roman jurist and writer. Attached to the sect of Proculus, to whom he addressed many letters.

References: Berger, 368; Clark, 108-11; Smith, William, *A Dict. Gk. Rom. Biogr. Myth.* Vol. I, 405.

**19. Attalus**

Greek stoic philosopher, orator, and writer during the reigns of Augustus and Tiberius. Seneca the Elder called Attalus the most acute and eloquent of the philosophers of his day.

References: Gummere, 5; Longman, 6; Morford, 157-8.

**20. Bassus of Corinth**

Philosopher and writer, corresponded with Apollonius of Tyana. Came from a well-to-do family, lived late first and early second century.

References: Anderson, *Sage, Saint, and Sophist,* 57, 139, 145; Penella, 51, 79; Philostratus, IV:26; Smith, William, *A Dict. Gk. Rom. Biogr. Myth.* Vol. III, 1160.

**21. C. Cassius Longinus**

Lawyer/jurist, became consul in 30 CE. Grandson of jurist Tubero. He was governor of Syria under Claudius, 45-50 CE. Wrote at least ten volumes on law, *Libri Juris Civilis*. Died c. 69-79.

References: Fowler, 192-3; Rutledge, 116; Sherman, 72.

**22. Calvisius Taurus of Berytus**

Teacher of A. Gellius, mid second century. Writer and member of a new school of Platonists including Thrasyllus of Mendes, Theon of Smyrna, Alcinous, Albinus, Plutarch, L. Apuleius of Mendaurus, and Maximus Tyrius. All were unaware of any Jesus Christ.

References: Enfield, 321; Rosse, 132; Tennemann, 161-163.

**23. Cassius Dio**

Cassius Dio Cocceianus (c. 155-64 to after 229) spent ten years (c. 220) writing his *Roman History* in 80 volumes, of the events year by year over the course of 1400 years up to 229 CE. Published c. 229, his treatise on the first century starts with Vol. 57, which comes down to us today, complete. Dio used the "c.u." date system (years since the founding of Rome) in his texts, not "AD," as he was, of course, unaware of the concept of *Anno Domini* (which would not come about until the sixth century). Dio was the grandson of Dion of Prusa.

References: Cassius Dio, *Roman History*; Platts, Vol. II, 174-5; Temporini, II, 484-5.

**24. Chaeremon of Alexandria**

Stoic philosopher and grammarian of the middle of the first century CE, flourished 30-65, teacher of young Nero. Author of a History of Egypt; of works on Comets, Egyptian Astrology, and Hieroglyphics; and of a grammatical treatise on expletive conjunctions. His original works are lost but we have a wealth of information on him from other authors from the first to twelfth century. Not to be confused with the Chaeremon mentioned by Strabo (Chaeremon was a common name, especially in Egypt).

References: Morford, 154; van der Horst; *Encyclopædia Britannica* (1910), Vol. V., 788.

**25. Claudius Agathemerus**

Greek physician and writer of first century. Born in Lacedaemon; contemporary of Christ, a pupil of the philosopher Cornutus. Lived past 50 CE.

References: Park, 488; Schmitz, *A History of Latin Literature*, 148; Smith, William, *A Dict. Gk. Rom. Biogr. Myth.* Vol I, 62.

**26. Claudius Ptolemaeus**

"Ptolemy," Native of Egypt, prolific Greek/Roman writer and mathematician, c. 83 – 161 CE, in Alexandria during the reigns of Hadrian (emperor 117 to 138) and Antoninus (emperor 138 to 161).

References: Platts, Vol. II, 106-10; Southern, 240; *The Encyclopaedia Britannica* (1910), Vol. 22, 618-26.

**27. Cleopatra the physician**

The name "Cleopatra" was common in ancient Egypt and Greece (Abbot, Plant). This Cleopatra (not "Queen of the Nile"), a physician, published many remedies in Latin c. 64 CE and was written about by Galen of Pergamum. Six fragments of her works, of significant length, are still extant.

References: Abbott, 45; Bates, 41, 47; Flemming, 257–279; Plant, 135-44.

**28. Cluvius Rufus**

Cluvius Rufus was an "eloquent and accomplished" historian, and governed Spain during the reign of Caligula. His writings were used by Tacitus, Suetonius, and Plutarch.

References: Platts, Vol. II, 14; Quill, 7 & 16.

**29. Cn. Cornelius Lentulus Gaetulicus**

Contemporary of Christ, consul in 26 CE, later Governor of Gaul and Germania. Corresponded with Tiberius in letters, and was a poet of note. Died 39 CE.

References: Baring-Gould, *Tragedy of the Caesars*, 363, 454; Bowman, Vol X, 226; Rutledge, 100.

**30. Columella**

L. Junius Moderatus Columella was an author, 4 – c. 70 CE, contemporary of Christ, wrote *Res Rusticae* and *De Arboribus.*

References: Bowman, 461; Loudon, 21; Morford, 154; Platts, Vol. II, 86; Schmitz, *A History of Latin Literature*, 144.

**31. Cornutus**

L. Anneus Cornutus was a writer during reigns of Augustus through Nero. Cornutus' allegory on stoic theology survives today. A teacher of Claudius Agathemerus and Persius, he was exiled by Nero in 68 CE.

References: Bréhier, 51, 151; Morford, 10; Rutledge, 42-3, 161-2.

**32. D. Haterius Agrippa**

Decimus Haterius Agrippa, Roman consul in 22 CE, contemporary of Christ, orator, and later senator. Son of senator and orator Q. Haterius. Died 32 CE.

References: Grant, *Annals,* 202-220; Rutledge, 92-3; Smith, William, *A Dict. Gk. Rom. Biogr. Myth,* Vol. 1, 77.

**33. D. Valerius Asiaticus**

Decimus Valerius Asiaticus (5 BCE-47 CE) ("Valerius 2"), contemporary of Christ, was a Roman consul twice (in 35 and 46), a Narbonian Gaul. He corresponded with Apollonius of Tyana. Valerius helped assassinate Caligula.

References: Bauman, 172-5; Frere, 52, Penella, 119-20.

**34. Damis**

Assyrian acolyte of Apollonius of Tyana, contemporary of Christ. Damis chronicled the travels and deeds of Apollonius, mid- to late-first century CE.

References: Penella; Philostratus, *Life of Apollonius;* Platts, Vol. II, 87.

**35. Demetrius**

"Demetrius the Cynic," cynic philosopher and friend of Seneca and P. Clodius Thrasea Paetus. Lived in Rome during Caligula through Vespasian (37-71 CE). Apollonius of Tyana corresponded with Demetrius (*Ep. Appol. 77e*).

References: Morford, 154; Penella, 132 (Ep. 77e); Philostratus, *Life of Apollonius,* IV.25.1; Platts, Vol. II, 88; Zeller, *History / Eclecticism,* 291-3.

**36. Demonax**

Cynic philosopher and orator at Crete, flourished under Hadrian. Lucian met and wrote of him, calling him "pointed and witty." His writings are extant with Lucian, and others.

References: Lucian, *Life of Demonax*; Platts, Vol. II, 88.

**37. Demosthenes Philalethes**

First century writer and physician, living in Turkey (ancient Anatolia), student of Alexander Philalethes.

References: Sarton, 244; Von Staden, 69-70; Smith, William, *A Dict. Gk. Rom. Biogr. Myth.* Vol. 1, 991.

**38. Dion of Prusa**

Dion of Prusa, aka Dio Chrysostom was a noted Greek rhetorician and philosopher, born at Prusa, living 40 – c. 120 CE, fl. 100. His famous speech was *Against Philosophers*; his eighty orations are extant. Dion corresponded with Apollonius of Tyana, and taught Favorinus. Exiled 83 CE.

References: Bréhier, 151-3; Bowman, 905; Davenport, 223; Morford, 204; Penella, 39; Platts, Vol. II, 101-2.

**39. Domitius Afer**

Born in Nîmes, contemporary of Christ, praetor under Tiberius, consul under Caligula, Domitius Afer was a brilliant and celebrated orator and writer under Nero. He was written about by the younger Pliny. Died 59 CE.

References: Capes, 75; Fyfe, 122-3; Lewis, 57; Rollin, 548; Rutledge, 220-1.

**40. Epictetus**

Greek Stoic philosopher, born as a slave at Hierapolis in Phrygia c. 55 CE. His master was Epaphroditus of the court of Nero. Died c. 135, his writing is extant. Epictetus wrote: "The good or ill of man lies within his own will."

References: Bradley, 174-6; Bréhier, 151, 159; Lietzmann, 172-4; Platts, Vol. II, 88-9, 148.

**41. Erotianus**

First century CE lexicographer, grammarian & physician, living during Nero's reign (54-68 CE). His works are extant.

References: Eschenburg, 496; Platts, Vol. II, 101; Smith, William, *A New Classical Dict. of Biog., Myth., and Geog.*, 248.

**42. Euphrates of Tyre**

Stoic philosopher of Tyre (Phoenicia, now Lebanon), middle of the first century CE, pupil of Musonius Rufus, friend of Pliny the Younger, and lifelong enemy of the peace-loving Apollonius of Tyana.

References: Jones, *Letters of Apollonius*, 4, 11, 13, 21; Jones, *The Roman World of Dio Chrysostom*, 10-14; Penella, 89; Platts, Vol. II, 88.

**43. Fabius Rusticus**

Roman historian Fabius Rusticus wrote during Claudius and Nero. A friend of Seneca, he was quoted by Tacitus.

References: Henderson, 428-9; Jahn, 13; Platts, Vol. II, 105; Wiseman, 47-8.

**44. Favorinus**

Favorinus of Arles, born c. 75 CE, wrote about philosophy, history, and rhetoric. He wrote at least five books of *Memoirs*.

References: Bréhier, 151; Platts, Vol. II, 100; Sandys, *A Short History,* 78.

**45. Flaccus**

P. Aulus Avilius Flaccus, contemporary of Christ, was chosen by Tiberius in 32 CE to be governor of Alexandria.

References: Philo Judaeus, *Against Flaccus;* Herzog, Vol. IX, 39.

**46. Florus**

P. Annius Florus, Roman historian and poet, born in Africa, flourished in the time of Trajan (98 - 117) and Hadrian (117 – 138). His works are extant.

References: Platts, Vol. II, 104; *Encyclopædia Britannica* (1910) Vol. X, 547.

**47. Fronto**

M. Cornelius Fronto, Roman orator and writer under Hadrian was consul under Pius. Preceptor of Emperor Aurelius and L. Verres. Son of T. Cornelius, born c. 90-5 CE, died c. 167. Aurelius made him consul, and erected a statue to his honor. Fronto taught M. Aurelius not only eloquence, but the duty of a monarch, and excellent morals. Most of his letters are extant. Fronto eschewed the modern Jewish and Christian religions, but apparently never heard of "Jesus."

References: Platts, Vol. II, 155; Sandys, *A Companion to Latin Studies,* 684-5.

**48. Gordius of Tyana**

Ti. Claudius Gordianus (or Gordius). Consul, native of Tyana, corresponded with Apollonius.

References: Penella, 18, 59, 114, I44; Bowman, 219; Van Dam, 54-5.

**49. Gnaeus Domitius**

Domitius (c. 6 - 67), was a Roman general, contemporary of Christ, was Senator, and a writer, son-in-law of Caligula. Domitius wrote voluminous accounts of his experiences as general.

References: Cassius Dio, *Roman History,* 58.14; Eggenberger, 29.

**50. Halicarnassensis Dionysius II**

Greek historian Halicarnassensis Dionysius flourished under Hadrian. He wrote a History of Musicians in 26 books, and Roman Antiquities in seven books.

References: Cary; Platts, Vol. II, 105.

**51. Heron of Alexandria**

Famed Greek mathematician, engineer, and inventor lived c. 10 to 85 CE. Prolific author of works on science, engineering, and mathematics.

References: Ceccarelli, 216-45; Landels, 199-202.

**52. Josephus**

Flavius Josephus, famed Jewish historian, lived c. 38-107 CE. Visited Rome in 64 (age 26 or 27). Joined the Essenes c. 53 CE. Published *Jewish War* c. 95.

References: Platts, Vol. II, 101-2; Thackeray, 1-22.

**53. Justus of Tiberias**

Justus of Tiberias was a Jewish author and historian living in the second half of the 1st century, contemporary of Josephus. While his writings are lost, they were extant in the ninth century and in the hands of Christian scholar Photius.

References: Cutner, 107; Temporini, II.21.2, 787-8; VanderKam, 145; Smith, William, *A Dict. Gk. Rom. Biogr. Myth.*, Vol. II, 687.

**54. Juvenal**

Decius Junius Juvenal, famed prolific poet and writer of the first and second centuries, wrote under Nero, and later years.

References: Highet; Platts, Vol. II, 92-3.

**55. Lesbonax of Mytilene**

Lesbonax, or Lesbona, rhetorician and philosopher, father of celebrated philosopher Potaman, was author of at least sixteen political speeches and other works, of which two are extant, plus other works. Lesbonax corresponded with Apollonius of Tyana. (The Lesbonax described in Suidas as the author of a large number of philosophical works is probably from a much earlier date.)

References: Platts, Vol. II, 83; Sherk, 103-4; Syme, *The Roman Revolution*, 262; Tredwell, 105.

**56. Lucanus**

M. Annaeus Lucanus, nephew of the younger Seneca, and writer of considerable excellence during the first century (39 - 65 CE). Lucanus was a friend of Persius, and childhood friend of Nero. Many of his works are extant.

References: Lawrence, 95; Middleton, 264.

**57. Lucian**

Also Lucianus: second century Greek author, born in Samosata (125-180 CE), one of the first novelists of western civilization.

References: Anderson, *Lucian*; Platts, Vol. II, 99; Sheldon.

**58. Lysimachus**

Alexander Lysimachus - patrician Judaism writing at Alexandria under Tiberius and Claudius, contemporary of Christ, brother of Philo, imprisoned by Caligula.

References: Abrahams, Vol. II, 102-4; Huidekoper, 98-9, 222; Platts, Vol. II, 45.

**59. M. Antonius Pallas**

A favorite of Claudius, secretary, recorder for the Roman empire under Claudius and Nero. Acquired enormous wealth under Claudius.

References: Platts, Vol. II, 9; Shotter, *Nero Caesar Augustus*, 57-8; Temporini, II, 1195.

**60. M. Vinicius**

Consul 30 CE, with C. Cassius Longinus, when Velleius Paterculus dedicated his work to Vinicius. Elaborate orator, Vinicius was a contemporary of Christ. He married Julia Livilla (daughter of Germanicus) in 33 CE and was put to death 46 CE.

References: Griffin, 48-9; Temporini, II, 902.

**61. Macro**

Praetorian commander, writing early/mid first century, contemporary of Christ. Macro was in charge at Alexandria, and met with Philo of Alexandria. Lived 21 BCE - 38 CE.

References: Dando-Collins, 127-8; Huidekoper, 102-5.

**62. Mam. Aemilius Scaurus**

Mamercus Aemilius Scaurus, son of Marcus Aemilius Scaurus, was a distinguished orator and poet, consul in 21 CE. A member of the senate during Tiberius, he was a contemporary of Christ. He killed himself in Rome c. 34 CE.

References: Crévier, 372; Cassius Dio, *Roman History*, 58:24; Hartley-Parker, 94; Rutledge, 98-100; Tacitus, *Annals*; Temporini, II, 3254.

**63. Marcellus Sidetes**

Marcellus Sidetes, physician from Pamphylia, flourished under Hadrian. He wrote 42 books on medicine which were deposited in the public libraries of Rome by the emperors. Some fragments are extant.

References: Anthon, 448; Platts, Vol. II, 114.

**64. Martial**

M. Valerius Martialis was a poet born at Bilbilis (modern Calatayud), 40 CE. He went to Rome c. 63, published many epigrams in Rome between AD 86 his death, c. 102 CE.

References: Dudley, 9747; Harrison; Platts, Vol. II, 91-2.

**65. Maximus Tyrius**

Greek rhetorician, writer, and philosopher of the second century CE. Forty one of his *Dissertations* are still extant. The new school of Platonists included Thrasyllus of Mendes, Theon of Smyrna, Alcinous, Albinus, Plutarch, L. Apuleius of Mendaurus, and our Tyrius.

References: Enfield, 321; Platts, Vol. II, 145-6; Tennemann, 161-3.

**66. Moderatus of Gades**

Greek philosopher of neo-Pythagorean of the first century, early, middle, and late. Moderates wrote volumes on the doctrines of the Pythagoreans. He flourished 80-90 CE. (Not to be confused with Moderatus Columella.)

References: Turner, 363-72; Zeller, *Outline / Greek Philosophy,* 307; *The Encyclopaedia Britannica* (1911) Vol XVIII, 642.

**67. Musonius**

C. Musonius Rufus, Roman philosopher, 1st century CE. Musonius wrote many philosophical works. A teacher of Euphrates, he was an inveterate enemy of Apollonius of Tyana, and corresponded with Apollonius. Born c. 14 CE, Musonius lived until at least 79 CE. His writings survive to this day.

References: Jagu, 7-8; Morford, 10, 204-5; Penella, 89; Platts, Vol. II, 86; Smith, William, *A Dict. Gk. Rom. Biogr. Myth.* Vol. III, 676.

**68. Nicarchus**

Greek writer of note, and poet, Nicarchus wrote in Alexandria during the reign of Nero.

References: Clausen, 105-6; Paton, 67.

**69. Nicomachus Gerasenus**

Pythagorean writer, philosopher and mathematician. He lived during the time of Tiberius until late first century. He wrote primarily on music and arithmetic. Several of his works are still extant, including *Introductio arithmetica.*

References: De Morgan, 17; Gow, 88-98; Hawkins, Bk II, 73-6; Hogendijk, 123, 125, 130-3, 166; Park, 488.

**70. Onasandros**

Onasandros (or Onasander, Onosander), first century philosopher, was a contemporary of Christ. Author of a commentary on Plato's *Republic* (lost), and a comprehensive work on the duties of a general dedicated to Q. Veranius Nepos (consul 49), which comes down to us today. A Platonic philosopher, he dedicated his work "The General" to Veranius, Roman consul in 49 CE

References: Park, 488; Platts, Vol. II, 97; Rose, 394.

**71. P. Clodius Thrasea Paetus**

Writer, stoic philosopher, Roman senator, lived during the reign of Nero. A prominent figure at Rome, friend of Demetrius, and hero of the stoics. He wrote a life of Cato. Died 66 CE.

References: Henderson, 100, 295, 297; Platts, Vol. II, 8; Rutledge, 133, 219-20; Shotter, *Nero*, 65.

**72. Palaemon**

Q. Remmius Palaemon was a Roman grammarian of the first century under Tiberius, Caligula, and Claudius, native to Vicentia, teacher of A. Flaccus Perseus, Jesus contemporary. Palaemon was the most celebrated grammarian of his time. Some of his works are extant.

References: Platts, Vol. II, 90; Swiggers, 257-8; Smith, William, *A Dict. Gk. Rom. Biogr. Myth.* 1890, Vol. III, 88-9.

**73. Pamphila**

Female historian from Egypt, and native of Epidaurus, Pamphila lived during Nero's reign. She wrote a history (*summikton historikon hupomnematon logoi*) in 33 books, as well as *An Epitome Of Ctesias* (3 books), and epitomes of histories and other works. Her works were used by Diogenes Laertius, Sopater, Photius and A. Gellius, among others. Pamphila worked diligently for 13 years, faithfully recording whatever she heard from her husband and other learned men who frequented their residence, as well as what she learned from her extensive reading.

References: Plant, 127-9; Platts, Vol. II, 105; Smith, William, *A Dict. Gk. Rom. Biogr. Myth*, Vol. III, 102.

**74. Pausanias**

Well-known, revered, and prolific Greek travel writer of the second century CE who recorded some of the Mystery rites practiced in the temples he visited.

References: Habicht; Platts, Vol. II, 174.

**75. Pedacus Dioscorides**

Physician and botanist during Nero. Pedacus wrote five books on the medical uses of plants.

References: Lemprière, 540; Platts, Vol. II, 113.

**76. Persius/Perseus**

A. Persius Flaccus (34-62 CE), Roman poet and satirist, went to Rome at the age of 12, and was taught by Remmius Palaemon and Verginius (Virginius) Flavus. Persius became friends with Cornutus and Caesius Bassus. He was the author of six satires on life in Rome during Nero.

References: Claridge, 34; Platts, Vol. II, 90.

**77. Petronius**

Petronius Arbiter (c. 27–66), great critic and writer, proficient in science, author of *Satyricon,* was a favorite of Nero, and disciple of Epicurus. Some of his works come down to us today.

References: Park, 583; Platts, Vol. II, 94-5; Smith, Martin S.

**78. Phaedrus**

Phaedrus flourished through the reigns of Augustus to Claudius. A contemporary of Christ, he died c. 50 CE. Phaedrus wrote at least 97 fables in iambic verse, which come down to us today.

References: Grant, *Roman Literature,* 218-20; Smith, William, *A Dict. Gk. Rom. Biogr. Myth,* Vol. III, 231.

**79. Philippus of Thessalonica**

First century poet of about 90 works, and compiled a Greek Anthology. Lived after the time of Augustus, flourished under Trajan.

References: Fitzgerald, 27; Smith, William, *A Dict. Gk. Rom. Biogr. Myth,* Vol. III, 292-3.

**80. Philo of Alexandria**

Philo Judaeus of Alexandria, 25 BCE - 50 CE, was a contemporary of Christ. He was considered the greatest Jewish philosopher of his age. Born in Alexandria, he received a complete education in Greek literature and philosophy as well as on the Old Testament. Wrote *Against Flaccus, De Vita Contemplativa,* and many more works.

References: Bréhier, 168; Finkelstein, Vol 3, 877-900; Platts, Vol. II, 95.

**81. Phlegon of Tralles**

Greek writer of the second century under Hadrian. Phlegon, a sports enthusiast, wrote at least sixteen books, chiefly about the Olympiads, but also containing essential historical events.

References: Luck, 235; Platts, Vol. II, 100.

**82. Pliny the Elder**

C. Caecilius Plinius Secundus (23-79 CE) was a member of the equestrian order. Natural historian, procurator rationalis in Spain, then praefectus of the fleet at Misenum by Vespasian. Wrote twenty books on the history of the German wars, thirty one books on *History of His Times,* and an encyclopedia, *Naturalis Historia,* which survives to this day.

References: Beagon; Hosbrooke; Park, 488; Platts, Vol. II, 97.

**83. Pliny the Younger**

C. Plunius Caecilius Secundus, son of Caecilius Plinius Secundus and his wife Plinia, b. 61 or 62 CE, d. 113 CE. Prolific author, member of a rich equestrian family. Taught by Quintilian and Nicetes Sacerdos.

References: Hosbrooke; Larson, 308; Park, 488; Platts, Vol. II, 97-8, , Radice, 12 & Appendix C.

**84. Plotinus**

Third century philosopher, teacher, writer. Died 270 CE, yet he seems to have never heard of Jesus Christ, or even of the "Christians."

References: Gerson; Platts, 209-10.

**85. Plutarch**

Roman historian, 46 - 125 CE, studied philosophy under Ammonius during the time of Nero. Famous for his *The Lives,* a series of biographies of famous Romans and Greeks. Priest of Apollo at Delphi for the last 30 years of his life.

References: Platts, Vol. II, 83-5; Smith, William, *A Dict. Gk. Rom. Biogr. Myth*, Vol. III, 429.

**86. Pompeius Saturninus**

Roman historian, poet, and orator. Flourished during the reign of Trajan. The younger Pliny speaks highly of him, exchanged letters with him, and always consulted him before he published his works.

References: Melmoth, 10; Platts, Vol. II, 105; Pliny, younger, *letter 16* (to Erucius).

**87. Pomponius Mela**

Author of a large compendium on geography, writing in the middle of the first century CE. Born in Spain. Nothing more is known of the man's life. Mela describes the customs and peculiarities of various countries. His three books of cosmology are still extant.

References: Bunbury, 352-70; Kish, 128; Platts, Vol II, 96.

**88. Pomponius Secundus**

Roman writer, tragic poet, and legatus of the middle of the first century CE. Friend of Sejanus and the elder Pliny.

References: Boyle, 184-92; Middleton, 282-4; Smith, William, *A Dict. Gk. Rom. Biogr. Myth,* Vol. III, 764.

**89. Potamon of Mytilene**

Potamon (or Potamo), philosopher of the 1st-2nd century, son of Lesbonax who corresponded with Apollonius of Tyana. Potatmon was the teacher and friend of Emperor Tiberius. The city of Mytilene erected a huge monument in honor of Potamon; its base contained a record of his activities. Fragments of documents written by the emperor, along with decrees and honors of Potamon were found in the old acropolis of Mytilene.

References: Cichorius, *Rom und Mytilene,* 62-6; Platts, Vol. II, 150; Rowe, 125, 139; Sherk, 103-4; Syme, *Roman Revolution,* 262; Tredwell, 105.

(Note that Wm Smith gets it wrong, calling Lesbonax the son of Potamon and father of "Polemon" in *A Classical Dictionary of Biography, Mythology,* p. 378.)

**90. Ptolemy of Mauretania**

1 BCE – 40 CE Prince, writer, contemporary of Christ, and the last Roman client king of Mauretania (Algeria/Morocco).

References: Smith, William, *A Dictionary of Greek and Roman Antiquities,*Vol. I, 3; *Encyclopedia Britannica* (1911) Vol. XIX, 697.

**91. Q. Asconius Pedianus**

Roman historian, author, and grammarian, b. Patauium c. 2 BCE, died c. 83-88 CE in Rome. Contemporary of Christ, acquainted with Livy. He wrote of Longus Caecina, as well as historical commentaries on Cicero's speeches; his works survive today.

References: Park, 487-8; Sandys, *A Companion to Latin Studies,* 665; Smith, William, *A New Classical dictionary of Greek and Roman Biography and Mythology,* Vol. I, 384.

**92. Q. Curtius Rufus**

Quintus Curtius Rufus, rhetorical historian, author of *The History of Alexander the Great* in ten books, written during the early reign of Claudius (all but the first two survive).

References: Platts, Vol. II, 103; Sandys, *A Companion to Latin Studies,* 668.

**93. Quintilian**

M. Fabius Quintilian, teacher of eloquence, born c. 42 CE during the reign of Claudius. He studied under Domitious Afer in Rome, and opened a school at Rome, being paid a salary by the state as public teacher. Quintilian wrote 145 "*Declamations,*" most of which are still extant. He lived until c. 95 CE.

References: Atchity, 208-9; Platts, Vol. II, 95-6; Winterbottom.

**94. Rubellius Plautus**

Lived 33-62 CE, descendent of Augustus, Roman nobleman, writer, rival of Nero, friend of Musonius Rufus. Rubellius was assassinated on Nero's orders, c. 62 CE.

References: Baring-Gould, *Nero,* 44-9, 216; Bréhier, 152; Henderson, 133-5.

**95. Rufus the Ephesian**

Physician under Trajan, Rufus wrote many works, on many subjects, still extant.

References: Bowman, 952-3; Platts, Vol. II, 113.

**96. Saleius Bassus**

Roman epic poet and satirist of mid- to late-first century CE, contemporary with Statius. His works do not survive to this day but Quintillian and Juvenal speak of his works, his genius, and morals.

References: Jones, *Plutarch and Rome;* Tacitus, Cornelius, *Dialogus, Agricola, and Germania*; Smith, William, *A Dict. Gk. Rom. Biogr. Myth,* Vol. III, 473.

**97. Scopelian the Sophist**

Scopelian was a noted sophist of late 1st c. CE, native of Clazomenae. Born c. 40 CE, he corresponded with Apollonius of Tyana. Scopelian went to Athens when Herodes Atticus (101-177) was a boy. He was given a fortune in talents for his oratory skills by the father of Herodes Atticus.

References: Jones, *Philostratus, Apollonius of Tyana,* 23 (Phlstr. 1.23.3); Penella, 45, 137-8; Phillimore; Walden, 180-2, 220-31.

**98. Scribonius**

Scribonius Largus, Roman historian, flourished c. 22-50 CE; wrote his famous *Annals*. Some of his works are still extant.

References: Carrick, 174-5; Platts, Vol. II, 101.

**99. Seneca the Elder**

Roman philosopher and writer, lived c. 54-57 BCE - c. 37-39 CE. Seneca wrote a series of works, many of which survive today. He wrote a history of Rome up to the death of Tiberius, which is lost. Father of Seneca the Younger.

References: Fairweather; Griffin; Grube, 257; Kennedy, 275-79.

**100. Seneca the Younger**

Roman philosopher, author, and politician 4 BCE - 65 CE. Seneca was educated in Rome, traveled extensively in Egypt. A vegetarian, he was a follower of Pythagoras in his youth. Consul in 55 and 56 CE, and became tutor and ghost-writer for Nero.

References: Griffon, 45-7; Kennedy, 279-81.

**101. Sex. Afranius Burrus**

Outspoken commander of the praetorian guard and writer, 51-62 CE. Very powerful Roman, helped Seneca control the early years of Nero. Suetonius wrote (*Nero,* 35:5) that he was ultimately poisoned by Nero.

References: Ball, Allan Perley, 179; Platts, Vol II, 10; Rosse, 9.

**102. Sex. Julius Frontinus**

Roman consul and prolific writer of at least two books, including *Strategematicon*, and *De Aquaeductu*. Born c. 32 in Sicily, died c. 103.

References: Platts, Vol. II, 29; Scott.

**103. Servilius Damocrates**

Writer, poet, and physician of Nero. Some of his works remain with us today.

References: Cichorius, *Römische Studien*, 432; La Wall, 58-9, 211; Nutton; Park, 488.

**104. Silius Italicus**

C. Silius Italicus, Roman poet and writer, born c. 15-25 CE, contemporary of Christ in his youth. Became consul in 68 CE. His great work was an heroic poem of seventeen books, *Punica*, which we have in its entirety.

References: Atchity, 200-1; Platts, Vol. II, 89-90.

**105. Soranus**

Physician of Ephesus, flourished under Hadrian, and wrote a treatise of female diseases, parts of which survive today.

References: Atchity, 284-98; Platts, Vol. II, 114.

**106. Soterides of Epidaurus**

Father of Pamphila, mid- to late first century; wrote a work on Orthography, and philosophical commentaries on Homer and Menander.

References: Blair, 155; Plant, 127; Smith, William, *A Dict. Gk. Rom. Biogr. Myth*, Vol. III, 889.

**107. Sotion**

Native of Alexandria. Philosopher, writer, and instructor of Seneca, lived during the reign of Tiberius. Plutarch quotes Sotion in *Life of Alexander*.

References: Pratt; Smith, William, *A Dict. Gk. Rom. Biogr. Myth*, Vol. III, 889.

**108. Statius the Elder**

Publius Papinius Statius, born in Naples, d. c. 80-86 CE. Father of P. Papirius Statius. Was a prolific Roman writer and poet of the Silver Age of Latin literature, tutor of a young Domitian.

References: Bailey; Browne, 381; Am. Acad. Arts and Sc., 114.

**109. Statius the Younger**

Publius Papirius Statius, prolific writer, son of Publius Papinius Statius, contemporary of Juvenal, born c. 45-60 CE, died c. 95-100 in Naples. Many of his works survive.

References: *Am. Acad. Arts and Sc.*, 36; Bailey, 1-8; Browne, 382; Platts, Vol. II, 93.

**110. Suetonius**

Gaius Suetonius Tranquillus, lived 69 - 140 CE. Roman historian and author of *The Twelve Caesars.* Friend of the younger Pliny. Suetonius mentions Christians c. 120 CE but no Jesus or Christ, or any acts or miracles.

References: Larson, 308; Osman, 141-2; Platts, Vol. II, 104.

**111. Sulpicia**

First century author and poet, wrote during the reign of Domitian. Some of her writings are extant.

References: Plant, 124-6; Platts, Vol. II, 93-4.

**112. T. Aristo**

Titus Aristo, Roman jurist, writer, and friend of Pliny the younger, Pliny speaking highly of Aristo's virtue and learning. Author of several books, and pupil of Cassius, died c. 105 CE. (Not to be confused with Aristo of Ceos, Aristo of Chios, or Aristo of Alexandria.)

References: Clark, Part I, 112-5; Melmoth, 33; Platts, Vol. II, 99; Sherman, 71-2; Thomas, 174.

**113. T. Statilius Crito**

Greek writer, and chief physician and procurator of Trajan, b. Heraclea. Also known as Criton of Heraclea; corresponded with Apollonius of Tyana.

References: Penella, 103; Wilcocks, Vol II; Wood, Vol IX.

**114. Tacitus**

Publius Cornelius Tacitus (c. 56 – c. 117). Well-known historian and senator in Rome. His many works survive to this day. His *Annals* span the years 18 to 68 CE. Tacitus wrote with passion to expose the lies produced by Roman Empire officials.

References: Mellor; Tacitus, *The Histories,* first century.

**115. Thallus**

Greek historian, possibly during Augustus and Tiberius. Wrote history from the fall of Troy to the first century CE. Fragments of his works exist.

References: Collins, 51; Holladay, 343; *Oxford Classical Dictionary,* 434.

**116. Theon of Smyrna**

Platonic Philosopher, mathemetician, and astronomer. Lived during the time of Trajan and Hadrian. Wrote c. 130 CE; three works are extant. Lived 70 – c. 135.

References: Ball, Walter William Rouse, 95; Trinity College, Vol. XIV, 261-79; Platts, Vol. II, 106; Tennemann, 161.

**117. Thrasyllus of Mendes**

Ti. Claudius Thrasyllus, lived under Tiberius. Alexandrian grammarian, editor of Plato and Democritus, philosopher, astrologer. Died c. 36 CE.

References: *Encyclopaedia Judaica,* 280; Tennemann, 161; Caius Plinius Secundus, *Naturalis Historia.*

**118. Ti. Claudius Pasion**

Tiberius Claudius Pasion, District judge under Claudius, mid first century CE. Extensive records were kept of all proceedings under his command.

References: Munro, 225; Parkin, 304.

**119. Ti. Julius Alexander**

Son of Alexander Lysimachus, nephew of Philo of Alexandria. Julius was a Jewish writer who lived during the time of Christ, and after. Married Herod's daughter Berenice, and became procurator of Judea (c. 46-48), then assistant to Titus (69-70).

References: Finkelstein, Vol. 3, 878; Landman, 174.

**120. Tiberius**

Roman Emperor Tiberius Claudius Nero Caesar, lived 42 BCE to 37 CE. Reigned 14 CE (after Augustus) until his death. Tiberius wrote Greek poems, a lyric poem on the death of L. Caesar, and a commentary of his own life, which Suetonius made use of for his *Life of Tiberius*. Tiberius also wrote many letters to princes and others (which Suetonius used), and Oratories to the senate.

References: Braund; Munro; Smith, William, *A Dict. Gk. Rom. Biogr. Myth,* Vol. III, 1123.

**121. Valerius Flaccus**

Gaius Valerius Flaccus (died c. 90 CE) was a Roman poet, dedicating a poem to Vespasian. Quintilian makes reference to Valerius, which is where we get the approximate date of his death. At least one significant work of his comes down to us today.

References: Sandys, *A Companion to Latin Studies,* 635-6; Middleton, 286-8; Platts, Vol. II, 93.

**122. Valerius Maximus**

Prolific first century Latin writer, flourished c. 31 CE. Contemporary of Christ. Wrote of Roman religious beliefs and morals largely in terms of historical anecdotes and vignettes. His treatise included not just morals, but the deities like Juno, Vesta, Jupiter, which he cites as rationale for morality.

References: Atchity, 190; Mueller.

**123. Vardanes I**

Ruled Parthia (Iran) from 40–45 CE, writing epistles and other texts not far from Judea. Corresponded with Apollonius of Tyana.

References: Yarshater, 75-6; Philostratus, *Life of Apollonius*, 1.21, 1.29.

**124. Velleius Paterculus**

Marcus Velleius Paterculus (c. 19 BCE - 31 CE). Contemporary of Christ. Velleius was born in Capua about BCE 19, traveled extensively, and wrote a compendium of Roman history down to his own time (*Historiae Romanae Duo Volumina ad M. Vinicium Cos.*), dedicated to consul Marcus Vinicium and completed around 30 CE.

References: Garnett; Grant, *Readings*; Rockwood, vii-viii.

**125. Verginius Flavus**

Virginius (or Verginius) Flavus, first century writer, rhetorician, and teacher (taught Persius and the younger Pliny), contemporary of Cornutus and Palaemon. Exiled by Nero along with Musonius Rufus.

References: Ballif; Cruttwell, 355; Duff, 190, 224, 336; Cornelius Tacitus, *Annals of Tacitus*; Platts, Vol. II, 90, 97.

**126. Vindex**

Junius (or Julius) Vindex, governor of Gaul. Christ contemporary, corresponded with Nero c. 65-67 CE.

References: Platts, Vol. II, 16; Plutarch, *Lives* ("Galba"); Schmitz, *A History of Rome*, 598-9; Syme, *Ten Studies in Tacitus.*

**Bibliography for the Index of Authors**

The following bibliography applies to this appendix.

Abbott, Jacob, *History of Cleopatra, Queen of Egypt*. Harper & Brothers, 1879.

Abrahams, Israel, *The Jewish quarterly review*. London: October, 1889.

Alberti, Antonina M., *Aspasius*. Walter de Gruyter, 1999.

Am. Acad. Arts and Sc., *Memoirs of the American Academy of Arts and Sciences*. 1857.

Anderson, Graham, *Lucian*. Brill, 1976.

Anderson, Graham, *Sage, Saint, and Sophist*. Routledge, 1994.

Anderson, R. Dean, Ancient Rhetorical Theory and Paul. Peeters, 1999.

Anthon, Charles, *A Manual of Greek Literature*. Harper, 1853.

Atchity, Kenneth John, *The Classical Roman Leader*. Oxford University Press, 1998.

Bailey, David Roy Shackleton, *Statius,* Loeb Classical Library. Harvard University Press, 2003.

Ball, Allan Perley, *Selected Essays of Seneca and the Satire on the Deification of Claudius*. Macmillan, 1908.

Ball, Walter William Rouse, *A Short Account of the History of Mathematics*. Macmillan and co., limited, 1908.

Ballif, Michelle, *Classical Rhetorics and Rhetoricians*. Praeger, 2005.
Baring-Gould, Sabine, *Nero*. A. L. Humphreys, 1907.
Baring-Gould, Sabine, *The Tragedy of the Caesars*. New York: C. Scribner's sons, 1907.
Bates, Donald George, *Knowledge and the Scholarly Medical Traditions*. Cambridge University Press, 1995.
Bauman, Richard A, *Women and Politics in Ancient Rome*. Routledge, 1994.
Beagon, Mary, *The Elder Pliny on the Human Animal*. Oxford University Press, 2005.
Berger, Adolf, *Encyclopedic dictionary of Roman law*. Diane Publishing, 1953.
Blair, John, Blair's Chronological Tables. H. G. Bohn, 1856.
Bond, John James, *Handy-book of Rules and Tables for Verifying Dates with the Christian Era*. London: Whittingham and Wilkins: 1875.
Bowman, Alan K., *The Cambridge Ancient History*. Cambridge University Press, 1996.
Bowra, C. M., *Greek Lyric Poetry from Alcman to Simonides*. Oxford University Press, 2001.
Boyle, Anthony James, *An introduction to Roman tragedy*. Taylor & Francis, 2006.
Bradley, K. R., *Slavery and Society at Rome*. Cambridge University Press, 1994.
Braund, David, *Augustus to Nero*. Taylor & Francis, 1985.
Bréhier, Émile, *The Hellenistic and Roman Age*. Chicago: University of Chicago Press, 1965.
Browne, Robert William, *A History of Greek Classical Literature*. Blanchard and Lea, 1857.
Bunbury, Edward Herbert, *A History of Ancient Geography*. J. Murray, 1883.
Caius Plinius Secundus, *Naturalis Historia*. c. 77 CE.
Capes, William Wolfe, *Roman History*. New York: Longmans, Green, and Co., 1897.
Carrick, Paul, *Medical Ethics in the Ancient World*. Georgetown University Press, 2001.
Cary, Earnest, *The Roman Antiquities by Halicarnassensis Dionysius*. Heinemann, 1943.
Ceccarelli, Marco, *Distinguished Figures in Mechanism and Machine Science*. Springer, 2007.
Cichorius, C., *Rom und Mytilene*. Leipzig: Teubner, 1888.
Cichorius, C., *Römische Studien, Historisches, Epigraphisches, Literargeschichtliches*. 1922.
Claridge, Amanda, *Rome*. Oxford University Press, 1998.
Clark, Edwin Charles, *History of the Roman Private Law*. Cambridge: University Press, 1906.
Clausen, Wendell Vernon, *The Cambridge History of Classical Literature: The Early Principate*. Cambridge University Press, 1983.
Collier, George Frederick, *A Translation of the Eight Books of Aulus Cornelius Celsus on Medicine*. London: Simpkin and Marshall, 1831.
Collins, John Joseph, *Between Athens and Jerusalem*. Wm. B. Eerdmans Publishing, 2000.
Crévier, Jean Baptiste Louis, *The History of the Roman Emperors*. J. and P. Knapton, 1755.
Cruttwell, Charles Thomas, *A history of Roman literature*. C. Griffin, 1878.
Cutner, Herbert, *Jesus: God, Man Or Myth?* San Diego: The Truth Seeker Co., 1986.
Dando-Collins, Stephen, *Blood of the Caesars*. John Wiley and Sons, 2008.
Davenport, Richard Alfred, *Dictionary of Biography*. J & B Williams, 1839.

De Morgan, Augustus, *Arithmetical Books from the Invention of Printing to the Present Time*. Taylor and Walton, 1847.
Dickey, Eleanor, *Ancient Greek Scholarship*. Oxford University Press US, 2007.
Dihle, Albrecht, *Greek and Latin Literature of the Roman Empire*. Routledge, 1994.
Dio, Cassius, *Roman History*. 228 CE.
Dodd, Henry Philip, *The Epigrammatists*. Bell and Daldy, 1870.
Dudley, Charles, *Library of the World's Best Literature, Ancient and Modern*. J. A. Hill, and Co., 1896.
Duff, John Wight, *A Literary History of Rome in the Silver Age*. Barnes & Noble, 1960.
Dzielska, Maria, *Apollonius of Tyana in Legend and History*. L'Erma di Bretschneider, 1986.
Edwards, Iorwerth Eiddon Stephen, *The Cambridge Ancient History: The High Empire, A.D. 70-192*. Cambridge University Press, 2000.
Eggenberger, David, *An Encyclopedia of Battles*. Courier Dover Publications, 1985.
*Encyclopædia Britannica*. 1911.
*Encyclopaedia Judaica*. 1982.
Enfield, William, *The History of Philosophy, from the Earliest Periods*. T. Tegg, 1837.
Eschenburg, Johann Joachim, *Manual of Classical Literature*. Frederick W. Greenough, 1839.
Fairweather, Janet, *Seneca the Elder*. Cambridge University Press, 1981.
Finkelstein, Louis, *The Cambridge history of Judaism*. Cambridge University Press, 1999.
Fitzgerald, William, *Martial*. University of Chicago Press, 2007.
Flemming, Rebecca, *Classical Quarterly*. 2007.
Fowler, Harold North, *A History of Roman Literature*. New York: D. Appleton, 1909.
Frazer, Sir James George, *The Golden Bough*, Oxford: Oxford University Press, 1998.
Frere, Sheppard Sunderland, *Britannia*. Routledge, 1987.
Fyfe, William Hamilton, *Tacitus Dialogus, Agricola, and Germania*. Clarendon press, 1908.
Garnett, Richard, *The Universal Anthology*. The Clarke Co., Ltd., 1899.
Gerson, Lloyd P., *Plotinus*. Taylor & Francis US, 1999.
Gow, James, *A Short History of Greek Mathematics*. AMS Bookstore, 1968.
Grant, Michael, *Readings in the Classical Historians*. Scribner's, 1992.
Grant, Michael, *Roman Literature*. Penguin Books, 1964.
Grant, Michael, *The Annals of Imperial Rome*. 1996.
Griffin, Miriam Tamara, *Seneca*. Oxford University Press, 1992.
Grube, G. M. A., *The Greek and Roman Critics*. Hackett Publishing, 1995.
Guignebert, Charles, *Jesus*. New York: Knopf, 1935.
Gummere, Richard Mott, *Ad Lucilium Epistulae Morales by Seneca*. Harvard University Press, 1934.
Gunnyon, William, *A Century of Translations from the Greek Anthology*. Dunlop & Drennan, Printers, 1883.
Habicht, Christian, *Pausanias' Guide to Ancient Greece*. University of California Press, 1998.
Harrison, S. J., *A Companion to Latin Literature*. Blackwell Pub., 2005.

Hartley-Parker, E., and Furneaux, Henry, *Subject Matter of Tacitus Annals, I-III*. James Thornton, 1908.

Hawkins, John, *A General History of the Science and Practice of Music*. Kessinger Publishing, 2006.

Henderson, Bernard William, *The Life and Principate of the Emperor Nero*. London: Methuen & Co, 1905.

Herzog, Johann Jakob, *The New Schaff-Herzog Encyclopedia of Religious Knowledge*. New York: Funk and Wagnalls, 1911.

Highet, Gilbert, *Juvenal the Satirist*. Clarendon Press, 1960.

Hinnells, John R., *Mithraic Studies*. Manchester University Press ND, 1975.

Hogendijk, J. P., *The Enterprise of Science in Islam*. MIT Press, 2003.

Holladay, Carl R., *Fragments from Hellenistic Jewish Authors*. Scholars Press, 1983.

Hosbrooke, George Otis, *Selections from the Letters of the Younger Pliny*. Boston: John Allyn, 1888.

Huidekoper, Frederic, *Judaism at Rome, B. C. 76 to A. D. 140*. Boston: George H. Ellis, 1900.

Jagu, Amand, *Musonius Rufus: Entretiens et Fragments*. G. Olms, 1979.

Jahn, John Nicholas Henry, *A Critical Study of the Sources of the History of the Emperor Nero*. New York University, 1920.

Jones, Christopher P., *Letters of Apollonius*, Loeb Classical Library, 2006.

Jones, Christopher P., *Philostratus, The Life of Apollonius of Tyana*. 2005.

Jones, Christopher Prestige, *Plutarch and Rome*. Clarendon Press, 1971.

Jones, Christopher Prestige, *The Roman World of Dio Chrysostom*. Harvard University Press, 1978.

Kennedy, George Alexander, *The Cambridge History of Literary Criticism*. Cambridge University Press, 1993.

Kish, George, *A Source Book in Geography*. Harvard University Press, 1978.

La Wall, Charles Herbert, *Four Thousand Years of Pharmacy*. J.B. Lippincott Company, 1927.

Landels, John Gray, *Engineering in the Ancient World*. University of California Press, 2000.

Landman, Isaac, *The Universal Jewish Encyclopedia*. 1938.

Larson, Martin A, *The Story of Christian Origins*. Tahlequah: Village Press, 1977.

Lawrence, Eugene, *A Primer of Latin Literature*. Harper, 1877.

Lemprière, John, *Lempriere's Universal Biography*. R. Lockwood, 1825.

Lewis, John Delaware, *The Letters of the Younger Pliny By Pliny*. Trübner & Co., Ltd., 1890.

Lietzmann, Hans, *A History of the Early Church*. Cleveland and New York: Meridian Books, 1961.

Long, George, *Plutarch's Lives*. London: George Bell and Sons, 1900.

Longman, *The Biographical Dictionary of the Society for the Diffusion of Useful Knowledge*. London: Longman, Brown, Green, and Longmans, 1844.

Loudon, John Claudius, *An Encyclopædia of Agriculture*. London: Longman, Green, Longman, and Roberts, 1860.
Luck, Georg, *Arcana Mundi*. Baltimore: JHU Press, 2006.
Luhtala, Anneli, *Grammar and philosophy in late anti*quity. John Benjamins Publishing Company, 2005.
Maximus Tyrius, *Dissertations*. Second c. CE.
Mellor, Ronald, *Tacitus*. Routledge, 1994.
Melmoth, William, *The Letters of Caius Plinius Caecilius Secundus*. London: George Bell and Sons, 1905.
Middleton, George, *The Student's Companion to Latin Authors*. Macmillan and Co., Ltd., 1896.
Mills, Abraham, *The Poets and the Poetry of the Ancient Greeks*. Phillips, Sampson, and company, 1858.
Morford, Mark P. O., *The Roman Philosophers*. Routledge, 2002.
Mossman, Judith, and Bowie, Ewen, *Plutarch and his Intellectual World*. 1997.
Mueller, Hans-Friedrich, *Roman Religion in Valerius Maximus*. Routledge, 2002.
Munro, Dana Carleton, *A Source Book of Roman History*. Heath, 1904.
Niebuhr, Barthold Georg, *The History of Rome*. J. Taylor, 1851.
Nutton, Vivian, *Ancient Medicine*. Taylor & Francis, 2005.
Osman, Ahmed, *Out Of Africa*. London: Arrow, 1998.
*Oxford Classical Dictionary*. Clarendon Press, 1949.
Park, Edwards Amasa, *The Bibliotheca Sacra*. W.F. Draper, 1891.
Parkin, Tim G., *Roman Social History*. Routledge, 2007.
Parkinson, G. H. R., *Routledge History of Philosophy*. Routledge, 2007.
Paton, William Roger, *The Greek Anthology*. London: William Heinemann, 1918.
Penella, Robert J., *The Letters of Apollonius of Tyana*. Leiden: Brill, 1979.
Penella, Robert, "An Unpublished Letter of Apollonius of Tyana to the Sardians." London: Harvard *Studies in Classical Philology*, Vol. 79, 1975.
Phillimore, J.S. (transl.), Philostratus, *in Honour of Apollonius of Tyana, in two volumes*. Oxford: Clarendon Press, 1912.
Philo Judaeus, *Against Flaccus*. c. 45 CE.
Philostratus, *Life of Apollonius*. c. 220-230 CE.
Plant, Ian Michael, *Women Writers of Ancient Greece and Rome*. University of Oklahoma Press, 2004.
Platts, John, *A Universal Biography*. London: Sherwood Jones and Co., 1825.
Plutarch, *The Lives of the Caesars*.
Pratt, Norman T., *Seneca's Drama*. Chapel Hill: UNC Press, 1983.
Prioreschi, Plinio, *A History of Medicine*. Horatius press, 1995.
Quill, Albert William, transl., *The History of P. Cornelius Tacitus*. 1892.
Reader, William W., and Polemo, Antonius. *The Severed Hand and the Upright Corpse*. Scholars Press, 1996.
Reitzenstein, Richard, *Hellenistische Wundererzählungen*. Leipzig: Teubner, 1906.
Rockwood, Frank Ernest, *Velleius Paterculus*. Sanborn, 1900.

Rollin, Charles, *The Ancient History of the Egyptians, Carthaginians, Assyrians, Babylonians.* New York: Harper and Brothers, 1870.
Rooke, John, *Arrian's History of the Expedition of Alexander the Great.* London: J. Davis, 1813.
Rose, Herbert Jennings, *A handbook of Greek Literature.* Methuen & Co., Ltd., 1934.
Rosse, J. Willoughby, *An Index of Dates.* H. G. Bohn, 1858.
Rowe, Greg, *Princes and Political Cultures.* University of Michigan Press, 2002.
Rutledge, Steven H., *Imperial Inquisitions.* Routledge, 2001.
Sandys, John Edwin, *A Companion to Latin Studies.* Cambridge University Press, 1913.
Sandys, John Edwin, *A Short History of Classical Scholarship from the Sixth Century B.C.* The University Press, 1915.
Sarton, George, *Introduction to the History of Science.* Williams & Wilkins Co., 1927.
Schmitz, Leonhard, *A History of Latin Literature.* 1877.
Schmitz, Leonhard, *A History of Rome.* London: Taylor, Walton, and Maberly, 1852.
Schneidewin, Friedrich Wilhelm, *Philologus.* O. Kleinecke's Buchhandlung, 1872.
Scott, Robert B., *Strategematicon of Sextus Julius Frontinus.* London: Thomas Goddard, 1811.
Sheldon, Winthrop Dudley, *A Second-Century Satirist.* D. Biddle, 1901.
Sherk, Robert Kenneth, *Rome and the Greek East to the Death of Augustus.* Cambridge University Press, 1984.
Sherman, Charles Phineas, *Roman Law in the Modern World.* New Haven: New Haven Law Book Co., 1922.
Shotter, David Colin Arthur, *Nero.* Routledge, 2005.
Shotter, David, *Nero Caesar Augustus: Emperor of Rome.* Pearson Longman, 2008.
Smith, Martin S., *Petronii Arbitri Cena Trimalchionis.* Oxford University Press, 1975.
Smith, William, *A Dictionary of Greek and Roman Antiquities.* London: John Murray, 1890.
Smith, William, *A Dictionary of Greek and Roman Biography and Mythology.* 1880.
Smith, William, *A New Classical Dictionary of Greek and Roman Biography, Mythology, and Geography.* Harper, 1895.
Smith, William, *A Classical Dictionary of Biography, Mythology, and Geography.* Harvard: J.Murray, 1883.
Smith, William, *A Dictionary of Greek and Roman Biography and Mythology.* J. Murray, 1890.
Southern, Pat, *The Roman Army.* ABC-CLIO, 2006.
Swiggers, Pierre, et al, *Grammatical Theory and Philosophy of Language in Antiquity.* Peeters Publishers, 2002.
Syme, Ronald, *Ten studies in Tacitus.* Clarendon, 1970.
Syme, Ronald, *The Roman Revolution.* American Council of Learned Societies, Oxford University Press, 2002.
Tacitus, Cornelius, *Annals of Tacitus.*
Tacitus, Cornelius, *Dialogus, Agricola, and Germania.*
Tacitus, Cornelius, *The Histories.*

Targa, Leonardo, *A Translation of the Eight Books of Aul. Corn. Celsus on Medicine.* London: Longman, 1840.
Taylor, Joan E., *Christians and the Holy Places.* Oxford: Clarendon Press, 1993.
Temporini, Hildegard, *Aufstieg und Niedergang der Römischen Welt.* Walter de Gruyter, 1986.
Tennemann, Wilhelm Gottlieb, *A Manual of the History of Philosophy.* Bell & Daldy, 1870.
Thackeray, H., *Josephus.* Kessinger Publishing, 2006.
Thomas, Joseph, *Universal Pronouncing Dictionary of Biography and Mythology.* B. Lippincott Company, 1915.
Trapp, Michael B., *Philosophy in the Roman Empire.* Ashgate Publishing, Ltd., 2007.
Tredwell, Daniel M., *Apollonius of Tyana.* Kessinger Publishing, 1992.
Trinity College, *Hermathena.* Dublin: Members of Trinity College, 1907.
Turner, John D., *Sethian Gnosticism and the Platonic Tradition.* Presses Université Laval, 2001.
Van Dam, Raymond, *Kingdom of Snow.* University of Pennsylvania Press, 2002.
van der Horst, Pieter Willem, *Chaeremon, Egyptian Priest and Stoic Philosopher.* Brill Archive, 1984.
VanderKam, James C., *An Introduction to Early Judaism.* Wm. B. Eerdmans Publishing, 2001.
Von Staden, Heinrich, *Herophilus.* Cambridge University Press, 1989.
Walden, John William Henry, *The Universities of Ancient Greece.* C. Scribner's Sons, 1910.
Wells, Colin Michael, *The Roman Empire.* Harvard University Press, 1995.
White, Horace, *The Roman History of Appian of Alexandria.* New York: The Macmillan Company, 1899.
Wilcocks, Joseph, *Roman Conversations.* Strand: P. Norman, 1797, Vol II.
Williams, Henry Smith, *The Historians' History of the World.* London: Hooper and Jackson, Ltd, 1908.
Winterbottom, Michael, *The Minor Declamations Ascribed to Quintilian.* Walter de Gruyter, 1984.
Wiseman, Timothy Peter, *Death of an emperor* by Flavius Josephus. Presses Université Laval, 1991.
Wood, William, *Wood's Medical and Surgical Monographs.* New York: William Wood and Company, 1891.
Yarshater, Ehsan, *The Cambridge History of Iran.* Cambridge University Press, 1983.
Zeller, Eduard, *A History of Eclecticism in Greek Philosophy.* Longmans, Green, and Co., 1883.
Zeller, Eduard, *Outline of the History of Greek Philosophy.* Longmans, Green, 1886.

# INDEX

Made in the USA
Lexington, KY
01 October 2014